# Visions of Social Control

# Visions of Social Control

*Crime, Punishment and Classification*

STANLEY COHEN

Polity Press

Copyright © Stanley Cohen, 1985

First published 1985 by
Polity Press in association with Blackwell Publishers Ltd.
Reprinted 1986, 1987 (twice), 1989, 1990, 1993, 1994, 1995

*Editorial office:*
Polity Press
65 Bridge Street, Cambridge CB2 1UR, UK

*Marketing and production:*
Blackwell Publishers
108 Cowley Road, Oxford OX4 1JF, UK

Blackwell Publishers Inc.
238 Main Street
Cambridge, MA 02142, USA

A CIP catalogue record for this book is available
from the British Library.

*Library of Congress Cataloging in Publication Data*

Cohen, Stanley.
    Visions of social control.

    Bibliography: p.
    Includes index.
    1. Social Control    2. Deviant behaviour—
Prevention.    3. Crime prevention    I. Title.
HM291.C595    1985        303.3'3    84–24882
ISBN 0–7456–0020–4
ISBN 0–7456–0021–2 (pbk)

Typeset by Styleset Limited, Warminster, Wiltshire
Printed in Great Britain by
T.J. Press (Padstow) Ltd, Cornwall

*For Ruth, Jude and Jess*

This is the first mention I've heard of these Control Officials and naturally I can't understand them yet. But I fancy that two things must be distinguished here: firstly, what is transacted in the offices and can be construed again officially this way or that, and secondly, my own actual person, me myself, situated outside of the offices and threatened by their encroachments, which are so meaningless that I can't even yet believe in the seriousness of the danger.

Franz Kafka, *The Castle*

The object of persecution is persecution. The object of torture is torture. The object of power is power. Now do you begin to understand me?

George Orwell, *Nineteen Eighty-Four*

You see control can never be a means to any practical end . . . It can never be a means to anything but more control . . . Like junk . . .

William Burroughs, *The Naked Lunch*

We must cease once and for all to describe the effects of power in negative terms: it 'excludes', it 'represses', it 'censors', it 'abstracts', it 'masks', it 'conceals'. In fact, power produces; it produces reality; it produces domains of objects and rituals of truth.

Michel Foucault, *Discipline and Punish*

# Contents

# Acknowledgements

I have been working and not-working on this book for much too long. This has meant accumulating more debts than I can remember, let alone repay. Still:

For all sorts of help — discussions which they don't remember, photocopies and references they sent at just the right time, comments on earlier papers and drafts or just nagging me to get finished — I would like to thank Richard Abel, Tony Bottoms, Bill Chambliss, Nils Christie, David Dery, Jason Ditton, Roger Friedland, Barbara Hudson, Steven Spitzer, Brian Stapleford, Ian Taylor, Andrew von Hirsh and Colin Ward.

For similar help but also for reading and commenting on all or most of the manuscript, I am deeply grateful to David Greenberg, Gary Marx, Sheldon Messinger and Andrew Scull. They helped me more than they realize.

I presented some of this material in a seminar course in the Sociology Department at New York University in September–October 1983. I am grateful to Eliot Freidson and the Department for inviting me and to him and the students for many helpful comments.

Parts of chapters 2 and 4 appeared in somewhat different forms as 'The Punitive City: Notes on the Dispersal of Social Control', *Contemporary Crises* 3 (October 1979) and 'Social Control Talk: Telling Stories about Correctional Change' in Peter Garland and David Young (eds) *The Power to Punish*, (London: Heinemann, 1983). I am grateful to the editors and publishers for permission to recycle some of this material.

Most of this work was begun in 1979–80 while I was a Lady Davis Visiting Professor at the Hebrew University, Jerusalem. I am grateful to the Lady Davis Trust for their financial support during this year and for the continued hospitality of my colleagues in the

Institute of Criminology at the Hebrew University. Thanks also to the Wechsler Fund for assistance with typing expenses and to Sylvia Farhi for her very efficient typing.

Michael Hay was a helpful and eternally patient editor.

# Introduction

This is a book about social control, that is, the organized ways in which society responds to behaviour and people it regards as deviant, problematic, worrying, threatening, troublesome or undesirable in some way or another. This response appears under many terms: punishment, deterrence, treatment, prevention, segregation, justice, rehabilitation, reform or social defence. It is accompanied by many ideas and emotions: hatred, revenge, retaliation, disgust, compassion, salvation, benevolence or admiration. The behaviour in question is classified under many headings: crime, delinquency, deviance, immorality, perversity, wickedness, deficiency or sickness. The people to whom the response is directed, are seen variously as monsters, fools, villains, sufferers, rebels or victims. And those who respond (by doing something or by just studying the subject — jobs which are too often confused) are known as judges, policemen, social workers, psychiatrists, psychologists, criminologists or sociologists of deviance . . .

My aim here is neither to provide a comprehensive textbook-like study of this field nor to argue for a single thesis, explanatory framework, theory, model, political line or personal grievance. I have simply selected what I take to be some key trends in recent Western social control patterns, and used them as a base from which to speculate on issues of wider social concern. Rather than being either descriptive or prescriptive — both fine sociological enterprises — my bias is theoretical and critical.

I am critical of a society which classifies too much. This book itself, however, is primarily an exercise in classification, in ways of looking, in modes of making sense. It belongs to the type of sociology which tries to make the world look different: a strange terrain appears imperceptibly to be familiar or, just as interesting, a familiar terrain begins to look a little strange. My book attempts this type of cognitive re-mapping. The rest of this introduction is a

brief academic description of and apology for my subject; readers
who prefer matters to speak for themselves should proceed
straight on to chapter 1.

The term 'social control' has lately become something of a Mickey
Mouse concept. In sociology textbooks, it appears as a neutral
term to cover all social processes to induce conformity ranging
from infant socialization through to public execution. In radical
theory and rhetoric, it has become a negative term to cover not
just the obviously coercive apparatus of the state, but also the
putative hidden element in all state-sponsored social policy,
whether called health, education or welfare. Historians and political scientists restrict the concept to the repression of political
opposition, while sociologists, psychologists and anthropologists
invariably talk in broader and non-political terms. In everyday
language, that concept has no resonant or clear meaning at all.

All this creates some terrible muddles. Historians and sociologists
are locked in a protracted debate about whether the history of
prisons, mental hospitals and the juvenile court can meaningfully
be studied in the same framework as the history of the factory and
the control of working class resistance to the state.[1] Analysts of
social policy spend time in deciding whether this or that measure
by the state is 'really' social control.[2] The question is asked,
whether teachers in schools, warders in prisons, psychiatrists in
clinics, social workers in welfare agencies, parents in families,
policemen on the streets, and even bosses in the factories are all,
after all, busy doing the 'same' thing.

The answer to these fascinating questions is, no doubt, that
'it depends' — it depends on our image of social control and on the
purposes of any definition. My own purpose is to classify, assess
and criticize some current changes (proposed or actual) and to
comment on other similar exercises. This purpose will be served
less well by any essentialist definition than simply by mapping out
those 'social control matters' which this book covers.

My interest is in planned and programmed responses to expected and realized deviance rather than in the general institutions
of society which produce conformity. I will use the term 'social
control', then, to cover matters considerably narrower and more
specific than the general sociological/anthropological terrain of

all those social processes and methods through which society ensures that its members conform to expectations. These normally include internalization, socialization, education, peer-group pressure, public opinion and the like, as well as the operations of specialized formal agencies such as the police, the law and all other state powers. But I am interested in something a little wider and more general than the restricted criminological terrain of the formal legal-correctional apparatus for the control of official crime and delinquency. My focus is those organized responses to crime, delinquency and allied forms of deviant and/or socially problematic behaviour which are actually conceived of as such, whether in the reactive sense (after the putative act has taken place or the actor been identified) or in the proactive sense (to prevent the act). These responses may be sponsored directly by the state or by more autonomous professional agents in, say, social work and psychiatry. Their goals might be as specific as individual punishment and treatment or as diffuse as 'crime prevention', 'public safety' and 'community mental health'.

I will talk about 'deviance' but my material comes mainly from crime control and, moreover, from ordinary 'bread and butter' adult crime and juvenile delinquency rather than such important types as organized, political, white-collar and state crime. Parallel issues arise in the control of drug abuse, mental illness and sexual deviance and where these are particularly relevant, I will draw on this literature. Another way of restricting my scope is to concentrate on certain societies, notably 'liberal capitalist' states such as the USA, Canada, Britain and other Western European countries. These have social control systems embedded in more or less highly developed commitments to 'welfare' and more or less sophisticated ideologies about 'treatment'. These are also the same societies in which these commitments and ideologies have been the object of so much scepticism over the past decade or so.

It is just these shifts in strategy and beliefs that interest me. This book is less a description of the social control apparatus as it stands, than an attempt to monitor recent visions and alleged or real master movements and predict their implications for the future: a sociological seismograph to detect fissures, cracks, quakes, tremors and false alarms. The textbook notion of 'correctional change' draws attention to movements of this sort:

(1) A transformation of the arrangements employed to deal with convicted offenders (for example, the establishment of the penitentiary system); (2) a change in the severity of punishment dispensed to

offenders (for example, an increase in the average length of time offenders spend in confinement); (3) a change in either the numbers or
the proportion of convicted offenders dealt with by various components
of the correctional system (for example, an increase in prison population or assignment of an increasing number of convicted offenders to
pre-trial diversion programmes); and (4) a change in the prevailing
ideologies employed to 'explain' or make sense of offenders and their
involvement in criminality.[3]

But this is a list of operational changes — shifts that are often
too minor and ephemeral to be of much concern to the non-spec-
ialist. I am interested in more dramatic and profound movements,
the genuine master shifts against those massively entrenched
patterns of organized social control associated with the birth of the
modern state: attacks on prisons and mental hospitals, the development of alternative forms of community control, attempts to
bypass the whole criminal justice system, scepticism about professional competence; disenchantment with the rehabilitative ideal,
the development of new forms of intervention and the ideologies
which justify them. I will keep returning to the profoundly
ambiguous and contradictory nature of these changes.

There are other control patterns, both of change and stability,
that also deserve attention: in the form, content and administration
of the criminal law; in the nature of civil law and other forms of
regulation or conflict resolution; in the organization and techniques
of policing. But these subjects I mention not at all or only in
passing. I focus less on detection, apprehension or judicial procedure, than on 'deployment', that is, the institutional tracks into
which populations about to be or already defined as deviant
are directed. It is here, particularly in the iconography of prison
against community, that visions, claims and changes have been
most dramatic. In brief, this book is about punishment and classification.

## THE SOCIOLOGICAL CONNECTION

Now is the time for the obligatory self-serving section about how
irrelevant, misguided or plain foolish the existing literature on the
subject turns out to be.

In truth, the standard literature on social control probably *is* a
little more irrelevant, misguided and foolish than it might be in

most other areas of sociology. The academic, sociology-of-knowledge reasons for this, lie in the already well-chartered argument about the severance of criminology and the sociology of deviance from the mainstream of sociological concerns.[4] This was not always so. In the classical nineteenth-century tradition of social thought, the concept of social control was near the centre of the enterprise.[5] The great problem of social order was how to achieve a degree of organization and regulation consistent with certain moral and political principles (for example, 'democracy' or 'civil rights') and without an excessive degree of purely coercive control.

In twentieth century, largely American, sociology this organic connection between social control and a contemplation of the state, became weaker and weaker. The concept lost its political thrust, becoming less structural and more social-psychological. That is, it became more concerned with the 'processes' (a key term) by which the individual was induced into becoming a more-or-less willing participant in the social order. The individual was seen as an actor who learnt scripts and internalized rules and roles or else was pulled or pushed back into shape by something vaguely called 'official' or 'formal' control. This was a reactive, 'trampoline' model of social control.[6] Usually things went pretty smoothly ('consensus'), but every now and then the play broke down, the actors departed from the script and the director was challenged. Then social control was needed to get things back into order.

The social and sociological crises of the sixties were to change all this. Oppression, repression and suppression now became the normal properties of society. Consensus was either non-existent or else precariously maintained by awesome and cunningly disguised systems of social control. The individual could barely breathe, let alone 'internalize'. The struggle was to survive in the belly of that monster, the state. And those old 'deviants' — the nuts, sluts and perverts of criminology and social pathology textbooks — could emerge from their dark closets into the sociological daylight. They were now to be awarded leading roles in the re-written drama of social reality, as exemplars (first victims and underdogs, then rebels and heroes) of the struggle against social control.

Slowly too, the 'new' sociologists of deviance then, a few years later, the 'new' criminologists came out. Leaving the deviants huddled in their closets with their custodians and healers, these intellectuals proclaimed their independence from 'correctional' interests. Their project was to distance themselves from the machine — not to make it more effective, nor even to humanize it, but to question and demystify its very moral legitimacy. Labelling theorists and their later, rather tougher successors (Marxist or radical criminologists) pushed the notion of social control towards the centre of the stage  It was not just a reactive, reparative mechanism produced when other methods failed, but an active, ever present, almost mystical force which gave crime and deviance their very shapes. Control leads to deviance, was the catechism, not deviance to control. And law and other systems of control were intimately linked with the whole business of maintaining social order, discipline and regulation.

Further, along with these largely academic developments in sociology, wider social movements, whose effects and ideologies I will examine closely, started registering these same changes. The very agents of social control themselves − the professionals who operated the machine − began to scrutinize their own roles. Successive waves of anti-psychiatrists, radical social workers, de-medicalizers, deschoolers and delegalizers began to nourish and draw nourishment from those more academic reappraisals of social control.[7] With varying degrees of commitment, credibility and success, they lent their support to movements dedicated to changing, reforming or (amazingly) even abolishing the very agencies and institutions in which they worked.

All these moves − whether within general sociology, specialized subfields such as criminology, or the control apparatus itself − contributed towards a massive theoretical and political reordering of the subject. But (as with the alleged master changes in the apparatus itself) these cognitive shifts have turned out to be much less clear than they seem at first sight. Many have been false alarms or tremors which have registered only slightly in the worlds of theory and practice. What this means − and here comes the criticism of the literature − is that the sociology of social control remains a lot more retarded than these academic rumblings would lead us to expect.

Thus, despite the enterprise of radical demystification, the study of social control shows a wide gap between our private sense of what is going on around us and our professional writings about the social world. This private terrain is inhabited by premonitions of *Nineteen Eighty-Four*, *Clockwork Orange* and *Brave New World*, by fears about new technologies of mind control, by dark thoughts about the increasing intrusion of the state into family and private lives, by a general unease that more of our actions and thoughts are under surveillance and subject to record and manipulation. Social control has become Kafka-land, a paranoid landscape in which things are done to us, without our knowing when, why or by whom, or even that they are being done. We live inside Burroughs' 'soft machine', an existence all the more perplexing because those who control us seem to have the most benevolent of intentions. Indeed we ourselves appear as the controllers as well as the controlled. Suspending all critical judgement, we accept readily – almost with masochistic pleasure – the notion that *Nineteen Eighty-Four* has literally arrived.

The professional literature, however, reveals little of such nightmares and science fiction projections. Textbooks – those depositories of a discipline's folk wisdom – still use an older and blander language of social control: how norms are internalized, how consensus is achieved, how social control evolves from pre-industrial to industrial societies. Marxist theories, to be sure, confront the concept in a more critical way. But seldom in these powerful and baroque abstractions about the 'ideological' and 'repressive' state apparatus do we get much sense of what is happening in the apparatus. We learn little about those 'transactions' and 'encroachments' going on in Kafka's 'offices'.

For this sense of what the social control apparatus is actually getting up to, the specialized literature is surprisingly unhelpful. Take, for example, the realm where the most formidable and irreversible of all master shifts is alleged to be taking place – the replacement of the closed segregated institution by some form of 'open' community control. Most criminological studies here are of a uniformly low level. They fall into three categories:

(1) *evangelical*, in which we are told that this or that project has achieved a breakthrough in reducing recidivism, in involving the community or whatever (and that further research is needed to confirm this result);

(2) *fudgy*, in which under the heading of 'evaluation' words such as process, control group, feedback, flow-chart, objectives, goals, inputs, and system are arranged in random order (and more research is called for); and

(3) *nihilistic*, in which it is shown that nothing, after all, works, everything costs the same (and more research is probably needed).

Little of this helps towards understanding the underlying picture, and much reading between the lines is required to see what these projects and programmes are about.

There are, of course, major exceptions to this dull collection.

Most notably, there are the various recent schools of revisionist history about the origins of eighteenth- and nineteenth-century control institutions and systems. I review this work in chapter 1. It includes Rothman's pioneering history of the origins of the asylum in early nineteenth-century America and, from quite a different intellectual tradition, Foucault's extraordinary 'archaeology' of deviancy control systems.[8] We have here at last a vocabulary with which to comprehend more recent changes. Already, such work has been extended into the contemporary scene, for example in Scull's writings on 'decarceration'[9] and those of Foucault's followers on the 'policing of families' and the 'advanced psychiatric society'.[10] Less penetrating theoretically, but equally compelling polemically, are the various formulations about the 'therapeutic state', 'psychiatric despotism', the 'psychological society', and 'mind control'.[11] Note, though, that this work, and other allied, but more ambitious social critiques,[12] tend curiously to concentrate on psychiatry — the form of intervention least visible as social control and (arguably) the least appropriate to conceive simply as social control.

The more obvious, everyday forms of control — police, prisons, courts — have been much less frequently chosen for this type of sophisticated theoretical scrutiny. They are no doubt less glamorous and romantic subjects for the social critic. There is much more fun (and theoretical mileage) in studying fashions in psychoanalytical theory, nude encounter groups, primal screaming and sensitivity training, than in peering down the corridors of a juvenile correctional institution. There are, of course, useful statistics and good ethnographies of these more mundane control agencies — police departments, juvenile courts, prisons, crime prevention programmes — but these studies tend to be fragmented and abstracted. They need locating in historical space (How did they get there?) in physical space (the city, the neighbourhood) and, above all, in social space (the network of other institutions such as school and family, broader patterns of welfare and social services, bureaucratic and professional interests).

There is yet another space in which I want to locate social control: the future. From classical nineteenth-century social theory onwards, speculation about the future has always been on the sociological agenda, whether in positivist theories about evolution and progress, in grand cyclical views of world history or recently in more pessimistic and apocalyptic visions of the future. The interest in prediction has been revived in the literature about postindustrial society, futurology and social forecasting. Despite, however, the continuing public sensitivity to the crime problem as an index to 'where we are going', such literature pays virtually no attention to the subject.[13] It is, as chapter 6 shows, in the less academic world of science fiction, that the more interesting futures of social control are to be found.[14]

### WHAT FOLLOWS

What follows, as I have said, is neither a textbook nor an exhaustive review of the field. The reader will not find detailed statistical support for each argument, though I am aware that just such support is needed at certain moments. Nor do I provide up-to-date bibliographical citation for each point though, being fond of a didactic style of writing, I use my many footnotes as signposts to further reading and thought (even if these lead to diversions or directions somewhat different from my own).

A word about my audience: I have two in mind, which is to run the risk of not pleasing either. The first consists of specialists in the crime and deviance area who are familiar with the technical literature, but less so with its wider sociological ramifications. The second consists of sociologists who are aware of general debates (in areas such as the welfare state, community and professionalism) but will be quite unfamiliar with the specialist (particularly 'criminological') literature. I try to provide each audience with signposts to the other's preoccupations.

This type of writing has its costs. One is a certain unevenness of level: I have to assume some signposts as known, while others need harder work to make them visible. Another cost is over-schematization: at certain points (notably chapter 3) my didactic fitting of ideas into boxes is much neater than reality. And finally (much against my personal preference for the concrete and the specific) the argument is often too general and abstract: 'western social control systems', for example, when the reference should be something like 'delinquency control in one province of Canada'.

A word about theory. This is a book which uses theory rather than being about theory. That is, with a few exceptions central to the argument, I have not laid out intellectual genealogies, internal contradictions or counter positions. These are fascinating and important matters but not on my agenda here. Instead, I have raided certain theoretical perspectives and adapted them for my own purposes. Ideas are part of the market place and not commodities to be fetishized by the privileged few. I am aware of the risks of appropriating and domesticating theory in this way — 'popularizing' as it is usually called. Most notably, an intellectual philistinism creeps in that misrepresents ideas by taking them out of their context. I can only say that I have tried to avoid such distortion.

In this regard, a special warning is due about Foucault, whose ideas I use extensively in this way. Foucault undoubtedly has to be 'situated', 'contextualized' and 'problematized' (as today's cabbalists would put it). The best minds of our generation are busy doing all this. On the Left Bank of Paris, in the Polytechnics of Britain and in the journals of American campuses, Foucault's relationship to Marxism, structuralism, hermeneutics, idealism and much else is being scrutinized. In particular, the question of whether he is Marxist, non-Marxist or anti-Marxist has been found particularly troublesome, and rightly so. Foucault himself admits to playing games with his critics here. He quotes concepts and phrases from Marx 'without feeling obliged to add the authenticating label of a footnote with laudatory phrase'. Somewhat disengenuously, he asks 'when a physicist writes a work of physics, does he feel it necessary to quote Newton and Einstein?' Or he wonders 'what difference there could ultimately be between being a historian and being a Marxist'.[15]

Given such pronouncements (and others even more gnomic), it is little wonder that theorizing about Foucault is so difficult or that for many of his critics he is not at all a Marxist but the most extreme idealist imaginable. I will refrain from all such debate, except to note here that what orthodox Marxists see as Foucault's greatest weakness — his conception of power as a 'thing' not reducible to the workings of labour and capital — is, for my purposes, his greatest strength. So I will use Foucault more or less uncritically, even though I am altogether unsympathetic to the intellectual climate in which his work flourishes and (being exactly the type of 'humanist' he is always attacking) totally opposed to his structuralist denial of human agency. But to write today about punishment and classification without Foucault, is like talking about the unconscious without Freud.

Finally, a word about my 'sources of data'. On the whole, these are the most visible and open possible: the actual stories and words used by the people who run the control system to describe what they are doing or would like to do. These are, of course, not just 'ordinary' people but politicians, reformers, academics, social workers, psychiatrists, custodians, researchers, official committee members, professionals and experts of all sorts. And they might not be 'running' or 'doing' very much at all. Most of their words are produced to describe, explain, justify, rationalize, condone, apologize for, criticize, theorize about, or otherwise interpret things which have been, are being or will be done by others. And all these words might bear only the most oblique relationship to what is actually happening in the cells, buildings, corridors, offices and encounters of the social control apparatus.

We will have to move continually between the realm of words and the realm of deeds. The relationship between these worlds is a problem for the student of social control no more nor less than it is in any other area of social inquiry. It appears in any interesting psychological contemplation of an individual human being or any interesting sociological contemplation of a whole society. This is what is meant in the debates, respectively, about 'motive' and 'ideology'. What is perenially at issue, is how surface reasons can differ from 'real' reasons, or how people can say one thing, yet be doing something which appears radically different. Perhaps such gaps between appearance and reality or between words and action, exist because people cannot ever comprehend the real reasons for their actions. Alternatively, they understand these reasons only too well, but use words to disguise or mystify their real intentions. Or perhaps the stated verbal reasons are indeed the real ones, but because of the obdurate nature of the world, things somehow turn out differently. These various notions about words and deeds, intentions and consequences, image and reality will be my recurring themes.

My chapters are ordered as follows. *Chapter 1* is primarily historical. It describes the original foundations of the deviancy control system in the late eighteenth and early nineteenth century, compares the competing historical models used to explain these developments and introduces the themes of change and discontinuity which appeared in the 1960s. The long *Chapter 2* is primarily descriptive. It condenses all sorts of statistical and other research information in order to map out the patterns and trends in crime control that have cmerged over the past two decades. *Chapter 3* considers how these trends have been and can be explained. It sets out, as a guide to the literature, five models of the relationship between intentions and consequences in the carrying out of social control policy.

A key element in such explanations is the focus of *Chapter 4* — the stories told by ideologists of the system in order to justify and make sense of what they are doing. The surface appeals and the deeper structures of some of these stories are analysed. *Chap-*

*ter 5* moves from these tales to their tellers. It considers the power and interests of professionals and experts in determining the nature of control policy. *Chapter 6* consists of speculation and projection. It moves beyond the boundaries of the control system into the space of the neighbourhood and the city. The problem of crime control is projected on to more general visions of order and disorder.

Finally, *Chapter 7* is addressed to those with more applied and practical interests in the business of social control. It looks at cracks and holes in the structures of social control depicted or projected in the earlier chapters. And it confronts this earlier analysis with the old question, 'What is to be done?' An *appendix* at the end of the book guides the novitiate through the vocabulary of social-control talk and suggests how a glossary of such talk might be constructed.

# 1

# The Master Patterns

There have been two transformations — one transparent, the other opaque, one real, the other eventually illusory — in the master patterns and strategies for controlling deviance in Western industrial societies. The first, which took place between the end of the eighteenth and the beginning of the nineteenth centuries, laid the foundations of all subsequent deviancy control systems. The second, which is supposed to be happening now, is thought by some to represent a questioning, even a radical reversal of that earlier transformation, by others to merely signify a continuation and intensification of its patterns.

The history and the 'revisionist' history of that original change has just about been written, and is not the subject of this book.[1] The cumulative picture we have been given is of the following four key changes.

(1) The increasing involvement of the state in the business of deviancy control — the eventual development of a centralized, rationalized and bureaucratic apparatus for the control and punishment of crime and delinquency and the care or cure of other types of deviants.

(2) The increasing differentiation and classification of deviant and dependent groups into separate types and categories, each with its own body of 'scientific' knowledge and its own recognized and accredited experts — professionals who eventually acquire specialized monopolies.

(3) The increased segregation of deviants into 'asylums' — penitentiaries, prisons, mental hospitals, reformatories and other closed, purpose-built institutions. The prison emerges as the dominant instrument for changing undesirable behaviour and as the favoured form of punishment.

(4) The decline of punishment involving the public infliction of

physical pain. The mind replaces the body as the object of penal repression and positivist theories emerge to justify concentrating on the individual offender and not the general offence.

There are, of course, differences of emphasis, detail, location and timing in the revisionist historiography of this transition, but there is agreement on the reality and clarity of these momentous changes. The really important disagreements, which I will soon examine, are about *why* these changes occurred.[2]

The second master correctional change — the subject of this book — is considerably more opaque. The very essence of the transformation — just *what* is happening — is open to dispute as well as its supposed causes. For some of us there have indeed been real changes — the increasing extension, widening, dispersal and invisibility of the social-control apparatus — but these have been continuous rather than discontinuous with the original nineteenth-century transformation. Moreover, these changes run in almost every respect diametrically opposite to the ideological justifications from which they are supposed to be derived. In other words, if we are in the midst of a 'second transformation', it is not quite what it appears to be.

This chapter, then, moves from a story of change that we think is clear (but have some trouble in explaining) to another story whose very plot is ambiguous. In the process, it gives a synoptic introduction to the themes elaborated in the rest of the book.

## THE ORIGINAL TRANSFORMATION

Before the middle of the nineteenth century, the four major features of today's deviancy control system that I have outlined above had already been established in most industrial societies. These features are elaborated in *table 1* in the column headed 'Phase Two'.

I begin with the past not just because of the obvious empirical point that any current changes can only be understood in terms of the system's original foundations. That is the most important justification for considering this history. Nearly as important, though, are the conceptual analogies with the present that have been thrown up by the extraordinarily interesting current debates about eighteenth- and nineteenth-century structures of punishment, justice and treatment. For these are not just competing versions of what may or may not have happened nearly two hundred years ago. They are informed by fundamentally different views about the nature of ideology and hence quite different ways of making sense of current policies and change.

The use of the past to illuminate the present makes more than dialectical sense: all these revisionist histories contain a hidden and sometimes not-so-hidden political agenda for the present. Rothman begins and ends with the dilemmas of the welfare state and modern liberalism.[3] Foucault and more orthodox Marxists are impelled by the current 'crisis' to understand the true historical origins and functions of the penal sanction.[4] In both cases archaeology is an opportunity for a contemporary critique, whether of the liberalism of good intentions or the whole of Western humanist tradition. This is a history of Leviathan itself rather than a simple history of prison reform.[5]

The lines of these historical debates have been so sharply drawn that we can use them as templates on which to mark current controversies about social-control policy. Each of these stories evokes and is derived from the contemporary issues discussed in later chapters.

I will caricature three somewhat different stories which emerge from a study of this historical literature. Each contains four complementary (if not always entirely synchronized) sub-plots: (i), a master theory of how correctional changes or reforms occur in general; (ii) an account of why this specific historical transformation occurred (that is, from Phase One to Phase Two); (iii) an account of how the reforms embodied in this transition actually 'failed'; and (iv) the contemporary political moral of the whole story.

In each case I will concentrate on the emergence of the prison. This, of course, was only one of the complex pattern of changes (in policing, in professionalization, in the form and content of the law, in theories of punishment) during this period, but I will take it as the paradigm for understanding the whole picture.

### Uneven Progress

The conventional view of correctional change in general and of the emergence of the prison and the early nineteenth-century crime control system in particular, is based on a simple-minded idealist view of history.[6] The motor force for change lies in the realm of

TABLE 1: Master changes in deviancy control

|  | Phase One (Pre-eighteenth century) | Phase Two (From the nineteenth century) | Phase Three (From the mid-twentieth century) |
|---|---|---|---|
| 1. State involvement | Weak, decentralized, arbitrary | Strong, centralized, rationalized | Ideological attack: 'minimum state', but intervention intensified and control extended |
| 2. Place of control | 'Open': community, primary institutions | Closed, segregated institution: victory of the asylum, 'Great Incarcerations' | Ideological attack: 'decarceration', 'community alternatives', but old institutions remain and new forms of community control expand |
| 3. Focus of control | Undifferentiated | Concentrated | Dispersed and diffused |
| 4. Visibility of control | Public, 'spectacular' | Boundaries clear, but invisible inside — 'discreet' | Boundaries blur and 'inside' remains invisible and disguised |
| 5. Categorization and differentiation of deviance | Hardly developed at all | Established and strengthened | Further strengthened and refined |

| | | |
|---|---|---|
| 6. Hegemony of law and criminal justice system | Not yet established; criminal law only one form of control | Monopoly of criminal justice system established, but then supplemented by new systems | Ideological attack: 'decriminalization', 'delegalization' 'diversion', etc. but criminal justice system not weakened and other systems expand |
| 7. Professional dominance | Not at all present | Established and strengthened | Ideological attack: 'deprofessionalization', 'anti-psychiatry', etc. but professional dominance strengthened and further extended |
| 8. Object of intervention | External behaviour: 'body' | Internal states: 'mind' | Ideological attack: back to behaviour, external compliance, but both forms remain |
| 9. Theories of punishment | Moralistic, traditional, then classical, 'just deserts' | Influenced by positivism and treatment ideal: 'neo-positivist' | Ideological attack: back to justice, neo-classicism, partly successful, though positivist ideal still present |
| 10. Mode of control | Inclusive | Exclusive and stigmatizing | Ideological stress on inclusion and integration: both modes remain |

ideas: ideals, visions, theories, intentions, advances in knowledge. All change constitutes 'reform' (a word with no negative connotations); all reform is motivated by benevolence, altruism, philanthropy and humanitarianism, and the eventual record of successive reforms must be read as an incremental story of progress. Criminology and other such disciplines provide the scientific theory (the 'knowledge base') for guiding and implementing the reform programme. Thus, the birth of the prison in the late eighteenth century, as well as concurrent and subsequent changes, are seen in terms of a victory of humanitarianism over barbarity, of scientific knowledge over prejudice and irrationality. Early forms of punishment, based on vengeance, cruelty and ignorance give way to informed, professional and expert intervention.

Changes occur when the reform vision becomes more refined and ideas become more sophisticated. Institutions do not so much 'fail' as adapt and modify themselves in the light of changing moral sensitivities, scientific knowledge or social circumstances. Not that this vision is at all complacent. The system is seen as practically and even morally flawed. Bad mistakes are often made and there are abuses such as overcrowding in prisons, police brutality, unfair sentencing and other such remnants of irrationality. But in the course of time, with goodwill and enough resources (more money, better trained staff, newer buildings and more research), the system is capable of being humanized by good intentions and made more efficient by the application of scientific principles. Failures, even tragedies, are interpreted in terms of sad tales about successive generations of dedicated administrators and reformers being frustrated by a prejudiced public, poor coordination or problems of communication. Good intentions are taken entirely at their face value and are radically separated from their outcomes. It is not the system's professed aims which are at fault but their imperfect realization. The solution is 'more of the same'.

A modern version of Enlightenment beliefs in progresss, this vision represents the mainstream of the rhetoric of penal reform. Its believers are the genuine heirs of the nineteenth-century reform tradition. I devote little space to this story not because it is unimportant: quite the reverse. As a view of history and a rationale for present policies, it is by far the most important story of all. The point is that it has been so taken for granted, and not challenged until the revisionism of the last decade, that it hardly needs exposition.

*Good (but Complicated) Intentions — Disastrous Consequences*

The second model, which might also be called the 'we blew it' version of history, is a more recent, more complicated and eventually much more ambivalent heir to the Enlightenment tradition. Roughly from the mid-1960s onwards, a sour voice of disillusionment, disenchantment and cynicism, at first hesitant and now strident, has appeared within the liberal reform camp. The message was that the reform vision itself is potentially suspect. The record is not just one of good intentions going wrong now and then, but of continual and disastrous failure. The gap between rhetoric and reality is so vast, that either the rhetoric itself is deeply flawed or social reality resists all such reform attempts.

The meta-view of history is less idealist than in the progress model. Ideas and intentions must still be taken seriously, but not as the simple products of humanitarian impulses or advances in knowledge. They are, rather, functional solutions to immediate social changes. The original and most influential version of this model, Rothman's *The Discovery of the Asylum*, tells a story that is now well established.

In Rothman's account, the asylum, which links the concept of rehabilitation to the practice of incarceration, emerged in Jacksonian America in response to social changes which began at the end of the eighteenth century. Up to that point, the criminal justice system had much more limited purposes — petty offenders were deterred, punished, shamed into conformity by the stocks, whipping, fining or banishment. The more serious offender was sent to the gallows. These punishments were directed at the body, and they took place in public. Starting in the period after the war of independence, attitudes and programmes changed dramatically. An inchoate anxiety developed about the new restless, socially mobile population, together with the sense that older forms of social control (family, community, religion) were decaying and becoming outmoded. A pre-Durkheimian version of anomie theory gained acceptance among reformers: deviants were seen as the products of an anomic social order, and attempts to control or change them came to involve segregating them away from the corrupting influences of the open society. The asylum was conceived as a microcosm of the perfect social order, a utopian experiment in which criminals and the insane, isolated from bad influences, would be changed by subjecting them to a regime of discipline, order and regulation.

This goal of changing the person was born of an optimistic world view. There was a patriotic enthusiasm to be free from the brutal European monarchical heritage, and a revulsion over the spectacle of public physical punishment. The pessimistic Calvinist view of innate depravity was replaced by a more optimistic post-Enlightenment view of people as plastic creatures who could be shaped by their environments. The prospects for reform seemed bright and these institutions proliferated, eventually dominating the social-control repertoire. Soon, though, there was failure: by the 1870s, and clearly by the 1890s, it was obvious that asylums had degenerated into mere custodial institutions — overcrowded, corrupt and certainly not rehabilitative. None of the early promises had been realized but the continuing story was 'legitimation despite failure'. The profound criticisms made no difference — the institutions were kept going because of their functionalism and the enduring power of the rhetoric of benevolence.

Rothman's next book, *Conscience and Convenience*[7] continues the chronicle of reform into its next phase: the progressive reform package of the first decades of the twentieth century. As closed institutions degenerated further, a new wave of reform energy devoted itself to the search for alternatives, administrative flexibility, discretion, a greater choice of dispositions. The ideal of individual treatment, the case-by-case method and the entry of psychiatric doctrines produced a whole series of innovations — attempts to humanize the prison, probation and parole, indeterminate sentencing, the juvenile court — which have remained virtually intact and, until recently, unchallenged.

But again the gap between promise and fulfilment was enormous. None of the programmes turned out the way their designers hoped. Indeed, so 'diluted' became the ideas, that practice bore no relationship to the original text. Closed institutions hardly changed and were certainly not humanized; the new programmes became supplements, not alternatives, thus expanding the scope and reach of the system; discretion actually became more arbitrary; individual treatment was barely attempted, let alone successful. Once again, however, failure and persistence went hand in hand: operational needs ensured survival while benevolent rhetoric buttressed a long-discredited system, deflected criticism and justified 'more of the same'.

'Convenience' is Rothman's crucial concept here: it does not simply dilute, undermine or diminish the original vision ('conscience') but actually facilitates its acceptance. Far from working against the new programmes, the managers of the system (administrators, caretakers, custodians all) actively embraced them and used them for their own ends. A symbiotic alliance thus is forged between the reformers and the managers – a political force which allows programmes to survive even if they seem abject failures.

For Rothman then, an appreciation of the historical origins of the original reform vision, the political interests behind them, their internal paradoxes and the nature of their appeal, creates a story far more complicated than terms such as 'reform', 'progress', 'doing good', 'benevolence' and 'humanitarianism' imply. And an appreciation of how reforms are implemented, shows that the original design can be systematically, not incidentally, undermined by managerial and other pragmatic goals. This is explicitly a history aimed at raising our consciousness. Both these reform episodes, from post-Jacksonian America and the progressive era, bear a heavy moral lesson for contemporary liberalism.[8]

Informed by a particular ideology about the desirable limits of state intervention and by the same intellectual currents as labelling theory's ironical view about social institutions, the warning from history is that benevolence itself must be distrusted. A guide to future policy might be 'do less harm' rather than 'do more good', or anyway, 'do less altogether' rather than 'do more of the same'. But if the reform enterprise is to be distrusted, it is certainly not to be dismissed as foolhardy or deceptive. No inevitable historical forces determine correctional change: 'choices were made, decisions reached; and to appreciate the dynamic is to be able to recognize the opportunity to affect it.'[9] There is an implicit identification between the analyst and the historical reformers being analysed – hence '*we* blew it'. A new type of liberalism unencumbered by the naive optimism of its historical predecessors still allows room for manoeuvre.[10] Things can still be improved.

### Discipline and Mystification

The third and most radical (and pessimistic) model, may be called the 'it's all a con' view of correctional change. The original transformation of the system was not what it appeared to be, nor should the subsequent history of institutions like the reformed nineteenth-century prison be explained as stories of 'failure'. Contrary to Rothman's sad tale, the system was and is continuously 'successful', not, of course, in line with the progress story, but in the sense of fulfilling quite other than its declared functions. The new control system served the requirements of the emerging capitalist order for continual repression of the recalcitrant members of the working class and, at the same time, continued to mystify everyone (including the reformers themselves) into thinking that these changes were fair, humane and progressive.

The motor force of history lies in the political economy and, in the more orthodox version of this model, the theory of social change is clearly materialist. There is little room for Rothman's 'choices', 'decisions' or 'preferences', and the story assigns a quite different significance to the matter of stated intentions and motives. The problem is neither an uneven realization of the reform vision, nor a tragic cycle of failure arising from the historical tension between 'conscience' and 'convenience'. Rather, everything has occurred as ordained by the needs of the capitalist social order. Ideals and ideologies cannot much change the story. Stated intentions are assumed *a priori* to conceal the real interests and motives behind the system. They constitute a facade to make acceptable the exercise of otherwise unacceptable power, domination or class interests which, in turn, are the product of particular politico-economic imperatives.

Ideology is important then, only insofar as it succeeds at passing off as fair, natural, acceptable or even just and humane, a system which is basically coercive. Unlike either of the first two models, the analyst can have little in common with the reformer or manager. Those who run the system are either knaves who are deliberately hiding their true intentions, fools who are sheltered from full knowledge by the vantage point of their class interests, or (in structuralist terms) do not exist at all. Only the outside observer, uncontaminated by false consciousness, can really know what is going on.

The earliest version of this model appeared in the work of Rusche and Kirchheimer.[11] For them and subsequent writers in this tradition, the original master moves reflected underlying transformations of the social structure associated with the growth of the capitalist market system. Specific kinds of punishments always conform to specific modes of production. The need for regulating labour, the rationalizing impact of the market place, the need to replace traditional authority and pre-modern outlooks, the fear of the rising proletariat, the emergence of the factory as a forcing house for transforming people — all these, in various combinations and at various times, render sheer physical force anachronistic. New systems of domination and discipline are needed to socialize production: to create a submissive, well-regimented work-force.

This is what the reformed prison does. It renders docile the recalcitrant members of the working class, it deters others, it teaches habits of discipline and order, it reproduces the lost hierarchy. It repairs defective humans to compete in the market place. Not just the prison but the crime system as a whole, is part of the larger rationalization of social relations in nascent capitalism.[12] The transition from a paternalistic social order to the capitalist market system calls for new forms of regulating economic and social relationships. A new technology of repression emerges to legitimate and strengthen ruling-class control of the work-force and to deal with various redundant, superfluous or marginal populations — those groups least amenable to the virtues of bourgeois rationality. Earlier *ad hoc*, inefficient, weak and decentralized forms of control are replaced. The state takes on a more and more active role in guiding, coordinating and planning a criminal justice system which can achieve a more thorough, rationalized penetration of the subject population.

The most resolutely orthodox version of this type of Marxist tale, is to be found in the work of Melossi and Pavarini.[13] For them, the functional connection between the prison and society lies in the concept of discipline. The point is to create a socially safe proletarian, that is, someone who has learnt to accept being propertyless without threatening the institution of private property. The penitentiary is 'like a factory producing proletarians not commodities'.[14] The capitalist organization of labour shapes the form of the prison as it does all other institutions: 'the entire system of social control is modelled on the relations of production.'[15] And nothing much can change the story line: the control system continues to replicate and perpetuate the forms needed to serve its original purpose: ensuring the survival of the capitalist social order. The only modifications are those required by the evolving exigencies of capitalism: changes in the mode of production, fiscal crises, phases of unemployment, the requirements of capital. Throughout the story, stated intentions are more or less irrelevant or only of derivative status.

A quite different, and somewhat 'softer', version of this model is to be found in *A Just Measure of Pain*, Ignatieff's history of the emergence of the penitentiary system in England. Here, and especially in subsequent reflections on his own work, Ignatieff explicitly rejects 'economic determinism' and 'left functionalism' and insists on the 'complex and autonomous structure of religious and philosophical beliefs' which led reformers to conceive of the penitentiary.[16] These beliefs, and not the functional necessity of the economic system nor the 'fiction of a ruling class with a strategic conception of its functional requirements', explain why the penitentiary was adopted to solve the 'crisis in punishment' in the last decades of the eighteenth century.

In this respect — a careful scrutiny of stated intentions — and in acknowledging that things could have turned out differently, Ignatieff is not too far from Rothman. Motives are indeed complex. Driven by a perceived disintegration of society as they knew and valued it, the reformers yearned for a return to what they imagined to be a more stable, orderly and coherent social order. They acted out of political self-interest, but also out of religious belief and a sense of guilt — an understanding that the wealthy had some responsibility for crime.

Although these motives might appear similar to those of Rothman's reformers, this story belongs to my 'discipline and mystification' box because of Ignatieff's insistence on seeing organized philanthropy as expressing a new strategy of class relations. Both the *property* nature of crime and the role of the prison in containing the labour force are essential to his account. The new disciplinary ideology of the penitentiary, with its attempt to isolate the criminal class from the rest of the working class, was a response to the crisis years of early industrialization. There was a specific *class* problem to be solved, not a vague sense of unease about 'social change'. The point of the new control system — reforming the individual through punishment, allocating pain is a just way — was to devise a punishment at once so humane and so just that it would convince the offender and the rest of society of the full moral legitimacy of the law. In this respect, Rothman's type of emphasis on 'failure' is quite misplaced — the reformed prison succeeded.

Finally there is Foucault, the most ambitious and enigmatic representative of the disciplinary model.[17] 'Ambitious' because the subject of his 'history of the present' is not the prison but (no less!) the 'human soul'. 'Enigmatic' because even in *Discipline and Punish* (the most 'Marxist' of his writings) he veers between a materialist connection between prison and emerging capitalism and an idealist obsession with the power of ideas. But he must belong to this category (or a category of his own) because of his theory of relentless discipline, his ridicule of the whole enterprise of liberal reform and his total rejection of conventional notions of success and failure.

To Foucault, power and knowledge are inseparable. Humanism, good intentions, professional knowledge and reform rhetoric are neither in the idealist sense the producers of change nor in the materialist sense, the mere product of changes in the political economy. They are inevitably linked in a power/knowledge spiral: forms of knowledge such as criminology, psychiatry and philanthropy are directly related to the exercise of power, while power itself creates new objects of knowledge and accumulates new bodies of information.

The 'Great Incarcerations' of the nineteenth century — thieves into prisons, lunatics into asylums, conscripts into barracks, workers into factories, children into school — are to be seen as part of a grand design. Property had to be protected, production had to be standardized by regulations, the young segregated and inculcated with the ideology of thrift and success, the deviant subjected to discipline and surveillance. The new disciplinary mode which the prison was to represent, belonged to an economy of power quite different from that of the direct, arbitrary and violent rule of the sovereign. Power in capitalist society had to be exercised at the lowest possible cost (economically and politically) and its effects had to be intensive and extended — 'relayed' throughout the social apparatus. This was power ' . . . that insidiously objectifies those on whom it is applied, to form a body of knowledge about these individuals, rather than to deploy the ostentatious signs of sovereignty'.[18]

The historical transition which symbolized the new order was from punishment as torture — a public, theatrical spectacle — to the more economically and politically discreet prison sentence. Punishment became 'reasonable' and the body disappeared as the major target of penal repression. Within a few decades, the grisly spectacles of torture, dismemberment, exposure, amputation and branding, were over. Interest was transferred from the body to the mind — a coercive, solitary and secret mode of punishment replacing one that was representative, scenic and collective. Gone was the liturgy of torture and execution, where the triumph of the sovereign was symbolized in the processions, halts at crossroads, public readings of the sentence and, even after death, when the criminal's corpse was exhibited or burnt. In its place came a whole technology of subtle power.

When punishment leaves the domain of more-or-less everyday perception and enters into abstract consciousness, it does not become less effective. But its effectiveness arises from its inevitability, not its horrific theatrical intensity. The new power was not to punish less but to punish better, to punish more deeply into the social body. A new army of technicians (wardens, doctors, chaplains, psychiatrists, educators, social workers, criminologists, penologists) took over from the executioner (the 'immediate anatomist of pain') and proceeded to provide theories which would justify punishment as an exercise in changing the mind.

At first, according to Foucault, the older corporal forms of punishment (scaffold, ritual torture, vengeance) were to be replaced not by the prison and the disciplinary mode, but by a more juridical form. The classicist reformers like Beccaria wanted power to be reorganized more justly, to be codified, subject to exact rules of procedure and allocated according to a strict proportional economy (the 'tariff'). With no evidence that this vision was ever widespread, Foucault suggests that the ultimate fantasy was of an exact 'semiotic' correspondence between crime and punishment, to be represented in rituals spread throughout the 'punitive city' — 'hundreds of tiny theatres of punishment'.

But, for reasons Foucault hardly makes very clear, this juridical vision was never realized. In its place came the carceral or disciplinary society: the subject was to be observed, retrained and rendered obedient, not just punished along some abstract scale of justice. And the prison, instead of being just one landmark in the punitive city, now came to monopolize and symbolize all forms of punishment. Surveillance and not just punishment became the object of the exercise. The all-seeing world of Bentham's panopticon is the architectural vision of the new knowledge/power spiral: the inmate caught in a power which is visible (you can always see the central observation tower) but unverifiable (you must never know when you are being looked upon at any one moment). The prison is the purest form of the panopticon principle and the only concrete way to realize it.

But this construction was not just an isolated human menagerie, laboratory or forcing ground for behavioural change. Rather, 'panopticism' emerged as a new modality of control throughout society. The reform of prisoners, the instruction of schoolchildren, the confinement of the insane, and the supervision of workers all became 'projects of docility' related to the new political and economic order. Hospitals, schools, clinics, asylums, charities, military academies became part of the panoptic world. Once the 'human soul' enters the scene of justice, the 'disciplinary' or 'carceral' society arrives. In a (typically) cavalier reading of cause, effect and sequence, Foucault argues that the more general forms of discipline — surveillance, classification, examination, ordering, coding – (i) precede the prison as the centre of punitive justice; (ii) become organized in their pure form in the prison; and (iii) are then diffused further in the shadow of the prison.

In any event, it is only in terms of this overall 'economy of power' that we can make sense of the supposed 'failure' of the prison. Of course there was failure, in the obvious and immediately recognized sense that the prison was not going to reform offenders into honest people. But this 'monotonous critique of the prison' has always been the same: 'for a century and half the prison has always been offered as its own remedy.'[19] That is, the stock solutions of prison reformers (useful work and education, scientific treatment, better classification) cannot at all be understood as the product of idealist cycles of ideas then implementation, followed by more reforms. Instead, each reform 'is isomorphic, despite its "idealism" with the disciplinary functioning of the prison'.[20]

What, then, are the 'real' purposes of the prison? The answer is that 'failure' is merely a drawback to be strategically exploited. Delinquents turn out, after all, to be useful and prisons to be successful: (i) the new forms of illegality which threaten the bourgeoisie are now isolated, enclosed, individualized and made manageable; (ii) the needs of the control mechanism itself, with its growing multitude of dependents are fulfilled; and (iii) a state of permanent conflict is maintained. All talk of success and failure totally misses the point: the prison invents the delinquent; it cannot 'fail' because, like all punishment, it 'is not intended to eliminate offences, but rather to distinguish them, to distribute them, to use them.'[21]

This type of 'left functionalism'[22] is less incompatible with Marxism than Foucault's insistence throughout that he is constructing a 'political economy of the body' which is not simply a reflection of 'the' political economy. Certainly it was the economic take-off of the West (the accumulation of capital, new relations of production, the new legal status of property) which required the political take-off to a different form of power. The prison, however, and all other new methods of control, eventually become micro-systems with their own momentum and logic not reducible to the working of capital. Thus, 'the growth of a capitalist economy gave rise to the specific modalities of disciplinary power, whose general formulas, techniques of submitting forces and bodies, in short "political economy" could be operated in the most diverse political regimes, apparatuses or institutions.'[23]

Progress, benevolence gone wrong or relentless discipline? This book is not the place to arbitrate between these different histories of the 'same' reality, each with its own grand theories, meta-theories, meta-physics and hidden agendas. As we start moving into the present, we will see how each of these stories echoes and mimics ways of understanding the current control system. These are all interesting stories, not in the sense that they are after all the same and can be 'integrated' by word magic, but because the events they chronicle are classically over-determined. There will be more than one answer to the same questions and few answers which make only one type of theoretical sense.

Take, for example, the differences between revisionist historians about the question of stated intentions. Rothman's model has attracted formidable criticism here:

- he is trapped within the limitations of idealism;
- he takes the reformers' explanations at their face value and is too fair to them;
- he gives the impression that the entire cause and outcome rests on the rhetorical skills of the reformers allied with the bureaucratic self-interest of the managers (while his own evidence shows powerful forces at work outside these groups);
- the gap between conscience and convenience is artificial (conscience, too, may have been an ideology of self-serving convenience),
- his own criticisms of penology are launched from a vantage point well within the progressive consensus — he is 'a progressive in spite of himself.'[24]

To these critics, Rothman's work, as much as the traditional progress model, is fixated with the power of free-floating ideas and intentions. Their warning is Marx's famous one about taking words too seriously: 'whilst in ordinary life every shopkeeper is very well able to distinguish between what someone professes to be and what he really is, our historians have not yet won this trivial insight. They take every epoch at its word and believe that everything it says and imagines about itself is true.'

Such critics probably do less than justice to the complexity of Rothman's view of intentions and they certainly underestimate the pragmatic lessons which the 'good intentions—disastrous outcomes' sequence can teach us. To reduce ideology to epiphenomenal status, a mere mirage, or to dismiss stated intent as an index of confusion, self-deception, delusion, partiality, class interest or whatever, is to ignore how institutions (like the prison) were seen as solutions to immediate problems.[25] It would be to underestimate what Berlin refers to as 'the terrible power over human lives of ideological abstractions'.[26]

Ideas, of course, do not exist in some numinous realm of their own, abstracted from political and material interests, but they do vary over time and one must argue seriously — as, in fact, do most of Rothman's critics — about why these ideas took particular and successive forms. Even independent of any supposed influence they might have, even if they are wholly spurious, they are still of sociological interest. The structure might indeed only 'allow' certain ideas to dominate at any one time, but once this facilitation occurs, the ideas take on something of a life of their own, a life which generates its own social facts. And these facts do not often take the form of conscious and intentional falsification and distortion.

Knowledge is its own form of power, whether or not the knowledge is self-deceptive. In the hands of the state intelligentsia, ideas obviously serve purposes other than those stated. But they must still be seen as lived-through solutions to certain political demands. And as Berlin suggests, our judgments of these solutions — past or present — cannot be made simply in terms of an *a priori* epistemology or even by an appeal to how things actually turned out, but in terms of dilemmas and contradictions actually seen and theorized at the time. Even if apologists for the system are *only* apologists, they cannot be consigned to represent abstract historical forces. It is unreasonable to assume that the reformers were propelled by class interests beyond their understanding, and then only afterwards drew on a plausible vocabulary of legitimation.

In practice, just as few of the liberal revisionist historians of social control 'take every epoch at its word', so most Marxist alternatives pay attention to these words. And, despite his ambivalent commitment to structuralism (*because* of this, his critics would say), Foucault very much deals with intentions. Indeed, *Discipline and Punish* draws more on stories, visions and plans than any other source.

But we cannot obscure the classical sociological debate about ideology by glossing over the very real differences between these positions. It is enough at this stage (chapter 4 returns to the problem) to say that all sides might agree to ground the study of social-control talk in terms of its actual working functions. This is a more mundane way of describing Foucault's knowledge/power spiral — the sense in which control ideologies are utilitarian forms of knowledge, 'alibis' for the exercise of power.

The rest of the revisionist package can be reduced to a series of claims which seem to me more or less self-evident[27]:

- that the motives and programmes of the reformers were more complicated than a simple revulsion with cruelty, impatience with administrative incompetence or sudden scientific discovery;
- that we cannot understand the emergence of the prison apart from similar institutions of the same period;
- that the aims and regimes of such institutions must be understood in terms of a general theory, whether of the social order, power, class relations or the state;
- that experts and professionals created and captured a monopoly for their services despite their demonstrable lack of cognitive superiority;[28] and finally,
- that control institutions can persist indefinitely despite their manifest failure.

All the revisionists confront these issues. It is only Foucault though, who does not have a *mimetic* theory of the control system. The prison for Rothman is a model of functional order and equilibrium; for orthodox Marxists like Melossi and Pavarini it is a model of capitalist relations of production; for Ignatieff it is a model of the emerging class hierarchy. Only Foucault sees it as a system of power in itself. Each 'project of docility', each 'subtle act of cunning' shows that the relation between penal practice and society cannot be reduced to a question of the state, class interests, benevolent intention or metaphors of property, disorder and contract, although it is continuous with them: 'there is neither analogy nor homology, but a specificity of mediation and modality.'[29]

THE ALLEGED CURRENT MOVE: DESTRUCTURING

Beginning in the 1960s (so the story goes) those massively entrenched transformations of the early nineteenth century began to be attacked. These attacks were not altogether new in content — the prison, for example, had been criticized virtually from its inception and on the same grounds as those used by current reformers[30] — but they became more radical, they emerged not just from the margins but from the actual centre of the crime control establishment itself and, moreover, they appeared to be successful.

I will conceive of the whole package of these attacks — criticisms, claims, visions, ideologies, theories, reform movements and all sorts of other talk — as taking the form of a profound *destructuring impulse*. There appeared to be a sustained assault on the very foundations (ideological and institutional) of the control system whose hegemony had lasted for nearly two centuries. An archaeology of post-1960s social-control talk would reveal a near complete ideological consensus in favour of reversing the directions taken by the system in the late eighteenth century. These supposed reversals are listed as Phase Three in table 1 and can also be expressed as four groups of destructuring movements or ideologies (table 2), each directed against one of the original transformations.

(1) *Away from the state*: 'decentralization', 'deformalization', 'decriminalization', 'diversion', 'non-intervention': a call toward divesting the state of certain control functions or at least by-passing them and creating instead innovative agencies which are community based, less bureaucratic and not directly state-sponsored.

(2) *Away from the expert*: 'deprofessionalization', 'demedicalization', 'delegalization', 'anti-psychiatry': a distrust of professionals and experts and a demystification of their monopolistic claims of competence in classifying and treating various forms of deviance.

(3) *Away from the institution*: 'deinstitutionalization', 'decarceration', 'community control': a lack of faith in traditional closed institutions and a call for their replacement by non-segregative, 'open' measures, termed variously 'community control', 'community treatment', 'community corrections' or 'community care'.

(4) *Away from the mind*: 'back to justice', 'neo-classicism', 'behaviourism': an impatience with ideologies of individualized treatment or rehabilitation based on psychological inner-states models and a call to reverse the positivist victory and to focus instead on body rather than mind, on act, rather than actor.

My focus in this book is principally on the third set of slogans but, as we will repeatedly see, these movements often overlap with each other, draw on the same rhetoric and can invariably

TABLE 2: The Destructuring Impulse

| Nineteenth-Century Transformation | 1960s: Counter Ideologies/ Destructuring Movements |
|---|---|
| (1) Centralized state control | Decentralization, deformalization, decriminalization, diversion, divestment, informalism, non-intervention |
| (2) Categorization, separate knowledge systems, expertise, professionalization | Deprofessionalization, demedicalization, delegalization, anti-psychiatry, self-help, removal of stigma and labels |
| (3) Segregation: victory of the asylum | Decarceration, deinstitutionalization, community control |
| (4) Positivist theory: move from body to mind | Back to justice, neo-classicism, behaviourism |

be traced to common societal origins. The prison—community contrast will work as a model for all the others.

The destructuring impulse here took the form of a radical attack on the very idea of imprisonment. The whole ideological consensus about the desirability and necessity of the segregative social-control institution appeared to break. The prison — we were widely assured — was an experiment whose time had come to an end, it had played out its allocated role, the long grim history of prison reform was over, alternative methods were at hand. This seemed to be not just the old 'monotonous critique', but something more total: the institution was 'necessarily always and absolutely a failure — a colossal mistake whose commission can only be redeemed by its abolition'.[31] It was not just a matter of administrative mistakes, lack of funds, prejudiced custodians, but rather a fundamental flaw in the vision itself.

This assault on prisons became widespread from the 1960s, was found throughout the political spectrum and, initially at least, led to a decline in some rates of incarceration. The assault on mental hospitals was more dramatic and had more obvious results. At the end of the eighteenth century, asylums and prisons were places of the *last* resort; by the mid-nineteenth century they became places of the *first* resort, the preferred solution to problems of deviancy and dependency. By the end of the 1960s they looked like once again becoming places of the last resort.

The extraordinary notion of abolition, rather than mere reform, became common talk even in the heart of the control system itself. With varying degrees of enthusiasm and actual measurable consequences, officials in Britain, the USA, Canada and some Western European countries, became committed to the policy labelled 'decarceration' — the state-sponsored closing down of asylums, prisons and reformatories. This apparent reversal of the 'Great Incarcerations' of the nineteenth century was hailed as the beginning of a golden age, a form of utopianism whose ironies cannot escape anyone with an eye on history: 'there is a curious historical irony here, for the *adoption* of the asylum, whose *abolition* is now supposed to be attended with such universally beneficent consequences, aroused an almost precisely parallel set of millenial expectations among its advocates.'[32]

What beliefs could justify this strange millenarian reversal? Decarceration and each of the other three destructuring movements drew upon and created a whole package of more or less integrated beliefs, facts and ideas. In ascending order of complexity and resonance, I will call these *cognitive, theoretical* and *ideological.*

*Cognitive* The first set is seen either as a matter of common sense — 'what everybody knows' — or the irrefutable result of empirical research: (1) prisons and juvenile institutions are (in the weak version) simply ineffective — they neither successfully deter nor rehabilitate. In the strong version, they actually make things worse by strengthening criminal commitment; (2) most institutionalized deviants can be managed just as safely by various community alternatives, (3) just as effectively, (4) almost certainly more cheaply and (5) without any doubt more humanely than the prison. Community alternatives, therefore, 'must obviously be better', 'should at least be given a chance' or 'can't be worse'.

*Theoretical* The second set of assumptions appeals to a number of sociological and political beliefs not as self-evident as the previous set, but taken by the believer to be just as well established. (1) Theories of stigma and labelling have demonstrated that the further the deviant is processed into the system, the harder it is to return him to normal life. Stabilized deviance is in fact a *product* of the control system. 'Therefore' measures designed to minimize penetration into the formal system (and especially the closed custodial institution) and keep the deviant in the community as long as possible, are desirable. (2) The causal processes leading to most forms of deviance originate in society (family, community, school, economic system). 'Therefore' prevention and cure must lie in community and not in artificially created agencies constructed on a model of individual intervention. Intervention must be aimed not at 'revenge' (supposedly the pre-progress slogan) nor 'rehabilitation' (the first fruits of progress) but at 'reintegration' (the new panacea).

*Ideological*     As we shall see in chapter 4 which is devoted to this subject, the decarceration movement derives its appeal from a much wider rhetoric than is implied by the limited question of how many offenders should be sent to closed institutions. De-structuring became a package deal for many more resonant ideologies: criticisms of centralization and bureaucracy in the criminal justice system; doubts about the expertise and good faith of the helping professions; disenchantment with the rehabilitative ideal; questions about the desired limits of state intervention and even the whole notion of the liberal, welfare state itself. Towards the prison in particular but also the whole correctional apparatus (especially liberal measures such as reformatories, the juvenile court and the rehabilitative ideal) the dominant tone became 'caution', 'pessimism', 'scepticism', 'realism' or 'nihilism'. The state should 'pull back' (this is how decriminalization, diversion and decarceration were visualized). The goal should be less harm rather than more good.

Each part of the destructuring package worked out its own version of these beliefs. The diversion movement, for example, was relatively modest. The talk was about the over-reach of the criminal law; the clogged up and impersonal court system; disenchantment with sentencing inequity; the need to minimize penetration into the formal system; the need for communities to assume responsibility and to mobilize their own natural resources.

The delegalization and informalism movements were, however, much more radical and ambitious, calling for justice 'outside the law' or 'without the law'.[33] This was not just an operational criticism of the legal system, but also an explicit attempt to transfer power from the state to the 'people' (victims, disputants, the local community), or even (at its most radical) to remove the coercive, constraining and dehumanizing features of the legal order. The talk included a criticism of the inefficiency, inaccessibility, injustice, cynicism and corruption of the formal legal system; the case for replacing formal adjudication by institutions which better evoke traditional adversarial relations; the need to preserve legality by eliminating unnecessary legal acts and actors from the formal system ('minimalism'); a libertarian and *laissez-faire* attack on government regulation and bureaucracy; the desirability of reproducing simplicity, intimacy, equality and security – the alleged small-town virtues of pre-industrial rural America; a romantic yearning for 'direct', 'traditional' or even 'tribal' forms of conflict settlement and dispute resolution (for example, negotiation, mediation, reparation and restitution). Abel has well described the promised land of informal justice: institutions, processes and rights which would be 'legal' but unofficial (dissociated from state power); non-coercive (dependent on consensus rather than force); non-bureaucratic; decentralized; non-professional; autonomous from the formal legal system and with substantive and procedural rules which are unwritten, democratic and flexible.[34]

Beyond these specific critiques and visions, the destructuring ideologies could draw on certain world views of the 1960s which came from well outside the confines of organized deviancy control system. These were the years of the 'greening of America', the 'third wave', the diffusion of counter-cultural values into the educated middle class. All sorts of radical populist ideas – the spirit of sentimental anarchism – entered into the intellectual supermarket: small is beautiful, people are not machines, experts don't know everything, bureaucracies are anti-human, institutions are unnatural and bad, the community is natural and good.[35] Radicals no longer had to shout about the evils of the standardized, synchronized, centralized nightmare of the 'system'. Everyone appeared to be listening. Society could be redeemed by what Illich nicely called 'organizational disestablishment'.

As we move along, we will see the problems, inconsistencies, contradictions and unintended consequences in this whole destructuring package deal. How could it be otherwise? Entirely opposed groups will deliver the same message, entirely opposed messages will be delivered by the same group. Take for example, the specific issue of programmes aimed at treating and rehabilitating offenders in the wake of the 'nothing works' critique. *For law-and-order conservatives* the message was 'we told you so' – criminals cannot be changed, we must just protect the public through hard punishment, deterrence, incapacitation. *For tender-hearted liberals and technocratic criminologists:* rehabilitation hasn't really been tried properly, if our present techniques don't work we should try to devise others. *For tough-minded liberals:* this shows that you must distrust benevolence, let us abandon rehabilitation and substitute less ambitious goals. *For civil libertarians and the justice lobby:* treatment is an attack on civil rights, an extension of the therapeutic state and a violation of the norms of justice and proportionality. *For Marxists:* treatment obviously won't work because it is just an ideological tool to focus on the individual, thus mystifying the real causal connection with the larger social and economic structure. *For Foucault (and similar theorists):* the whole idea of treatment 'working' is absurd — it is simply another twist in the self-contained spiral of power, classification and knowledge.

But whatever the byzantine internal differences between social-control talkers, the 'same' destructuring impulse was recorded in all parts of the machine. The apostles, apologists and futurists of crime control mouthed the same clichés, used the same slogans. Magic words like 'community', 'neighbourhood' and 'reintegration' rolled off the tongues of correctional administrators, guards and judges, state legislators in America, Home Office civil servants in Britain as easily as they had in the rhetoric of radical community activists, reformers or prison abolitionists. And everyone could point to real changes. Some institutions were physically closed down and their inmates thrown out ('decarceration' or 'excarceration' as this was called). An amazing range of new community agencies proliferated. Fiscal shifts took place as funds were syphoned from institutional building programmes and financial bribery was used to encourage community 'alternatives'. Some laws were changed, status offences partially decriminalized. Publishers paid authors to produce scores of new textbooks on 'community corrections'. Foundations paid anthropologists to travel to Africa to come back with blueprints for new modes of conflict resolution. Something was happening.

### FIRST DOUBTS, SECOND THOUGHTS

The gap between the rhetoric of the destructuring movement and the reality of the emerging deviancy control system is the subject of the rest of this book. For, indeed, something *was* happening.

Instead of any destructuring, however, the original structures have become stronger; far from any decrease, the reach and intensity of state control have been increased; centralization and bureaucracy remain; professions and experts are proliferating dramatically and society is more dependent on them; informalism has not made the legal system less formal or more just; treatment has changed its forms but certainly has not died . . .

Unevenly to be sure, and in some parts of the system much more clearly than others, there has been an intensification, complication and extension of these early nineteenth-century master patterns, not their reversal. Those original patterns — rationalization, centralization, segregation, classification — were not born fully grown. They were trends which are still going on and the more recent changes are also trends yet uncompleted. But it was as if the destructuring impulse revealed how deep were those original structures.

These sorts of doubts were to emerge almost simultaneously with the impulse itself. The very same intellectuals and reformers who had been apostles of the new order now cast themselves as prophets of doom. This language of doubt drew on many sources: the tendency of a self-reflective culture to immediately reflect on itself and then reflect on these reflections, the mood of scepticism in which good intentions no longer command automatic assent; a harsh monetarist economic climate looking for any excuse to cut back on 'innovations' in social policy; a gigantic research establishment obsessed with questions of evaluation; a distrust by political radicals of all reforms as disguised measures of coercion.

Later chapters will examine each of these sources. They combined to produce a series of unhappy new stories.[36] Some gains were conceded, but the final status of the destructuring movements came to be seen as ambivalent, ambiguous or wholly negative:

(1) Decarceration and community control were not being carried out for good reasons (revulsion against institutions or the search for 'reintegration') but mainly in response to fiscal pressures and a retrenchment of welfare policies.

(2) In regard to crime and delinquency at least — if not mental illness — decarceration anyway was hardly even happening. Rates of institutionalization simply were not diminishing as rapidly as they should have.

(3) It has not been established that community alternatives are any more effective in reducing crime (by preventing recidivism) than traditional custodial measures.

(4) These new methods are not always much cheaper.

(5) They are not necessarily any more humane and, indeed, they might be less humane by disguising coercion, increasing invisible discretion or (for the mentally ill) simply dumping deviants to be neglected or exploited.

(6) Overall, the system enlarges itself and becomes more in-trusive, subjecting more and newer groups of deviants to the power of the state and increasing the intensity of control directed at former deviants.

So it was not merely a question of reform 'going wrong'. The benevolent-sounding destructuring package had turned out to be a monster in disguise, a Trojan horse. The alternatives had merely left us with 'wider, stronger and different nets'.[37]

How these sad messages were, are and will be decoded is another matter, and depends of course on the observers' political pre-delection, theoretical acumen and, above all, their degree of vested interest in the system. Some voices professed to be amazed, dis-mayed or appalled at the 'excesses', 'distortion' and 'paradoxical transformations' of their original vision.[38] Others merely recorded this as another chapter in the long saga of 'unmet promises'.[39] Many of the benevolent reformers who themselves sponsored the original rhetoric took a while to register that their *own* good in-tentions and progressive ideals, might be subject to the same iron law of 'good intentions going wrong' which they uncovered in history. For yet other critics, of course, reaction was slightly more *knowing* — not 'we blew it, yet again' but 'we could have told you so'. With the right theory and the right grasp of history everything could have been predicted: 'beware the Greeks bearing gifts!'[40]

I will soon be scrutinizing these interpretations and the reality they are supposed to be interpreting. All these critics share the sense that things have not worked out too well, that there are contradictions, discrepancies, inconsistencies, gaps between rhetoric and reality. But these first doubts, these second thoughts, however interesting intellectually, however rich theoretically, emerge from the margins of the correctional enterprise. At the heart of the system one message and one message alone can dominate — that from the 'uneven progress' story. There have indeed been advances and changes; things are going well, slow progress is being made, all such changes take time, mistakes will soon be rectified, more of the same is needed (more resources, money, patience, tolerance and, of course, research). All the signs are the same: 'business as usual'.

Our histories should have taught us to expect just this: 'legitimation despite failure' was Rothman's lesson; 'failure never matters' was Foucault's. But before we try to fit such interpretations on to the present, the emerging system has to be described more carefully.

# 2

# Inside the System

Imagine a complete cultural dummy — the Martian anthropologist or the historian of centuries to come — picking up a textbook on community corrections, a directory of community agencies, an evaluation study, an annual report. How would he or she make sense of this whole frenzied business, this *mélange* of words?

There are those agencies, places, ideas, services, organizations, and arrangements which all sound a little alike, but surely must be different:

- pre-trial diversion and post-trial diversion;
- all sorts of 'releases' — pre-trial, weekend, partial, supervised, semi-supervised, work and study;
- pre-sentence investigation units and post-adjudication investigation units;
- community-based residential facilities and community residential centres;
- all sorts of 'homes' — community, foster, small group, large group or just group;
- all sorts of 'houses' — half-way, quarter-way and three-quarter-way;
- forestry camps, wilderness and outward-bound projects;
- many kinds of 'centres'; attendance, day, training, community, drop-in, walk-in and store-front;
- hostels, shelters and boarding schools;
- weekend detention, semi-detention and semi-freedom;
- youth service bureaux and something called 'intermediate treatment';
- community services orders, reparation projects and reconciliation schemes;
- citizen-alert programmes, hot-line listening posts, community radio watches and citizen block watches;

- hundreds of tests, scales, diagnostic and screening devices . . . and much, much, more.[1]

All these words at least give us a clue about what is happening.[2] But what of:

GUIDE (Girls Unit for Intensive Daytime Education);
TARGET (Treatment for Adolescents Requiring Guidance and Educational Training);
ARD (Accelerated Rehabilitative Dispositions);
PACE (Public Action in Correctional Effort);
RODEO (Reduction of Delinquency through Economic Opportunity);
PREP (Preparation Through Responsive Educational Programs);
PICA (Programming Interpersonal Curricula for Adolescents);
CPI (Critical Period Intervention);
CREST (Clinical Regional Support Team);
VISTO (Volunteers in Service to Offenders); not to mention
READY (Reaching Effectively Acting Out Delinquent Youths);
START (Short Term Adolescent Residential Training); and
STAY (Short Term Aid to Youth).

Then who are all those busy *people* and what might they be doing? Therapists, correctional counsellors, group workers, social workers, psychologists, testers, psychiatrists, systems analysts, trackers, probation officers, parole officers, arbitrators and dispute-mediation experts? And the para-professionals, semi-professionals, volunteers and co-counsellors? And clinical supervisors, field-work supervisors, researchers, consultants, liaison staff, diagnostic staff, screening staff and evaluation staff? And what are these parents, teachers, friends, professors, graduate students and neighbours doing in the system and why are they called 'community crime control resources'? To find our way through all this, let us begin with an over-elaborate, somewhat arch and even, occasionally, quite misleading metaphor.

Imagine that the entrance to the deviancy control system is something like a gigantic fishing net. Strange and complex in its appearance and movements, the net is cast by an army of different fishermen and fisherwomen working all day and even into the night according to more or less known rules and routines, subject to more or less authority and control from above, knowing more or less what the other is doing. Society is the ocean — vast, troubled and full of uncharted currents, rocks and other hazards. Deviants are the fish.

But unlike real fish, and this is where the metaphor already starts to break down, deviants are not caught, sorted out, cleaned, packed, purchased, cooked and eaten. The system which receives the freshly caught deviants has some other aims in mind. After the sorting-out stage, the deviants are in fact kept alive (freeze-dried) and processed (shall we say punished, treated, corrected?) in all sorts of quite extraordinary ways. Then those who are 'ready' are thrown back in the sea (leaving behind only the few who die or who are put to death in the system). Back in the ocean (often with tags and labels which they may find quite difficult to shake off), the returned fish might swim around in a free state for the rest of their lives. Or, more frequently, they might be swept up into the net again. This might happen over and over. Some wretched creatures spend their whole lives being endlessly cycled and recycled, caught, processed and thrown back

Our interest is in the operation of this net and the parent re-cycling industry which controls it: the whole process, system, machine, apparatus or, as Foucault prefers, the 'capillary network' or 'carceral archipelago'. The whole business can be studied in a number of quite different ways. The fishermen themselves, their production-line colleagues and their managers profess to be inter-ested in only one matter: how to make the whole process *work better.* They want to be sure, they say, that they are catching 'enough' fish and the 'right' fish (whatever those words might mean); that they are processing them in the 'best' way (that the same fish should not keep coming back?); that the whole operation is being carried out as cheaply and (perhaps) as humanely as pos-sible. Other observers, though, especially those given the privileged positions of intellectuals, might want to ask some altogether dif-ferent questions.

First, there are matters of *quantity*: size, capacity, scope, reach, density, intensity. Just how wide are the nets being cast? Over a period of time, do they get extended to new sites, or is there a contraction — waters which are no longer fished? Do changes in one part of the industry affect the capacity of another part? And just how strong is the mesh or how large are its holes, how intensive is the recycling process? Are there trends in turnover? For example, are the same fish being processed quicker or more new ones being caught?

Second, there are questions about *identity*. Just how clearly can the net and the rest of the apparatus be seen? Is it always visible as a net? Or is it sometimes masked, disguised or camouflaged? Who is operating it? How sure are we about what exactly is being done in all the component parts of the machine?

Third, there is the *ripple* problem. What effect does all this activity — casting the nets, pulling them in, processing the fish — have on the rest of the sea? Do other non-fish objects inadvertently get caught up in the net? Are other patterns disturbed: coral formations. tides, mineral deposits?

Time to switch metaphors to something less elaborate, but more abstract. The deviancy control system occupies a space in any society — both a real space (buildings, technology, staff, clients) — and a social space (ideas, influences, effects). Of any physical object in a space, we may ask questions of *size and density* (how much space is being taken up?); *identity and visibility* (what does the object look like and where are its boundaries?) and *penetration* (how might the object — by magnetism, gravitational pull, radiation or whatever — affect its surrounding space?). These are the three sets of problems which this chapter will address. Whether or not visions of fishing nets and objects in space help very much, my task is to describe the new patterns of crime control established over the last decades. Again, the focus will be on the ideal of community control.

## SIZE AND DENSITY

By definition, the destructuring movements were aimed at decreasing the size, scope and intensity of the formal deviancy control system. All the visions were abolitionist, destructive or at least reductive: decreasing reliance on the treatment ideology, limiting the scope of the criminal law, ending or radically decreasing incarceration, restricting the full force of the criminal justice system, minimizing formal system intervention whenever possible, screening out offenders into less intrusive alternatives. To return to the net analogy: the size and reach of the net should be decreased and so should the strength of its mesh.

I focus here on the two most established and popular strategies to achieve these ends: deinstitutionalization/community alternatives and diversion. Leaving aside for the moment questions about causality, consequence and failure, the size and density questions can be answered quite simply:

(1) there is an increase in the total number of deviants getting into the system in the first place and many of these are new deviants who would not have been processed previously (wider nets);

(2) there is an increase in the overall intensity of intervention, with old and new deviants being subject to levels of intervention (including traditional institutionalization) which they might not have previously received (denser nets);

(3) new agencies and services are supplementing rather than replacing the original set of control mechanisms (different nets).

No one who has listened to the historical tales of the last chapter, particularly about the results of earlier alternatives and innovations such as probation, parole and the juvenile court,[3] should be altogether surprised at any of this. But these patterns need careful scrutiny, are not always self-evident and, as I will show in the next chapter, are never easy to explain.

### The Old Institutions Remain

Let us start with the (apparently) simple question of whether the decarceration strategy has worked in reducing the rates of juvenile and adult offenders sent to custodial institutions. The obvious index of success is not simply the proliferation of new programmes, but whether custodial institutions are being replaced, phased out or at least are beginning to receive fewer offenders overall. The statistical evidence here is by no means easy to decipher and there are complicated methodological problems in picking out even the crudest of changes. But all evidence here indicates failure — that in Britain, Canada and the USA rates of incarceration are not at all declining and in some spheres are even increasing. Community control has supplemented rather than replaced traditional methods. We may approach this data in a number of ways.[4]

First, by using official national statistics, we might simply look at overall rates of custody. The picture here is quite clear. In none of the countries we are considering, has there been any appreciable decline in the number of adult or juvenile offenders in traditional, closed custodial institutions. These numbers have either been constant or, more often, have increased either steadily or dramatically. Each standard index of imprisonment — numbers of inmates in custody at any one time, rates of custody per 100,000 of the population, numbers or rates of annual admissions, length of time in custody, building programmes, custodial budgets or staff numbers — shows a slightly different pattern, but the overall picture is indisputable: the continuation or expansion of the custodial institution. Here is a crude summary and a few examples from the mass of statistics covering the period from the late 1960s to the present.[5]

*Britain* For adults, with the exception of a slight decline in 1974, there has been a steady upward spiral in the number and rates of imprisonment. In 1982 the average daily prison population was 43,700; 11,000 of these were crowded into two per cell and 3,600 into three per cell. This was the ninth successive year in which more adults were received under sentence of immediate imprisonment. Average sentence length has increased. An estimated £80 million was spent that year on a prison building programme, not enough to accommodate the estimated number of 49,000 prisoners expected by 1991. The prison population nearly doubled over the 'decarceration' period and, by 1982, according to the Home Office Minister of State, the country was 'in the middle of the biggest prison building programme for a century'.

For juveniles, where the anti-institution and pro-community rhetoric was stronger, the increased use of custody during this period has been even larger and more dramatic than for adults. This included even the hardest and most traditional forms of custody — young adults in prisons (under-21s constituted 30 per cent of the custodial population in 1982), Borstal (up by 136 per cent between 1969 and 1977) and detention centres (up by 158 per cent during this period) — as well as the softer, more welfare-oriented institutions. Overall, a massive increase in custodial sentences to juveniles throughout this period.

*USA* For adults, the pattern is quite clear — a slight drop in incarceration rates from the mid-sixties to the early seventies (102 prisoners per 100,000 of the population in 1968 to 93 in 1972), then a dramatic increase over the 1970s (a 54 per cent increase in number between 1972–9) and continually rising. By 1981, the rate of imprisonment per 100,000 of the population was 153 and by 1982, some 175. The rise (on an annual basis) in the first half of 1982 was 14.3 per cent — the highest rate ever recorded since 1926. In 1981 alone, the net annual gain in inmates admitted to State and Federal Prison was 37,309 — nearly 90 per cent of the total gain from 1977 to 1980. At this rate of increase, there will be 500,000 prisoners by 1985. During this period there has been an incremental increase in corrections expenditure, reaching 6,361 billion dollars in 1979. Custodial staff similarly increased (more than the inmate rate, thus giving a more intensive staff : inmate ratio).

For juveniles, there was some reduction over this period of numbers of residents in public (state and local government) facilities, and incarceration rates for categories such as status offenders decreased. Much of this overall decrease however, has been offset by the increase in the number of state or privately run welfare and psychiatric establishments. Even in the conventional sector, from 1971–9, the cost of juvenile detention facilities rose from $92.1 million to $228.8 million — an increase of 148.5 per cent. The budgets of training school increased by 60 per cent in this period. And, at the hard end, locking up juveniles in adult jails had not declined; by the end of the 1970s at least 500,000 juveniles were still processed in this way.

*Canada* After a slight drop in the early seventies, incarceration rates began to climb back to the late sixties level and, by 1982, rates (in Federal and provincial prisons) were showing an all-time high, both in the standing population and those flowing through the system. Correctional service personnel increased by 84 per cent between 1966 and 1979 (as with the USA, an increase that exceeded the number of inmates).

These data are extremely complex and there are all sorts of internal variations which need explaining, for example: changes according to different types of offences, the differences between Britain and the USA, the dramatic success of other reasonably similar countries (such as Holland)[6] in cutting incarceration rates. It is important also to note that, although overall imprisonment rates are not declining, there has been in most places a proportionate decline in the use of imprisonment as a percentage of all sentences. In other words — to take the British example — although more identified offenders are being sent to prison each year, fewer of the total being sentenced (a decline of about 25 per cent in 1965 to 15 per cent in 1980) are being sent to prison. Only in this respect can decarceration be said to have 'worked' — a slight decline in the reliance on imprisonment in the overall sentencing repertoire. Yet even here there are doubts because many of these alternative sentences are ways of deferring or suspending imprisonment. In every other sense, though, there has been an exponential rise in the use of imprisonment: prison populations in the USA and Britain have roughly doubled since 1950.

A second empirical strategy in looking at net size, is not to use global rates, but to compare systems with differing degrees of commitment to the community ideology. This is logically the most useful research strategy but for obvious reasons the most difficult. This sort of comparison between different states in the USA clearly shows that increased reliance on community programmes is not accompanied by a corresponding decrease in the use of institutional programmes. The reverse is true: the states which score high on use of community programmes, also have an above-average use of institutions.[7]

A third strategy — a refinement of the simple reliance on official statistics — is a detailed follow-through of the overall dispositional patterns of one correctional system over time. Exemplary work of this kind is Hylton's time-series analysis of trends in the Saskatchewan province of Canada from 1962–79. At the end of the 1950s, the province adopted a clearly articulated philosophy of community control, there was a massive investment in the new programmes and a clear belief that they would replace institutions.

The results showed no reduction at all in reliance on custody, whether measured by numbers and rates of admission or number and rates incarcerated on any given day. The average daily inmate count per 100,000 of the population increased from 55.23 in 1962 to 84.87 in 1979 — a 54 per cent increase in incarceration rates on any given day over 18 years. The rate of admissions rose over this same 18-year period by 58 per cent. Institutions now process more offenders than at any time in the province's history and all trends indicate that this expansion is increasing. Again, decarceration has worked only in the sense that the relative reliance on custody compared to other dispositions has decreased — from about two-thirds of all sentences in 1962 to about a quarter in 1979. Some potential inmates are syphoned off but the institution remains and expands.

A final research approach is to narrow down even further to case studies of particular legislative acts, projects or programmes. The most publicized (and evaluated) series of programmes in the USA have been the Massachusetts reform, the California Probation Subsidy programmes, DSO (Deinstitutionalization of State Offenders) and Community Corrections Acts in states such as Minnesota. These are mainly variations on the strategy of providing economic incentives (bribes) to local authorities to switch from custody to community. There have been some notable successes here, for example the DSO programme in certain states and the well-known and dramatic Massachusetts strategy of closing down all juvenile training schools.[8] Although there are important reservations, which I will consider later, about the nature of the alternatives, it is clear that traditional custody has declined in these cases. These exceptions are important for social policy. Overall assessment of other programmes, however, suggests far more negative or equivocal results.

In California, for example, initial reported decreases in commitments to the Youth Authority have been interpreted differently by later research and do not seem to have been sustained.[9] While the programme shifted control of juveniles destined for state institutions to local jurisdiction, this did not reduce the state's overall reliance on custody. That is to say, the form and location of confinement changed and these new forms of commitment 'compensated' for any reductions in conventional admissions. Commitments shifted to local country levels, there was more detention by the police and (as we shall see) the notion of 'intensive treatment in the community' actually glossed over a degree of hidden custody within the community programmes themselves. Overall, offenders ended up spending more time in institutions.

Little research of equivalent sophistication is available in Britain, but the Intermediate Treatment (IT) experience certainly fits this general pattern.[10] Implemented from the beginning of 1971, this is a system of intensive supervision in the community designed to provide care and control for a whole range of juvenile offenders and 'children in trouble' who would otherwise have been sent to 'residential care' (the English euphemism for custody). Quite the opposite has happened. As the national data suggest, there has been a massive increase in custodial sentences for juveniles from 1968 to the present. The greater the IT provision, the larger become the institutional populations.

From all these sources then — with isolated exceptions — the story is of stable or increasing institutional populations over the last twenty years. As one analyst of the British evidence notes, the institution has not only survived the ethos of the 'era of decarceration' but has actually become stronger.[11]

## Overall the System Expands

If the use of community control is increasing and if traditional custody is either increasing or only remaining constant, an inescapable conclusion suggests itself — that the system overall is getting larger. This, in fact, is the trend reported from all research.

Again, we might approach the problem by examining global statistical trends or by trying to isolate specific effects of community strategies. The total correctional caseload in the USA (adults and juveniles incarcerated or under supervision) increased from 1,281,801 (661.3 per 100,000 of the population) in 1965 to 1,981,229 (921.4 per 100,000) in 1976. This was an absolute increase of 54.6 per cent and a rate increase of 39.3 per cent. By 1983, it was estimated that some 2.4 million persons were under some form of correctional care, custody or supervision — a rate of 1,043 per 100,000 of the population (leaving out allied forms of welfare and psychiatric tracking). Three-quarters of these were somehow 'in the community'. Twenty years after 1965, the overall system will have nearly doubled its reach.

Other indices from the USA, Britain and Canada also show overall increases in rates 'under correctional sanction or supervision'. Hylton's data on one province in Canada are a microcosm of the trend to expand in systems committed to community control. The rate per 100,000 of the population under supervision of the Saskatchewan correctional system increased from 85.46 in 1962 to 321.99 in 1979 — 277 per cent in 18 years. The admissions rate increased in these years by 179 per cent — a rate of increase each year of about 44 per cent. In simpler terms, the rate of persons under supervision by the correctional system on any given day more or less tripled during these 18 years.

This type of finding is duplicated throughout the research literature. The system overall expands relentlessly while the relative proportions sent to prison rather than community programmes declines (in that Canadian case, from two-thirds down to one-quarter over 18 years). The obvious inference then, strongly supported by correlational evidence, is that the use of community alternatives actually causes an overall system expansion which might not otherwise have occurred. The correlational logic is simple enough: if community programmes were *replacing* institutions, then systems high in community places would show a less-than-average use of institutions. But if community was *supplementing* institutions, then systems high in community would also have an above-average use of institutions and this is just what seems to be happening. Such tricky statistics aside, how does all this happen? (Later chapters try to explain why.)

*New Deviants are Drawn in and Intervention Intensifies on the
same old ones*

The simplest way of visualizing the non-reduction of incarceration
rates and the concomitant expansion of the whole system, is to
argue that the 'wrong' populations are being swept into the new
parts of the net. 'Wrong' in the sense of being inappropriate,
'inappropriate' in the sense of not being the populations for whom
the original reforms were meant — in other words, not the populations who would otherwise have been incarcerated if the new
programmes did not exist.

Clearly, of course, some of the new 'clients' *are* being kept out
of institutions; the changes in relative disposition rates show this.
But large proportions of these populations — the literature sometimes shows between a half and two-thirds — are 'shallow-end'
or soft delinquents,[12] minor or first offenders whose chances of
incarceration would otherwise have been slight. As long as the
strategy is not being used for genuine 'deep-end' offenders and as
long as institutions are not literally closed down or phased out,
incarceration will tend to increase, the system will be more interventionist overall and a substantial number of community clients
— perhaps a majority — will be subjected to a degree of intervention higher than they would have received under previous non-
custodial options such as fines, conditional discharge and ordinary
probation or parole.

There are considerable research problems in showing all this
and especially in estimating the shallow-end : deep-end ratio.
Macro-research on how the system changes overall will not necessarily produce the same results as micro-research trying to show
that particular offenders on a new 'alternative' programme would
not have been sent to an institution anyway. And as Klein suggests
in regard to status offences, the total confusion about the original
definition of such terms makes it almost impossible to know
whether the right clients have been 'targeted'.[13] Nevertheless,
there is overwhelming consensus that a considerable number of
community clients, perhaps the majority, are shallow-enders. To mix
these aquatic metaphors: the old nets keep on catching most of
the original deep-end fish, while the new nets take up the remain-
der but mostly catch the original shallow-enders (the minnows).

All these spatial trends can be observed even more clearly in
regard to diversion. Because the idea itself is more radical than
deinstitutionalization — deflection from the whole system and not

merely its deep custodial recesses — studies of the diversion strategy demonstrate failure even more radically.[14] Diversion was hailed as the most radical form of destructuring short of complete non-intervention or decriminalization. At the height of the diversion 'fad' (as it is now being called) official estimates and hopes were that as many as 70 per cent of juveniles passing through the formal system could be diverted away into less intrusive options. (The figure 70 per cent seems to have a magically radical ring. At the crest of the decarceration wave, this was the figure most often quoted as the proportion of inmates who do not 'need' to be locked up.) The grand rationale is to restrict the full force of the criminal justice system to more serious offences and either to eliminate or substantially minimize penetration for all others. By diverting people at the 'front end' of the system, it is hoped that more reductions can take place at later stages. The strategy has been most systematically adopted for juveniles (a remarkable development, as the central agency from which offenders were to be diverted, the juvenile court, was itself the product of the Progressive's reform movement aimed at 'diversion').

Clearly all justice systems, particularly juvenile ones, have always operated with a substantial amount of diversion. Real diversion has always occurred in the sense that by far the majority of delinquent acts noticed by parents, teachers, social workers, neighbours, employers and casual observers are simply not acted on in any way at all. And at the earliest formal part of the system's front end, police discretion has always been widely used to divert juveniles: either right out of the system (by dropping charges, informally reprimanding or cautioning) or by informal referral to social service agencies. Most research routinely quotes figures as high as 70 per cent for this type of police diversion.

What has now happened, is that these discretionary and screening powers have been formalized and extended and, in the process, quite transformed. Diversion is no longer something that just 'happens': it takes the form of a massive infrastructure of programmes and agencies: throughout the 1970s, the US Federal Government, through the Law Enforcement Assistance Administration (LEAA), funded over 1,200 adult and juvenile diversion programmes, at a cost of $120 million.

It is this infrastructure which calls for the distinction between *traditional* or *true* diversion — removing the juvenile from the system altogether by screening out (no further treatment, no service, no follow-up) — and *new* diversion which means screening plus programme (formal penetration is minimized by referral to programmes in the system or related to it). Only traditional diversion is true diversion in the sense of diverting *from*. The new diversion diverts — for better or worse — *into* the system. Cressey and McDermott's laconic conclusion from their evaluation of one such set of programmes might apply more generally:

> If 'true' diversion occurs, the juvenile is safely out of the official realm of the juvenile justice system and he is immune from incurring the delinquent label or any of its variations — pre-delinquent, delinquent tendencies, bad guy, hard core, unreachable. Further, when he walks out of the door from the person diverting him, he is technically free to tell the diverter to go to hell. We found very little 'true' diversion in the communities studied.[15]

In other words, to return to the example of police discretion, where the police used to have two options — screen right out (the route for the majority of encounters) or process formally — they now have the third option of diversion into a programme. It is this possibility which allows for net extension and strengthening. For what happens is that diversion is used as an alternative to screening out and not as an alternative to processing. The system thus expands to include those who, if the programme had not been available, would not have been processed at all (genuine new fish). Or if the diversion programme is located at a later stage of the machine, the clients are those who would otherwise have received less obtrusive options like fines, conditional discharge, suspended sentence or traditional probation (old shallow-enders). Both phases are examples of what the literature now calls 'accelerated penetration'.

In either case, diversion simply has not occurred: 'diversion means to turn away from and one cannot turn someone away from something toward which he was not already heading.'[16] As with community 'alternatives', the exact proportions of such wrong clients (their 'transitional probability rating', to use the approved term) are difficult to estimate. Such averages hide massive variations from one programme to another, but the research consensus is that at least half the divertees are what American police sometimes call 'cream puff' cases — young people who would otherwise have been 'counselled and released' by the police or would never have been inserted this far into the system. Compared to other offenders, they tend to be younger, have committed less serious offences or status offences (which might include matters such as 'incorrigibility', running away and truancy) have a less serious (or no) past record and are more likely to be female.

Moreover — an even more radical form of net extension — these diversion clients might not have committed any offence at all. The ideology of early intervention and treatment and the use of psychological or social-work selection criteria, allows diversion to be incorporated into wider preventive strategies. Legal definitions and due process give way to low visibility, 'discretionary decision making' by administrative or professional agencies. The drift is to work with parts of the population not previously reached, variously defined as young people 'in trouble', 'at risk' or 'in legal jeopardy', 'pre-delinquents' or 'potential delinquents'. These trends are not primarily a widening of social control into 'empty' spaces, but an intensification and formalization of previous methods. Populations who once slipped quickly through the net are now retained much longer; many innovative alternatives become adjuncts to established sanctions such as probation and fines.[17]

We arrive then at something close to a total reversal of all the supposedly radical justifications on which the original diversion strategy was based: reduction of stigma and labelling, non-intervention, decreased emphasis on individual treatment, more justice and reduction of system load. Instead, intervention comes earlier, it sweeps in more deviants, is extended to those not yet formally adjudicated and it becomes more intensive. And all this takes place in agencies co-opted into the criminal justice system (but less subject to judicial scrutiny), dependent on system personnel for referrals and using (as we shall see) more or less traditional treatment methods.

The whole topic of net space and density is altogether fascinating and complex. I have given only a glimpse of the intricate ways in which the system grows, renews itself and mutates, and how all this might be studied. Note, for example, what we can learn from the characteristics of the new clients of these community and diversion programmes. These clients are not simply mistakes who enter the system because screening has been relaxed. Quite the contrary. It is only because screening is so careful and successful that the shallow-enders and cream puffs are pulled further in. They come from precisely those backgrounds — fewer previous arrests, minor or no offences, good employment record, better education, younger, female — which all research suggests to be overall indicators of greater success. The point is to find as clients for community services those who have the strongest community ties and commitments in the first place. Behind the elaborate ritual of psychological testing and diagnoses, this is, in fact, how selection takes place. Many agencies, such as various pre-trial bail release schemes, simply use a crude points system which guarantees acceptance on to the programme to those who score best on length of residence in one place and employment record. This, presumably, goes according to the old principle of giving more to those that have more.

Of course, as the statistics indicate, some bad risks (the 'real' target clients) do get in. Certain programmes do give the offender a genuine choice about entry and there is pressure to make the programme look impressive by really rescuing offenders from the deep end. In these cases, some of the old losers — who probably prefer anything to returning to the traditional system — will enter the programme.[18] But too many of them will make the programme look bad and lead to pressure for a clamp down. If there is little room for such self-selection (the normal state of affairs) then only the shallow-enders will be let in — those who will make the programme less risky. This process repeats itself at all the increasing stages in the system: each level creaming off the clients it wants — those who are amenable, treatable, easy to work with, the good prospects. The rest are 'diverted' to the next level up.

All this ensures a steady clientele. And the more benign, attractive and successful the programme becomes defined, the more it will be used, the more staff and budgets will be needed and the wider it will cast its net (nearly everyone could do with a little 'help'). Police will divert because this is less risky than outright release and much less trouble than fighting the case through the courts (especially as the courts become more legalistic and therefore make it difficult to secure a conviction). Judges are attracted to the new programmes because this avoids unnecessary incarceration, while at the same time ensuring that 'something constructive' is done.

To use yet another metaphor (fishing nets? objects in space?), we have here a benevolent kind of suction machine, driven by the principle of *incremental eligibility.* Each stage retains its own eligible material, leaving another body — in a deeper or shallower part of the system — to operate its own eligibility criteria. Of course things might not always run so smoothly. Agencies within the criminal justice system might compete over the same potential clientele, or clients might be tracked and retracked between crime, welfare and psychiatric systems. These moves in the game of re-labelling and moral passage then might be formalized in administrative or legal changes.

A typical example would be status offenders. They can be relabelled 'downwards' as being in need of care, treatment or resocialization and thus the property of welfare or treatment agencies. But just as likely, youths previously defined as status offenders and hence eligible for decarceration, diversion or even decriminalization, can now be relabelled upwards as real delinquents. The police might push up the arrest rates of such offenders in order to compensate for the loss of the status offender market. As Lemert says, they are simply doing what comes naturally and easily to them: dipping into the reservoir of youths who might otherwise have gone free.[19] And this dipping does not occur randomly. Research evidence is mounting, for example, that *girls* with little prior system contact are a particularly vulnerable group for further processing by the new programmes.[20]

The suction principle is even more complicated by the fact that as the system changes, so all its component parts adjust themselves, in good cybernetic fashion, to take into account the new feedback. The disposition received by an offender arriving at a particular level is now affected by the knowledge that he was 'diverted' at an earlier level. The most severe punishments go not just to the worst offenders in legalistic terms, but to those who foul up at their previous level. In 1981, for example, about one out of every five admissions to prison in the USA were for conditional release violations rather than as direct sentences from the court.

Sometimes, with radical system changes, whole stages might be skipped. This appears to be one of the effects of Intermediate Treatment in Britain. Some previous shallow-enders (who might have received probation, fines or conditional discharges) become defined as unsuitable for the new programmes and are sucked straight into the custodial end of the system. The new 'care order' (a custodial sentence based on welfare rather than legalistic criteria) permits some marginal delinquents to go to custody while the new system prefers to take others who might not have committed offences at all but come from 'deprived backgrounds'. Many of the care orders which fail to demonstrate the supposedly objective criteria for care (one study found as many as 89 per cent were in this category)[21] are renewed not because of further offences, but because the client fouls up in the system (by being uncooperative or by absconding).

In summary, net expansion occurs through a series of what Illich nicely called 'iatrogenic feedback loops'. The juvenile court diverted from the adult system; diversion agencies divert from the juvenile courts; new diversion agencies divert from the diversion agencies. Each stage creates the deviant it wants and constructs its

programmes accordingly. These organizational loops thus do more
than enlarge the capacity of the system, they also change its
character. For example, as the community rhetoric becomes accepted (even if it is not what it might seem) traditional agencies
change their operating principles. Prisons now become defined in
more negative terms: warehouses for the incorrigibles, hard cases,
those which the soft end of the system has been unable to reach.
They have been given their chance in the community, now they
have reached the bottom of the barrel.[22]

There are also such feedback loops to networks of deviancy
control, care and treatment right outside the criminal justice
apparatus. As I will describe in the next section, boundaries
between these systems are now less clearly defined and therefore
gains and losses are virtually impossible to estimate. The flow
occurs in both directions: former offender groups are retracked
into the welfare or mental health system and previous patients
(notably decarcerated mentally ill adults) come into the criminal
justice system.

This is merely one example of the technical complexity of
describing changes in the size and density of the control network.
But the broad outlines are clear — the older and discredited parts
of the system (particularly traditional custodial institutions)
remain. Overall, the system enlarges itself and some, at least, of
this enlargement is due to the proliferation of the newer community alternatives. I will raise later the obvious question of the
relationship between this expansion and increasing crime rates. It
is enough to say here that in every case system expansion is larger
than crime expansion.

### VISIBILITY, OWNERSHIP AND IDENTITY

Most forms of net widening are perceived as largely unintended
consequences of destructuring reforms. Or at least, as the notion
of 'unintended consequences' already implies a particular theory,
these effects could not be predicted in any simple way from the
ideology. I turn now to three properties of the machine: the visibility of its boundaries; its ownership or sponsorship; and the
identity of its operations. The first two of these could certainly
have been predicted and understood from the ideology.

## Boundaries are Blurred

The segregated and insulated nineteenth-century institutions made the actual business of deviancy control invisible, but its boundaries visible. That is to say, what went on inside these places was supposed to be unknown. Institutions like prisons gradually became wrapped with an impenetrable veil of secrecy.[23] Segregation came to mean insulation and invisibility. This was the transition which Foucault charted — from the visible, public spectacle (torture, execution, humiliation) to the more discreet form of penitentiary discipline. The public trial remained the only visible part of the system.

But a condition for internal invisibility was to have the boundaries of the punitive system more visible and obvious. We should not see or know what went on behind the walls of the prison, but we should definitely know that these were walls. Whether prisons were built in the middle of cities, out in the remote countryside or on deserted islands, they had clear spatial boundaries to mark off the normal from the deviant. And these spatial boundaries were reinforced by ceremonies of social exclusion: prisoners were sent away or sent down, their 'bodies' were symbolically received at the prison gate, then — stripped, washed and numbered — they entered another world. Those on the outside would wonder what went on behind the walls, those inside could try to imagine the 'outside world'. Inside/outside, guilty/innocent, freedom/captivity, imprisoned/released — these were all distinctions that made sense.

In the new world of community corrections, these boundaries are no longer nearly as simple. The way *into* an institution is not clear (it is just as likely to be via a post-adjudication diagnostic centre as a police car) the way *out* is even less clear (graduated release or partial release is just as likely as full freedom) nor is it clear what or where *is* the institution. There is, we are told, a 'correctional continuum' or a 'correctional spectrum': criminals and delinquents might be found anywhere in these spaces. And so fine, and at the same time so indistinct, are the gradations along the continuum, that it is by no means easy to know where the prison ends and the community begins or just why any deviant is to be found at any particular point. Even the most dedicated spokesmen for community treatment have some difficulty in specifying just what 'the community' is; one early report confessed that the term community treatment 'has lost all descriptive usefulness except as a code word with connotations of "advanced correctional thinking" and implied value judgements against the "locking up" and isolation of offenders.'[24]

Even the most cursory examination of the new programmes reveals that many varieties of the more or less intensive and structured 'alternatives' are virtually indistinguishable from the real thing. A great deal of energy and ingenuity is being devoted to this problem of definition: just how isolated and confining does an institution have to be before it is a prison rather than, say a 'residential community facility'? Luckily for us all, criminologists have got this matter well in hand and are spending a great deal of time and money on such questions. They have devised quantitative measures of internal control, degree of community linkage, normalization (harmony with neighbourhood, type of building, name of programme) and the like. There are now any number of standardized scales for assigning programmes along the 'institutionalization–normalization continuum' or awarding them PASS (Program Analysis of Service Systems) or MEAP (Multiphasic Environmental Assessment Procedure) scores.[25]

But these are not just untidy loose ends which scientific research will one day tie up. Community control is a project explicitly devoted to changing traditional ideas about punishment. The ideology of the new movement quite deliberately demands that boundaries should not be made too clear: the metaphor of 'crumbling walls' implies an undifferentiated open space. The main British prison reform group, the Howard League, once called for steps to 'restore the prison to the community and the community to the prison'. Less rhetorically, here was an early enthusiast for a model 'community correction centre': 'the line between being "locked up" and "free" is purposely indistinct because it must be drawn differently for each individual. Once the client is out of Phase I, where all clients enter and where they are all under essentially custodial control, he may be "free" for some activities but still "locked up" for others.'[26]

There is no irony intended in using inverted commas for such words as 'free' and 'locked up' or in using such euphemisms as 'essentially custodial control'. This sort of blurring — deliberate or unintentional — may be found throughout the complicated networks of 'diversion' and 'alternatives' which are now being set up.

The half-way house might serve as a good example. These agencies — called variously, 'residential treatment centres', 'restitution shelters', 'rehabilitation residences', 'guidance centres', 'reintegration centres', 'community training residence programmes' or (with the less flowery language preferred in Britain) simply 'hostels' — invariably become special institutional domains themselves. They might be located in a whole range of odd settings — private houses, converted motels, the grounds of hospitals, YMCAs, beach clubs, the dormitories of university campuses or even within the walls of prisons themselves. Their programmes turn out to reproduce regimes and sets of rules very close to the institutions themselves: about security, curfew, passes, drugs, alcohol, permitted visitors, required behaviour and surveillance.[27] Indeed it becomes difficult to distinguish a very 'open' prison, with liberal provisions for work release, home release and outside educational programmes, from a very 'closed' half-way house.

Any number of half-way houses, for example, can be found to be more 'institutional' than the Vienna Correctional Centre, a minimum security institution in Illinois which counts as a prison.[28] Here, inmates:

- are trained as emergency technicians and operate radio-directed ambulances;
- learn fire fighting and constitute the local fire department;
- serve as umpires on a Little League baseball field;
- make up a band to entertain at concerts and high school games;
- meet local residents who come to fish in the prison lake, play basketball in its gym or join in its adult education centre or vocational training programme.

The prison, we are told, looks like a suburb or college campus, paths lead to separate 'neighbourhoods' and prisoners have the key to their own rooms. Many hostels 'in the community' are more restrictive and artificial than this sounds.

To confuse matters further: half-way houses may be half-way *in* for those too serious to be left at home, but not serious enough for the institution — and hence are a form of 'diversion' — or half way *out* for those who can be released from the institution but are not yet 'ready' for the open community — and hence are a form of 'after care'. To make life more difficult the same centre is sometimes used for both these purposes, with different rules for the half-way in inmates and the half-way out inmates.

Even this degree of blurring and confusion is not enough: one advocate draws attention to the advantages of *quarter-way* houses and *three-quarter-way* houses.[29] These 'concepts', we are told, are already being used in the mental-health field, but are not labelled as such in corrections. The quarter-way house deals with people who need supervision on a near permanent basis, while the three-quarter-way house is designed to care for persons in an 'acute temporary crisis needing short-term residential care and little supervision'. Then, taking the opposite tack from devising finer and finer classification schemes, other innovators argue for a 'multi-purpose' centre. Some half-way houses already serve as a parolee residence, a drop-in centre, a drug-treatment programme and a non-residential walk-in centre for after care. And in the absence of a handy multi-purpose centre in the neighbourhood, a package deal is worked out around the offender himself, shuttling him from probation, a day training centre, a hostel, a service for alcoholics and a job creation programme.[30]

Behind all this administrative surrealism, this manic activity, some more significant forms of blurring are happening. For many of these 'multi-purpose' centres, bureaux, services and agencies are directed not just at convicted offenders, but are preventive, diagnostic or screening enterprises aimed at potential, pre-delinquent or 'at risk' populations. The ideology of community treatment and the preventive thrust of the diversion strategy allows for an altogether facile evasion of the delinquent/non-delinquent distinction.

A good example of this evasion is the British system of Intermediate Treatment (IT). This is not just an intermediate possibility between sending a child away from home and leaving him in his normal home environment, but also a new way 'to make use of facilities available to children who have not been before the courts, and so to secure the treatment of "children in trouble" in the company of other children through the sharing of activities and experiences within the community.'[31] Note the wording of these accounts of IT projects: 'a provision for young people at risk of institutionalization, unemployment, homelessness, family breakup and lack of work skills'; 'community based provision for adolescents and children who are deprived or who are more at risk of getting into trouble than their contemporaries'; 'a continuum of care . . . with intensity increasing according to the degree of deviancy or perceived needs'.

There is a deliberate attempt here to evade the question of whether a rule has actually been broken. 'Illegal behaviour' (degree of deviancy?), we are assured, 'merges almost imperceptibly with behaviour which does not contravene the law' (perceived needs?). The 'deprived' are not very different from the 'depraved'. The point is to devise a service flexible enough to deal with both − a service which is simultaneously a response to delinquency and to other 'crises' (family breakdown, deviant leisure styles, school problems, unemployment) in the 'normal life cycle'.[32]

This type of definitional 'flexibility' is ensured by the tendency of the new agencies to operate in a closed circuit free from legal scrutiny. While the traditional screening mechanisms of the criminal justice system have always been influenced to a greater or lesser degree by non-offence related criteria (race, class, demeanour) the offence was at least considered. Except in the case of wrongful conviction, some law must have been broken. This is no longer clear: a delinquent may find himself in custody ('short-term intensive treatment') either because of welfare/treatment criteria (at risk, deprived) or by programme failure (violating the norms of some other agency in the continuum, for example by non-attendance at a therapy group or 'acting out'). By 1981, through a classic form of net widening, at least 45 per cent of participants on all IT programmes were not subject to any court order at all.

The definitional blurring which occurs in regard to individual judgements (referral, diagnosis, screening, eligibility) is reproduced at the organizational and personnel level. Agency names like 'Youth Service Bureau' or 'Intermediate Treatment Centre' and staff titles such as 'counsellor' or 'supervisor' are interchangeable and they might just as easily be managed by the educational, welfare or health sectors as by criminal justice authorities. All this again is intentional: 'as institutional walls disintegrate, figuratively speaking, the boundaries between the various human service areas will disappear as well — and correctional problems will come to be the problem of a range of professionals serving communities.'[33] Crime and delinquency nets thus not only become blurred in themselves but get tangled up with other welfare, treatment and control nets. In Britain, social workers are the most powerful human service professionals operating in these waters, while in the USA the mental-health net is more important.

For adults, the mental health/crime interchange has been reported from two quite opposite directions. With the successful decarceration of the mentally ill ('successful' because whatever the damaging criticism of the end result, average daily mental hospital populations in the USA declined dramatically from 600,000 in 1955 to 100,000 in 1980) and the development of more stringent civil liberty requirements, many offenders with records of mental illness get into hospitals. This is because the crime-like notion of 'dangerousness' is increasingly being used to decide on commitment standards. Commitment is thus used in lieu of arrest. From the opposite direction, however, many recently decarcerated mental patients who do not seem dangerous, but certainly are troublesome and bizarre, might be arrested on minor public order charges (like loitering) because the police can think of nothing else to do with them.[34]

For juveniles, there are even more intricate patterns of re-tracking, between delinquency, mental illness and welfare systems. Besides hybrid services such as intermediate treatment, the most significant development is a hidden correctional system (largely, as we will see in the next section, privately owned) which operates along psychiatric lines. There is a network of agencies — in-patient psychiatric settings, residential treatment centres, out-patient clinics — that redefine delinquency in terms such as 'disruptive behaviour', 'acting out', 'adjustment reaction' or 'runaway reaction by adolescents'. Lerman has described in detail the various levels of relabelling now taking place in the juvenile system in America: how terms such as 'voluntary admissions', 'other non-offenders' or 'dependency' are used to retrack petty offenders from the old training schools into 'community treatment' in a private facility; how child welfare and social service workers use psychiatric rather than juvenile court labels to justify removal of the child from family; and how the child welfare, mental health and juvenile correctional systems are drawing on overlapping populations.[35]

These forms of de- and re-labelling are extremely difficult to demonstrate empirically. It is already clear, however, that a probable outcome of this blurring (especially with regard to juveniles) is the creation of a hidden custodial system, under welfare or psychiatric sponsorship, which official delinquency statistics simply ignore. This is what is meant by the accurate (if clumsy) term 'transinstitutionalism'.

But leaving aside these intricate overlaps between the crime, mental illness and welfare nets, it is evident that even within the criminal justice system itself, we are witness to something more than just the proliferation of agencies and services, finely calibrated in terms of degree of coerciveness or intrusion or unpleasantness. The uncertainties are more profound than this: voluntary or coercive, formal or informal, locked-up or free, guilty or innocent. Those apparently absurd administrative and research questions — When is a prison a prison or a community a community? Is the alternative an alternative? Who is half-way in and who is three-quarter-way out? — beckon to a future when it will be impossible to determine who exactly is enmeshed in the formal control system, and hence subject to its jurisdiction and surveillance, at any one time.

## Public Merges with Private

The notion that the state should be solely responsible for crime control only developed in Britain and the USA in the nineteenth century. The key changes then — the removal of prisons from private to public control and the creation of a uniformed public police force — are taken as the beginning of the continued and voracious absorption of deviancy control into the centralized apparatus of the state. And this process indeed seems endless: increasing state control in the form of more laws, regulations, administrative and enforcement agencies.

In parts of the system, though, there are important developments which are moving in a different direction. Particularly with regard to the police, some observers have claimed that 'the spheres of public and private have actually become progressively less distinct,' that there has been a 'privatization of social control'.[36] This interpenetration between public and private is even seen as going back full circle to the link between crime control and other forms of profit making at the end of the seventeenth century. Today's forms of 'privatization' are obviously not quite the same as those of that earlier era, nor can they ever be in the rationalized, centralized state. It is apparent, though, that along with the other types of blurring, there has been some merging of the obviously public and formal apparatus of control with the private and less formal. The ideology of community control implies this: on the one hand, the repressive, interventionist reach of the state should be blunted, on the other, the 'community' should become more involved in the day-to-day business of prevention and control.

At the macro-political level, particularly in the USA and under the influence of monetarist economic policy, the increasing attempt to shuffle social services from the public to the private sector is transparent enough. Indeed, as we shall see, the impetus for the whole decarceration movement itself has been attributed by theorists like Scull to the 'fiscal crisis' in which the state divests itself of expensive crime-control functions allowing private enterprise to process deviant populations for profit.

In the case of mental illness, the trend to privatization is now beyond dispute. Those chronic mental patients whose previous fate was to be assigned to the back wards, are now (if they are not in the back alleys) commodities to be exploited as a source of income. As Scull suggests, this commodification (or rather re-commodification) of social junk marks a sharp break with the pattern of state responsibility for the mentally ill, even the beginning of a 'new trade in lunacy'.[37] Today's network of private clinics, nursing homes and welfare hotels, run on a direct private basis or under contract from the state, is the twentieth-century equivalent of the madhouse — that profitable business in eighteenth- and early nineteenth-century *laissez faire* capitalism.

The retracking of some forms of delinquency into the mental-health system gives an additional boost to the entrepreneurial boom in private mental hospitals for adolescents — 'transinstitutionalism'. Overall, however, privatization is a much more complicated business for crime control than for mental illness. Strictly speaking, 'privatization' means that the state ceases to supply a particular service and it is supplied instead by private enterprises which are directly paid by the public as customers. With the important exception of the private security industry (to which I will return) there is not much room for this form of privatization in the crime-control system. The recipients of the 'service' are, to say the least, somewhat unwilling customers.

But there is far more room for the weaker form of privatization where the state contracts out certain services to private enterprise, retaining some measure of control. There is now considerable evidence on how this type of arrangement is taking place. Helped by fiscal changes at the local,[38] state and federal levels, commercial entrepreneurship has now joined the more traditional forms of moral entrepreneurship.[39] A significant proportion of community agencies and diversion projects are financed and contracted in this way. Lerman in fact argues that through shifts in federal and state budgeting, the entire policy of community alternatives has been made possible by the increasing dominance of the private sector.[40] The public sector takes up the more secure (hard-end) facilities while the private sector moves into the less restrictive facilities such as special schools, ranches, group homes and foster homes.

By the end of the 1970s, one-third of all delinquents, even in the official custodial system, were in privately owned facilities. And in the private sector overall, the majority of youth were either status offenders or fell into categories such as 'voluntary admissions', 'dependency' or 'other non-offenders' — euphemistic labels for petty delinquency. These traditional soft-enders (younger and more often girls) have become the major clients for the private sector. There is a new division of labour then — public funding of a profitable private business in 'community control'. In Massachusetts, for example, the sudden 'decarceration' led to a near monopoly by the private sector. Spending on 'privately purchased human services' increased from $25 million in 1979 to $300 million in 1981 (the number of separate facilities increasing from 9 to 164 over this period). Over 90 per cent of residential programmes for 'court-involved youth' (mainly for CHINS — children in need of supervision) are now privately run.[41] And this is genuine commodification — not 'Little House on the Prairie' families looking after deprived children, but large corporations, experienced contract lawyers and organized lobbying of the state legislature.

Indirect privatization of this type ('third-party funding') is likely to develop in other parts of the American system as a result of the massive post-1979 cutback in LEAA budgets. Not only did individual agencies go private, but so did coordinating and planning projects such as the NCCJPA (National Clearing House for Criminal Justice Planning and Architecture). Between 1969 and 1978 this body was involved in interpreting and writing LEAA standards for some 1500 adult and juvenile correctional projects. Now, in the form of a private corporation, 'Centre for Justice Planning Incorporated', it advertises for business like any other private enterprise. There are also new groups of criminal justice professionals, calling themselves 'clinical' or 'forensic' criminologists, who prepare private pre-sentence reports for defence attorneys. Claiming to do a better job than a probation service reduced by budgetary cuts, such private organizations as 'Criminological Diagnostic Consultants Inc.' in California, are now employed as hired guns (like private psychiatrists), charging fees of up to $2000 for a pre-sentence court report.[42]

There is no shortage of such schemes for moving other services into the private sector, even going back to pure Benthamite utilitarianism by negotiating contracts with payment conditional on some agreed measure of success. Private agencies would receive bonus payments for each recidivism-free client or (in true monetarist terms) offenders could be given 'treatment vouchers' to spend where they want, thus driving out unsuccessful treatment from the 'market'.[43]

The fate of most private agencies though, especially if they prove successful, is not to remain very 'private' but to be co-opted and absorbed into the formal state apparatus. This has happened even to some radical self-help organizations which originated in an antagonistic relationship to the system. In the case of diversion, the ideal non-legal agency (free from system control, client-oriented,

with voluntary participation, independent of sponsor's pressure)
often becomes like the various 'para-legal' agencies closely connected to the system and dependent on it for space, referrals,
accountability and sponsorship.[44] Various compromises on procedure are made as temporary tactics to deflect suspicion and criticism, but are then institutionalized. The private agency might
expand by asking for public funding and in turn changes its
screening criteria to fit the demands of the official system. It
becomes increasingly difficult to assign the status of private or
public to these agencies.

The recruitment of volunteers is another rapidly growing form
of privatization. Whatever the reasons for this growth — filling
service gaps created by budget cuts, the ideology of community
involvement, the perception that volunteers are often as effective
as paid professional staff — volunteers are to be found in every
part of the control system. Ex-offenders treat offenders; indigenous
community residents are recruited as probation 'aides' or to voluntary 'big brother' schemes; family members and teachers are
used in behavioural contracting programmes and university students
take on counselling functions to obtain credits for their course
work.

There is obviously very little new in the voluntarism principle
itself. Probation, prison visiting and other such schemes often
originated as volunteer efforts. But the combination of an expanding community network and declining social services budgets ensures an even greater future role for volunteers. The community
setting, with its emphasis on the supposed 'naturalness' and 'norm-
ality' of the intervention process is particularly suitable for volunteer workers. As with private agencies themselves, the potential
for volunteers to be absorbed into the official system is high.
Often the volunteers are retrained or formalized into para-profes-
sional or professional status, either in fact or else by giving a new
name to what they were already doing. This last practice is nicely
illustrated by calling jailhouse lawyers 'para-legals'.[45]

All this, though, is fairly far removed from pre-nineteenth-
century forms of privatization. The parallels, however, are closer
in the area of policing, where four developments are worth singling
out: (i) the private police industry, (ii) pro-active policing, (iii)
community police relations; and (iv) citizen policing.

In all Western societies, private policing has become a massive
growth industry. Already by 1975, in the USA and Canada, private
police began to outnumber their counterparts in the public sector.
This growth is usually attributed to the increasing involvement of

the ordinary police with 'non-crime' work: peacekeeping, traffic control, disguised social work, social sanitation and various other forms of human-services dirty work.[46] This leaves large corporations dependent on the private sector for all sorts of protective and investigative operations, both of the 'hard' and visible type (security forces, personal bodyguards, etc.) and for less visible work (employee pilferage, industrial espionage, computer fraud investigations, security checks and credit card scrutiny).

All this might not be quite the same as seventeenth-century thief catching by piecework, but it certainly represents a massive transfer of costly crime-control functions to the profit-making private sector. Far from being an 'adjunct', a mere 'junior partner' to the criminal justice system, the private security system operates in its own realm of justice. The implications of this may be quite profound. As Shearing and Stenning note, the enormous growth of contract security has taken place in public rather than purely private places. There has been an increase in what they call 'mass private property' (shopping centres, residential estates, campuses, airports) where the maintenance of public order as well as the protection of private property is at issue. Huge areas of public life previously under state control are now in the hands of private corporations. The result, this analysis suggests, is 'an unobtrusive but significant restructuring of our institutions for the maintenance of order, and a substantial erosion by the private sector of the state's assumed monopoly over policing and, by implication, justice.'[47]

At the same time as these forms of privatization are taking place, certain changes in ordinary public policing might be leading to directions with other curious historical parallels — to the time when the dividing lines between the civilian population and a uniformed, centralized police force were not at all clear. There has been an increasing emphasis on proactive rather than reactive policing, that is operations aimed at anticipating and preventing crimes not yet committed, particularly through the use of informers, secret agents, undercover work, *agents provocateurs*, decoys and entrapment. Besides the particular (and traditional) practice of the infiltration of social movements by informers and *agents provocateurs*,[48] observers of undercover work[49] note a more fundamental switch in police strategy. The move is not to decrease illegal opportunity structures (by patrolling, etc.) or target hardening, but actually to *increase* the opportunity structure for crime.

These techniques go beyond 'anticipation' towards actually

trying to facilitate the controlled commission of crime. Routine forms of undercover work include cooperation with others in illegal activities, secretly creating opportunities and generating motives for crime. Standard methods range from buying or selling illegal goods and services (police posing as prostitutes seeking customers, as customers seeking prostitutes, buying or selling drugs, setting up fencing operations, running pornographic book shops); using decoys to draw street crime (posing as elderly citizens, physically handicapped, derelicts) and various forms of intelligence gathering and 'morality testing'. (A much publicized recent example was the FBI 'Sting' operation designed to expose corrupt judges. This included the use of false defendants, false attorneys, the invention of crimes and the bugging of Judges' chambers.)

All this is not so much privatization as a form of boundary blurring through the deliberate use of deception. As Gary Marx suggests, the move (for pragmatic rather than ideological reasons) is from coercive to deceptive forms of social control − not only making the police look more like citizens, but to make citizens believe that any one of their fellow citizens could be a police officer in disguise.

But while these parts of police work are becoming more underground and secretive, others are reaching out more openly into the wider community. Movements to strengthen community police relationships, to improve the public image of the police and to develop schemes for 'community-based preventive policing' have become standard. Community relations officers, juvenile liaison bureaux, school-linked officers are all trying to establish closer links with the community, humanize the face of police work and encourage early reporting. Policemen are now 'friends' (who help neighbourhood kids with sports activities and take them on weekend hikes) or social workers who are trained in 'human relationships'.

Besides general image building, all this is directed to obtaining greater citizen cooperation in the form of reporting and informal surveillance. In the USA especially, a much more formalized type of enlistment of private citizens into police work has been taking place. Volunteer work such as driving cars, traffic control and escort services is provided to overloaded police forces, but more particularly there has been a formalization of neighbourhood surveillance and reporting systems: crime-stoppers groups, neighbourhood patrols, citizen crime-reporting projects, whistle-alert neighbourhoods, citizen-band radio reporting, block-watch projects.[50] More dramatically (and certainly closer to early forms of privatization) there has been the growth of various forms of local 'auxiliary justice'. With overload on the formal criminal justice system and the perception among victims and potential victims that the state is 'letting them down', new forms of private and vigilante justice — fanned by racialism and community tensions — have developed.[51] Whether they see themselves as 'by-passing' or as 'helping' the police, these activities are easily blurred with the formal system.

All these forms of policing appeal to the same community involvement vision which informs the destructuring movement as a whole. Once again though, new structures are being created rather than old ones being replaced. Nor can attempts to reproduce pre-urban systems of mutual responsibility, peacekeeping and good neighbourliness be very successful. Citizens of today's suburbia or inner-city slum cannot through an effort of will recreate the conditions of an eighteenth-century rural parish. Closed-circuit television, two-way radios, vigilante patrols, private security companies and police decoys hardly simulate life in a pre-industrial village. This is not for want of trying. In some large stores, private security police are posing as employees. They conspicuously steal and are then conspicuously 'discovered' by the management and ceremonially disciplined, thus deterring the real employees. They then presumably move on to stage somewhere else another such Durkheimian ceremony of social control.

But Durkheimian theory notes the functions of social control in clarifying and strengthening boundaries. All our examples in this section point to the increasing *invisibility* of the net's boundaries.

### Inside, the Same old Things are Being Done

If I were being processed by the machine ('my own actual person, me myself') few of the matters contemplated so far would be of very great interest: not how big the net might be, nor what it is called, nor what it looks like, nor who runs it. Only one thing matters: what is actually going on inside all these 'offices'?

The promise was a form of intervention that would be less intrusive, onerous, coercive, stigmatizing, artificial and bureaucratic; more humane, just, fair, helpful, natural and informal. What are we to make of these good intentions? Is the new system subject to the same commonplace of those historical tales about the old system recounted in chapter 1 — that the most benign innova-

tions come to mask the most coercive of practices and consequences?

At first sight, the benevolence of the new agencies seems
obvious. The very language of the community and diversion movements speaks of good things happening. And without doubt, the
end results are often humane, compassionate and helpful. Some
'clients', at least, are kept out of the harsher recesses of the system,
many are offered a wider range of services than they would have
received before and almost all would prefer the new variety of
agencies to the stark alternative of the prison. (I return to such
considerations in chapter 7.)

But the word 'alternative' should alert us to the immediate
problem of the new nets. The claim to be doing more good (or less
harm) is somewhat less valid if the alternatives are not real alternatives at all, but supplements. The size and density evidence shows
that many offenders are exposed to the new system *in addition* to
traditional processing or else instead of not being processed at
all. The mystifying nature of the idea of alternatives may be nicely
illustrated by the curious justification of agencies like half-way
houses: being just as successful in preventing recidivism as direct
release into the community. As Greenberg notes, when participation in such programmes is a condition of release from prison,
'the contrast between the brutality of the prison and the alleged
humanitarianism of community corrections is besides the point,
because the community institution is not used to replace the
prison; instead the offender is exposed to both the prison and the
community "alternatives".'[52]

Even when the notion of 'alternative' is not phony, the idea of
'preference' or 'choice' most often is. At the deep end of the
system, choice is seldom offered while at the shallow end, the
generation of new treatment criteria and the pervasiveness of the
social welfare and preventive rhetorics, often ensure an erosion of
traditional rights and liberties. In a system of low visibility and
accountability, where a high degree of discretion is given to administrative and professional bodies (in the name of 'flexibility')
there is often less room for such niceties as due process and legal
rights. Police diversion programmes are the most notable examples
here: juveniles usually proceed through the various filters on the
assumption or admission of guilt. As one critic of such programmes
comments: 'to force a youngster to participate in a diversion
program under the threat of adjudication, has most of the elements
of the formal justice system save due process.'[53]

Making future status contingent on programme participation

is only one form of hidden coercion. Overall, the rhetoric of welfare and treatment allows all sorts of invisible discretion about referral, recall, resentencing, reallocation, and so on. Lerman's often-quoted research on Californian community projects showed that offenders in the experimental (community) groups, spent much more time in traditional custody than was generally believed, and could be locked up for reasons quite unrelated to their legal offence: violating treatment expectations, administrative convenience, missing a group meeting, sassing a teacher, the threat of 'emotional explosion' or 'acting out', community pressure or even diagnostic purposes. As Messinger comments on this research:

> When subjects failed to comply with the norms of the intensive treatment regime, or even when a program agent believes subjects might fail to comply, then, as they say in the intensive treatment circles, detention may be indicated. Both these features, and the extensive use of home placements as well, suggest that the term 'community' like the term 'intensive treatment' may come to have a very special meaning in programs designed to deliver 'intensive treatment in the community'.[54]

Phoney choice, problems of legal rights and hidden custody aside, we might still want to ask whether most bona fide forms of community programmes are not, after all, experienced as more humane and helpful by the offender. There is little evidence either way on this, beyond the rather bland common-sense assumption that most offenders would prefer not to be 'locked up'. What tends to happen is that deep-end projects — those that are genuine alternatives to incarceration — make a trade-off between treatment goals (which favour an integrated community setting) and security goals which favour isolation. The trade-off under these conditions, especially given widespread community reluctance to open its arms to the joyous project of reintegration, will invariably favour security. The result is programmes which simply recreate the institutional domains under a different name, regimes which simulate or mimic the very custodial features they set out to replace. Even when the security trade-off is less important, community treatment is often just 'semantic trivia' for traditional programmes whose physical location in an urban area is the sole basis for identifying the programme as community-based.[55]

This is certainly the case with the many half-way house programmes which contain stringent security conditions, compulsory therapy, intensive observation and surveillance and continual requirements to 'avoid undesirable behaviour sequences' and to 'develop and display positive attitudes'.[56]

Let me give a specific example of a 'community correctional facility' which is part of a wider community corrections programme. This is Fort Des Moines, a 50-bed non-secure unit, meant for adult offenders not stable enough to be granted probation, but not dangerous enough to be sent to a traditional locked institution.[57] The unit is housed in the converted barracks of an ex-army base, the clients work in ordinary jobs in the community and there is only minimal physical security such as bars and fences. The security trade-offs, however, result in an intensity of intervention at least as high as that in most maximum-security prisons. The following are some examples.

(1) The low 'client–counsellor' ratio of one staff person for every two clients allows for intensive 'informal observation' of the clients for security purposes. A 'staff desk person' signs clients in and out, recording their attitudes and activities. And a 'floating staff person' circulates throughout the institution, observing client behaviour, taking a count of all clients each hour (called the 'eye check') and recording the count in the log. The staff have total discretion in granting furloughs, visits, searching for contraband and administering a urine analysis or breath test at any time.

(2) The client has to 'contract' to behave well and participate actively in his rehabilitation and the sanction of being returned to prison is always present. From the beginning of his stay (when he has to sign a waiver of privacy granting the programme access to information in confidential agency files) he is closely scrutinized. Besides obvious offences like using drugs, fighting or trying to escape, the failure to maintain 'a significant level of performance' is one of the most serious offences a client can commit and results in immediate return to jail.

(3) The court retains jurisdiction over the client, receiving detailed rosters and programme reports and having to authorize internal requests for work, schooling or furloughs. In addition, the local police and sheriffs' departments receive weekly listings of the residents, indicating where each has to be at specified hours of each day. This information is available to patrol officers who may see inmates in the community.

Every item of behaviour and attitude is recorded on the Behaviour Observation Report. It is this panopticon principle, together with the commitment to a compulsory programme of behaviourist conditioning which casts the most doubt on the humanity and non-intrusiveness of the new programmes. This is true even when the project is more genuinely 'in the community' than the unfortunately named Fort Des Moines. Let us consider a few examples of this kind, community projects genuinely not anchored in a custodial base.

One well-described example is the Urbana Champaign Adolescent Diversion Project (ADP). Juveniles considered as 'beyond lecture and release and clearly headed for court' are referred by the police to a programme of behavioural contracting organized by a university psychology department. The volunteer staff monitor and mediate contractual agreements between the youth and his parents and teachers — privileges in return for his compliance with the curfew, doing house chores and maintaining his personal appearance. Here are extracts from a typical day in the life of Joe, a 16-year-old who had come to the attention of the juvenile division for possession of marijuana and violation of the municipal curfew laws:

| *Joe agrees to* | *Joe's parents agree to* |
|---|---|
| 1. Call home by 4.00 p.m. each afternoon and tell his parents his whereabouts and return home by 5.00 p.m. | 1. Allow Joe to go out from 7.30 to 9.30, Monday through Thursday, evenings and ask about his companions without negative comments. |
| 2. Return home by 12.00 midnight on weekend nights. | 2. Allow Joe to go out the subsequent weekend night. |
| 3. Make his bed and clean his room daily (spread neat; clothes hung up). | 3. Check his room each day and pay him 75 cents when cleaned. |
| 4. Set table for dinner daily. | 4. Deposit 75 cents per day in a savings account for Joe. |

*Bonus*

If Joe performs at 80% or above ## 1 though ## 4 above his parents will deposit an additional 3 dollars in his account for each consecutive seven-day period.

*Sanction*

If Joe falls below 60% in ## 1 and ## 2 above in any consecutive seven-day period, he will cut two inches off his hair.[58]

Variations of the two main elements in this project — close surveillance and behavioural contracting — are being used throughout the USA, Canada and Britain. The Intensive Probation Program in Georgia includes regular contacts with the officer, an 8.00 p.m. curfew, community service, and registration on the state computer system (for which service the offender pays a monthly fee!).[59] In Florida, community control takes the form of residential house arrest: armed community officers, equipped with urine analysis kits and surveillance devices, are empowered to enter the offender's home at any time.

In Britain, the favoured solution for 'heavy-end' offenders deflected from custody has become Intensive Intermediate Treatment (IIT). Directly exporting the technique (and terminology) from the system developed in Massachusetts, projects such as PACE (Project for Alternative Community Experience) are using a complex system of 'tracking'.[60] An infinite number of IIT permutations have already appeared: 'full-time IT', 'IT Plus', 'short-term holding', 'long-term holding', 'intensive tracking' and 'booster tracking'. But the basic model is something like this: the 'trackee' starts off in a carefully graded 'residential component'; he or she passes through close supervision in a residential unit, then 'supervised and monitored outside contact', and then 'increasingly unsupervised but still monitored outside contacts' (with curfew, spot checks, regular phone reports). The amount of time in each phase depends on progress made.

This is followed by the 'community/intensive supervision' or tracking component (some projects only start at this stage). This again entails decreasing levels of intensity according to progress. The 'young person' is linked to a tracker who knows where he is at all times, ensures that he follows a structured and approved routine, teaches him social skills, advises him about work, school and family and generally monitors his behaviour. As in the ADP model, offenders have to agree to a written behavioural contract and this usually calls for direct involvement by the family. Breaking any clause in the contract (in one project this includes filling in a log book for each hour of the day between 9.00 a.m. and 11.00 p.m and 'acting like an adult in arguments'), can result in a series of graded sanctions, including more intensive tracking, return to the court or recall to a 'short-term residential experience'. One project describes how a trackee's 'persistent acting-out behaviour' could lead to a weekend in the 'residential flat' in the company of his tracker. Supervision is gradually decreased until the 'lad' can function on his own. The programme might end, as it did for 'John' on the Coventry PACE project, with a staged incident in a local community setting (a pub). Now, the interactionally skilled and properly socialized offender does not explode into uncontrollable rage.

It should be absolutely clear that whatever else these community programmes might be and, as we move along, we will see all sorts of justifications for them, they are not examples of normal, integrated community life. Moreover, because of the increasing dominance of the just-deserts rhetoric for allocating punishment, these programmes are required to look to the courts as credible alternatives to custody. That is, they must be controlling and intrusive enough to be a response in good faith to the judicial demand for sentences that do actually punish and restrict. The uncomfortable policy dilemma is that it is very difficult to think of a 'credible capacity to incapacitate' besides imprisonment.[61]

Meanwhile, there is no problem in finding criminologists, psychologists, social workers and others who will justify all these community alternatives as humane, kindly and even 'therapeutic' — as they have historically justified anything that could be called treatment. This is the particularly wondrous advantage, as I will suggest in chapter 4, of those programmes which use the explicit rationale of behaviourism.[62] But leaving such considerations aside, the most fundamental fact about what is going on in the new agencies is that it is much the same as what went on and is still going on in the old system. The new 'service delivery modalities' — as the evaluation pros call them — are dominated by the same forms of individual or group treatment used in custodial institutions or traditional one-to-one encounters such as probation. Whether it is individual counselling, vocational guidance, encounter groups, role playing or behaviour contracting, it is one person doing something to another person or group of persons. And however normal, banal and everyday the activity might be (in other words, however close it might come to what happens in real communities) it is justified with the old (and supposedly discredited) rhetoric of treatment.

This is the real, awful secret of community control. Not the old closely guarded secrets of the penitentiary (the brutality, the chain gangs, solitary confinement). These things cannot occur in the community — and this is, by any measure, progress. The secret is a much less melodramatic one: that the same old experts have moved office to the community and are doing the same old things they have always done. Once again, we do not know *what* they are doing, not because they are hidden behind walls but because they are camouflaged as being just ordinary members of the community.

Picture a lake on which a duck tranquilly floats. On the grass edge sits a happy pre-adolescent boy chatting to a laid-back, bejeaned, student-looking young man. Brothers? Friends? No, this is just one of the activities of CREST — the Clinical Regional Support Team in Gainesville, Florida. The older boy is a 'volunteer' graduate psychology student, gaining some course credits by counselling a young probationer on this community programme. What are they doing by the lake? The caption on the photo tells all: 'A relaxed comfortable environment sets the stage for meaningful counsellor—client dialogue.'[63]

### PENETRATION AND ABSORPTION

With that happy image of the dialogue by the lake, we arrive at the third and last of the inquiries I posed about the machine: the extent and nature of its penetration beyond the known space it occupies. For Foucault, it was precisely the redistribution of the penal power into a wider social space that marked the great disciplinary projects of the nineteenth century. It was not just that disciplinary establishments increased, but that 'their mechanisms have a certain tendency to become "de-institutionalized", to re-emerge from the closed fortresses in which they once functioned and to circulate in a "free" state: the massive compact disciplines are broken down into flexible methods of control which may be transferred and adapted.'[64]

For the ideologists of today's control system, not a glimmer of this history is visible. Theirs is a classic story of progress: the gradual dawning of the light in the mid-twentieth century. The magic word is 'reintegration' — the new 'R' in the history of corrections. This was the ritually quoted sequence: we are in the middle of a third revolution in corrections: the first from Revenge to Restraint (in the first part of the nineteenth century), the second from Restraint to Reformation (from the late nineteenth to the early twentieth century), and now from Reformation to Reintegration.[65]

Although, as history, this story is quite absurd, as ideology it does proclaim a preferred change quite profound and radical. What is being proposed is a greater direct involvement of the family, the school and various community agencies in the day-to-day business of prevention, treatment, and resocialization. But this means something more than simply recruiting more volunteers, improving communication with schools or encouraging citizens to report more crime. It implies some sort of reversal of the presumption in positivist criminology that the delinquent is a different and alien being. Deviance rather is with us, woven into the fabric of social life and it must be 'brought back home'. Parents, peers, schools, the neighbourhood, even the police should dedicate themselves to keeping the deviant out of the formal system. Together they should constitute a gigantic shield of diversion: deflecting, absorbing, integrating the deviant back into the community where he belongs.

This master notion also informs the many other 'Rs' of contemporary corrections — reparation, restitution, repayment, reconciliation. If crime results from the estrangement of the individual from meaningful community contacts, imprisonment can only make this worse. These new modes of control allow the offender to undo the damage he caused (thus responding to the demands of justice) while, at the same time, integrating himself by working in and for the community.

The ideology of reintegration (buttressed usually by some variant of labelling theory) signifies, as my later chapters will show, a move more portentous than 'operational changes in the correctional system'. The vision was of an inclusionary rather than an exclusionary mode of social control. The asylum represented not just isolation and confinement, like quarantining the infected, but a ritual of physical exclusion. Without the possibility of actual banishment to another society, the asylum had to serve the classic social function of creating a scapegoat: the animal driven into the wilderness, bearing away the sins of the community.

In the new ideology of corrections, there is no real or symbolic wilderness, just the omnipresent community into which the deviant has to be unobtrusively 'integrated' or 'reintegrated'. Boundary blurring implies both the deeper penetration of social control into the social body and the easing of any measures of exclusion and stigmatization. Deviants must remain in their own natural society as long as possible.

In operational terms — as they say — what all this means is that the overburdened, inefficient and inhumane formal system (doing things it should not be doing) must shift its load to the primary institutions of society. They (schools, family, neighbourhood) and not the experts and professionals must take responsibility for deviancy control. Instead of depriving them of their potential, they should be strengthened and used as natural resources in the war against crime. They should prevent the deviant from getting into the machine, they should substitute for the machine, they should look after him when he gets out of it.

So much for the vision. The reality does not look quite the same. Far from *avoiding* the touch of the formal system, the primary institutions have, in various metaphors, been invaded, penetrated, besieged or colonized by the formal system. Far from there being any less reliance on experts, these same experts are simply working within the primary institutions. If there has been any 'absorption' it is not that the deviant has been absorbed by community institutions, but that the community institutions have been absorbed by the formal control system. The spaces surrounding the net — to return to my old metaphor — are increasingly drawn into its orbit.[66]

The historical sequence, then, is a little different from the story of the four Rs. First, there is control in the community; second, control is concentrated in the prison — an isolated, specially constructed model of what the good community should look like; third, prisons are reformed (this is what the Progressives visualized) to make them less artificial and more like ordinary communities — the community is brought into the prison; then, fourth, the modality of the prison is dispersed and exported back into the community.

In chapter 6, I look at the broader implications of the reintegration ideology, projecting it on to the whole space of the city and the imaginary space of the future. Here, I just want to give a more limited idea of how the new network is making itself felt in its surrounding space, using family, school and neighbourhood as examples.

### Family

The role supposedly being reallocated to the family is, perhaps, the clearest example of the integration and inclusion ideology at work. As part of a wider movement of the rediscovery of the family in social policy, this is a variation on the standard theme that the 'lost' functions of the family should be restored. The family is not only a natural way of preventing and containing the deviance of its own members, but is an obvious source for treating the deviance of others.

Thus recent years have seen the extension of established methods of community treatment such as foster care, substitute homes and family placements. One enthusiast even looked forward to 'the day when middle class American families actually wanted in large numbers to bring juvenile and pre-delinquent youths into their homes as a service commitment'.[67] The family having a delinquent living with them is seen as a 'remarkable correctional resource' for the future. In Britain and Scandinavia a number of alternative systems of family placement besides salaried foster parents have been tried, for example 'together at home' — the system of intensive help in Sweden in which social workers spend hours sharing the family's life and tasks. Other programmes require selected adults to act as parent models or surrogates. Once these parents are trained, children with 'behavioural problems' are placed in their model homes.

The delinquent's own family is also used in this way. This is standard practice in various behavioural contract programmes. Joe's family, in the ADP programme, becomes a 'correctional resource' and under the watchful eye of the university psychologist, it learns the correct behavioural sequences and reinforcement schedules. In Intensive IT and other tracking or befriending programmes, parents and siblings are parties to the behavioural contract and are expected to play an active role in retraining their errant child. In the regions of the system not influenced by behaviourist psychology, the fashion is for family sensitivity groups, weekend marathon family encounters, conjoint family therapy, PET (Parent Effectiveness Training) and the like. One must assume that a family with a member under house arrest is also a 'treatment resource'.

But the purposeful use of families in this way is less significant — statistically and socially — than the overall senses in which the contemporary family has become a site for expert invasion and penetration. As Lasch argues, the same market forces which undermined the traditional functions of the family are now — far from restoring these functions — undermining them still further.[68] The increasing array of guidance, instruction, therapy, counselling and advice now being offered to the family strengthens the process of its 'proletarianisation', which started well before the era of 'reintegration'.

*School*

The discovery by reintegrationists that most children go to school as well as live in families, coincided with the emergence in the 1970s of the school as a major site where crime, delinquency and violence actually took place. This has meant that the penetration of the school has taken both a soft and a hard edge. The soft, liberal, thrust comes from the community-integration ideology and takes the form of incorporating the school as a preventive, diagnostic, screening or diversion agency. The hard thrust, provoked by concern over violence, disruption, vandalism, unruliness or indiscipline in school, takes the form of target hardening, drug or behaviourist controls and increasing segregation of troublemakers. As these movements often share common technologies, such as behaviourism and early prediction techniques, it is not always easy to keep them apart in practice.[69] The discovery of hyperkinesis nicely illustrates the convergence of the benevolent treatment rhetoric with the need for a technology of pacification.[70]

At the soft edge, an increasing array of professionals, paraprofessionals, counsellors, social workers, psychologists and experts of all sorts have attached themselves to the school. Their task is to 'pick up' deviancy problems at their source and, where possible, contain them without formal referral to the system. The fact that these personnel are themselves part of the machine is not usually seen as a contradiction, despite the increasing formalization of their methods, for example the use of diagnostic rating scales to weed out the potential delinquents, the inclusion of schools in behaviour-contract agreements with criminal justice agencies and the incorporation of token economy programmes into the routine of the classroom.

At the hard edge, the legendary vision of the blackboard jungle has dominated social control policy. In Britain, the strategy has been exclusion and isolation — the setting up over the seventies of special units for the segregation of disruptive pupils.[71] From 1947—1977 alone, the number of these units (on or off the site of the school) increased from 40 to 239. The model is the classic one of individual pathology. The benevolent rationale was to 'help young people who find it difficult to adjust to schooling' while at the same time saving the rest of the class from being disturbed by these troublemakers. Referral takes place on the vaguest of diagnostic criteria (including restlessness, 'potentially disruptive behaviour', answering back, irritability, not wearing uniform or 'difficulty in making relationships') and pupils might spend anything from a month to a few years in the segregation unit before being returned to the ordinary school or the outside world. The units are given names such as sanctuaries, withdrawal groups, and even pastoral care unit (see appendix).

The harder forms of school 'controlization' in the USA have little room for such euphemism. From the 1978 'Safe School Study' onwards, the entrepreneurial direction has been towards a massive investment in hardware and preventive technology: video surveillance, ultrasonic detectors, hot lines to the police, redesigning buildings into clusters of manageable space. Problems such as bomb threats, arson, vandalism, violence, drug pushing, 'mass disruption' and 'rumour control' are stressed, the object of the exercise being a safe, secure school. Parts of the relevant literature read like blueprint for converting the school into a closed-security prison. This is the message of 'involvement' directed at school administrators by such private agencies as the Institute for the Reduction of Crime.[72]

Compared with the family, the school is obviously more of a 'public' institution and its connections to the state are more direct. This will allow an even greater degree of penetration, soft or hard, in the future.

## Neighbourhood

The ideology of reintegration and the strategies of community and diversion demand a physical relocation of the business of deviancy control: not the wilderness and not the closed fortress, but the immediate physical space in which ordinary people live and go about their business. So the growing network of new agencies enters the city and tries to normalize its presence there. A conscious attempt is made to locate half-way houses, hostels or day centres in the most inconspicuous and normal environments, on the assumption that this will reduce stigma and social distance. The local 'community' is not always so enthusiastic about these encounters and legal action, media pressure and restrictive zoning regulations often force the new agencies back into the social badlands of the city. Despite these counter forces though, this kind of physical penetration is slowly taking place.

There are, in addition, some less visible forms of penetration — like that relaxed counselling session next to the lake. Anxious to avoid the stigma of the office, the agency corridors and the waiting room, the new professionals and their aides increasingly try out more normal community settings for their encounters. Detached youth workers and street corner workers have, of course, traditionally used such 'reaching out' methods. The literature now is full of stories of clients being encountered or contracted in bars, cafes, parks, cars and even rock concerts. Least visible of all are the *linkers* (local leaders used to break down mistrust between the community worker and the neighbourhood deviant sub-culture) and the *befrienders, trackers* and *shadows* — workers in high-intensity community programmes who attach themselves to individual clients and make sure they get out of bed in time, get to work and attend their therapy sessions.

Outside the city, who knows whether that happy group of kids hiking up a mountain, building a campfire or swimming in a river are not taking part in a delinquency programme such as ACTION (Accepting Challenge Through Interaction with Others and Nature)?[73] The only way to tell that these are not, after all, boy scouts, would be to know that the participants had been pre-tested and then, after coming back from the wilderness, would be post-tested about their self-concepts, their relationship with their peers and their perception of the role of authority figures.

Back in the city, there are other forms of treatment such as community-service orders which offer further opportunity for the normalized presence of the offender. Satisfying the aims of both integration and reparative justice, offenders on such schemes are sentenced to useful (usually supervised) work in the community: helping in geriatric wards, driving disabled people around, painting and decorating the houses of various handicapped groups, building children's playgrounds.

These are all the softer forms of the reintegration strategy at work, and are directed at the individual offender *after* his apprehension and conviction. Other forms of neighbourhood penetration are not only 'harder', but move from the individual offender to preventive and proactive strategies directed at whole groups or environments (a move which, as we shall see, some observers consider the most significant of all changes in social control).

Obvious examples come from the new forms of community and preventive policing I reviewed earlier. In addition to the now-routine technologies of prevention, detection, deterrence and surveillance in public and private space (stores, airports, shopping malls), the reintegration ideology demands a more active form of participation. Citizens are urged to provide neighbourhood centres for potential delinquents, organize all sorts of surveillance and early reporting schemes, take part in 'court-watching programmes' and conduct crime prevention seminars in their homes.[74] Through programmes such as CAPTURE (Citizens Active Participation Through Utilization of Relevant Education) and national organizations such as the National Centre for Community Crime Prevention, neighbourhoods are absorbed into general crime-prevention strategies. Some projects call for collective surveillance and reporting (block clubs, neighbourhood watch, radio-alert networks, tenant patrols, secret-witness programmes) while others teach personal survival and protective techniques (though seminars and booklets with such titles as 'Safe Passage in City Streets' or 'Mugging Avoidance Techniques'). The neighbourhood now becomes an 'untapped human resource for delinquency prevention'.[75]

The police on their side are also more actively 'reaching out', by joining neighbourhood organizations, serving on local committees, and helping in school and youth groups. Increasingly, as I describe in chapter 6, urban design and planning decisions (about shops, streets, housing estates, parking areas) are made with reference to crime-control needs. Planners routinely use the rhetoric of defensible space, target hardening or illegal-opportunity structure. And we must add to all this the activities of private security companies, as well as the possibility that the beggar on the pavement, the old lady crossing the street, a client in the local massage parlour and your friendly neighbourhood dope dealer might all be policemen in disguise. The city streets take on a different look.

Let me summarize this section on 'penetration and absorption' by drawing the lines a little bit more sharply than the reality. The system penetrates the space of the family, the school and the neighbourhood; it tries to buttress their existing control processes by exporting the modes of discipline and control which characterize its 'own' spaces; it rationalizes all this by appealing to a vision of what the real family, school or community looked like once or should look like now — and these institutions are then changed further rather than restored to their pristine state.

CONCLUSION: THE EMERGING PATTERNS

Let us now forget fishing nets, suction machines and objects in space. Forget also the question of whether or not what is happening is what was intended. We have arrived at a point where this long chapter needs to be summarized: can today's master patterns of social control be picked out in the same way as those of the early nineteenth century? Any answer must be highly qualified and tentative. Some of the patterns I described are indeed clear enough, some are highly contradictory and ambiguous, yet others are merely hints of what might come.

But these are the main outlines: a gradual expansion and intensification of the system; a dispersal of its mechanisms from more closed to more open sites and a consequent increase in the invisibility of social control and the degree of its penetration into the social body. My selection of examples to arrive at even this crude outline are obviously open to dispute. On the one hand, for instance, I might have overplayed the element of novelty. A reading of correctional stories gives an exaggerated notion of how much innovation there has been: novel alternatives such as tracking or house arrest involve only a minority of offenders. Many such programmes started in the heyday of the community movement have now closed through lack of funding and most offenders under supervision receive traditional forms of probation and parole. And, most important of all, it is the continued persistence of the prison, as well as the 'dispersal' of its mechanisms which has to be explained.

On the other hand, certain critics of the 'dispersal of discipline' thesis would pick out a quite different set of changes.[76] To them, the *proportionate* decline in the use of imprisonment is a noteworthy achievement as well as its replacement by modes of punishment (such as fines, suspended sentences, victim compensation and support schemes) which are not 'disciplinary' in the sense of demanding continuous supervision and attempting to change behaviour.

I will be returning to the implications of such arguments. But it seems to me that beyond all the complex empirical problems, historical comparisons and implied value judgements which terms such as 'discipline' and 'dispersal' might hide, there is the over-riding fact of proliferation, elaboration and diversification. No one, least of all that proverbial Martian anthropologist with whom this chapter started, cannot but be impressed by all this bustling, frenzied activity, all these busy people doing so many things in so many places to so many others.

While it may be difficult to know which of these activities are old or new, vague or definite, there is no doubt that the logic of these master patterns, as opposed to their particular current forms, is not at all new. Their antecedents can be traced, though, not to their supposed model — the idyllic pre-industrial rural community — but to the very same patterns of punishment and classification laid down in the nineteenth century.

Foucault, we remember, reconstructed (or rather fantasized) the vision of the eighteenth-century judicial philosophers: power dispersed throughout the 'punitive city' — not the vengeful and arbitrary power of the sovereign, concentrated in the spectacle of torture, but a discreet dispersal of social control through 'hundreds of tiny theatres of punishment', each a perfect arithmetical representation of the bourgeois social contract. A right and just arithmetic of punishment, no more and no less. The juridical project, however, was never fully realized. It was replaced, or rather overlaid, with the carceral or disciplinary vision. The offender is observed, judged, normalized — something is done to him. He is returned to society, if at all, not as the requalified subject of the social contract, but the retrained, obedient subject.

But where was this new disciplinary project to be put into practice? Here, Foucault confuses us. On the one hand there was concentration: punishment becomes concentrated in the coercive institution of the prison — a single uniform penalty varied only according to length. On the other hand, there was dispersal — not of judicial semiotics but of projects of docility. The same microphysics of power reproduces itself in the prison and the community: hierarchical surveillance, continuous registration, perpetual assessment, partitioning and repartitioning, discipline and resocialization. 'The prison transformed the punitive procedure into a penitentiary technique; the carceral archipelago transported this technique from the penal institution to the wider social body.'[77]

To describe today's system as simply a continuation of the disciplinary society — nothing more and nothing less — is mistaken. This would be to ignore the real differences outlined in this and later chapters. The attack on positivism, for example, in the name of 'neo-classicism' or 'back to justice' (the early 'judicial' vision) certainly does not fit Foucault's history of the present. Nor do all those innovations in policing and crime prevention which denote a move from the individual offender to opportunity structures and the control of whole populations.

But every one of the major patterns I have described in this chapter — expansion, dispersal, invisibility, penetration — is indeed continuous with those original transformations. The prison remains — a stubborn continuous presence, seemingly impervious to all attacks — and in its shadow lies 'community control'. Together, they make up what appears in Foucault as the 'carceral archipelago' or (to list all his images) 'net', 'continuum', 'city', 'circle' and 'pyramid'. The creation of all those new agencies and services surrounding the court and the prison, the generation of new systems of knowledge, classification and professional interests (the subject of chapter 5), is little more than a widening and diversification of the last century's archipelago, made possible by resources, investment, ingenuity, technology and vested interest on a scale that befits 'post-industrial society'.

All these agencies — legal and quasi-legal, diversionary and alternative, administrative and professional — are marking out their own territories of jurisdiction, competence and referral. Each set of experts produces its own 'scientific' knowledge: screening devices, diagnostic tests, treatment modalities, evaluation scales. And all this creates new categories and the typifications which fill them. Where there was once talk about the 'typical' prisoner, first offender or hardened recidivist, now there are typical 'clients' of half-way houses or community correctional centres, typical divertees, trackees or pre-delinquents. These creatures are then fleshed out — in papers, research proposals, official reports — with sub-systems of knowledge and new vocabularies. Locking up becomes 'intensive placement', dossiers become 'anecdotal records', rewards and punishments become 'behavioural contracts'.

The enterprise, I will argue, justifies itself: there is hardly any point in asking about 'success', this is not the object of the exercise. Research is done on the classification system *itself* — working out a 'continuum of community basedness', prediction table or screening devices.

This is not to say that the classification is in any sense random. From the foundation of the control system, a single principle has governed every form of classification, screening, selection, diagnosis, prediction, typology and policy. This is the structural principle of binary opposition: how to sort out the good from the bad, the elect from the damned, the sheep from the goats, the amenable from the non-amenable, the treatable from the non-treatable, the good risks from the bad risks, the high prediction scorers from the low prediction scorers; how to know who belongs in the deep end, who in the shallow end, who is hard and who is soft.[78]

Each individual decision in the system — who shall be chosen? — represents and creates this fundamental principle of bifurcation. The particular binary judgements which have come to dominate the present system — who shall be sent away from the custodial institution and who shall remain in it, who shall be diverted and who shall be inserted — are but instances of this deep structure at work. And if we ignore individual decisions and look at the system as a whole — as it extends and spreads itself out — we will be seeing how this same bifurcation organizes all its movements.

# 3

# Deposits of Power

So far I have mapped out the contours of the emerging social-control system, speculated on their continuities with the master patterns established in the last century and noted their apparent divergence from the ideologies which are supposed to inform them now. The subject of this chapter is not mapping, but explanation. We cannot presume however — as does the progressive vision of history — that what has to be explained is 'failure' or 'unintended consequences'. Such terms already assume a particular theoretical commitment. We can only start with a clear lack of fit, a measure of incongruence between the new system and the rhetoric with which it usually justifies itself. It is this incongruence and the emerging patterns themselves which have to be explained.

An obvious starting point in the search for the 'right' explanation would be to use those historical theories reviewed in chapter 1. Indeed, one justification for looking at that history was to find an appropriate lens with which to view the present. But to interrogate this past and to try to project it on to the present is a difficult business. Current deviancy-control patterns are much less clear than their predecessors, there are major disagreements about their implications, and the societal structures in which they are embedded are far more complex. Still, the differences between those theoretical visions are permanent ones and a slight adaptation will easily yield the five models which this chapter distinguishes. They are set out in table 3. The two matters to be explained are, first, the causes and nature of the destructuring rhetoric (intentions) and, second, the causes of the emerging master patterns and their correspondence with the rhetoric (outcomes).

The highly condensed, even caricatured, nature of this typology fulfils one purpose of this chapter — a purely didactic attempt to set out different ways of looking at the same reality. Like all such exercises, this results in certain oversimplifications, even distor-

TABLE 3: Intentions and consequences: five models

| Model | Original Intentions | Status of Eventual Consequences |
|---|---|---|
| 1. Progress | Benevolent — taken entirely at face value | More or less according to plan |
| 2. Organizational convenience | Somewhat mixed but on the whole benevolent — things could have worked out | Things not quite working out: unmet promises, unintended consequences. Organizational convenience snarls up the original plan |
| 3. Ideological contradiction | Contradictory and mixed and, for this reason, virtually impossible to realize | Because of contradictions, the emerging pattern bears little relationship to the plan. The policy area is a site in which contradictions are resolved |
| 4. Professional interest | Some benevolence, but on the whole, intentions are highly suspect and eventually self-serving | Just what you would expect: the system is shaped by professional self-interest |
| 5. Political economy | Intentions are more or less irrelevant or simply a mask for undeclared needs of the system | Just what you would expect: the system is shaped by the demands of the political economy |

tions: complicated theories are reduced to a few sentences and theories which I squeeze into one model often overlap with other levels of explanation. The more sophisticated 'organizational' theories, for example, take into account changes at the general social level; many 'political economy' theories look at internal organizational processes; theories of all types talk about the power of professionals. Some theorists try, eclectically or more thoughtfully, to combine all levels. So these boxes must be viewed with caution.

But this chapter has another purpose. I would like these models to be seen not just as competing abstract explanations, nor as different schools of thought to be contemplated and then purchased in the academic supermarket. Each of these systems of thought is connected with a corresponding system of power. That is to say, the stuff of which the theory speaks, represents certain real social 'deposits'. The metaphor of a deposit (and similar terms such as vessel, site, holding, accumulation, reservoir, reserve, resource or residue) conveys a dual meaning: it is something which is *left behind* and something which is *drawn upon*. At each level — ideas, organizations, professionals and political economy — these deposits take the form of descriptions (stories) and causal theories, which are drawn upon and leave behind real forms of power. While the deposits appear to be contradictory, they, in fact, rely on each other.

To express all this less metaphorically: each of these models in table 3 speaks of different parameters of social action. Each can be emphasized for different purposes, and all might be needed for something like a complete explanation. Thus:

(1) the notion of progress is always present in the sense that things can obviously be better;
(2) organizations which try to implement each new good idea start with (and then generate more of) their own demands;
(3) whatever these demands, we will tell stories (ideologies) to justify and rationalize what we are doing;
(4) these ideologies will justify action in such a way as to give a privileged position to their tellers and to safeguard their interests; and, finally,
(5) these stories and interests exist and must be located in a particular social structure or political economy.

This chapter, then, is meant to work at two levels: for didactic reasons, each model is treated separately but in the theoretical sense these models should be seen as interdependent. I pay particular attention here to models 2 (Organization) and 5 (Political Economy), as models 3 (Ideology) and 4 (Professions) respectively form the basis of the next two chapters.

PROGRESS

As with its historical counterpart, there is not very much to be said about the progress model. The truth is self-evident — there is nothing to be explained. In response to the same combination of benevolent intentions and advances in knowledge which have always propelled correctional change, a spirit of innovation and reform somehow gripped the social-control system in the 1960s. Old practices seemed outmoded in the light of new ideas. The destructuring ideology appeared, offering not just novelty but a genuinely radical reversal of traditional assumptions. Diversion, deinstitutionalization, reintegration and the move to community all signalled a new era in deviancy control.

This model sees the end result turning out more or less according to the vision. There are, of course, some gaps, some deficiencies, but this is only to be expected. They result from problems of misunderstanding, lack of resources, the fact that the pace of the reforms is just too rapid for the old system to absorb. In the course of time, these problems will be resolved.

The source material for this model can be found in all the official commissions, enquiries and reports, the project descriptions and evaluations, the journals, textbooks, work-shops and conferences which are ground out by the control system (power) and the academic establishment (knowledge) to which it is symbiotically linked. In sheer volume and importance, the weight of these productions far exceeds that for all our other models combined. But for the moment, there is nothing to be said about them: original intentions are accepted as self-evident, while failures or discrepancies are either denied or explained away. In chapter 4, I will look at these stories more carefully. The fact that they might bear little relationship to reality is unimportant. They are important as deposits: they draw upon previous ideologies and abstractions in order to solve new problems, leave behind powerful new deposits which serve to justify new changes, rationalize existing ones, guide individual decisions and insulate the system from any criticism.

There is one particular aspect of this model, however, which does need brief comment here. Its strength is that it sees the control system as a direct and *rational* response to the problem of crime. This is a 'strength' not because the explanation is correct, but simply because other models, for whatever reason and, notably, because of their conceptual bias towards seeing social control as an independent variable, play down this type of rationality.

'Rationality' says nothing about boundary blurring, dispersal or invisibility, but it does appear to account for expansion. The relevant literature here, on the relationship between the amount of crime and the amount of punishment, is vast and complex. This is not just because of technical reasons (questions about the reliability and validity of the statistics), but because of the very issue on which the other models are united: crime rates are not just generated autonomously but, partially at least, reflect control policy. Still, it would be a bizarre type of theory that completely ignored the possibility that the expansion of the crime-control system over the last two decades (as measured, say, by increasing rates of custody and supervision per 100,000 of the population) is a direct response to increasing official crime rates over this period. Even if some of this increase is explained by a greater willingness to report crime rather than a real increase in victimization,[1] this cannot explain away the real structural factors that would lead one to an increased crime rate during this period. To ignore these factors — economic and political, unemployment, demographic shifts or whatever — would indeed be bizarre.

This is not to say that 'logical' explanations for the amount of punishment are self-evident. Quite the contrary. One influential body of thought (associated with Blumstein and his colleagues) has accumulated evidence for the Durkheimian theory of the stability of punishment. Another theory argues that crime rates expand to satisfy organizational capacity. Yet others suggest that there is no relationship whatever between crime rates and system size. International comparisons of correlations over time between crime and imprisonment are as bewildering as they could possibly be.[2] They show (i) increases in crime rates followed by proportionate increases in imprisonment (England); (ii) increases in crime followed by lower rates of imprisonment (some European countries and Australia); (iii) increases in crime associated with stable rates of imprisonment (other European countries and Canada); and (iv) increases in crime followed by disproportionately higher rates of imprisonment (the USA). None of these correlations have been constant over the last 50 years, each is open to multiple interpretations. My own impression is that over the last 25 years, at least, the case of the USA is quite clear and perhaps paradigmatic: an annual growth of prison populations which has consistently outpaced the annual growth of arrests. One recent analysis of the aggregate correlations over the last 20 years between offences reported to the police and changes in the prison population in each of the 6 years before and after the crime rates were reported, found that the correlations were 'not significantly different from zero'.[3]

There is probably no way of proving a constant and direct causal relationship between the amount of crime and the amount of imprisonment (or total supervision). But while the progress model overall cannot really explain the size of the current system (still less, its form or lack of fit with its own rhetoric) the notion that there is, after all, an 'input' into the system, is too obvious to ignore.

### ORGANIZATIONAL CONVENIENCE

Like the progress model, this one has its exact counterpart in the historical literature on deviancy control. It is the closest contemporary echo of accounts such as Rothman's of the emergence of the asylum and its early twentieth-century alternatives. The plot is just a further twist to the old story of good intentions going very wrong. The well-intentioned plans of reformers (conscience) are systematically transformed by the obdurate nature of social reality. The real block lies at the organizational level. When reforms reach the existing system, they confront a series of powerful managerial, administrative and organizational imperatives. The reform impulse is resisted and blocked or (more frequently) it is welcomed, only to be absorbed and co-opted (for the wrong reasons) and in the process completely transformed, even in directions diametrically opposed to the original vision.

Almost every one of the sceptical evaluations I relied upon in my last chapter (those first doubts and second thoughts) draws upon one or other version of this model. The note is a poignant one. Very frequently, these critics were, a few years earlier, the apostles and apologists for these very same changes. The good intentions were their own. What could have happened, they now cry, to programmes with such 'impressive pedigrees' as diversion and deinstitutionalization — theoretically justified, legislatively mandated, responsive to powerful social movements and representative of full professional consensus?[4] Or, in a more explicit personal identification with the original ideology, Lemert asks, what hath been wrought in my name?[5] Insofar as his own writings contributed to the proliferation of diversion programmes, he can only express 'scholarly chagrin and dismay' over the 'entrepreneurial excesses' diversion programmes may have wrought in juvenile justice. All sorts of things have 'gone wrong', his original conception has gone 'wide off the mark'. There have been 'oversights', goals have been 'distorted', 'displaced' or 'perverted'. A 'paradoxical transformation' has taken place. Instead of judicious non-intervention, diversion has turned into a happy means of ensuring a steady supply of young clients for treatment: 'what began as an effort to reduce discretion in juvenile justice became a warrant to increase discretion and extend control where none existed before. If nothing else is learned from this, it is the fearsome difficulty of trying to understand how even a segment of our highly contrived society works'.[6]

A 'litany of impediments' then, as Klein terms the problem. The trouble is not with the original vision. The real issue is 'programme integrity' — strategies like diversion and deinstitutionalization, cannot even be evaluated properly, because they have not been properly implemented, or given a chance to fulfil their promise. Somewhere in between the original or ideal programme rationale and the eventual outcome lies the awful business of implementation — what the programmes actually do. This is where things start going wrong: goals are displaced, manifest functions give way to latent functions, vested interests operate. As Eliot told us: 'Between the idea and the reality, Between the notion and the act, Falls the Shadow'.

There are different ways of explaining just what this Shadow is. In the most primitive version, there is some mysterious constant force, an organizational Murphy's law, which keeps fouling things up. Social reality is a complex business — fearsomely difficult indeed — and what happens in 'the field', is invariably more complicated than anything which the reformers could have anticipated. We must simply learn to live with the sad knowledge that things never turn out quite as they are planned.

At the next step upwards in explicitness, the implementation problem is seen as a matter of consistent *error*. For all sorts of reasons — often unexamined — the programme is implemented in a clumsy, thoughtless, over-eager or (alternatively) over-cautious way. Mistakes are made about priorities or timing, the wrong clients are targeted, the wrong tactics are used, opponents are alienated. To quote one analysis of the failure of the 1969 Children and Young Persons Act in England to achieve its objectives of decarceration and diversion: 'quite simply, cumulatively, these disparate bodies of professionals made the wrong decisions about the wrong children at the wrong time.'[7]

The disciplines of organizational and public-policy analysis provide a more complicated conceptual apparatus with which to approach the implementation problem: 'something happens when programs enter the implementation structure.'[8] On the one hand there are goals, objectives, strategies, ideals and intentions. On the other, there is a series of powerful organizational constraints and constraints on organizations — technology, budgets, inter-agency competition, public opinion, system interdependence, political interference, etc. These all ensure that the original goals are (variously) sabotaged, undermined, distorted, manipulated, frustrated, co-opted, displaced, neutralized or resisted. These organizational restraints, together with any vulnerable features of the goals themselves, eventually set up impediments so powerful that the programme, to all intents and purposes, is not even tried at all.

Klein lists five such impediments to deinstitutionalization and diversion.[9]

(1) insufficiently developed programme rationales — the knowledge base of the theory is too vague;

(2) inappropriately selected client groups — the clients targeted are often not the ones to whom the rationales most clearly apply;

(3) development of insufficient and narrowly conceived services and agencies — the 'service modalities' (such as individual treatment) are not the appropriate ones for realizing the programme goals;

(4) professional resistance to attempts at reform — traditional groups such as correctional staff, judges and police undermine the original strategy; and

(5) placement of programmes in inappropriate settings — the programme is set up either in an unfavourable setting or where 'success' would have been likely even without it.

This is a powerful list. And if Klein is correct in his evaluation, there is indeed little 'programme integrity' in the 200 or so programmes he examined. The 'relative non-occurrence' of deinstitutionalization and diversion is thus easily understandable. With the exception, however, of point 4 — professional resistance —

these impediments are all results rather than causes of faulty implementation. The question remains, why do things go so terribly wrong?

The most persuasive answer is given by those who come (knowingly or not) somewhere close to Rothman's original historical model. The problem lies in what Austin and Krisberg call the 'dialectics of reform'.[10] Each separate reform movement (from the liberal direction — diversion, decarceration, due process and decriminalization; from the more conservative direction — deterrence and just deserts) represents a series of 'unmet promises'. The criminal justice system, propelled by its own organizational dynamics, functions to resist, distort and frustrate the original purposes of these reforms. These 'dynamics' are both internal to the system (interactive processes by which changes in one segment trigger off changes in another or the operation of interest groups trying to expand their sphere of power) and external or 'dialectical' (contradictions in the surrounding society, ideology and political economy).

Austin and Krisberg — and other accounts like theirs — are not, then, simple proponents of the organizational model. They are well aware of all those 'external' ideological, professional and political forces (my next three models). But their main emphasis remains on the organizational dynamics within the criminal justice system. It is the interactive quality of the system (the complex sequence of trigger→resistance→transformation→unintended consequences) which determines the end result. Of particular importance here is the struggle between component parts of the system for power, influence, resources, even survival: 'agencies compete with one another and reactions to a given reform depend on the perceived value of that reform to the agency's survival.'[11]

It is a Manichean view of the system: good intentions are sacrificed in this bitter struggle for survival, for resources to protect, create or expand programmes and for budgets, prestige and power. And the struggle is an unequal one: the old guard — police, judges, prosecutors, custodial staff — remain the most powerful actors in the system. They are the ones that define, that call the tune. All the others — the forces of progress and reform — have to make deals, compromises and trade-offs in order to make a few gains: 'compromises on policy and procedure may be made as temporary tactics to mitigate suspicion and fear on part of the traditional system personnel but such compromises often become rigorously observed organizational guidelines, thereby changing the nature of the alternatives.'[12]

Depending on the setting, different groups of 'traditional-system personnel' are more powerful. For Lemert (and most other critics of diversion) the villains are the police. He argues that the whole sad diversion story should serve to instruct us about the tremendous power of the police in the scheme of American justice. Law enforcement agencies (traditional probation departments as well as the police) simply took charge of the new programmes, pre-empting and co-opting them into their own 'in-house' programmes, with their own personnel, selection criteria and operating procedures. Instead of diversion away from the system, the outcome was 'little more than an expansion in the intake and discretionary powers of the police and a shuffling of such powers from one part of the organization to another.'[13]

A research literature is now being built up with variations on this theme. Reparation and community service are used to enhance the legitimacy of other more-criticized sanctions such as fines and probation. Post-incarceration programmes are absorbed into a strategy which increases the level of intervention. New patterns of funding give power to the very sectors of the system from which clients were supposed to be removed. Private agencies start re-labelling their clients as divertees in order to attract funds. An apparently radical decarceration strategy ends up only shifting custody from state to local level and becoming a revenue sharing carve-up between local agencies.

These examples could be multiplied. In each case, the struggle is perhaps a little less melodramatic than the term 'Manichean' implies and is something more like a parlour game of musical chairs. There is an undignified scramble which contributes to the mixed results of most programmes. Some things turn out right, others do not. This process is nicely described in the organizational research on the Illinois DSO programme.[14] Something worked — fewer youths were referred to detention — but more than expected were classified as detainable and subject to court and agency processing. This happened because agencies which only partly supported the deinstitutionalization strategy, were all competing for the same contract funds. Each sponsoring organization (court, police, probation, welfare) was concerned primarily with achieving its own objectives and only secondarily with the project rationale. But the project had to rely on these agencies (despite their minimal commitment to the ideology of decarceration) and in so doing had to make deals and compromises. Two crucial objectives were compromised: (i) that deinstitutionalization would be accompanied by real diversion; and (ii) that the community-based services would be as non-intrusive as possible.

The pay-off for the traditional groups is sometimes explained in purely organizational terms. Each group is simply looking after its interests by hanging onto its own turf. Faced with loss of power and status, with threats to organizational growth, these groups will resist adapting to innovation; this is a 'bureaucratic imperative'.[15] A relentless organization logic ensures, then, that strategies like diversion are doomed to be implemented not as 'true diversion' but as 'new diversion', and thus expand the system by increasing personnel and budgets, protecting and redefining the boundaries of the machine. This was exactly Rothman's historical tale: in every single setting — parole, probation, juvenile court, indeterminate sentencing — the reform vision was transformed into a caricature to serve the interests of the caretakers and managers.

In other versions, the pay-off is explained in more ideological terms. A good example of this is the co-option of fixed-sentencing reform — how the original radical thrust of the just-deserts model (the attack on discretion, the call for fairness and justice) was neutralized by powerful law-enforcement interests and absorbed into the conservative movement towards harsher and harsher punishment.[16] But whether it be self-interest or ideology, the story is always more complicated than a simple one of the forces of light being routed by the forces of darkness. The eternal thread which binds together the participants of this type of reform movement is that everybody means well. The ideology of innovation in the name of progress allows each stage to lend credibility to the other: 'every level of interaction is defended as a more humane or efficient means of averting something more severe.'[17] This encourages eternal expansion — the more benevolent a programme is defined, the more it will be used, and the wider it will cast its net:

> developing and administering community programmes can be a source of gratification to sincere correctional administrators and lay volunteers who believe they are 'doing good' by keeping people out of dungeons and helping them obtain social services. Judges, reluctant to send difficult children to a reformatory and equally reluctant to release them without an assurance that something will be done to prevent them from returning may be especially enthusiastic about the development of alternative dispositions.[18]

The lesson from most organizational studies, then, is not quite that which their authors (well-intentioned reformers themselves) want us to learn. It is not so much that good intentions are frustrated by obstinate (or malevolent) reality, but rather that good intentions actually dominate the course of events. A triumph, rather than a failure of benevolence. This is illustrated by the following example: how the 'selective application' of the 1969 Children and Young Persons Act in England led, 10 years later, to a near-total failure in the realization of any of its decriminalizing or deinstitutionalizing objectives. In the end, 'a new system came in but the old one did not go out'.[19] Thorpe and his colleagues nicely describe this as 'vertical integration'. Something intended as a replacement is grafted onto the old system, not through conflict, but accommodation: 'an implicit set of demarcation agreements and neutral zones . . . the sector served by the old system simply expands in order to make way for the newcomer.'[20]

So far, the story looks familiar. But what this study shows is that both the expansion of the new system (the soft end) and the integration between the two systems, was made possible by the triumph of the child-saving rhetoric. As the new professionals became more powerful, so the vocabulary of social work was used to widen all the nets. If the root causes of delinquency lay in the failure of community control, then an institution to compensate for this lack of control was necessary. There was a *need* for 'structure', 'care and control', 'care and protection in a planned environment' — the same diagnosis and the same remedy used by Rothman's reformers 150 years ago. So the feeder mechanisms worked even faster: social workers were not only inspired by the rhetoric of 'need' but found the old system a convenient way of disposing of *their* hard cases. This gave a rationale to the notion of prevention (there must after all be something you are trying to prevent) and allowed them to get on with the business of attracting completely new clients into the soft end.

This was not a story then, of hard-hearted traditionalists overruling soft-hearted progressives. (Social workers in this research actually made three times more custodial recommendations than probation officers.) It is by making the system appear less harsh, that people are encouraged to use it more often. Far from each benevolent intermediate option slowing down the career of delinquency, it facilitates, promotes and accelerates it by making each consecutive decision easier to take: 'putting more rungs in the middle of the ladder makes it that much easier to climb'.[21]

In strictly organizational terms then — no changes in input, no changes in the wider social structure — it is difficult to see how modern social-control systems can do anything but expand. Organizational logic must lead to a more voracious processing of deviant populations – in new settings, with different names, run by different professionals. Strategies like diversion allow for ever greater elaboration of what Illich calls 'iatrogenic feedback loops'. Each stage creates the 'correctional clients' it wants, ministers to them and then sets up benevolent loops to send elsewhere those whom it does not want.

To return now to those master patterns. There is little doubt that the organizational model explains these emerging patterns only too well. Expansion and dispersal are readily understandable in terms of agency self-interest, feedback loops from one part of the system to the other, all the deals, shuffles and boundary disputes between various organizations. Clients are brought into the system because more alternatives exist. Bifurcation also makes sense: the hard and soft ends are symbiotically related to each other. The hard end is the back up – to reassure the public, to serve as a deterrent to trouble-makers in the soft end, to be a dumping ground for its unamenable clients, to serve status degradation functions by emphasizing the boundary between good and bad.

The model is of little use, however, in explaining the original good intentions themselves. These are simply unexamined and taken entirely at their face value. The reason for this is obvious: the analyst as reformer identifies with these intentions. The devil lies in the machine, and not in the ideas which are fed into the machine. Even when the ideas themselves are scrutinized, either to point to the paradoxical quality of benevolence or to the 'inadequate conceptualization' behind the theory, this is only to call for better thinking, an awareness that social reform is a tricky business. In the simple version of the model (there are many others which indeed go beyond the organizational box and talk about wider ideological or economic changes) there is not much attempt to locate either the ideas or the reform enterprise itself in a wider social context.

The model also contains a strand of organizational nemesis – the doom-laden prophecy that the best of ideas will *inevitably* be fouled up. But for the most part, the world view of organizational analysis remains optimistic. All those formidable impediments to Proper Programme Implementation are not necessarily insurmountable, they have merely not been surmounted to date: 'it should be possible to develop and implement programs which have well developed theoretical rationales of some conceptual merit.'[22] No need for despair — and certainly no need for criminologists, researchers, reformers, programme evaluators and theoreticians to go out of business.

For a more detached and more pessimistic note about intentions and reality, we have to move to our next three models.

One of the main criteria for distinguishing between the various historical accounts of that original early nineteenth-century transformation was the different weightings each one assigned to the power of talk. In the last instance (as they say), how much did talk really matter in producing correctional change? What was the status of ideas, theories, knowledge, beliefs, intentions, and ideals?

I ended with a pragmatic alternative to the extremes of idealism and materialism. Ideas were not merely froth, mystification, 'so many words', but neither did they come from nowhere. Humanitarianism, benevolence, scientific progress — these were neither free floating abstractions, nor did they actually correspond to what was happening. To switch to this chapter's guiding metaphor: ideas draw upon existing social, political and economic arrangements (as well as previous ideas) and then, in turn, leave behind their own deposits which are drawn up to shape later changes, reforms and policies.

All this makes the question of ideology (or, to be more specific, the original reform ideas) a lot more complicated than the progress or organizational models allow. We must listen to the talk very, very carefully, but not credulously. What we might discover, then, are not mistakes, sloppy conceptualization or instructions which are not properly followed. The contradictions, distortions, paradoxes, anomalies, impurities or whatever, are internal to the ideology. And it is at this level that we have to understand *both* the original appeal of the ideology and the way in which the master patterns are eventually working themselves out.

We must go back in time to trace the sources of these contradictions and forward in time to see the policy arena as a site in which these contradictions work themselves out. All this is like negotiating a particularly subtle double bind: talk must be understood at its face value, but only by not taking it at its face value. It may well be — to take an example from the recent critical literature on informal justice — that the ultimate status of ideology

is to serve as a 'rhetorical device', a mere 'conforting facade'.[23]
Ideology becomes 'Orwellian newspeak', an Alice-in-Wonderland
in which everything is its opposite. 'Informal' means created and
sustained by the formal state apparatus; 'decentralized' means
centrally controlled; 'accessibility' means rendering justice more
inaccessible; 'non-coercive' means disguised coercion; 'community'
means nothing; 'informalism' means undermining existing non-state
models of informal control; 'benevolent' means malignant.

But to say all this is not to strip ideology of its power. Quite the
reverse. It is only, as Orwell reminded us, in resolving contradictions that power is retained indefinitely. We have to revisit all that
control talk we so easily dismissed when criticizing the progress
model. Here is the place to find both the power of ideology and
why it contains its own contradictions and mirror images.

This the task of the next chapter. In it, I take three exemplary
current ideologies (the ideal of community, the notion of the
minimal state and the psychology of behaviourism), examine their
internal messages and speculate on how they are used.

### PROFESSIONAL INTEREST

So concerned have I been with the structural dichotomies between
the prison and the community, between being in the machine
and being out of the machine, that I have virtually ignored one of
the other great patterns laid down in the control system's original
foundation. This was the emergence of those distinctive bodies of
people — specialists, experts, professionals of all sorts — each of
which took over its 'own' category of deviants and established a
monopolistic claim over their lives. Only the experts know what to
do (knowledge); only they should be allowed to do it (power).

This fourth model is quite straightforward. It suggests that the
original line of professional knowledge and power has never been
broken — not by deprofessionalization, delegalization, anti-
psychiatry, decategorization, the distrust of benevolence or anything. The enterprises of classification (diagnosis, screening, selection) and intervention (control, treatment, punishment) remain as
interlocked as they have always been. The new destructuring
ideologies and their eventual outcomes are understandable merely
as further twists in the long spiral which has symbiotically linked
the control system with the behavioural sciences. The new professionals are the link people, doing the jobs they have always

done. The reform programme was part of a job description that had already been written, and it left behind yet another layer of power and knowledge.

In this model then, the focus is not on the tales but their tellers, not on the ideology but its producers and carriers. And, unlike in the organizational model, these people are not merely players of occupational roles, nor participants in a bureaucracy, nor actors in the drama of progress versus reaction. Their significance is not as individuals, but as members of a particular class or strata — the 'new' middle class of service professionals. Their ideas reflect shared cognitive systems of the wider society. We shall have to go well outside the offices and corridors of the control machine in order to understand all this.

In the process I must raise an issue which I have so far ignored, the one issue which the professionals themselves claim is their one and only interest: Does any of this *work*? That is to say, what eventually are the results of all these strategies in terms of their manifest and declared objectives? Do overall rates of crime come down? Are individual offenders less likely to recidivate? If the answers to these traditional correctional questions are in any way positive, then, claim the professionals, everything else is more or less irrelevant. Never mind nets, ladders, feedback loops, monopolies, self-interest or expansion; in the end the intervention really works. As in medicine (so the argument goes), even if there are unsubstantiated claims, damaging side-effects or iatrogenic illnesses, *on balance* the good outweighs the harm, the enterprise ultimately is rational and benevolent. The helping and healing professions are not, after all, self-interested monopolies or 'disablers'.

These are the sorts of issues taken up in more detail in chapter 5, which is organized around the theme of professional power and knowledge.

POLITICAL ECONOMY

For many observers, the shift from the erratic and uncoordinated local enterprise of the seventeenth and eighteenth centuries to the eventual dominance of the centralized, rationalized state was not just one of several patterns of crime control established in the nineteenth century, but the key transformation which explains and subsumes all others. Correspondingly, the argument goes, any current ideological changes and actual control patterns must be explained at the level of the overall political economy.

These explanations reflect variations and disagreements within contemporary Marxist-type theories (which correspond closely to the differences between the disciplinary models of prison history). The differences lie particularly in the degree of 'relative autonomy' given to the state and the relative emphasis assigned to the political and the economic. There are, though, common features which make such models quite distinct. Crucially, these are that benevolent rhetorical intentions are of little or only derivative significance, that while professionals and organizations might be important their autonomy is strictly controlled and limited by the state, and that the notion of 'failure' so central to the organizational model is meaningless. Such theories tend towards a left functionalism: what is there must be there to ensure the success of the state in reproducing capital and to deflect any threat to its stability. Now, as ever, the motor force for change lies not within the crime-control system itself, but at the level of national (or even 'world-system') political and economic developments.

Leaving aside for the moment the anomalous case of Foucault, we can divide theories which more or less share this approach into two groups — the first veering towards the economic, the second to the more political edge. In both cases, remember what the deposit metaphor conveys: the political economy is a source of power which then leaves behind new forms of power.

### Economic Rationality: Business as Usual

The first group of theories might be called 'business as usual' or 'shuffling the cards'. There is no break, no new phase to explain; the crime-control apparatus is part of the continuous drive to rationalization which began with capitalism itself. Capitalist development encounters internal crises and contradictions which impede or resist its flow and these have to be resolved: 'as it moves along its twisted course, capitalism requires an ever changing ensemble of strategies to meet new crises.'[24] If these crises and contradictions are understood, then a political economy of crime control can be constructed to explain each element in the ensemble.

The stress throughout this group of theories is on economic sources and expressions of the crisis. Liberal democratic theory may assume a separation of the economic from the political and legal but, the argument goes, the state will hardly operate to undermine its own economic base: all its operations will be directed to maintaining the viability of the economic system. The state will, thus, only create the type of crime-control system which in the long run supports the existing division of labour. As the spheres of interest of the modern state expand, so all institutions on which the system depends — health, education, welfare, crime control, etc. — will tend to become more interventionist overall. Exactly how this happens and why the results are accepted as legitimate or even humane, just and progressive, varies from theory to theory.

What also has to be explained, though, is the exact *form* which state intervention might take. Why, for example, the apparent move against the closed institution and towards the community? Here, the best known and most influential account is Scull's analysis of the decarceration movement.[25] He starts by dismissing standard progressivist approaches which see decarceration as caused by a new sensitivity towards the liberal critique of the institution. Such critiques, however, were voiced nearly a century ago, and in Scull's view they functioned more recently as liberal froth to cover changes required by the new exigencies of welfare capitalism. New forms of pacification and control are now needed.

The socialized cost of segregative social-control systems, he argues, could previously be borne by the state without much effort. There were, anyway, no real alternatives to the policy of dumping and isolating the most difficult, troublesome or incapacitated members of the disreputable poor. In the early 1970s, though, welfare capitalism was caught in a fiscal crisis: on the one hand it had to continue to socialize the costs of production and on the other, structural pressures were generated to curtail spending on costly (and ever-increasingly so) institutions such as the asylum and prison. In relative terms, these expenses became harder to justify and these surplus populations could, by this time, be managed (as they could not be at the end of the nineteenth century) through subsistence systems of welfare payment in the community.

So, as part of a more general retrenchment, the state divests itself of expensive institutions and diversifies elsewhere. This move most clearly affects the mentally ill, but as overall fiscal pressures intensify, so programmes under the liberal banner of community control look more and more attractive elsewhere. Money can be saved, and benevolent intentions proclaimed. The state thus withdraws, leaving various deviant and problem populations to be treated like industrial waste. They are left alone, repressively tolerated in restricted zones of the city, or fed into the private sector where they are reprocessed for profit. Deviants find themselves in the communities most intolerant or least able to look after them; decarceration is another burden heaped on the back of those people most obviously the victims of society's inequalities.

Scull now concedes a number of empirical problems in his original account of what happened to the mentally ill: notably, that the relationship between decarceration and the fiscal crisis is not automatic and deterministic. Comparative statistics, for example from Britain where instead of privatization there was increased public spending, or from European countries where time sequences were quite different, show a much more erratic pattern. Other critics claim that even in the USA it was an optimistic political liberalism, committed to expansion, which caused the most dramatic initial phase of decarceration, and that retraction and public spending cuts only took place later.

But more important, as Scull now recognizes, is the difference between crime and mental illness. While non-interventionism and benign (or not so benign) neglect has indeed been the fate of many of the mentally ill, none of this applies to crime and delinquency. As we saw in chapter 2, control policies are becoming more, rather than less interventionist, prison populations are not declining and community control is responsible for the overall system increase. While financial considerations certainly were important in building up the new community programmes, and while relative expenditure on prisons declined (in *some* places) as a proportion of the human services budget, the net saving produced by community control is dubious.[26] Even the (expanding) forms of privatized community control in the USA are funded along 'third party' lines, that is the state contracts out to a private supplier.[27]

Scull continues to insist that the modern welfare state infrastructure was a necessary condition for the age of decarceration, but now emphasizes the particular ideological nature of crime. Crime is not a sickness which calls for humane 'community care' but a voluntary action – which demands more rather than less intervention. Old-fashioned law-and-order politics – the pressure to 'get them off the streets' – rather than any reform going wrong, accounted for the increasing reach and intensity of the system. This pressure is almost entirely absent for mental illness – no one much cares about the crazies on the streets and buses – so decarceration 'works' here (with whatever grim results).

The error was simple: many early theorists and harbingers of decarceration (and the rest of the destructuring package) accepted, more or less at face value, progressivist visions of what was happening. So we tried to explain something which hardly existed. It soon became apparent that community control was mostly not an alternative to doing and spending more, but to doing and spending less. This is not at all what one might expect from a model stressing economic rationality. It is far more plausible to argue for another type of rationality – that an increase in what is variously termed the 'reserve army of labour', the 'relative surplus population', the social marginals, leads to a corresponding enlargement in the state 'ensemble' of social strategies. Deviants thus become *overproduced*.[28]

An objection of a quite different order to the fiscal-crisis model is raised in Melossi's explanation for changing strategies of social control.[29] For him the fiscal crisis could not have had its powerful effect if, on a wider societal level, the disciplinary functions of the prison had not become obsolete. For Melossi, the new strategies are not qualitatively different from the old; there has simply been 'a shuffling of cards in the deck',[30] a reshuffle which only takes place because of overall changes in capital and the mode of production. He sees the control system as modelled all along on relations of production, and 'social control' as always and only 'learning of discipline'. The changes we are witnessing are simply the ways in which the prison 'follows' or 'feels' the movement of capital from within the factory to the community outside.

This theoretical approach sees the disciplinary functions of the prison as reaching their peak when the labour force was relocated into the city under the guidance of the self-regulating market of nascent capitalism. Already in the last century, the prison's malaise began, oscillating between a productive institution modelled directly on the factory and a mere instrument of terror. Under welfare capitalism, these institutions start becoming obsolete. Capitalism – the reproduction and socialization of labour power – extends itself outside the factory gates and tries to regulate more and more areas of life. The monopoly of the small segregative institutions makes no sense, and capitalism's disciplinary modes follow the deviant into the community, developing new sites for discipline and surveillance.

At the same time, the work ethic itself became less relevant because of mass unemployment and a questioning of rationality and scientific management. There is no point in teaching discipline to those who want no part of it and know that they do not need it in the future anyway. The profound connection between social control and the capitalist organization of work is reflected in the 'mass struggles' of the 1960s against authoritarian institutions such as the prison and mental hospital. The state counteracts this movement by strengthening its repressive apparatus, but the prison cannot be saved. It fades away into mass society, into all the other new forms of control now being developed. Gradually, the complex machinery created by the bourgeoisie in its rise to power begins to be disassembled. This is seen as the meaning of decarceration: the closed institutions invented as a monument to the factory become redundant, their walls are opened up and their functions integrated into the rest of the community. Yet we are still in a transitional period as the agencies of capitalist control try to respond to the crisis in all sorts of diversified and tentative forms. So the pack continues to be shuffled.

This is aesthetically an extremely powerful theory, though unfortunately it produces little or no evidence to support its main idea: the homologous relationship between control systems and the organization of capital. It is also somewhat far-fetched to describe the destructuring ideologies of the sixties as being in any way 'mass movements' or expressions of the 'class struggle'. Finally, there is the embarrassing problem of the prison itself, which is in no way becoming 'obsolete'.

## Political Crisis: The Cunning State

In my second group of political economy theories, the notion of a crisis also appears, but this time, although the crisis has economic roots, it is *expressed* closer to the political than to the economic edge of the state. I will summarize here two converging streams of writing. One comes from a group of British criminologists using Gramscian notions about the legitimation or hegemonic crises of the state,[31] the other comes from a North American group (associated with the journal *Crime and Social Justice*) trying to connect the crisis in world capitalism with the rise of the new right.[32] For the American group in particular, there is less interest in the new parts of the system (matters like community control and diversion are virtually not mentioned) than in analysing the general move to a larger and harsher apparatus of crime control. The overall story is one of increasing state repression: the rise of the 'exceptional state'.[33]

'Crisis' appears on the stage as both cause and effect: the crisis in the world economic order produces a particular crisis of authority for the liberal democratic state. Or, in other terms, a shift at the centre of the political economy (at national and international levels),

causing crises, recession, and unemployment, is registered at the
political level. A new authoritarian consensus emerges (or is
engineered) about what must be done. In current electoral terms:
Reaganism in the USA, Thatcherism in Britain, signs of right-
wing populism in Canada. In broader political terms: the rise of
the new right, neo-conservatism, the 'moving right show', even
'friendly fascism'.[34]

Traditional economic issues are, thus, shifted on to the common-
sense ideological space of law and order, justice, authority, discipline, control, and welfare. It is on this terrain that the post-Keynes-
ian assumptions of welfare liberalism begin to be dismantled in favour
of an austere, technocratic conservatism. Taylor well describes
the dual move in Britain away from the traditional wisdoms of the
post-war Labour/social democratic consensus and towards reviving
old-fashioned moral virtues and hierarchies: it is 'increasingly
suggested that the promised orderliness of conventional social
democracy could only be assured by a reversion to the use of
containment and coercion.'[35]

In the sphere of crime control, indices of the move towards
'containment and coercion' (in Britain and North America) are
taken to be:

- increasing rates of imprisonment;
- increasing severity of punishment (renewed emphasis on deterrence and incapacitation and longer, determinate sentencing);
- a widening net of criminalization;
- an expansion of the repressive parts of the apparatus to deal
  with political and industrial unrest;
- a cut-back of liberal 1960s gains in areas such as abortion and
  women's rights, with a corresponding ascendance of right-wing
  moral crusaders;
- greater publicity given to street crimes; and
- a transformation of the discrete moral panics of the 1960s into
  a deliberate climate of hostility to marginal groups and racial
  minorities, who become scapegoats for the crisis.

As this drift to repression becomes clear, state expenditure is
not so much reduced as redirected. This takes place along familiar
bifurcatory lines. The hard side of the system becomes harder,
with a greater investment in police, prison, crime control, hardware, military spending — the 'tools of domestic pacification' (as
they are termed). The soft side contracts in response to fiscal
crises or general monetarist economics. Health, education and

welfare budgets are cut; certain social services shifted to the private sector; ideals such as treatment or rehabilitation become irrelevant and expensive – even if they 'worked', they would be pointless because the economy could not absorb those who had been 're-formed'. What remains of the soft edge (community projects, diversion, social work) is understood either as just benign watchfulness or as symbolic exercises of legitimation, serving to 'cover' and deflect attention from the repressive moves happening elsewhere.

The critical writing on informal justice assigns a similar mystificatory role to the soft parts of the system. The dominant interpretation here is what might be called the 'theory of the cunning state'. The trend to informalism is really part of a cycle in which the managers of the system need new ways of legitimation, especially to resolve the contradiction in legal liberalism between formal equality and substantive inequality. The whole repertoire of informalism (community justice, dispute mediation, neighbourhood conflict resolution, and so on) is a cunning way of justifying domination. State control is extended, conflict is neutralized and coercion is disguised. In the process, state and capital are legitimated. Just when there is widespread public cynicism about the possibility of justice, 'informalism responds to public hostility towards and mistrust of the state by simulating its withdrawal from civil society, purporting to relieve citizens of oppressive regulation and to expand their freedom of choice.'[36]

In these and similar theories of 'crisis' or 'legitimation', any hard/soft bifurcation remains subservient to the general principle of more repression and more intervention. Rising crime rates and increasing recalcitrance can be expected under the impact of monetarism and mass unemployment. In response, the system keeps on expanding remorselessly, and shifts the expenses which the state cannot pick up onto the private sector. The liberal welfare state, it is assumed, has failed to solve its own internal contradictions; its demise is imminent.[37]

In the next chapter, I will return to many of these general questions about the role and nature of the state. Let me here note a few general problems in these two variants of the political-economy model. Besides the occasional exaggerations and rhetorical excesses – the price we sometimes pay for political awareness – a continual problem is the contradictory status assigned to the newer and softer forms of social control. They are seen either as taking over from the prison (which is patently not true) or else as shrinking in response to welfare cut-backs (also patently not so).[38] In either case, the particular appeal of the new ideologies, their internal contradictions, organizational transmutations and the way they are used by state professionals all tend to be ignored. This gap probably arises from the theoretical concentration on more obviously political forms of repression and on the hard end (surveillance, law-enforcement technology, long sentences) of the criminal justice system.

There are, of course, exceptions to this tendency. Despite its commitment to the meta-theory of the cunning state, for example, the 'radical' evaluation of informal justice pays considerable attention to the ideological appeal and professional interests behind informalism. And, as in each of my other models, there are explanations here which draw on other levels. Chan and Ericson, for example, start with the notion of the fiscal crisis, move to the ideological need for the state to reproduce order while maintaining the appearance of being just and rational, and then suggest how this need is 'translated' by control agents at the day-to-day organizational level. Thus, 'appreciation of the competing demands on control organizations to reproduce order, legality and their own interests makes it possible to understand why the consequences of reform are typically different from what was originally intended.'[39] 'Intentions' are explained at the structural level, consequences at the organizational level.

This type of combination theory, however, is seldom used. The great strength of the political-economy model, compared with any of the others, lies in its ability to move right outside the machine into the wider society. Whatever we might think of any of its specific variants — fiscal crisis, socialization of production, endless repression or whatever — the model shows that crime-control policies cannot be seen simply as consequences (intended or unintended) of social-control talk or internal organizational loops. Receptivity to talk and the ways in which professional decisions are made must be understood in terms of clear structural impediments or imperatives. When the element of economic determinism is tempered by an awareness of the changing nature of state intervention, the model picks up major changes in social-control strategies not detectable at organizational or professional levels. Spitzer, for example, notes how growing state intervention, especially in the process of socialization is likely to produce an emphasis on 'general-preventative (integrative) rather than selective reactive (segregative) controls'.[40] That is, instead of waiting for troublemakers to surface then managing them through segregative techniques, the state uses 'assimilative' control — trying to normalize or absorb deviants. This contrast between segregation and integration is, as chapters 6 and 7 show, a major difference in social-control strategy.

If the model's strength is that it moves outside the machine, its corresponding weakness is to discount the day-to-day workings of the system by seeing them only as mirror images of the political economy itself. This is to insist on too tight a fit, to look for rationality — and even conspiracy — where it hardly exists. The new professionals and visionaries of crime control are something more (and less) than 'high level state functionaries (and their surrogates in the academy)' who cleverly recognize the limitations of capitalism and devise policies accordingly.[41]

In this respect it seems to me that Foucault's image of a self-reproducing power system — a political economy of the body which is not directly related to 'the' political economy — is more plausible. The endless current projects of diversion and deflection, alternatives and supplements, destructuring and restructuring are variations of the same 'deinstitutionalization' of power revealed by Foucault's archaeology of the last century. The original compact methods of discipline are still being broken up and made more flexible as they circulate into the new 'regional outposts' of the control network. As power is reorganized (the disciplinary or positivist project) each new form is legalized (the classical project) according to a finely tuned calibration of punishment.

To Foucault, none of these microsystems of power (a diversion agency, shall we say, or a tracking project) can be seen as a mere reflection of the great systems of politico-economic power. He either refuses to look for a centre of power (this certainly makes him non-Marxist) or argues that the centre is relatively indifferent to these 'subtle' and 'cunning' projects. But here (and not only here) Foucault is inconsistent. His account appears to work at the same level as the organizational or professional models, but only makes sense if 'power' and 'discipline' are the determining forces at some global, even supernatural level.

Foucault's most deceptive appeal, however, is that of the most banal of historical 'lessons' — the idea that there is nothing new and therefore there is nothing to be explained. The conventional political-economy models are altogether more satisfactory in this respect. For there are, indeed, some new matters to be explained:

at the political level, for example, the demise of traditional welfare liberalism, or at the economic level, the growing significance of the private sector. On such matters, Foucault is silent.


CONCLUSION


The easy part of this chapter has been its textbook quality — conveying, that is, through a series of highly condensed summaries, that there are different and competing ways of looking at the same social reality. The difficult part is to convey the idea that these explanations are somehow complementary without at the same time falling into the intellectual slush of 'integration' in which all theories, ideas or philosophies imperceptibly merge with each other.

My deposit metaphor tries — inadequately, I fear — to convey this dual sense of distinctiveness and mutual interdependence. The progress vision draws on endless previous stories about progress, and then leaves behind another *mélange* of benevolent rhetoric to rationalize current policy and guide further innovation. Organizational dynamics and interests are indeed powerful impediments to any programme realization, and in the process of transforming each programme into their own ends, organizations create yet a further set of impediments. The contradictory nature of control ideologies explains much of what happens to policies carried out in their name, and then deposits new ideological residues to be resolved in the next cycle of change. Professional and managerial classes generate and then mould reforms to meet their own interests, and this leaves behind new and permanent interests to be protected. And the political economy takes any autonomous power away from words, organizations and professionals, dictates the limits of any changes, and leaves behind yet more powerful residues.

Any satisfactory account of control policy must find some way of sifting through these deposits and assigning them relative weight. Take the 'simple' matter of net expansion. Even if this did not happen quite as planned, it is actually 'progressive' for the net to widen if you believe that this is a way of doing more good to more people. It is also true that organizational feedback loops can explain exactly the way this expansion takes place. And this explanation is even more plausible if we consider the dominant vested interest of the people running these bureaucracies, namely to create a dependency on more people just like themselves. It is also true that contradictions in the ideologies of community and state interventionism (which I examine in the next chapter) explain very well why expansion tends to take place. Finally, there are unmistakable tendencies in the political economy which simultaneously create more problematic, deviant and marginal groups as well as expand the size and range of methods to deal with them in an orderly way.

Let me give two specific examples of how any plausible story must uncover each of these five deposits. First, Lerman's account of the retracking and hidden institutionalization which takes place under the rubric of the community control of juvenile delinquency.[42] To understand how a system (child welfare) traditionally associated with dependent, neglected and abused children started placing delinquents into its facilities, we start at the level of organizational and professional interests. But this move was only possible because of the convergence of two 'progressive' ideologies: the benevolent and therapeutic expansionism of the child welfare system and the new vision of community, An ideological trade-off results: the just-deserts idea limits the amount of traditional custody, but the private sector provides longer and more intensive services for the old shallow-enders. And this could only happen because of changes in state and federal funding – a new division of labour in which a publicly subsidized private sector totally dominates the field of community control.

Second, an example which (much more explicitly than the first) ends up at the wider societal level. Greenberg and Humphries' account of what happened to the justice model of sentencing, starts at the ideological level: the progressive, even radical thrust to the original 'struggle for justice' movement; the stress on social harm and distributive justice; the demand in the prisoners' movement to attack the abuses of the treatment ideology.[43] But as the reform agenda was fed into the system, it was transformed by powerful interests. Only one element of the ideology was abstracted – the individualistic, moralistic notion of justice – and the rest was discarded. There was success – restriction of parole, cutting down some areas of discretion, more scepticism about treatment, the move to fixed sentencing based on rough principles of offence severity – but failure lay in this very success. Discretion was shifted elsewhere, substantive justice became hidden even more by the rhetoric of formal justice and, above all, the effect of much legislative reform was to increase the average length of sentences and the time actually spent in prison. In the new political alliances thrown up by overall economic changes, neo-classicism emerged as an unmistakable victory for conservatism. Its hidden agenda is now becoming clear — to punish harder.

But perhaps my deposit metaphor is making things much too complicated. Control and welfare systems are not different from any part of a complex civilization in which institutions go about doing what they have to do, while at the same time saying they are doing many other things. Contrary to all those dire warnings about harshness, fascism and the new right, I believe that the ideology of doing good remains powerful. In a century which has witnessed the most terrible of atrocities being accompanied by the most exquisite of moral justifications, why should such innocent matters as punishing rule-breakers in the name of justice and helping potential rule-breakers in the name of welfare, not continue to be seen as benevolent? In comparison to real atrocities, these matters are indeed often naive and innocent, benevolent and benign, just and helpful, as well as all the other deposits they might reveal and leave behind.

This is the essence of a humanistic civilization: to exert power and to do good at the same time. This is what parents mean when they say that they are only punishing their children to help them. It needs, perhaps the cultural detachment of another civilization to see all this more clearly. Here is V.S. Naipaul's East African Indian trader, Salim in *A Bend in the River*:

> If it was Europe that gave us on the coast some idea of our history, it was Europe, I feel, that also introduced us to the lie. Those of us who had been in that part of Africa before the Europeans had never lied about ourselves. Not because we were moral. We didn't lie because we never assessed ourselves and didn't think there was anything for us to lie about; we were people who simply did what we did. But the Europeans could do one thing and say something quite different; and they could act in this way because they had an idea of what they owed to their civilisation. It was their great advantage over us. The Europeans wanted gold and slaves, like everybody else; but at the same time they wanted statues put up to themselves as people who had done good things for the slaves. Being an intelligent and energetic people, and at the peak of their powers, they could express both sides of their civilisation; and they got both the slaves and the statues.[44]

# 4

# Stories of Change

I have already announced the purpose of this chapter. This is to
listen carefully to social-control talk: the inconsistent and varied
words used by the workers, managers and ideologues of the system
as they explain what they think they are doing and announce what
they would like to do.

I have also made some preliminary judgements about the status
of all this talk. Words neither 'come from the skies' (as Mao reminds us) nor can they be taken as literal explanations of what
is happening. Nonetheless, we must still listen to them very carefully. Words are real sources of power for guiding and justifying
policy changes and for insulating the system from criticism. In
this sense, they are Naipaul's 'statues' which are built to reassure
the powerful about their intentions. But these stories are important
in another sense: as ideological constructions, they are full of
contradictions, anomalies and paradoxes. These internal impurities
reveal a hidden agenda, a message which is not as simple as the
surface tale. The arena of social policy is the place where such
hidden contradictions are resolved. Leaving aside any putative
'implementation gap' between rhetoric and reality, it is the rhetoric
itself which becomes the problem.

But let us reserve for the end of the chapter a further assessment
of how words work. I will now set out separately three representative stories of control: the quest for community, the ideal
of the minimum state, and the return to behaviourism. There are,
of course, other stories being told, but these seem to me to be the
most important. In each case I will look at the surface message,
the popular appeal of the tale, its deeper structures and then the
ways in which it is being used.

THE QUEST FOR COMMUNITY

Each one of the destructuring ideologies which appeared in chapter 1 (decarceration, diversion, decentralization and the rest) and their implied or actual preferences (community control, informalism, reintegration, etc.) are sustained by, and owe their public appeal to, the rhetorical quest for community. It would be difficult to exaggerate how this ideology — or, more accurately, this single word — has come to dominate Western crime-control discourse in the last few decades.

As I showed in chapter 2, it is not at all clear what community control (or treatment, alternatives, corrections, care, placement) actually means. This conceptual and actual blurring is, if not always deliberate, certainly part of the appeal. Almost anything can appear under the heading of 'community' and almost anything can be justified if this prefix is used.

At first glance, though, the surface ideal looks simple enough: to replace, wherever possible, individualistic modes of intervention (as represented by cellular confinement behind the walls of the classic penitentiary) by forms of control in the community. These new forms are described, theorized about or idealized primarily in negative or abolitionist terms: that is to say, they are not segregative, not behind walls, not in an artificially created institution, not individualistic. When the imagery is positive, the terms used are 'natural', 'open', 'integrative' or simply 'in the community'. In the hagiology and demonology of 'progressive' crime-control talk, the contrast is between the good community — open, benevolent, accepting — and the bad institution — damaging, rejecting, stigmatizing.

This is the iconography in its purest form: closed prison against open community. But the ideology of community spreads well beyond the restricted issue of the physical location of punishment. The talk refers not just to 'institution' in the lay sense, but to the sociological sense of the whole structural network (law, police, courts) of deviancy control. Community, then, is not simply the preferred alternative to the cell as a place for doing things to offenders, but the physical (and metaphysical) space in which the whole network is to be bypassed (diverted) or replaced.

Before looking for any deeper or hidden messages, let us remind ourselves of the surface intellectual supports for the community ideology. These converged from four directions:

(1) *Pragmatic and utilitarian*: the system was simply not working. Treatment regimes, in particular, and closed institutions, in general, were ineffective in preventing recidivism, reducing crime rates or whatever they were supposed to do.

(2) *Humanitarian and civil liberty*: these institutions were brutal, degrading, inhumane. Their systematic deprivation of individual rights and freedom was unnecessary and unjustifiable. Internal reform was pointless.

(3) *Social-scientific*: labelling and stigma theory and studies such as Goffman's *Asylums* had shown the potent and irreversible effects of isolating and segregating deviants. Institutionalization was the extreme form of labelling, and would inevitably create secondary deviation and the reinforcement of deviant self-imagery.

(4) *Cost benefit*: if the other messages came from within the left-liberal consensus, conservatives as well could claim that closed institutions were costly and unproductive. The same results — good or bad — could be achieved at a lower cost in the community.

The positive message was that community control would be more effective, more humane, less stigmatizing and cheaper. These were matters of faith — either evangelical (the community was self-evidently good) or modest (at least nothing could be much worse than the institution). There was also a vision of new technologies (behaviourist, drugs, electronic) which would supposedly allow a degree of surveillance and control outside the walls of the institution. This, then, was the story at its first hearing.

### Deeper Structures

For a first probe beneath the surface, we might start with the word 'community' itself. Not only is this a word rich in symbolic power, but it lacks any negative connotations. This is true of its everyday usage and its political appeal to both left and right. It is also true of its social-science connotations. Who cares about 'structure', 'function', 'process' or even 'relationship' and 'values'? These words can be used in a neutral way; they usually do not in themselves conjure up images of good or bad.

In all these contexts — popular, political and social-scientific — much of this symbolic power derives from a profound sense of nostalgia. Now nostalgia is a rather more complicated phenomenon than it first appears; nor is it quite the same as sentimentality or romanticism.[1] The form it takes in crime-control ideology is a look back to a real or imagined past community as providing the ideal and desirable form of social control. This impulse is reactionary and conservative, not in the literal political sense, but in always locating the desired state of affairs in a past which has now (usually *just* now) been eclipsed by something undesirable. As in all forms of nostalgia, the past might not really have existed. But its mythical qualities are profound. The iconography is that of the small rural village in pre-industrial society in contrast to the abstract, bureaucratic, impersonal city of the contemporary technological state.

This iconography is, of course, as old as sociology itself. Every first-year sociology student is introduced via the work of Durkheim, Weber, Marx, Tonnies, and Simmel to the classic set of contrasts between the face-to-face, *Gemeinschaft* traditional community and the impersonal, urban, mass society dominated by the cash nexus. Conventional histories of the sociological tradition have regarded community not only as 'the most fundamental and far-reaching' of sociological ideas but also have seen the 'rediscovery of community' as 'unquestionably the most distinctive development in nineteenth century social thought, a development that extends well beyond sociological theory to such areas as philosophy, history and theology to become indeed one of the major themes of imaginative writing in the century.'[2] This view might be slightly tinged by what today's conventional sociology wants to find in its own history, but the intellectual preoccupation was clear enough. And community continued in classical social theory both as fact and as value. It was not just a neutral concept, but a moral quest, not just a classificatory term to designate how life is led in a particular geographical or social space, but how life *should* be led.[3]

Already in the early nineteenth century, well before its formalization in social theory, this iconography was available to shape social-control ideologies. It was this same ideal of community which Rothman's and Ignatieff's reformers used — the sense of a lost social order which had to be reconstructed. The exact properties of this lost order were often as vaguely sensed then as they were now: 'community is often defined in much the same way as God was in medieval Jewish theology — that is to say by the *via negativa*, that is, saying what God is not rather than describing his particular attributes.'[4] Nostalgia though, does not depend on intellectual rigour; what matters is the symbolic evocation of a lost world.

For some, the original inspiration might have been something like the Greek *polis*, the homogeneous participatory democracy of Periclean Athens. There the 'whole man' of German romanticism could flourish. In control ideology, however, the most resonant vision was the small rural village, the world which (supposedly) had just been lost and whose traces still existed in living memory. Here, there could be a sense of belonging, shared values and rules, commitment to the group, mutual aid, intimacy and stability. In community lay all that was the opposite of alienation, estrangement, rootlessness, loss of attachment, disintegration of the social bond. These were the products of the city, of mass society, technology, industrialism, and the state itself.

The idealization of community was part of a deep strain of nineteenth-century conservative thought. Individualism, secularization, and rationalism had released ordinary people from restraint and obedience, from the traditional bonds of community. The result was not 'freedom' but unrest, loneliness, anomie. The most vulnerable social groups would break down; they had to be restrained for their own good. The most labile social groups would rebel; they had to be restrained for the wider social good. In the new institutions they would all be able to learn the meaning of order, discipline and authority — the good community.

Radical critics of industrialism and capitalism drew on the same imagery. To them, the community offered fraternity, the devolution of power, emotional involvement, participatory democracy. If anomie implied a lack of regulation, alienation implied too much of the wrong sort of regulation. The late nineteenth-century radical utopia was the self-help community.

As we move into the twentieth century, the actual memories of these worlds might begin to fade, but the nostalgia is continually reinforced. The rich iconography of the small rural village is contrasted to a powerful *via negativa*: the sense of urban confusion and degradation, the squalors of the big city. This sense was the driving force behind progressive crime-control ideology: children and other vulnerable groups were to be saved from urban vice. The traditional intellectual distaste for the city, combined in American sociology with the classical European tradition to create a particularly powerful influence on social-control theory. This was what Mills called 'the professional ideology of social pathologists', a view of social problems in which 'all the world should be an enlarged Christian democratic version of a rural village'.[5]

By the 1960s, of course, this simplistic vision had been largely disowned in sociology itself. The ascendancy of abstract structural functionalist theory and then, from the opposite direction, the fragmenting of the sociological enterprise by interactionism, phenomenology, Marxism and feminism, all replaced that naive moralism with the more complicated theories and values. Social workers, criminologists and other 'social pathologists' might indeed have continued being influenced by the older, more 'primitive' nostalgia, but the theorists around them were responding to more sophisticated chords.

Sophisticated,' but not radically different in their underlying vision of the good society. For the sixties witnessed yet another renewal of the quest for community. The diffusion throughout the educated middle class of bohemian, underground, radical and counter-cultural values turned into movements for demodernization and destructuring. Traditional forms of authority were questioned and utopian alternatives evoked from a lost past or from societies as yet untainted by the fatal touch of industrialism. The demodernization impulse (while continuous with nineteenth-century movements of disenchantment with secularization and rationality) took on new forms: interest in Eastern religions, a professed anti-materialism, the move back to natural foods and holistic health, the commune movement. The destructuring impulse was more genuinely novel, and sanctioned powerful emotional attacks on traditional social institutions such as the family and the school. The time had come to question these structures and replace them with looser, more open and flexible arrangements — 'participatory democracy'. Prefixes such as 'open', 'free', 'people's' and of course 'community' took on a renewed and unquestioned resonance: *these* were the sorts of parks, schools, hospitals, clinics, universities and political groups that would replace the old ossified structures.

In social-control talk this destructuring impulse took the form of what Beck calls an 'anti-institutional sentimentality'.[6] Anarchist (and other such ideologically consistent critiques) were lifted, and vulgarized by otherwise quite unsympathetic people. Sentimental anarchist ideas — such as bureaucracies are impersonal, the state is evil, small is beautiful — could be relied upon to win support for any policy which appeared to create free, collective living space, liberated zones where you could do your own thing outside of the 'system'.

The appeal of deinstitutionalization, Beck argues, lay in invoking this ideal not on behalf of the self but of some other oppressed or disadvantaged group, especially those behind the walls of the closed institution.[7] For many middle-class radicals, the message from the counter-cultural heroes of the time — Illich, Kesey, Marcuse, Laing, Szasz, Goffman — was that the benign terminology and pretentions of all these places (helping, nurturing, healing) was a fraud and had to be exposed. These places could only be brutalizing and degrading, and their staff (custodians, counsellors, therapists, all) had to be attacked at every opportunity. A great mistake had been made by trying to change deviants by forcing them to adjust to these artificial institutions; their salvation therefore was seen to lie in reintegration into the benign community. In the meantime, all the walls had to be broken down 'of prisons, hospitals, asylums, correctional centres, reformatories and homes for the handicapped, retarded, neglected, abused, abandoned, dependent, incompetent, misguided, not yet productive, no longer productive and never could be productive.'[8]

As we have seen, and as Beck is well aware, the entry and co-option of this radical rhetoric into official social-control talk depended on certain objective changes — the institutions were under strain from overcrowding, administrative difficulties, fiscal pressures and periodic scandals. Anarchist sentimentality might have been genuinely subscribed to by liberals and radicals, but it could be used as an alibi by the new cadre of foundation directors, managerial consultants and professionals at the forefront of correctional change. Theirs of course, was the more conservative vision of community and their interest was to clear the prisons of all but the hard cases. But pragmatists, progressive reformers and fiscal conservatives alike could all make the same sentimental claims to be doing good.

This is not to say that we must be entirely cynical about these motives and the reasons for these statues of benevolence being erected. Social-control talk is always more complicated than mere deception, the images of community are deep and historically resonant enough to have been genuinely believed as well as genuinely influential. It is more in the directions of self-deception and contradiction that we now have to turn. The question is less why the reality of community control has turned out so very unlike the vision but why we could not have expected much else.

The most immediate problem lies in the idealistic flaw of trying to base a social-control ideology on visions derived from other societies. In the first place, the content of the visions themselves is often historical and anthropological nonsense: neither the pre-industrial rural village nor the tribal or folk society were exactly communities in the ways that are idealized. In the informal justice literature, for example, radicals often underplay the paternalism, the fixed lines of authority and the arbitrary nature of justice.[9] Conservatives forget the high degree of conflict and disorder that were tolerated. Both sides tend to ignore the implicit threat of violence (natural or supernatural) which often lay behind the submission to community or informal justice.[10] And despite the evidence from revisionist historiography,[11] about the unequal, arbitrary and random nature of eighteenth-century policing and punishment, there is still a tendency to look for a 'Golden Age' of pre-capitalist 'community control'.

But even the authentic features of the vision – and one must grant that the ideal typical community did exist – simply cannot be recreated mimetically in another society, reproduced intact like the lifelike exhibits in a historical or folk museum. It is almost too obvious to point out that the overall societal conditions which made community control possible – pre-capitalist markets, fixed hierarchies, the pervasiveness of ritual and traditions – do not exist in industrial society.

If the past is viewed through a romantic lens, the present is no less so. Radicals and conservatives alike, at the same time as mourning the end of community, have disseminated a bizarre and disingenuous notion of what contemporary urban communities were like. To make the ideology persuasive, a patently false picture of ordinary 'community' life outside the walls of the institution is painted. Society is seen as potentially a series of little organic villages, in which ideas of integration, mutual help and good-neighbourliness are dormant but waiting to be revived: 'recognizable, flourishing and self conscious communities' to which clients and inmates have 'enduring and reconstitutable ties'.[12]

Some clients, of course, are only too well integrated into their communities – subcultures which supported and justified their deviance before they were sent to institutions and will continue to do so on their return. But, for most, there is simply no community to which to return. As Beck reminds us: 'the very fact that they have fallen among state officials is eloquent testimony to the lack of social, political and economic resources that support the kind of household and community life that protects the individual from the hard edge of the state.'[13] To recreate such resources, a lot more is needed than an invocation of the past and the establishment of a network of community agencies.

Most attempts to recreate community in fact constitute evidence of the end of community. The central impurity at the heart of the community-control ideology lies in the role of the state. For the essence of community, when it appeared as an ideal in classical political philosophy, was of something apart from the state. The eighteenth- and nineteenth-century defenders of the community ideal saw well enough how the modern industrial state was antithetical to community life. The quest for true community would have to take place on a voluntary basis, it would be a retreat from the all-embracing state.[14]

But the most obvious and incontrovertible feature of current correctional policies is that they are the creatures of the state: they are sponsored, financed, rationalized, staffed, and evaluated by state-employed personnel. It is unlikely, to say the least, that the very same interests and forces which destroyed the traditional community — bureaucracy, professionalization, centralization, rationalization — can now be used to reverse the process. There are, indeed, community workers, but they are usually people employed to tell other people that they do, after all, have a community.

The contrast between the new creations of community control and what traditional community control looked like, is close to Abrams' nice distinction between neighbourhood care as 'service delivery' and neighbourhood care as 'neighbourliness'.[15]. The one means the efficient delivery of bureaucratically administered welfare services to neighbourhoods, a more vigorous reaching out by the welfare state to those in need; the other means, as an alternative to the welfare state, the cultivation of effective informal caring activities within neighbourhoods *by* local residents themselves. These are two quite different, even incompatible conceptions and, as Abrams suggests, attempts to realize either one are likely to militate directly against the realization of the other. But in practice most projects find themselves trying both at once: using formal means (agencies, organization, professions) to promote informal relationships, neighbourliness and reciprocal care.

This is not simply a neat academic contradiction but a policy double-bind in which all the new projects find themselves. Like neighbourhood care as 'service delivery', community control must involve the addition of structures or even the demolition of existing natural-control systems. As much as all this is justified with the vocabulary of 'anti-institutional sentimentality' (community, home, house, work-shop, drop-in centre) and even 'anti-treatment' treatment methods (encounters, dialogues, meaningful interactions), nothing can disguise the fact that such projects have very little to do with the evocative model of community to which they continue to appeal. They are created by the state and every stage of the client's contact with them — entry, performance, departure — is heavily controlled and monitored by state professionals or (increasingly) by private entrepreneurs financed by the state. Under these conditions, the communities to which the decarcerated inmate is decanted, are hardly organic, free or autonomous.

Many handicapped, mentally ill, helpless or deprived groups have, indeed, been successfully decarcerated. For them, dispersal into the nooks and crannies of the 'community' did result in a degree of non-intervention — the state began to leave them alone. But for the criminal and the delinquent, as chapter 2 has shown, the story has been one of further and finer-graded intervention. In other words, the destructuring and abolitionist elements in the community ideology are largely illusory. The illusion derives, as I will soon show, from the obvious paradox of the state appearing to sponsor a move to disestablish itself. The rhetoric of destructuring is, in fact, used to justify the creation of new structures — a movement from the established closed institutional domains to new territories in the open parts of society.

This implies not simply constructing new formal domains (such as diversion agencies) but colonizing the master institutions. And none of this is new, surprising or particularly subtle. It is difficult to think of the historical evolution of social control in terms other than a decline in private space and an increase in public regulation. It is not that institutions like the family, education and the community have lost their social control functions — the metaphor of 'emptying' — but that the state is filling or entering into their traditional space. I will return in the next section to such metaphors as emptying, filling, invading, besieging and entering.

The reason why destructuring must lead to restructuring can be understood in a number of ways. The negative thrust of the anti-institution movement is impossible to sustain because it ignores the problem of *why* these people were labelled as deviant in the first place and hence candidates for social control. As Beck eloquently reminds us, these are populations already certified inadmissible to the world of work for one or other reasons (unwillingness, incompetence, disability, moral blemish, etc.). They are marginal, residual, embarrassing groups, and the development of alternative control strategies neither eliminates these populations nor the processes whereby they were initially identified and classified.[16]

Sensitive as it appears to be to the social rather than individualistic notions of deviance causation, the community ideology picks out only one element of the social. This is the idea that the main cause of deviance lies 'in' the community, especially in the form of weak or defective social control exercised by the family, school, religion, neighbourhood and other such institutions. The state, therefore, has to compensate by creating new external controls.[17] The founders of the nineteenth-century asylum had similarly and correctly diagnosed the causes of deviance in community breakdown but had incorrectly located the solution in a simulated, artificial setting. The compensatory controls which the state now has to create might be physically located in the community, but they remain external and compensatory in the sense that they could hardly emerge organically from the very institutions which had caused the problem in the first place.

'But so what?' the community ideologue might ask, 'Even if the vision is romantic or unrealistic, even if the reality must turn out so different from the rhetoric, surely the very novelty of the programmes and their physical location in the community, allows constructive intervention in a range of social settings right out of the institution's reach? Isn't this broader social intervention just what sociological theories of deviance always called for?'

This is a persuasive line of defence, and I will return in chapter 7 to the supposed benefits of community control. But this defence applies only to an insignificant part of the new endeavours. The combination of welfare cut-backs and the illusory qualities attributed to 'community' has meant that the ill, the inadequate and the defective, receive little in the way of constructive social intervention. Shunted between public welfare roles and the private sector, they find themselves in communities unable to tolerate or look after them. For criminals and delinquents, there is indeed intervention, but the new agencies can hardly be said to be responding to the wider social contexts (class, race, power, inequality) in which crime and delinquency are located. As I will show (later in this chapter), the rejection of individual pathology which is supposedly at the heart of the community ideology, is almost wholly spurious. While the notion of 'internal' individual pathology appears to have been discredited, the offender is still someone with a defect to be corrected — not his psyche, but his ties to the external social world, his social and vocational skills, his role competence, his presentation of self.

Under the ideology of 'reintegration', the offender has to be taught some lessons in reality: he has to cope and find a legitimate role in the community. And this is supposed to be done using 'modalities' which look suspiciously like the old one-to-one treatment relationships which have dominated the system since its inception. It is still the offender who has to change, not the community. Community control emerges as another round in the game of blaming the victim. Ryan's original expose of the ideology which justifies inequality and injustice by finding defects in the victims of inequality and injustice, still applies.[18] The new control agencies are less interested than the old in rooting out original causes — faulty psychic plumbing or subcultural status frustration — but in other ways they are the same. The community is deemed to be vaguely responsible but intervention skills are directed at the individual, resulting in what Ryan calls the 'terrifying sameness in the programmes that come from this sort of analysis'.

There is, though, one ironic difference. Certain older victim-blaming strategies actually allowed for genuine forms of social intervention in the form of compensatory education, neighbourhood-renewal projects, attacks on racial discrimination, improving health care and creating job opportunities. Whatever their problems or results, these programmes had the central virtue of connecting with the real master institutions of society. The new community professionals think of prevention in a quite different way. The stress is either on disembodied 'situations', 'behaviour sequences' or 'environments', or else remains individualistic. There is now *less* room for genuine reform and social intervention — who needs this if the offender is, after all, more or less ambulatory and back in the community? Away from the prying eyes and narrow minds of the old custodians, the offender's values, behaviour, cognitive skills or cultural defects can now really be corrected.

Of all the modes of community control, only 'community service' (restitution, reconciliation, reparation, compensation) evokes most directly the vision of community. These schemes have been heavily criticized as forms of net-widening, cheap labour, new sanctions in the sentencing tariff, and as a version of the same ideology of work and discipline developed in the prison, but they do come close to the original vision of involvement and integration. This is particularly so when punishment takes the form of direct victim compensation — vandals repairing the windows they have broken.

There is another quite different sense, however, in which the move from individual to 'community' is happening. All the forms of community control I have discussed here are punitive or treatment efforts directed at individual (usually 'soft-end') deviants after they have offended. For many more visionary ideologues and observers, however, the day is ending for all forms of individual intervention. The real master shift about to take place is towards the control of whole groups, populations and environments — not community control, but the control of communities. In this movement technology and resources, particularly at the hard end, are to be directed to surveillance, prevention and control, not 'tracking' the individual adjudicated offender, but preventive surveillance (through closed-circuit television, for example) of people and spaces.

To the extent that this sort of shift is already taking place, it also draws, as I show in chapter 6, on the community ideology. But it is at the soft end that the vision is most influential. And here, the strength of the community ideology is the strength of all ideology: its persuasive ability to keep us believing that we are doing one thing while we might really be doing something else. But this strength (and the whole destructuring impulse in which it is embedded) cannot — as de Sousa Santos reminds us — be dismissed as 'sheer manipulation and state conspiracy'.[19] Ideas such as informalism and community justice evoke powerful symbols of participation, self-government and real community. There are 'utopian transcendental', even 'potentially liberating' elements here, even if they are imprisoned and distorted in the overall state structure of social control. The quest for community is no less real than its results.

## THE IDEAL OF THE MINIMUM STATE

The segregative mode of control, signalled by the 'Great Incarcerations' of the early nineteenth century, was the object of reform and criticism from its very inception. In a sense, there have always been 'alternatives' — conceptual and actual — to the prison and asylum. But the master correctional change in which the victory of the asylum was embedded — the development of a centralized state monopoly for the control of crime and delinquency — has only recently appeared to be questioned explicitly. In the last few decades and in response to the same ideological currents which inform current talk about community, a new story has been told which blames the failure of crime control on an over-zealous extension of state power. The post-welfare, liberal democratic state, we are told, has over-reached itself. It must pull back or withdraw from selected areas of deviancy control. The ultimate and most fantastic destructuring idea of all has appeared: the state itself must loosen its grip.

This is the resonant appeal of such movements as decriminalization, diversion and delegalization. There should be changes in the substance of state control (selected areas such as crimes without victims should be patrolled less or even not at all) as well as formal changes: diversion or deflection to new agencies outside the state system. As with the overlapping quest for community, 'minimal statism' is an appeal which united an extraordinary collection of ideological bedfellows. It is worth listing each separately.

*Pragmatists*   Parallel to the 'nothing works' critique of prison and rehabilitation, the whole centralized apparatus is attacked on pragmatic grounds. The system is inefficient and full of unnecessary delays: bureaucracy is its worst; clogged up with minor cases; incapable of using discretion in any rational way. Justice and the very legitimacy of government itself is being discredited by this irrationality. The answer lies in a pragmatic bifurcation: the soft cases which are jamming the system should be filtered away into forms of control somehow 'outside' the machine. Resources could then be rationally concentrated on the real business of crime control.

*Disillusioned liberals*   The historical model of the 'distrust of benevolence' both draws upon and amplifies a particular contemporary ideology about the desirable limits of state intervention. We must be wary of good intentions; organized benevolence might do more harm than good; the zeal of liberal reformers and moral entrepreneurs of all sorts must be curbed. This was the explicit moral lesson which Rothman invited us to draw from his history of the asylum and which he and his fellow sceptics of 'doing good' warn us about today.[20] 'How is it', we must continue to ask, 'that good people − decent, upright and well meaning citizens − can contrive when they act on behalf of others and in the name of some higher principle or of some benign interest, to behave so harshly, coercively and callously, so at odds with what they understand to be their good intentions?'[21]

But these are not just any 'citizens': the particular target of criticism is benevolent *state* intervention — the notion of the state as parent. It was state paternalism which legitimated the juvenile court, parole, the indeterminate sentence and the whole package of progressive penology. It was state paternalism which allowed the rhetoric of *needs* to obliterate basic civil and human rights, and the return to rights was the rallying call of civil libertarians and deviant groups of the sixties: 'the commitment to paternalistic state intervention in the name of equality is giving way to a commitment to restrict intervention in the name of liberty. If our predecessors were determined to test the maximum limits for the exercise of state power in order to correct imbalances, we are about to test the minimum limits for the exercise of state power in order to enhance autonomy.'[22]

It was this identical strain of thinking (and this identical group of thinkers) that moved from the dual attack on the closed institution and the treatment ideal to the advocacy of the justice model of punishment. The Committee which drew up the 'doing justice' programme was motivated not by hope but despair at having to renounce the impulse to benevolence. But their new, restricted vision might at least 'do less mischief and perpetuate less inequity than the system with which we now live. But if we can deflate the rhetoric and limit the reach of programs that now pretend to do good, then our time and energy has been well spent.'[23]

*Neo-conservatives* With the appeal to do less harm rather than more good — deflating, limiting, restricting the reach of state paternalism — this powerful strain in contemporary liberalism increasingly begins to resemble the conservatism to which it was originally opposed. The problem with most liberal critiques of liberalism is that they sound conservative.

From the Second World War onwards, most capitalist societies took for granted a Keynesian state interventionism in the economy. The socialization of production was associated with a belief in reformism, amelioration and benevolent state intervention which even most conservatives shared. Over the 1970s, though, this tendency came under severe attack by a loose consensus labelled 'neo-conservatism' or the 'new right'. We have already seen how political-economy theorists have dissected the recent appeal of this ideology in Britain and the USA: populist support for law-and-order policies and for a monetarist-inspired retrenchment of the welfare state. Faced with the 'same' sources of disenchantment upon which liberals drew, the old conservatives could say 'we told you so'. The new conservatives could draw their strength from the fragmenting of the treatment ideal, and the apparent failure of social-reform programmes. Liberal crime-control solutions were attacked as tried, found wanting and hopelessly optimistic. The message here is again 'realistic' and again in favour of a selective state retreat: concentrate on the hard cases and let the soft take care of themselves.

*Anti-professionals*    Outside the arena of crime-control policy, one of the most popular of the destructuring ideologies of the sixties was a questioning of professional monopolies and claims to expertise. This was the era of demystification and debunking: slogans such as 'deschooling', 'demedicalization' and 'anti-psychiatry' moved from the counter-culture and the universities into the very state professionals being attacked. In place of state licensed and controlled monopolies there would be 'anti', 'counter' or 'alternative' services; self-help groups of deviants would heal and nurture each other; switchboards, networks and crisis centres would take the place of the old state bureaucracies.

Professionals were not just emperors without clothes but had been doing damage by their pretentions to omniscience and benevolence. Groups like social workers had their moral licence to be doing good severely questioned: they were now just agents of social control, disguised storm-troopers of the state.

*Sentimental anarchists*    The same sentimental anarchism invoked against the closed institution was extended more generally to other forms of state interventionism. A popularization (and usually distortion) of such philosophical writings as those of Rawls and Nozick found its way into both left- and right-wing versions of libertarianism. On issues such as state deregulation of all forms of drug use and on the rights of mental patients, a joyous coalition was forged between counter-cultural freaks, left radicals and extreme individual-rights conservatives like Szasz. All were agreed: the monster was the state and its ever increasing inroads into individual 'freedom'.

Both this simple-minded libertarianism and the more complicated stream of disenchanted liberalism, drew theoretical dignity from labelling theory. If deviance was sustained and shaped by the forces of social control, then the solution was radical non-intervention: a curtailment of well intentioned but eventually malignant labelling by state busy-bodies.

*Deeper Structures*

Given the diversity of these inputs, it could hardly be otherwise that all sorts of impurities, contradictions and anomalies appear in the ideology of minimal statism. Indeed, even if we stayed at the level of all these words, we should not be at all surprised to find that current correctional change is occurring in precisely the opposite direction to the story. We are seeing an increase rather than a decrease in the level and degree of state intervention, and in professional and bureaucratic power. I will explore three tensions within minimum-state ideology which go some way towards explaining these apparently paradoxical results.

*The welfare state*    First, there is the complicated nature of the terrain which neo-conservatives and disenchanted liberals seem to share. On one level, there is genuine common ground: the move over the twentieth century against enlightenment faith in reason and progress. Utopias become displaced by dystopias – a sense that industrialism is played out, that the machine will devour us, that we must conserve and retract rather than expand. Chapter 6 looks at these visions of the future.

There is little doubt that contemporary liberalism is responding to this wider ideological mood. Way beyond questions of welfare and control policy, there is a note of severe revisionism, self-doubt and retrenchment about the basic premises of the liberal tradition. Shifting perspectives on crime and punishment can be seen just as illustrations of the shattering of the post-war American liberal consensus that programmes for a better society could be devised.[24] The vigorous and self-confident strain in liberalism which dismissed conservative and pessimistic formulations as backward or stupid, has given way to an altogether more uncertain and pessimistic mood about crime and punishment, and about changing people or the world.

This pessimism, however, results not simply from a disappointment with the results of benevolence ('we blew it') but a contradiction between believing in liberal ideas and living in a capitalist society which cannot achieve them. Older interventionist ideals – treatment, reform, rehabilitation, individualized justice – make much less sense in a deteriorating economy. What is the point of vocational rehabilitation when employment itself is the issue? In this context it makes sense to retrench, to adopt the slogan 'less harm rather than more good', to call for, at least, a protection of human rights against the hard edge of the state.

This is not to say that the reasons which liberal control theorists themselves give for this change in mood are not deeply believed in. They are, and their talk shows a genuine and healthy distrust of authority and state power, a refusal to take good intentions at their face value, a dislike of disguised discretion under the name of treatment, a sense that no community of interests exists and that the best way to recognize conflict is to formalize legal rights, liberties and obligations. The problem, though, with these complementary themes of minimum intervention and civil rights, is that only in areas such as mental illness will the state allow them to be applied. Here, the destructuring ideology was stronger and had immediate results, in the attacks on the asylum and on the medical model.[25]

But as a general political ideology, minimal statism is a somewhat more superficial commitment than it appears. There are some notable exceptions — Szasz's extreme *laissez-faire* approach to problems of mental illness and drug abuse — but few neo-liberals or even neo-conservatives advocate a total retreat to non-interventionist social policy. Neo-conservatism is something more complicated than a reactionary impulse to escape back into the past, out of some sense of crisis, apocalypse, imminent or actual loss.[26] True, in the voices of Bell, Glazer, Kristol, Moynihan et al. (and their less intelligent and articulate counterparts in Britain) one does detect a sense of crisis, the collapse of authority, the disintegration of community ties, the erosion of traditional values. But, unlike traditional conservatives, they remain committed to many of the political and economic arrangements which cause the transformation they so bewail.

And in the area of crime control, far from being non-interventionist, neo-conservatives have in fact filled the policy vacuum created by liberalism's self-mortification, its obsession with civil rights and its hopeless timidity about using state power to 'correct imbalances'. As Waltzer suggests, the neo-conservative answer to the problem of fostering moral habits and communal ties that could check an unbridled individualism and hedonism, is to shore up the 'non-political' attachments of society: church, family, school, welfare, neighbourhood. By another route we return to the state having to compensate for weak social control. Whether this takes the form of heightening the visibility of the hard edge of the system (law and order) and/or decreasing the visibility of the soft edge, the end result can only be increased intervention. We need only pause for a minute to see that while in areas like mental illness, the private sector might genuinely displace the state, this would be an impossible outcome in crime control. For the state to give up here would be to undercut its very claim to legitimacy.

Although they exaggerate the garrison state mentality of the 'new realists of crime control', Platt and Takagi are surely correct in noting that behind the 'veneer of negativism' with which the state is criticized, there is a deep appreciation and promotion of the interventionist capitalist state.[27]

In other words — and these words are too clear to require much decoding — the anti-state critique was less directed at the state itself than at certain of its soft, progressive, paternalistic or liberal parts. All Western industrial societies over the last fifty years have shown a steady growth in the size and relative significance of public and social expenditure as a percentage of the Gross Domestic Product. Whether this is seen as a 'genuine commitment to welfare' or a 'socialization of capital', it nonetheless happened. The economic crises of the early seventies resulted less in an overall cut in social expenditure (there has for example been a continued increase in public-sector workers) than a redistribution from the soft to the hard edge of the system. Justice became more important than welfare.

All this can be seen most transparently in Britain, which has such an obviously different history from the USA of welfare state commitment. Minimum statism appears most starkly in the economic sphere: the selling-off of public industry. But otherwise the true meaning of the minimum state is the minimum *welfare* state. As Taylor shows, the ideological offensive is not on the state, but on the post-war Labour/social democratic consensus.[28] When 'nothing worked' and crime and delinquency actually increased in amount and visibility, it was professional liberals and do-gooders who were blamed. The left and the liberals could only respond with a vague prescription for more of the same and the defeatist theory that crime, after all, is an inevitable property of all industrial societies. Basic social arrangements could not be changed. A policy void once again, and in this void, as Taylor correctly notes, those on the right become the 'social reconstructionists', taking the interventionist offensive that had previously been the ground of social democracy. It does this by hardening its hard edge, while allowing the new professionals to look after and expand into the soft end.

Far from 'pulling back', the socialist alternative to conservatism is seen — correctly — as a reinforcement of liberal state interventionism. Here is Waltzer's American 'democratic socialist' alternative:

> politics can be opened up, rates of participation significantly increased,
> decision-making really shared, without a full scale attack on private life
> and liberal values, without a religious revival or a cultural revolution.
> What is necessary is an expansion of the public sphere. I don't mean by
> that the growing of state power — which will come anyway, for a strong
> state is the necessary and natural antidote to liberal disintegration —
> but a new politicising of the state, a devolution of state power into the
> hands of ordinary citizens.[29]

This is an appealing ideal of community — though its vision of a strong state which simultaneously allows power to devolve to ordinary citizens, raises some familiar problems.

*Public and private domains*   It is the contrast between the public and private sphere, though, which leads to the second of my contradictions in minimum statism. What does it mean to call for the modern state to reduce its 'public' reach and interfere less in the private?

In the classic political philosophies of Western democracies, the public/private distinction appears to be clear. The state is seen as creating and managing the public sphere and the emergence of the idea of civil society strongly depends on the separation of politics from private and social life.[30] In its classic nineteenth-century form, the liberal democratic state was liberal in the sense of being limited: a public device to protect and foster individual liberty based on private property. The notion of a self-regulating market which state power merely protects, is a model for the limited role of the state elsewhere. The private sphere is also to be protected: the family, and even the school are merely intermediary agencies, 'buffers' between the public and the private.

This vision, with its dual insistence on the limitations of state power and the separation between public and private, is invariably contrasted with totalitarianism or fascism. Here, the ideological function of the state is precisely to unify public and private. The nightmare of fascism, and of all science-fiction dystopias, is the total fusion of the public and private — the child informing on his parents. 'A *functioning* police state,' Dr. Benway reminds us, 'needs no police.'[31] This is the world of *Nineteen Eighty-Four.*

Back to reality. Whether the modern bourgeois state ever achieved either strict limitation or radical separation of public and private is another matter. For at least this century, economic and social state intervention have gone well beyond any model of the self-regulating market. For even longer, the notion of a self-contained private realm has made little sense. In crime-control talk this erosion is quite clear. Classical criminology was sustained by a series of separations: act from actor, procedure from substance, the rule of law as a protection from the state. Once these broke down, the public and private began to overlap. Positivism merges act from actor: judgements about private life (family, personality, toilet training, even dreams), become part of the public sphere. Probation officers have little difficulty in reading out to an open court details of their client's innermost anxieties, sexual fantasies or feelings about 'authority'.

This was Foucault's meaning when he talked about the emergence in the nineteenth century of the disciplinary society: the increasing surveillance and regulation over the most minute areas of social life. As Donzelot suggests, the control system actually creates its own hybrid domain of the 'social': a separate realm which is neither public nor private.[32] Under the impact of the juvenile court, social workers and psychiatrists, the family in particular is 'encircled', 'suffocated' or 'invaded'. And all along, these forms of intervention – philanthropic, professional, humanistic, psychiatric – increase in intensity without looking as if they are violating the tenets of the liberal 'public' state. Starting from the end of the nineteenth century, a whole 'tutelary complex' emerges, dominated by the social-work ideology but based on a series of graduated interventions which refer back to the hard centre of the state: the criminal law. Donzelot's vivid image is of a nest of Russian dolls in which the initial model is the judicial one and the others – social work, educational, therapeutic – are only enveloping copies.[33]

With a somewhat different imagery and theory, and interested much less in the judicial centre, this is what Lasch describes as the family 'besieged'.[34] Instead of being a refuge from the harshness and impersonal competition of the outside world ('haven in a heartless world') the family is now being besieged by the very same market forces which made it necessary as a refuge. Experts, counsellors, therapists of all sorts have weakened parental authority and subjected the family to a special sort of social management. Parents are still being 'proletarianized': freed from the repressive scrutiny of church and state, they are now taught that they cannot provide for their own or their children's needs without the advice and scrutiny of the trained expert.

The continual story, then, is of the erosion and, in a sense, politicization of private space. The very nature of the crime-control apparatus, with its classifications, bifurcations, layers, Russian dolls or whatever, depends on this type of penetration. All the moves I described in chapter 2 — boundary blurring, the public/private confusion, the control of space, the ideology of integration — only make sense in terms of the overall erosion of the public/private distinction. This is not to say that the original critique of benevolent state intervention was not genuine. But it was curiously beside the point. There is no need for the state to act as parent and teacher if parent and teacher can be made to act like the state.

Such metaphors as 'penetration' and being 'besieged', do little justice to the ambiguities of the public/private distinction. As my discussion of boundary blurring and privatization suggested, we are not witnessing a straightforward takeover by the state of previously private space. 'Privatization', hints at a *diminished* direct role of the state: the commodification of certain deviant populations and their management by private entrepreneurs; the massive growth of the private security industry with large corporations now regulating areas of public life previously controlled by the state. The phenomenon of private security is particularly interesting because the ideological confusion between public and private is mirrored by an actual ecological blurring between these realms. As Shearing and Stenning note, the emergence of privacy and private property as guarantees of state intrusion into individual liberty, required some congruence between private property and private space.[35] With much private property now made public and given over to mass corporations, not only are there more intrusions on to individual space, but a degree of sovereignty switches from state to capital, which is an authority far less subject to regulation and scrutiny.

When combined with more general corporatist tendencies in post-liberal societies, these specific patterns on deviancy control — integration, penetration, privatization, boundary blurring and the like — make some of the traditional distinctions between public and private obsolete.

*Minimal crime control?*   Returning to the more prosaic territory of crime control, it should be clear that the *laissez faire* or minimalist rhetoric, with its quantitative metaphors of 'withdrawing' 'cutting back' or 'pulling out', makes little sense. The state involvement in the business of crime control as well as the symbolic political significance of crime can hardly allow anything like this to happen. The notion of 'cutting back' might well have been appealing in areas of health and welfare, but conservative crime-control strategy was explicitly aimed at extending and strengthening the reach of the law.

It is this political thrust which explains the 'co-option' of the back-to-justice model. There is little doubt that the original liberal version of this model originated in the ideology of minimum statism. The neo-liberal attack on rehabilitation, the therapeutic state and doing good, emerged from a particular reading of the troubled politics of the America of the Sixties. The lesson was not that the social order needed fortification, but that the state and its agents could not be trusted to do good, that discretionary authority was inevitably arbitrary and government, repressive. The solution was the justice model: not benevolence (which had 'failed') but at least fairness, decency and protection from the arbitrary authority of the state.

But, as liberal critics of neo-liberalism now ruefully note, the just-deserts model merely re-entered into the political arena of the state — an arena now dominated by conservative law-and-order politics. The irony was obvious: those who mistrusted the state to administer rehabilitation in a just and humane manner, were now placing total faith in the state to punish justly and humanely.[36]

I will return in chapter 7 to the troublesome questions of justice and humanity, but this analysis is clearly correct in showing that whatever else was achieved by the justice model (the move for example to fixed sentencing), this has not cut down the power of the state. Quite the reverse: 'a system is created where the whims of the administrators are exchanged for an enormously powerful, simple and centralized system of state control.'[37] Neo-classicism needs a strong centralized state more than does positivism.

To these ideological twists must be added the question of professional interests. The very same state workers who run the control business — professionals, experts, bureaucrats, managers — were now supposed to be rallying around the libertarian, non-interventionist and 'hands-off' flags. The likelihood, as we will see in chapter 5, that such groups would support policies which resulted in anything other than more work, prestige and power for people just like themselves, was not very high.

Whether or not this was 'ironical', it was certainly odd that the adherents of reforms to curtail state power also believed that these reforms would be implemented with the assistance of the state: 'In other words, the targets of change (criminal justice agencies) were expected to use monetary rewards to reduce their nets. Since this reform strategy functioned to increase the resources available to the crime control apparatus, most of the funds went to buttress law enforcement operations and expand their capacity to process offenders.'[38]

All these ironies in minimal statism apply also to the more pragmatic criticisms of the system, not the grand destructuring vision but the attempt to merely ease the system's burden or overload. The image is one of dismantling the soft bits which have somehow attached themselves like leeches to the core. If one could only dislodge these soft bits (status offences, crimes without victims, minor disputes and conflicts), then the apparatus could concentrate on the real hard stuff of dangerous crime. This dislodging is the main guiding principle of movements towards diversion, delegalization, extra judicial dispute processing and so on.

Unlike the other elements in the ideology, this notion is not only logically consistent, but corresponds to what is actually happening in most Western crime-control systems. It is a restatement of the dominant bifurcation principle: the soft offenders are to be eased out of the system and the hard core are to be the target for the full (and now concentrated) weight of the state.

But in terms of the overall minimal state ideology, this model has a fundamental flaw: the dislodged soft bits are hardly being left to move in a free floating voluntaristic realm, far away from the scrutiny of the state. The new agencies responsible for the dislodged residues are dependent on the selection procedures, discretion, financing and back-up authority of the core parts of the system. And, as we have seen, the populations of the new agencies are not simply the cast-offs from the old system, but new groups who might otherwise never have found themselves in contact with the official system at all. The form taken by bifurcation, then, is not all in line with minimum state ideology: in the context of overall state expansion, the hard side gets harder (neo-classicism, strict punishment, target-hardening, technology), while the soft side (still under direct or indirect state control) takes up some of its human and ideological slack (progressive ideas such as reintegration), and also keeps expanding.

This flaw in the dislodging imagery is shown clearly in the informal justice movement. Abel argues that many 'extra-judicial' innovations extend the reach of the state by formalizing the settlement of disputes and conflicts that might otherwise have been resolved on their own.[39] The relationship between formal and informal is not cyclical or complementary (one contracts while the other expands) but additive: by 'dislodging', the formal institutions increase their capacity. And informal institutions maintain a steady case load by undermining genuine extra-state modes of informal control. The state remains the only legitimate form of authority and grows, rather than contracts, by 'delegation and devolution'.

What often happens here is that the extra-judicial ideology gets mixed up with the 'access to justice' ideology. Both visualize a 'centripetal movement' of cases to courts: the overflow image implies trying to relieve the system of its load, the access image implies allowing more cases to reach the court.[40] But most disputes (like most 'diverted' criminal acts) are 'resolved' (whether by resignation, self-help, withdrawal or whatever) through various forms of 'indigenous' ordering or law: in the home, work-place, neighbourhood, school, hospital, professional association or other institutional setting. The courts provide what Galanter calls the 'legal shadow' in which all these other activities take place. Thus judicial action is centrifugal: it moves outwards, sending its messages and effects (deterrence, threats, promises, legitimacy) into the wider world of disputing and regulating, rather than simply receiving a centripetal flow of cases.

The overall paradox of minimal statism (and all destructuring ideologies) is that they call for, and invariably result in, something being done. And this something, to borrow Galanter's imagery, must increase *both* the centripetal and centrifugal movements of the system. The ideal of the minimal state reveals only the extent of the maximum state; destructuring reveals the original structures. As a political slogan, minimum statism is either phoney or, when it is real, is vulnerable because it does not offer any *positive* solution, least of all to 'crime on the streets'. It is, thus, easily co-opted by interests which fill the policy vacuum it leaves.

## THE RETURN TO BEHAVIOURISM

By the end of the eighteenth century, the move from body to mind was well under way. The 'social' had been constituted as a special domain in which people could be scrutinized, supervised and changed. This transformation incorporated and facilitated the victory of positivism. As the mind rather than the body became the object of penal repression, so the actor rather than the act became the object of criminological attention. Those developments, seen as specific products of the twentieth century – rehabilitation, the treatment ideal, the 'therapeutic state', the medical model, the whole baggage of progressive penology — are all fully continuous and consistent with that original transformation. From the files of the early asylum managers to the case histories and diagnostic tests of the contemporary therapeutic professionals, runs an unbroken thread of knowledge and power.

In the 1960s, though, the same destructuring impulse which we have been monitoring, with its same strange coalition of political interests, looked to be questioning this inexorable move to the mind. Overlapping with the critique of the institution, and drawing upon a common stock of facts and values, the whole ideal of rehabilitation and treatment came under assault:

- pragmatists could point to evaluation studies of treatment which showed that 'nothing works';
- cost-benefit analysis could easily demonstrate that treatment was expensive;
- disenchanted liberals could mourn yet another set of mischievous results from trying to do good;
- liberals, radicals and civil libertarians could draw on the powerful emerging critique of the therapeutic state to show the dangers of unbridled discretion, disguised coercion and how social problems get blamed on the individual;
- conservatives could say what they have always said about do-gooders, and also point gleefully to the 'nothing works' literature.

By the seventies, everyone seemed agreed that the 'treatment model of corrections' was dead and buried. In its place were coming restricted horizons and less ambitious goals, a return to justice, neo-classicism or (in more conservative terms) deterrence, incapacitation, law and order and a new version of social defence. Of course, treatment personnel fought back, tried to retain parts of their empire or colonize new territories, even claimed that their methods were, after all, effective and that they only needed better resources to get on with the job. But everyone sensed that an era was over. The last few decades, though, have been a bit more complicated than this. Unlike the tales of community and minimum state where words so often are diametrically opposed to reality, here we find a number of opposing tendencies working at the same time.

### Deeper Structures

To understand these opposing tendencies, let us start not with pragmatism, but with the ideological attack on the therapeutic model of social control. Gathering momentum from the end of the Second World War, intellectual commentary from every conceivable political direction — liberal, humanist, radical, socialist or conservative — began to suspect the increasing power of psychiatry. There were two dangers — the substitution of medical for moral judgements (the 'therapeutic state' critique) and the prospects of total thought control.[41]

The nightmare was a new psychological technology with which the benevolent (or not so benevolent) eye of the state would be able to know and control all. *Brave New World, Nineteen Eighty-Four* and *Clockwork Orange* provided an immediate fictional iconography and the elements in this futuristic scenario could be found in every intellectual supermarket over the last few decades: electronic surveillance, data banks, informers and agents, brainwashing techniques, behaviour modification, drug control and psychosurgery. We have been taught to fear that our innermost private thoughts will soon be open to scrutiny and will be made to conform to the political dictates of the state. To the prophets of doom this has already happened: society is drugged into conformity, its members subject to endless psychological manipulation to prevent them from doing what 'the authorities' decide is bad or unhealthy.

It was, of course, Orwell's vision that captured all these elements. 'Big Brother' watches you through the telescreen which receives and transmits; there is no way of knowing when you are being watched. the 'thought police' are in total control. Not only can they penetrate beyond behaviour to thought, but 'thought crime' is 'the essential crime that contained all others in itself'. The state is well on the way to mastering the secret of finding out what another human being is thinking. The great aim of the Party is to extinguish the possibility of independent thought, to achieve not just external compliance but uniformity of inner thought. There is that famous chilling moment in Winston's interrogation when he is informed that a simple punishment is not the point. Neither passive obedience, nor even abject submission is enough — he must be made to think in a particular way. As O'Brien tells him: 'we are not interested in those stupid crimes that you have committed. The Party is not interested in the overt act: the thought is all we care about.'[42]

Whether, in the real 1984, Big Brother is watching us or not, is another matter. What is clear, though, is that many intellectuals have absorbed this vision in a highly simplistic and selective way.

From their own contact (or fantasies about contact) with the political edge of the machine, they have generalized 'social control' into a one-eyed monster which cannot distinguish between act and thought, and which has no sense of the political. In their warnings about the arrival of the new right, Marxist criminologists routinely quote analysis of 'friendly fascism' or the 'Americanization of *Nineteen Eighty-Four*' which dwell almost entirely on the political edge of the machine.[43] The argument is either that the same 'face of power' turned to political dissent is now turned to street crime or (with a somewhat inflated sense of self-importance), that the new strategies of coercion are only *superficially* aimed at street crime, but are really a warning to political dissidents.

To be sure, we are talking about the same machine; to be sure, there are common techniques and, to be sure, the definition of the political is a shifting one. But this critique greatly exaggerates the political identity of crime and delinquency. Telephone tapping, *agents provocateurs*, censorship of political writing, interference with academic freedom are not, after all, part of the everyday experience and concerns of the vast bulk of the population of Western democracies. Nor do they form much part of bread-and-butter crime control. The daily business of the social-control machine does not consist of processing thoughts rather than overt acts. It is, indeed, 'stupid crimes' that matter and those who commit them, and always have, are not treated as traitors or thought-criminals.

With characteristic prescience — but in a forgotten part of his vision — Orwell saw this quite clearly. To control the proles — the 85 per cent of the population outside the Party and the Inner Party — the state in *Nineteen Eighty-Four* did not really need thought police or telescreens. The proles could be segregated within ghettoes, 'the whole world-within-a-world of thieves, bandits, prostitutes, drug peddlars and racketeers of every description', subjected like animals by a few simple rules. They had no political significance at all and left to themselves they could continue 'working, breeding and dying'. Their thoughts did not matter. Their belief in Party ideology was unimportant.[44]

The bifurcations in Western crime-control systems are perhaps not too far away from all this: deviant thoughts of the party members being monitored and changed, deviant behaviour of the proles being punished or contained. But leaving aside the subject of political thoughts, what I want to argue is that, *within* the 'ordinary' crime-control system, a similar but finer bifurcation between thought and act is taking place. At the hard end of the system there has indeed been a partial withdrawal from the rehabilitative ideal. But this has taken the form of an attack on Freudian-derived 'inner states' models of treatment: a move from mind to body in which behaviourist models have become more influential, rather than treatment abandoned altogether. All this time at the soft end of the system, while behaviourism is making some inroads, the old treatment ideal is not only alive and well, but making incremental gains as the system itself expands.

These current variations of the dichotomies between mind and body, thought and behaviour, actor and act, Freudianism and behaviourism, positivism and classicism are, of course, hardly novel. Indeed they were prefigured exactly by the early nineteenth-century battle between different prison systems. The Philadelphia system, we remember, stressed change through internal spiritual insight and rebirth. The object of change was mind, thought, actor. In the twentieth century, this was the vision to be captured in the Freudian model of rehabilitation. The Auburn system (or Brockway's Elmira prison) stressed, on the other hand, change through external compliance. The object of change was body, behaviour, act — and the mode of change was the strict enforcement of rules. In the twentieth century, this became the Skinnerian model of behaviour control. Ideologies of control have always sustained these contradictory images and oscillated between them. At the hard core of the system, behaviourism became dominant and it is at the centre of the core, the prison itself, that we must look to understand this tendency.

It was in the prison that the rehabilitative ethic first came under attack. Here was concentrated the full force of the 'nothing works' rhetoric, the anti-treatment movement, liberal disenchantment and the 'back to justice' and prisoners' rights movements, with their emphasis on procedural safeguards and their critique of untrammelled therapeutic discretion. Of course, the ideology of decarceration encouraged the belief that prisons would soon be cleared of all but the hardest cases, for whom warehousing was the only answer. But just when everyone else seemed to be abandoning the goal of rehabilitation as unobtainable or even harmful, so behaviour modification reappeared on the scene.

'Reappeared' because, as Rothman rightly argues, the history of total institutions has been inextricably linked with the notion of behaviour modification.[45] Now, when the old treatment personnel deserted the prison for the more fertile fields of the community, the behaviour modifiers were only too willing to take over. Far from being 'anti-treatment' in any sense whatsoever, they were, as Rothman notes, 'the most aggressive and optimistic of the lot'. Rehabilitation was to be given another turn — not change through internal insight this time but change through external compliance. Never mind that this was still treatment and never mind that this offered even weaker safeguards to civil liberties than psychodynamic methods. The move made both managerial and ideological sense. Compared with psychoanalytically derived models, behaviour modification is simply the better technology and is uniquely suited to settings like the prison. You can observe behaviour in a way that you cannot observe insights; you do not have to rely on verbal skills or indeed any talking at all and, above all, methods such as aversive therapy and operant conditioning regimes allow you to continue doing what you have always done.

Those who believe that the burial of treatment was premature and that 'effective correctional treatment' is, indeed, attainable have openly acknowledged the reasons why behaviour modification so rapidly and dramatically became the fashionable form of treatment from the later sixties through the seventies.[46] As Ross and McKay note, operant conditioning was adopted so eagerly because it was 'new', but also because it was a fancy, socially acceptable, professionalized version of what generations of wardens had been doing for decades. Overnight the much-abused custodians could become treaters, experts and scientists. The new theorists were so different from the old ones: they talked a simple everyday language; they worked with easily observable and measurable variables; and they suggested things which could easily be done, indeed always *had* been done. No need for esoteric ideas about repression, sublimation, guilt or whatever; no need to turn the prison into a hospital, no need to transfer authority to 'shrinks'. Instead, 'a psychologist who actually behaved more like an administrator than an administrator.'[47]

There was also no reason to view the inmate as a poor, sick person who needed love, care, warmth or understanding. Though no harsh regime or punishment for its own sake: it was to be a scientifically managed programme of behavioural change. Even the old hard core — the poorly motivated, behaviour-disordered and inarticulate, abandoned by the psychodynamic therapists as 'untreatable' — could be accepted. And all this economically feasible, quick and administratively efficient (lots of standardized forms to check).

For Ross and his colleagues, determined to save behaviourism from this zealous co-option and to claim for it more modest goals than 'rehabilitation', many of these operant programmes are revealed as fakes, masquerades, mere euphemisms for tyranny. Anything — marches, meditation, diet — became scientific. (They cite this description of reduced diet as a punishment for inmates already punished by segregation: 'Behaviour Mod: Meat Loaf'). And the actual record of behaviourism in prison — token economies, programmed learning, contingency management or whatever — is altogether unimpressive in terms of conventional treatment criteria.

But whether all this resulted from an abuse of the theory and whether the behaviour model is a panacea which needs deflating in favour of more limited goals such as management and improving educational skills, is besides the point. For a while, at least, the paradigm was dominant and it left its traces throughout the correctional system. To be sure, these traces were uneven, and could be found more in talk (in journals and conferences) than in practice. Prison regimes are highly conservative: the original nineteenth-century disciplinary regimes persisted, unadorned by the jargon of behaviourism, while the few regimes modelled explicitly on operant- or aversive-conditioning models were closed down after public exposure.

Beyond the prison walls, in the new community control settings, behaviourism also began to leave its influential, if uneven, traces.[48] The pure rehabilitative model, after all, was always trying for something extraordinarily difficult: to change attitudes or even the whole person. The ideology which informs community agencies such as diversion centres, tracking projects, hostels or half-way houses is altogether more modest and limited. The offender is not asked to change, but to show an ability to maintain the overt demands of a conforming life. The stress is on retraining and providing skills; the delinquent is someone who has not learnt the rules of the social game. He can be presented with 'game situations' replicating life in miniature, eased into social life via institutions such as half-way houses (whose programme objectives are defined as 'no serious behavioural incidents') or, better still, closely observed as he experiments with real community living. There — like for John in Coventry (see page 74) — incidents can be staged to test his ability to conform or he can be 'reinforced' to behave in the proper way. Remember Joe in Illinois: all he had to do was get home on time, keep his room tidy and set the dinner table. All this is a long way from personality change and even further from 'insight'.

But if behaviour *modification* in the community is a relatively modest business, then behaviour *surveillance* is a much more ambitious prospect. The attraction of all those schemes for tracking, shadowing, and mediating is that they offer intensive methods of monitoring and supervising behaviour. If the clients of these programmes keep freer of police contacts or 'behavioural incidents' than their matched experimental groups, this is not too surprising. They are too busy being contracted or watched by their counsellors, Big Brothers, trackers, 'friends' or parents. And as long as they are watched carefully enough, who cares what might be going on inside their heads?

It was precisely the prospect of intensive surveillance in the community which many of the 'nothing works' brigade held out as the alternative for rehabilitation in prison, the ultimate dream being a one-to-one supervisor : offender ratio.[49] For the real futurists of crime control, even this was too limited and technologically naive. With electronic surveillance techniques, the prospect was the virtual abolition of imprisonment. From the early seventies onwards, the idea surfaced every now and then of 'humane alternatives' to prison: radio telemetry devices, externally worn or implanted on the subject to allow for 24-hour monitoring of behaviour.[50] Recent enthusiasts who have pointed out the advantages of this method compared with human 'field officers', have stressed the goal of incapacitation and have argued that such methods are neither permanent, stigmatizing, expensive nor cruel.[51] 'Orwellian' objections are easily dismissed (Lehtinen finds it 'incredible' that anyone would think that prisons are more acceptable) and the crucial advantage stressed — complete protection while the offender remains a productive tax-paying citizen. Community control indeed!

But despite their own assertions to the contrary, these programmes are closer to science fiction than immediate large-scale social policy.[52] Note, contrary to the popular version of *Nineteen Eighty-Four*, that none of these plans make any reference to *thought* control. What is being monitored is behaviour (or the physiological correlates of emotion and behaviour). No one is interested in inner thoughts. Even the most sacrosanct of the discourses of positivist criminology, the search for the criminal personality, has been touched by the new behaviourism. Most current versions of this search are part of a revival of interest in the behaviourist ideas of social defence and dangerousness.[53] Screening and surveillance depend on the identification of certain wrong behaviours which are then tied to particular people. And the treatment to be directed at this hard core has little to do with traditional rehabilitative change through insight. The whole point of the exercise is to identify those intractable offenders who are beyond change.

The 'renaissance' of the concept of dangerousness in contemporary penology depends on the decline of the rehabilitative ideal, together with the acceptance of a policy of hard—soft bifurcation.[54] While old treatment modalities based on mentalistic concepts are discredited, new behavioural experts are given more power to perform the crucial role of separating out the dangerous from the rest and then devising suitable technologies to contain their behaviour ('predictive restraint') or change it through 'last ditch' treatment modalities (drugs, electronic control, psychosurgery). All forms of clinical prediction, notoriously inefficient because of the 'false-positive' problem, are being abandoned in favour of actuarial prediction based on observable criteria — a clear move in the behaviourist direction.

Leaving aside all possibilities for the behaviourist-inspired treatment and surveillance of these *individual* offenders, the trend towards 'applied behaviour analysis' or 'behavioural criminal justice' has signalled a new way to evaluate correctional policy in general. Behaviour is the problem, not words, motives, attitudes or personality: 'the focus of the approach is not on what people report they do, but on how they actually behave and the conditions under which that occurs.'[55] The target for attack is 'behaviours' in daily living — the offence itself but also social, vocational and learning skills. The weapon is an applied technology, with procedures consistently replicable by other similarly trained personnel.

For some time, now, the few criminologists who have looked into the future have argued that 'the game is up' for all policies directed to the criminal as an individual, either in terms of detection (blaming and punishing) or causation (finding motivational or causal chains).[56] The technological paraphernalia previously directed at the individual, will now be invested in cybernetics, management, systems analysis, surveillance, information gathering and opportunity reduction. This might turn out to be the most radical form of behaviourism imaginable — prevention of the act of crime by the direct control of whole populations, categories and spaces.

As we saw earlier, much of this appears under the guise of community control. This approach, however, is not at all a move to the 'social' and is quite antagonistic to traditional liberal social reform. As one leading ideologue makes clear, the point is *direct* control over behaviour, to be set in motion before any offence. This rules out 'indirect devices' such as 'anti-poverty programmes, ego development and education'.[57] 'Environment' means the physical and not the social environment. What I term 'new behaviourism' is just as opposed to social reforms as it is to mentalistic psychologies.

The talk now is about the 'spatial' and 'temporal' aspects of crime, about systems, behaviour sequences, ecology, defensible space, environmental psychology, situations, opportunity structures, feedbacks, target hardening, spatial distribution of offenders. Crime is something which can be 'designed out' by changing the planning and management of the physical environment,[58] and massive financial and intellectual investment has been devoted to this effort.[59] Grandiose claims are even made for the emergence of a new 'paradigm' for crime prevention in which architects and planners, or else geographers, mathematicians and economists, have become the new experts. Unbelievable as it may sound (though only marginally less believable than what happened in the heyday of the psychodynamic enterprise), governments and universities are *actually paying money* to researchers to fit robbery trip-frequencies into Pareto exponential curves, to find that the average distance between criminal origin and eventual destination is 1.93 miles and to measure the time and space differences between robbery and armed robbery trips.[60]

From token economies in prisons to electrodes implanted in the skull, from aversion therapy with electric shocks to simulating offender spatial patterns, from behaviour contracting between client and counsellor to redesigning parking lots — these are some of the many manifestations of the new behaviourism. Only the observable act matters; older mentalistic concepts such as mind, thought, intention, motivation, guilt and insight are edged right out of the discourse.

The success of the change depends, as I have said, not just on its appeal to managerial goals, but its potential fit with wider ideological currents. In that common zone of pessimism shared by embittered liberalism and neo-conservatism, ambitions are to be limited and scaled down. As Rothman showed originally, the belief that deviants could be changed as people was essential for the initial victory of the asylum. It depended on a switch from the pessimistic Calvinist view of human nature to the optimistic enlightenment view that the psyche could be changed. The decline in fatalistic world views such as innate depravity, racial inferiority or divine will, removed the conceptual obstacles to intervention.[61]

To be sure, that original optimism was never quite so simple: at the heart of all therapeutic and punitive systems might have remained something of the Calvinist bifurcation — the elect who could be saved and helped, the doomed who were 'unamenable'.[62] But the helping professions were strong enough to receive a collective licence from the new faith in change, reform, treatment and perfectibility.

This conceptual licence has now been questioned in the 'new realism' of contemporary corrections. Treatment does not work, the liberal state does not deliver the goods. So, it is back to pessimistic theories such as sociobiology or else settle for horizons so limited that failure rather than success must be assumed:

> Heretofore, at the heart of the penal system or of parole and probation was a 'success' model: we could reform the deviant. As an alternative I believe that we could accomplish more by frankly adopting a 'failure' model by recognising our inability to achieve such heady and grandiose goals as eliminating crime and remaking offenders. Let us accept failure and pursue its implications.[63]

In the influential conservative version of the failure model, not only does rehabilitation not work, but the whole enterprise of searching for root causes — psychological or social — is a waste of time. Causes are too difficult to deal with and are, anyway, irrelevant to policy formation: 'ultimate causes cannot be the object of policy efforts, precisely because being ultimate they cannot be changed.'[64] For Wilson and other conservatives, trying to find out why people commit crime is futile: the point is to design a system of deterrence which will work, without knowing what factors would promote crime in the absence of deterrence.

This does not mean that the conservative model rules out the idea of treatment as such.[65] Some bifurcatory sorting must be done. The 'amenables' (young, anxious, verbal, intelligent and neurotic) can remain on the soft, counselling-type programmes. The non-amenables (the power-oriented psychopaths who foul up all the evaluation studies) must be subject to traditional custody or else strict surveillance and supervision in the community. 'Treatment' means not mind-therapy but any planned intervention, and becomes the same as special deterrence: 'behaviourally, it is not clear that a criminal can tell the difference between rehabilitation and special deterrence if each involves a comparable degree of restriction.'[66]

Leaving the conservative political element aside, there are more general tendencies in criminology away from traditional (positivist) questions about causation. One leading American criminologist, Wolfgang, cites with approval the decline of interest in causes in favour of the neo-classical concerns with justice, rights and policy. He advocates a 'behavioural science approach' which 'suggests that we react to correlative consequences and seek to alter known effects rather than to reach into the enormous chain of variables from proximate to first cause.'[67] An equally distinguished colleague, Cressey, has criticized the shift away from the whole scientific enterprise of generating valid causal propositions towards simply 'increasing the efficiency of the punitive legal apparatus'. He sees this as turning the typical modern criminologist into a 'technical assistant to politicians bent on repressing crime'. If this 'know nothing criminology' continues, by 1990 sociological criminology will be 'gasping its last breath'.[68]

The 'new realism' of crime-control talk and the 'unjoyful message' of the whole critique of liberal treatment and social reform comes, we are told, from 'confronting the uncomfortable possibility that human beings are not very easily changed after all'.[69] For those bringing this message, the lesson of the optimistic sixties was that solving social problems by changing people is simply unproductive. People are not amenable to persuasion, resocialization, counselling, treatment, re-education. We have to accept them as they are, modify their circumstances or deal with the consequences of their intractability.

Here is where the new behaviourism is so ideologically perfect.

- it is uninterested in causes (the result is what matters — causal theories are either contradicted by the programme or are irrelevant);
- it is not at all incompatible with management, control and surveillance (indeed this is what it is about);
- it offers the modest prospect of changing behaviour sequences rather than people;
- it works at the 'realistic' level of situations or physical environments rather than institutions which touch the social order.

The original and pure Skinnerian model was, certainly, a highly ambitious one — no less than a totally synchronized and predictable environment. But the realists of crime control will settle for a derivative, pragmatic version of the original: the most important matter is not to allow mind or consciousness to be taken into consideration. As long as people behave themselves, something will be achieved. This is a vision which will quite happily settle for sullen citizens, performing their duties, functioning with social skills, and not having any insights.

It is in these terms, I believe, that the back-to-justice, neo-classical movement must be understood. The initial victory of positivism was the victory of mind over act: it was to admit questions of mental states into the discourse about crime. Actions could be interpreted, motives imputed, complex debates allowed about responsibility and culpability. In its more sociological versions, even the wider structural influences on the individual were assigned importance. Though positivism was later to be justifiably criticized for its inhumane scientism, the depersonalization in its extreme medical model, and its removal of choice, we must remember that it unambiguously made room for the human. It added an agent to the act.

The conservative, neo-classical movement now gaining dominance in crime-control politics, looks forward to a return to an undiluted behaviourism: no discretion and no discussion of motivation or causation; only fixed and determinate sentencing, deterrence and incapacitation based on the gravity of the act. The original radical thrust in the struggle for justice movement, is now almost fully co-opted. To repeat Nils Christie's point: the hidden agenda of neo-classicism is simply to punish harder. If the eighteenth-century idea of crime as infraction became reconstituted in the nineteenth century by the intervention of the delinquent actor, we are now moving back to a revised version of crime as infraction, pure illegality.

To be sure, this move is a complicated one. We understand very little about the relationship between theories of control and the dominant social order. Is it clear, for example that today's 'legitimation crisis' can best be resolved by external compliance, whereas in nascent individualistic capitalism, Freudian inner-directed models fitted better?[70] Note also, that neo-classical, just-deserts theories are not exactly the same as pure Skinnerian behaviourism. As commentators on Skinner have suggested, his professed aim was a 'non-punitive society'.[71] He was explicitly opposed to the older, utilitarian, behaviourism of Bentham, Beccaria and Mill. Operant reinforcement — the proper arrangement of environmental contingencies — differs both from the pleasure—pain calculus of contemporary deterrence theory and the Kantian scaling of contemporary retributionist theory. The common ground is more the shift from causes to consequences, from inner states to behaviour and from individual to environments. Foucault's theory suggests yet another complication: that the formal code of classical justice was always supported by the 'dark side', the 'underside' of discipline (positivism). Somewhere in everyday life 'below the level of the emergence of the great apparatuses and the great political struggles',[72] the disciplinary mode continues. Quite incorrectly, I think, he ignores the formal neo-classical move altogether.

Leaving such complications aside, I would still read behaviourism, realism and just-deserts as complementary trends — and as indicators of the move from 'mind' back to 'body'. I must conclude this section, however, by noting some opposite tendencies — continuities, not breaks, from the nineteenth-century 'discovery' of the mind. Remember, above all, that behaviourism offers a replacement therapy, not no therapy at all. In the same way that 'minimum state' really meant a minimum *type* of state, so only the psychodynamic *type* of therapy has been cut down at the core of the system. The new behaviourism uses different words, but the old model of one person doing something to another has hardly been altered. And, as we saw, this is true even in the new community settings. Methods such as reality therapy, behaviour modification, milieu therapy and client contracting, might all have introduced new vocabularies, but much the same groups of experts are doing much the same business as usual. The basic rituals incorporated in the move to the mind — taking case histories, writing social enquiry reports, constructing files, organizing case conferences — are still being enacted.

As we move further from the hard core of the criminal justice system into the softer community and diversion agencies and then the more-or-less voluntary counselling and therapy business, we find that mind-treatment is intact and expanding massively. Ever since the nineteenth century, the institutional base and the world view of the mental health profession has been consistently expansionist. Moving from specific and limited areas of competence to the creation of new categories of illness and then the colonization of new sites of interest, the achievement has been the 'psychiatric society'.[73] Far from arresting this growth, all the 'alternative' or anti-therapies of the sixties added a new part to the empire.

The mental-health network contains its own hard—soft bifurcation exactly parallel to that in the criminal justice system. At the core remains the classic asylum, relegated by the ideology of community to a dumping ground for chronic clients and favouring drug and behaviour therapy. In the next circle come the community mental-health services and clinics, taking in a mixture of the old decarcerated patients and an increasing number of newer cases brought in by the net-widening ideology of preventive psychiatry and community mental health. These patients receive a mixture of drug therapy and traditional but watered down psychodynamic modalities. Then, in the widest circle, come the clients of the neo-Freudian health movement: healthy neurotics or the worried well, the YARVIS clients (Young, Attractive, Rich, Verbal, Intelligent and Successful).

It is this outer ring which behaviourism appears to have penetrated least. Here, the question 'who you are' still seems more important than 'what you do'. Behaviour is not the stuff of discourse but rather feelings, insight, emotional growth, awareness, self-actualization. Indeed, for many critics of this movement, the cult of the self implies a narcissistic denial of the importance of rules, morality and the existence of anything or anyone outside the self.[74] The comparison here is also with classical, pure Freudianism. The never-ending quest for well-being, psychic energy and true self is not an attempt to bring unconscious wishes to light and analyse the causes of repression. It is, rather, to dissolve the very machinery of repression, to put an end to all inner restraints, inhibitions and hang-ups.

The awareness movement is more ambitious and optimistic than behaviourism. That whole army of psychiatrists, therapists, clinical psychologists, social workers, counsellors, sensitivity group leaders, transactional analysts, mystics, EST operators and recycled Dale Carnegie and encyclopaedia salesmen which gathered force over the sixties, holds out all sort of grandiose attractions to its clients. For the healthy neurotic, the prospect is not just less anxiety, but total psychic well-being and self-actualization. This Americanization of Freud removes the pessimism, the irresolvable conflicts, the dark forces of the id and the death instinct. Now, the self to be liberated is essentially good. There is a little OK person trapped inside every non-OK shell.

These are altogether more rewarding areas of work than the hard edge of the criminal justice apparatus or the back wards of the mental-health system. The business is much more lucrative, these clients are only too willing to 'refer' themselves, and they seem quite satisfied with talking and being talked to, massaged or stroked in other ways. They need no persuasion to volunteer for help well before the first signs of psychic unease or deviation: devouring each new fashion in the self-help literature; attending all sorts of groups, sessions, meetings and encounters; submitting themselves to regular mind check-ups; visiting stress clinics for rest and recuperation before reaching breaking point or the next predictable cycle, passage of life crisis. There is no need to wait till the thought police come. 'Turn yourself in' is the motto of the movement.

With this crucial difference — the voluntary nature of the self-help movement — these self-actualizing ideologies have also penetrated the softer parts of the community-control system. Rather than giving up on treatment, these new community agencies are operating with an ill-digested mixture of behaviourism and neo-Freudian psychologies. Given the lack of interest in causality, the dominant philosophy is that 'anything goes'. It is easy to find a single agency which lists as its 'methods': role playing, transactional analysis, problem solving, task setting, reality therapy, behaviour modification, operant reinforcement, video game skills, remedial education and camping trips. The dominant ethos — the learning of social skills — remains, however, behaviourist. Even many self-actualizing psychologies, despite their apparent stress on feelings, insights and growth, actually complement behaviourism. Influential methods such as transactional analysis are explicitly opposed to the classic Freudian emphasis on the unconscious, 'deep' insights or the importance of early childhood. The stress is on learning in the here and now; morality is not the stern old superego, but a matter of observable conformity to the rules of the social game. Wolfgang, thus, is correct to note that the behaviourist move in the criminal justice system 'is the same kind of change noted in private psychiatric practice: the reduction of psychoanalytic probing of cause to cognitive therapy of current effects'.[75]

To summarize this long section: what I call the new behaviourism is an uneven move away from internal states to external behaviour, from causes to consequences, from individuals to categories or environments. Overlaid on the structural principle of bifurcation, this results in a complex hierarchy of intervention — the current version of Orwell's *Nineteen Eighty-Four*. The party members — the middle class — are scrutinized for extreme or violent political dissent, but are mostly left quite free to obtain neo-Freudian self-scrutiny or are encouraged to do their own thing. The proles — the old deviant classes — are contained in their defensible spaces, closely observed in public and not allowed to have too much insight or awareness. If they offend, they are inserted into the lower reaches of the correctional system, where their behaviour patterns (not their thoughts) are carefully tracked or else they are changed by being taught social skills through traditional behaviourist techniques, sometimes accompanied by the rhetoric of cognition and self. If they persist, they find themselves in the deep end: locked up in the old custodial institutions, most often just warehoused ('humane containment', 'selective incapacitation') or (occasionally) receiving behaviourist 'treatment'.

CONCLUSION: TELLING STORIES

What sense can we make of these three stories — community, state, behaviour — and all the other talk we overhear from the control system? What can now be said about those recurrent debates about words and reality, ideology and practice?

Remember the three contrasting positions which emerged from both the historical and contemporary debates: first, all is going more-or-less well and according to plan; second, there is a radical but unintended gap between rhetoric and reality; third, the words are mere camouflage behind which another plan is unfolding. There is no denying the radical theoretical differences between these positions. There appears to be no common ground at all. As Scull has written, 'the ideological proclamations of the proponents of current reforms are about as reliable a guide to the antecedents, characteristics and significance of what is happening in the real world as the collected works of the brothers Grimm.'[76]

This chapter suggests that Scull is quite right. But in another sense this uncompromising contrast between 'ideological proclamation' and 'real world' misses the essence of Controltalk. The contrast is false, because each side is obsessed with the same quixotic search for fit, congruence and consistency. Everything we know about the way social-control ideologies originate and function, should warn us about the delusion of ever expecting a synchronization of words with deeds. If progressives are like children who believe that fairy stories are actually true and that those who tell them always good, then radical demystifiers are like adults who laboriously try to prove that fairy stories are not really true, and that those who tell them are always bad.

No doubt there are some tellers of social-control tales who are either well-intentioned fools or ill-intentioned knaves. We might imagine someone running a community-control project who actually believes that everything he does is fostering values of personal intimacy, emotional depth and social cohesion, and simply cannot understand suggestions to the contrary. Or imagine a private management consultant drafting a crime-control programme in which he cynically inserts the word 'community' on every second page. But the social world is not usually like this. My own reading of these stories and my own contact with these story-tellers conjures up a much more opaque set of images: the same people sometimes knowing what they are doing, sometimes not; believing in what they are doing, yet at the same time sceptical about the whole enterprise; succeeding in some ways, totally failing in others.

An informed sociology of social-control talk can afford neither to be deceived by appearances nor to be obsessed by debunking. The notion of demystification is based on an inadequate understanding of the contexts, sources and functions of Controltalk. Abstract ideologies of the type I have analysed only make sense when grounded in the day-to-day operating philosophies of control agencies. They constitute working or practice languages. For the most part, the workers and managers – who are simultaneously the apostles and architects of the new order – cannot explain very well what they are doing or what is happening. So they improvise a vocabulary, drawing on those abstractions, which invests and dignifies their daily organizational imperatives and contingencies with the status of a theory.

What should be asked is less whether these theories are correct or not, or whether they came before or after the policy, but how they can be made to work. We must begin neither with a simple congruence (whose presence or absence then has to be demonstrated) between words and deeds, nor with the existence of abstract forces which will render any such congruence illusory. The best working strategy is to assume (for perfectly concrete sociological reasons) that most of the time there will be anomalies, incongruence, lack of fit, contradictions, paradoxes, impurities – all the deeper structures which this chapter 'revealed'.

There are any number of good theories which make reasonable sense of all this. We can range from Mao's conception of the contradictory nature of ideology to Becker's more mundane account of what officials do when the institutions for which they are responsible (like schools, prisons or hospitals) do not work in the way they are supposed to: 'officials usually have to lie. That is a gross way of putting it, but not inaccurate. Officials must lie because things are seldom as they ought to be.'[77] Interactionist studies teach us how these officials organize their talk (denying failures, explaining failure which cannot be hidden, saying what they would really like to do); Marxist theories guide us to the external conditions under which such talk — however internally implausible — gains acceptability in a certain social order.

In both these forms of collective language, it is tempting to apply Goffman's famous aphorism about the sad tales which individuals tell: there are no true stories or false stories, only good stories or bad stories. This relativism, however, is too extreme. If 'things are seldom as they ought to be', this means that we can sometimes know what they really are. We have to assume a quite radical distinction between the 'public realm of representations, significations and symbolic practices' (words) and the 'operational realm of sanctions, institutions and practices' (deeds). The first is not a theory of the second nor its 'ideational reflection', but a 'separate realm of penal discourse'.[78]

To put it more simply: what the social-control system does is invariably accompanied by much talk. These 'good stories' stand for or signify what the system likes to think it is doing, justify or rationalize what it has already done and indicate what it would like to be doing (if only given the chance and the resources). This talk also has other functions: to maintain and increase the self-confidence, worth and interests of those who work in the system, to protect them from criticism and to suggest that they are doing alright in a difficult world. These stories constitute sociological data as much as the motivational accounts of individuals (sad tales). This is the theoretical double-bind: to take these stories seriously (seldom are they based on total delusion, fantasy or fabrication), but also to explore their connections with the reality they are meant to signify.

We have seen how opaque and paradoxical these connections are. Practices are carried out for reasons quite different from their accompanying stories. Incompatible stories are used to justify the same practice. The sociological task is to understand how these discrepancies arise, how Naipaul's colonizers could have both 'slaves and statues'.

The problem is, thus, political, and social-control talk is a particularly good example of what Edelman calls the symbolic language of politics.[79] The language which the powerful use to deal with chronic social problems like crime is very special in its banality. Invariably, it tries to convey choice, change, progress, and rational decision making. Even if things stay much the same, social-control talk has to convey a dramatic picture of breakthroughs, departures, innovations, milestones, turning points — continually changing strategies in the war against crime. All social-policy talk has to give the impression of change even if nothing new is happening at all. As Sedgewick nicely notes about psychiatric policy: 'what is particularly striking about the long history of psychiatric medicine is its capacity to produce quite different rationalizations for a relatively constant practice.'[80]

The people who produce this talk of change — professionals, politicians, administrators, committees, fund-raisers, researchers and journalists — are all mounting a complex sociodrama for each other and their respective publics. This takes the form of shamanism: a series of conjuring tricks in which agencies are shuffled, new names invented, incantations recited, commissions, committees, laws, programmes and campaigns announced.[81] All this is to give the impression that social problems (crime, mental illness, pollution, alcoholism, etc.) are somehow not totally out of control. Promises and gestures can be made, anxieties can vanish away or be exorcised, people can be reassured or mesmerized. So magical is the power of the new languages of systems theory, applied-behaviour analysis and psycho-babble, that they can convey (even to their users) an effect opposite to the truth.

All this means that we need a model much looser than any of those we have considered: not the simple idealist, nor the simple materialist, nor even Foucault's complex spiral of power and knowledge. To Foucault, theoretical knowledge (in psychiatry, criminology, all the human sciences) is wholly utilitarian; it functions *only* as an alibi for power. Sedgewick correctly points out, however, that Foucault's 'infatuation' with the terms of each stage of therapeutic logic (the story of an epistemological break, of the eruption of rationalism) does not form the patient's-eye-view of psychiatry. This was the 'medical attitude', the doctors' accounts of what in any particular epoch they thought they were doing. While patients experience continuity, doctors talk of change. There is no necessary fit between these languages.

The deep structures of our three tales, then, elude all these theoretical models: consequences so different from intentions; policies carried out for reasons opposite to their stated ideologies; the same ideologies supporting quite different policies; the same policy supported for quite different ideological reasons. And any possible correspondence between ideas and policies will become even harder to locate as the system announces its own 'end of ideology'. While previous phases of crime control also exhibited ideological inconsistencies (classicism allowed some determinism, positivism allowed punishment) there was, at least, a dominant set of ideas from which departures could be noticed. Now, in the cheerless anti-theoretical realism of contemporary crime-control ideology, anything goes. There is no need even to pretend that policies have anything to do with causal theories.

On the principle that metaphors and analogies are often more helpful than substantive models themselves, let me conclude this chapter with stories about a quite different type of social change. In his classic analysis of Kachin society, Leach presents a highly suggestive analysis of how mythology can be said to justify changes in the social structure.[82]

Structure is usually seen as being 'represented' in certain rituals while myths are the verbal statements which accompany and sanction ritual action. That is to say, the ritual (practice) and the myth (talk) are consistent with and complement each other. Both idealist and materialist theories contain their own versions of this complementary relationship between ritual and myth. But this neat complementarity, Leach argues, hardly ever exists. Indeed, in Kachin mythology, contradictions and inconsistencies are fundamental: they are more significant than the uniformities and cannot be eliminated. Inconsistencies are not occasions to select one version as more correct than another. Even the 'simple' Kachin society is more complex than this: particular structures can assume a variety of interpretations, different structures can be represented by the same symbols. And ritual expression of agreement (in our example: that there has been a move from prison to community) does not mean that this is actually happening.

The explanations given by certain members of society about how particular institutions actually function. Leach argues, necessarily constitute a fiction. Moreover, such fictions are quite different from the language used by outside anthropological observers. Members do not use such scientific verbal tools as 'exogamy' or 'patrilineage' (any more than they talk of 'hegemonic crisis' or 'neo-classicism'); they become aware of structure only through performance of ritual acts and reciting tales of ritual implications. As Leach shows, actual crucial changes in particular communities are not at all reflected in the stories these communities tell about themselves (in the same way as real correctional changes, especially when caused by 'external' political or economic pressures, are often not picked up). Kachin mythology, then, is not a simple kind of history. The same characters and symbols are used, but story-telling is a ritual which differs according to the teller and justifies the attitude adopted at the moment of the telling:

Kachins recount their traditions on set occasions, to justify a quarrel, to validate a social custom, to accompany a religious performance. The story-telling therefore has a purpose; it serves to validate the status of the individual who hires a bard to tell the story, for among Kachins the telling of traditional tales is a professional occupation carried out by priests and bards of various grades . . . But if the status of one individual is validated, that almost always means that the status of someone else is denigrated. One might then almost infer from first principles that every traditional tale will occur in several different versions, each tending to uphold the claims of a different vested interest.[83]

Analogously, we must study not just the content of social-control talk, but the particular set occasions (enquiries, speeches, reports, evaluations) for which it is produced and the interests of the professional priests and bards who do the telling. Further, we must expect the tales to be 'unrealistic'. As Leach comments on one example: 'at the back of the ritual, there stood not the political structure of a real state, but the "as if" structure of an ideal state.'[84] When pushed, participants themselves will understand quite well that they are not talking about an actual society. Nobody running a community dispute mediation centre in New York actually believes that this recreates the conditions of a Tanzanian village court any more than 'house-parents' in a 'community home' believe that they are living in a family with their own children. And criminologists who mount research projects to determine whether an agency is 'in the community' or not should know that they are busy with magic, not science.

But this 'as if' quality of Controltalk (which renders it so vague, ambiguous or contradictory) derives from the ideal rather than idealistic nature of ritual. 'Ritual and mythology "represents" an ideal version of the social structure. It is a model of how people suppose their society to be organized. But it is not necessarily the goal to which they strive. It is a simplified description of what is, not a fantasy of what might be.'[85]

This means that the mythology of crime-control talk, even at its most fantastic and utopian moments, is very much grounded in the real world. And in this real world, there are tellers – with distinctive structural positions, with vested interests, with a preferred language – and not just tales. These tellers are the subject of the next chapter.

# 5

# The Professionals

The professionalization of deviancy control which began in the middle of the nineteenth century is a story of continual expansion and diversification. There have been no real breaks, slow-downs or dramatic changes. This is true despite the real achievements of those destructuring movements of the 1960s, aimed at weakening or by-passing professional power: deprofessionalization, demedicalization, delegalization, anti-psychiatry, client self-help. These movements created and sustained certain enclaves of help and care, for example rape-crisis centres, free drug clinics and gay-counselling networks, which managed to continue to function without professional dominance. And, just as important, they raised a sceptical consciousness about the more grandiose of professional pretensions to omnipotence and omniscience.

But no overall destructuring took place. Many reform movements were co-opted; others were allowed to establish their enclaves apart from (rather than instead of) professional control or else — most frequently — were ignored altogether. In every part of the deviancy control system, professional control is stronger than it was twenty years ago.

This chapter is not directly addressed to these questions of success and failure. It returns, rather, to the 'professional interests' model identified in chapter 3 and asks what deposits of power professionalism leaves behind. I suggest some features of care-and-control professionals and their academic auxiliaries — their power base, distinctive modes of working, preferred language and the ways they justify themselves — that might go some way to explain how control systems grow.

The debate about the distinctive social role and class position of professionals is part of the standard literature on contemporary social structures, whether the framework is post-industrial society or advanced capitalist society.

Post-industrial society theorists suggest that theoretical knowledge is the central principle of the new society.[1] Planners, technocrats, researchers, scientists, predictors, systems theorists and computer experts have replaced the old industrialists and entrepreneurs. The universities, research organizations and professional schools have become the axial structures of the new society, superseding the classic business firm. This is the 'knowledge society' and systematic professional knowledge is its main resource. Simultaneously, it has become a 'personal service society': more of the economy is given over to the human services, and more power is given to the expanding group of welfare, helping, therapeutic or service professionals.

Both these classifications — the 'knowledge society' and the 'personal service society' — have been intensely debated. Many doubt whether 'the knowledge classes' are capable of the degree of power, initiative or control (even over the welfare sector) which the post-industrial thesis requires of them. Neither the explosion of scientific knowledge and its increasing share of the gross national product, nor the growth of the service sector, proves much about the autonomous power of these groups. Much of the expansion of professionals in the occupational distribution has, anyway, been at the lower ends of the status scale: teachers, social workers, counsellors, various semi-professionals. These groups are dependent employees of public bureaucracies and, despite their pretensions or aspirations, have little power in determining major policy decisions.

If we come to this debate not from the post-industrial society direction, but from neo-Marxist formulations about advanced capitalist society, the focus is on how structural arrangements have generated a new and distinctive middle class. This is the professional managerial class (PMC): salaried mental workers who do not own the means of production and whose major function in the social division of labour is (in Marxist terms) to reproduce capitalist culture and class relations.[2] There is considerable disagreement in the literature on just what role this group plays in the state. And in the same way as the 'knowledge society' formulation allows this group too much power, so some Marxist accounts exaggerate the PMC's total subjection to economic imperatives.

In Marxist theories of social control, the people-processing professionals tend to be seen merely as part of the emerging administrative state. This is a system which stresses rationality, expertise, knowledge and problem solving in order to conceal an increasing state involvement in the accumulation process and also to deflect democratic participation (by co-opting radical impulses such as the destructuring reforms). Professionals in systems such as mental health, crime control or social work are locked into a network of bureaucratic and corporate interests. They are 'mind bureaucrats' – a new class whose interests range from universities, foundations, professional associations, corporate legal firms, pharmaceutical companies, crime-technology manufacturers and central or local government bureaucracies.

Managers are the key sector of the administrative class: they command the battalions of psychiatrists, psychologists, social workers, correctional staff, researchers and all sorts of dependent groups who do the dirty work of control and mopping up. They control large budgets, and bestow patronage through research grants, project funding, the appointment of boards, panels, enquiries and commissions. And the ultimate access to knowledge and power is controlled by the crime and welfare branches of government (the Department of Justice or Health and Human Services in the USA and the Home Office or Department of Health and Social Security in Britain), through 'command centres' such as the Law Enforcement Assistance Administration.

This perspective does well to remind us that low-level helping and controlling professions are indeed part of wider managerial and administrative systems. But we must take care not to see them simply as 'tools of the state'. To Gouldner, in his stimulating theses on the new class, intellectuals and technical intelligentsia (and particularly their 'humanistic' sectors) have a 'morally ambiguous' relationship to the state.[3] They are not the benign and already dominant technocrats of the post-industrial theorists (or of the progressives) but neither are they an exploitative master class, allies of the old class or cynically corrupt servants of power. They are elitist and self-seeking, they use their knowledge to advance their own interests, but they have some functional autonomy from the older elites and established institutions. In addition, they have access to 'CCD' – the Culture of Critical Discourse – a particular style of speaking and thinking which potentially makes for alienation and radicalism. The new class thus, is morally ambivalent 'embodying the collective interest but partially and transiently, while simultaneously cultivating their guild advantage.'[4]

The notion of 'guild advantage' brings us to the core of the professional model. Whatever their cognitive radicalism or ambivalent class position, professionals and experts continue to increase their monopolistic reach and their ability to make people dependent on them — in health, education, welfare, life-styles, family policy, deviancy control. To connect this extension with the growth of the control system itself, we must understand the complicated nature of guild advantages and interests. Professional dominance is the process by which occupational groups seek to gain and maintain control over their work:[5] protecting their 'cultural capital' (the technical knowledge possessed neither by wealth nor common sense), rising up economic and status ladders, controlling their work conditions. This process is neither purely instrumental nor selflessly dedicated: 'The New Class's occupational culture is neither the caricature of the devoted professional selflessly sacrificing himself in the service of his client, nor is it the stereotype of the venal elite that prostitutes its skills for gain.'[6]

Even those professional groups closer to the economic centre of the state, such as architects, planners and engineers ('APEs' as Finlayson calls them),[7] are not the slaves they were in early societies, nor the servant-craftsmen of the Middle Ages, nor even the wealthy members of the urban middle class they were in the nineteenth century. Their expertise and technocracy can be used to their own advantage — by-passing clients, officials, bureaucrats and politicians. Unlike the homogeneous, autocratic Victorian bourgeoisie, the APEs have been exposed to some strange values and experiences not always consonant with the dominant ideology.

This is all the more true for the people-processing professionals. These groups might vary in their efficiency, humanity, commitment and politics but, as Sedgewick notes about psychiatrists, their growth cannot be correlated with changing class relations, modes of production or political systems. What he terms the 'medical attitude' has its own autonomy. It is 'a separate instance of the domination of mental over manual labour, undertaken as part of the conditions of any society's reproduction.'[8] This 'attitude' is not free from ideology, but nor is it simply a form of ideology.

Thus, professionals in various state-welfare, health, educational or control systems are not directly nor necessarily acting in the best interests of the state. As one observer in Britain notes, although these agencies are used in cooling out, neutralizing and hiding problems, they also

> maintain spaces and potential oppositions, keep alive issues and prod nerves which capitalism would much rather were forgotten. Their personnel are in no simple sense servants of capitalism. They solve, confuse or postpone its problems in the short term very often because of their commitment to professional goals which are finally and awkwardly independent from the functional needs of capitalism.[9]

In addition to sticking to such professional goals, these workers might also be bearers not exactly of Gouldner's 'new consciousness' but of the very same radical and counter-cultural values which were used to attack them in the sixties. The most energetic attacks on professionalism came from professionals. No nineteenth-century charity organization worker could have joined a squat, a radical tenants organization, a welfare-claimants union or a gay liberation rally. These groups live and work with all sorts of contradictions between their socialized radicalism and their day-to-day job demands. They might dissociate themselves, for example, from the very same life-styles and values to which (as 'agents of social control') they have to persuade their clients to conform.[10]

It is for these two reasons — the peculiar autonomy of the professional ethic and the contradictory values in professions like social work — that the actual exercise of power at the lower levels of the system is so anarchic and unpredictable. There is no firm knowledge base, no technology, nor even any agreed criteria of success and failure. In addition, low-level professionals are often poorly supervised, and can easily deviate from organizational norms (for or against their clients). In the last couple of decades, therefore, to take the best-documented examples, the therapy business in the USA and social work in Britain have looked prone to all sorts of extraordinary fads and fashions. One cohort is 'into' client advocacy and civil rights, the next one discovers radical therapy and community work, yet another is suddenly attracted to behaviour-contracting. Thus, behind the ideology of 'professionalism', discretion is used in quite random and arbitrary ways.

To the hapless 'client' this might all sound much the same. It might not make too much difference what theory his worker subscribes to or where he or she went to graduate school. What does matter, is the common denominator of all forms of professional power, that is the 'technical fix' which awards professionals with knowledge and technique which no one else is capable of mastering. The rise of psychiatry has become the paradigmatic case for understanding the emergence during the last century of various experts in deviancy control, each with its own elaborate ideology and systems of classification.[11] The success of psychiatry was to establish a radical, legally formalized monopoly on its services and to be able to claim esoteric knowledge, effective technique and the right to treat.

All subsequent extensions of professional power and privilege derive from this monopoly — an increased intensity of formal training; more and more finer specializations (marriage counsellors, sex therapists, suicidologists); strengthening of professional associations (certification, credentialism and finer gradations of rank). With their institutional base in the asylum, their powerful set of analogies to physical and preventive medicine, and with their claims to unique knowledge and skill, psychiatrists have been able to conquer more and more areas of social life. The apotheosis of the 'rise of the therapeutic' is seen as the eventual replacement of the older moralities of right and wrong with the newer ethic of health and illness.[12]

The relevant sociological literature about medicine, psychiatry and therapy (sometimes called the 'madness network' or the 'mental illness establishment') is rich and interesting. By contrast, the crime-control establishment has been most unevenly analysed. More attention has been devoted to the hard end: the police, the judiciary, prison staff and various law-enforcement agencies and policy bodies. We know very little about the professionals at the soft end: all the counsellors, therapists and social workers of the new community programmes, the clinical psychologists and programme evaluators and the lower-level policy makers.

The best information here has to be drawn from areas of overlap with the mental health business. The story here is how a marginal occupational group became, in one generation, a massive industry employing half a million people in the USA.[13] This number includes workers in clinics, hospitals, mental-health centres, nursing homes, half-way houses, drug and alcoholic treatment settings, etc. and excludes psychiatrists, psychologists and social workers in private practice.

Community-control professionals fall between and overlap with the hard-end crime control establishments and the madness network. It is extremely difficult even to estimate their gross numbers and their formal characteristics.[14] One source of information is the overall statistics on criminal justice education which show a continual tendency towards more formal qualifications and an up-grading of job requirements.[15] It is not clear, though, just where community-control professions fit into this overall growth. Some of them are custodial or therapeutic staff displaced from closed institutions, others come from more traditional counselling, therapy and social-work backgrounds. The pool of unemployed social-science and arts graduates since the beginning of the seventies has been a major source of recruitment. We lack, however, basic information about the background characteristics of these groups, or of the effects of such important changes as the privatization of certain forms of social control.

Whatever this information, there is every reason to suppose that community control will continue to be professionalized along familiar lines. The new agencies (including the private ones) are much concerned with accreditation standards, goals and professional guidelines; new professional sub-specialties are being developed and associations set up (for example, the National Intermediate Treatment Federation and the International Halfway House Association); new qualifications are demanded (for trackers, community-service officers, community-based correctional administrator). And as the academy senses where the action is, so conferences, courses and textbooks proliferate.

THE LOGIC AND LANGUAGE OF CONTROL

The lack of solid information about lower-end care and control professionals is matched by the lack of good theory to explain their exact role in shaping the emerging control system. The most direct explanations draw on the general theory of professional growth, aggrandizement and self-interest. To put it simply, it is in the best interests of professions to enlarge the system and attract more clients. In a recent analysis of new forms of social control taking place through net-widening and 'transinstitutionalism' (moving inmates from the public to the private sector), Warren uses the term 'social-control entrepreneurship' to cover this direct type of economic self-interest.[16] Instead of Becker's 'moral entrepreneurs' we have various forms of direct programme, profit and professional interests. To keep your job, to justify your existence, to attract grants and subsidies, you must keep on expanding.

Like many simple theories, this one works well enough. Much system expansion can be explained in terms of relentless professional self-interest. There are, however, obvious limits to this theory. For one thing, it works better for the new private sector where, unlike the public correctional system, there is a direct incentive to seek out funding and clientele. But professional interests, as we have seen, are always more complicated than this. More importantly, professional growth only takes place when it is allowed by the political economy. Professional values might be self-contained but the conditions for expansion (budgets and man-power) are determined by wider political interests. Even the most self-serving of professional groups — academics are a good example — cannot expand indefinitely without appropriate financial and political support.

Moreover, it might simply not be in the immediate interests of all control agents to keep on expanding. Correctional bureaucrats for example, are more concerned with control than capacity. Prestige goes to the manager who can boast of a secure prison not a prison with the largest number of inmates. Prison managers correctly complain that they have little control over the actual numbers of clients they receive. This is determined by sentencing policy, internal self-regulating mechanisms and external changes such as increases in the rate of crime or the fear of crime.

The contrast between mental illness and crime shows that professional entrepreneurship can take quite different forms.[17] The mental-illness market allows more direct opportunity for privatization and profit making — either from the traditional high-income private clients or the new decarcerated clients dumped from the public sector. Correctional officials have to stick with the offenders provided for them by someone else, and their collective interests are more directly tied up to the public sector. Here, as Scull suggests, occupational self-interest in expansion coincides with the public and political demand to 'do something', a demand which does not exist in regard to mental illness (thereby allowing less rather than more state intervention).

Both in cases of direct commercial interest and dependence on the state, however, we need a good working model to explain the internal logic and language of professional expansion. A well-known example is Illich's critique of medicalization, the disabling impact of professional control.[18] This model has been justly criticized for its rhetorical excesses, the exaggerated power it gives to professionals and its fateful political ambiguity. And it has left virtually no impact on social policy. I believe, though, that it deserves more than relegation to the intellectual history of failed ideas. The logic of 'medicalization' and the prospect of 'medical nemesis' have some curious equivalents in the area of deviancy control.

Illich's central concept is iatrogenesis — disease caused by medical intervention. He sees medical progress as a myth: the major determinants of health are political and technological transformations and not progress in medicine — not status, training, knowledge, expertise, equipment or any other index of professional advancement. The great killer diseases of the nineteenth century peaked and declined in response to environmental changes and not advances in medical treatment. The idea of medical effectiveness is an illusion. Not only is much prestigious and expensive medical treatment useless, it actually *causes* pain, dysfunction, disability and anguish. This is what Illich calls 'clinical iatrogenesis'.

The parallels here to deviancy control are obvious. It is almost certain that rises and falls in the amount of crime are more responsive to macro social changes than to progress in control theory or technology. Most forms of intervention demonstrably do not work very well (and we certainly cannot be sure that the most sophisticated and advanced methods are any better than the crudest and simplest). Moreover, as 20 years of labelling theory (with somewhat less research evidence) has tried to show, many forms of intervention are iatrogenic: they make things worse (through secondary deviation, amplification, self-fulfilling prophecies, etc.). These effects have been suggested at both the hard (imprisonment) and soft (doing good) ends of the system. In the same way as the health industry implies that iatrogenic illness is the patient's fault, so crime-control ideologues blame failure on offenders. A special group of offenders is particularly to blame: the incorrigibles, the hard cores, the career criminals who so ungratefully persist in keeping recidivism rates so high. If only they would co-operate!

'Social' and 'cultural' iatrogenesis are for Illich the deeper effects of over-medicalization. The idea of health is appropriated by professionals, paralysing normal responses to pain, suffering, death and grief. This dependency feeds and grows on itself, creating 'impairments to health that are due precisely to those socioeconomic transformations which have been made attractive, possible or necessary by the institutional shape health care has taken'.[19] Budgets become medicalized (by over-prescription of drugs), expensive research is carried out and — above all — there is diagnostic imperialism. New categories of illness are generated, expensive treatment wasted on the incurable, the spheres of 'prevention' and 'at risk' are dramatically enlarged. New disorders are 'discovered' and attributed to particular individuals. This is not simply scientific advance nor is it even analogous to the sorcerer determining whether a hallucination (or other symptom) is a sign of good or evil magic. The physician rather invents the categories to which he assigns people and then controls the access to these categories. The key processes are diagnosis, selection and allocation.

The best known of the fables which Illich used to illustrate this point is worth quoting — again and again. This is the famous 1934 American Child Health study of diagnostic and referral procedures.

> In a survey of 1,000 eleven-year-old children from the public schools of New York, 61 per cent were found to have had their tonsils removed. The remaining 39 per cent were subjected to examination by a group of physicians, who selected 45 per cent of these for tonsillectomy and rejected the rest. The rejected children were re-examined by another group of physicians, who recommended tonsillectomy for 46 per cent of those remaining after the first examination. When the rejected children were examined a third time, a similar percentage was selected for tonsillectomy so that after three examinations only sixty-five children remained who had not been recommended for tonsillectomy. These subjects were not further examined because the supply of examining physicians ran out.[20]

The study was conducted at a free clinic and thus the results could not be explained simply in terms of commercial entrepreneurship. Diagnosis has its own autonomous status within the logic of professionalism. It takes little imagination to see how crime-control agencies operate in similar ways. Indeed the relative nature of deviance, as opposed to the more absolutist qualities of most medical categories, gives greater weight here to the labelling process. This, of course, is the whole basis of the functionalist claim that the boundary-maintaining nature of social control ensures that only the 'right' amount of deviance is selected and filtered through.[21]

There is no need to generalize too literally from the tonsillectomy study. Of course there are objective structural factors which affect the amount of crime (inflation, unemployment, immigration patterns, demographic changes, political contradictions), and of course these same factors account for such changes in the control system as more severe punishments. But it is equally self-evident that not all system changes are exogenous in these ways. Much system expansion is *endogenous* (filling or creating categories) or *iatrogenic* (mopping up the casualties created by its own operations). These forms of expansion can be understood neither in market terms nor as direct responses to objective changes or moral panics.

Endogenous expansion depends rather on the professional ideology of social problems. The whole social-problems industry is organized, staffed and financed on the assumptions of *permanence* and *long-term growth*. Every problem has to be seen simultaneously as more or less intractable, yet more or less under control. This is the dilemma of the rule enforcer which Becker originally described: be assured, we are doing our job, things are under control, but unless we are given more resources, things will get completely out of hand. Insolubility is built into the language of social-problem definition. This is precisely how the textbooks define a social problem — the sort of problem which is so messy and so complex that it really cannot be solved.[22]

Seeley has well described the functional necessity to define social problems as vaguely as possible. 'Poverty', 'health' and 'crime' become shifting, ambiguous terms. There are hints about vast numbers of undiscovered deviants — dark figures. We are told to watch out for early warning signs, latent problems, potential and at-risk populations. These groups must be brought into the net. And the hardest group to reach or to do anything about will always be the '5 per cent' (or whatever amount can be absorbed at the lower tail of whatever distribution curve we are talking about). These are the hard core, the dangerous, the deep end, the sickest (the ones who really need their tonsils removed). Here is Seeley's macabre example: 'if we were to attempt a radical solution by simply shooting those now held to be mentally retarded, it is unthinkable that anything would happen to the problem except that psychologists would need to rescore present intelligence tests so that they again found mean, mode and median at 100'.[23]

Mental retardation is one of the few forms of deviance where the metrics of professional definitions are so obvious. But the logic applies throughout the whole deviance-control and social-problems network. As organizations become more complex, so the interplay between professional logic and self-interest allows for even further elaborations of those 'iatrogenic feedback loops' described in chapter 2. These are positive feedbacks analogous to the escalating destruction generated by polluting procedures which are used as anti-pollution devices. Almost the entire alternatives, diversion and community movements can be seen as loops of this kind — new systems being created to deal with the damage caused by the old systems, but then inflicting their own kind of 'damage' from which clients have to be further saved, diverted, delabelled or decategorized. Diversion agencies loop clients away from the criminal justice system, then screening procedures have to be developed to loop the 'wrong' clients away from the diversion agencies. Theoretically, there is no end to this process.

Obviously, these (and other such iatrogenic processes) do eventually come to an end because of interests and resources outside the system. In this respect, the sociological and Marxist critiques of the professional power model are correct. But much expansion is indeed endogenous and self-perpetuating – there is no need to go out of this system to grasp its nature. This is what Burroughs meant: control only leads to more control. It is addictive, like junk. Far from leading to 'self-reliance', 'integration' or 'community' (that is, getting off the drug), the new feedback loops lead us back into the system, creating another network of dependence. To pursue the drug analogy: this is like moving from heroin addiction to methadone addiction and claiming it to be a 'cure'.

The redeployment of power along bifurcatory lines is another feature of professionalism. Policies like community-control, diversion and privatization, have allowed the hard-end professionals to concentrate their power (long fixed sentences, deterrence, selective incapacitation), dumping their soft-end cases elsewhere for more efficient preventive screening and the 'correct' bifurcatory classification. In medicine, this takes the form of 'planned patient dumping'. All sorts of uninteresting and time-consuming victims of diagnostic fervour (the new-born, the dying, the sexually inadequate) are transformed into clients of non-medical therapists (counsellors, social workers, auxiliaries, nurses psychologists). To quote Illich again:

> Whenever medicine's diagnostic power multiplies the sick in excessive numbers, medical professionals turn over the surplus to the management of non-medical trades and occupations. By dumping, the medical lords divest themselves of the nuisance of low prestige care and invest policemen, teachers or personnel officers with a derivative medical fiefdom. Medicine retains unchecked autonomy in defining what constitutes sickness, but drops on others the task of ferreting out the sick and providing for their treatment.[24]

This type of 'dumping' is another version of what happened in the nineteenth century when psychiatric medicine moved from being a threat to judicial power to becoming its ally. Donzelot describes this as a 'relay': the migration which brought the psychiatrist from playing a minor and infrequent role of last resort in difficult cases, to being the 'specialist of the invisible' who was now allowed his own fiefdom of jurisdiction, even allowed to *instigate* referrals This power in turn was dumped on to the lower-level educators and social workers, who were sent by the judicial authority on their missions of care, prevention and child-saving.[25] Similarly, Abel argues that judges supported informalism because it was seen as a repository for 'junk' cases. This enhanced their own status, while the substratum of new workers (arbitrators, mediators, conciliators) themselves became professionalized.[26]

Borrowing from Illich, I have given here a series of examples — feedback loops, diagnostic fervour, dumping and so on — of typical ways in which professional power is dispersed. While the centres — the medical lords for mental illness, the judicial lords for crime — retain ultimate jurisdiction, the lesser tasks of screening, diagnosis, prevention, counselling, casework, group-work, contracting and so on are each granted their own fiefdoms. These micro-systems of power reproduce themselves independent of control by the overlords or even by political economic imperatives.

Systems which expand in this way — and this critique would include medicine, education, social services and crime control — lack the rationality which materialist theories attribute to them. Pragmatic as their ideology often is, this is 'ritualistic pragmatism',[27] the ritual of the nurse waking the patient to take his sleeping pill on time. Budgets are spent, manpower increased, resources continually used, evaluation research commissioned without any of this being dependent on success. Indeed, even when failure is apparent — Illich's 'second threshold', the point beyond which costs outweigh benefits — investment will still increase irrespective of the quality of the services.[28] Despite periodic 'crisis talk' in the crime-control establishment (it would be impossible to count how many commissions, conferences and papers have been organized around the themes of crisis, turning point and crossroads), continual failure is a condition for survival.

We are back at the history of the prison itself — Rothman's story of 'legitimation in spite of failure'. Most theories find the sources of this legitimation at the level of the whole society. But we must also look at the daily discourse of the professionals and managers. At the soft end, it is the rhetoric of 'doing good' which functions now, as it did historically, to insulate the system from criticism, to explain away failure and to justify more of the same under the guise of novelty. This was how diversion and community control could expand: each rung of the ladder was benign, each of the new control and helping technologies promised salvation from the next.

In the therapeutic empire as well as the crime-control empire, the theory which so plausibly justifies this incremental growth, is the notion of an anticipatory syndrome which, if not dealt with properly, will lead to something worse. Those feedback loops in the organizational model depend, that is, on a particular theoretical loop. Such theories constitute the language, the 'cultural capital' of the helping professions. Words such as 'treatable', 'amenable', 'dangerous', 'pre-delinquent', 'at-risk', 'deserving' or 'pathological' become authoritative scientific definitions. They call for intervention, expansion, separate agencies and services.

But, as Edelman has so eloquently shown, such words are really 'mythic cognitive structures'.[29] Like words such as 'community', 'counselling', 'client', 'contracting', 'mediating' and 'training' they manage through metaphor, metonymy and syntax to convey 'rhetorical evocations' very far from their actual meaning. Edelman argues that, because the helping professions define other people's status, the terms which they use to categorize their clients and justify regulating or restricting them, reveal the essentially political function of language. Language creates multiple realities and, in particular, the bifurcatory reality of who is worthy and who is not, who should be sent straight to the hard end and who can be saved at the soft end: 'just as any single numerical evokes the whole number scheme in our mind, so a professional term, a syntactic form, or a metaphor with scientific connotations can justify a hierarchy of power for the person who uses it and for the groups that respond to it.'[30]

In the appendix, I refer again to Edelman's analysis of the professional language of helping and treating. The point is that the 'political' does not just belong to the realm of the macro. Here, in the language of the helping professions, the political system is also evoked, but this evocation is so subtle that both sides (the definers and the defined) can play out their roles without ever thinking in political terms. This is the power of the technical fix: 'when the power of professionals over other people is at stake, the language employed implies that the professional has ways to ascertain who are dangerous, sick or inadequate; that he or she knows how to render them harmless, rehabilitate them or both; and that the procedures for diagnosis and treatment are too specialized for the lay public to understand or judge them.'[31]

The great flexibility and potential of this language lies in its evocatory symbolism. It is this, as Edelman shows, that distinguishes it from simple deception. It is naive to think of terms such as 'community', 'diversion' or 'in need of care' as standing for particular places, objects or behaviour. They are symbols which condense, rearrange and mix up beliefs, speculations, perceptions, verified facts, expectations, memories and emotions. Most of the terms used by the helping professions combine a high degree of unreliability (in their diagnoses, prognosis and prescription of the right treatment), with an unambiguous set of constraints upon clients.

Any ambivalence about such constraints is resolved by appealing to the ultimate ends — treatment, mental health, welfare, law and order — which the professional wants us to share.[32] And, despite attacks on professions, this appeal is largely successful: 'the lay public by and large adopts the professional perspective; for its major concern is to believe that others can be trusted to handle these problems, which are potentially threatening to them but not a part of their everyday lives.'[33] Public reaction thus confers a licence on professionals and it allows them to spread their power.

The resolutions are not always as convincing as Edelman suggests, and they vary in their degree of tightness. Compare the USA to Britain, for example. In the USA, the psychobabble of treatment (Freudian or behaviourist) and the cultural obsession with naming everything, combines to provide a more total and unselfconscious linguistic insulation. Jargon, neologisms and acronyms are universally used to disguise reality. In Britain, euphemism rather than professional babble is the major form of linguistic mystification ('training', 'supervision', 'sanctuaries'). Social workers devote a great deal of tortuous self-reflection in deciding whether what they are doing is authority, influence, persuasion, advice, exhortation, intervention, enforcement, regulation, sanctioning or alas, after all, just plain 'control'.[34]

These vocabularies of helping and controlling belong to practitioners — those at the face-to-face edge of the system. But what about the more theoretical forms of knowledge? Here we have to look at criminology itself, conceived by many of its practitioners all over the world not just as a 'discipline' but as a profession.

COGNITIVE PASSION

For Foucault, the role of theoretical knowledge in the control system is obvious. Discourses like criminology were only called into being and are now only necessary to justify the imposition of punishment. They are alibis which allow the functionaries of the system to work with a semblance of good conscience, humanitarianism, even scientific status. 'Have you ever read any criminological text?' Foucault asks,

> They are staggering. And I say this out of astonishment, not aggressiveness, because I fail to comprehend how the discourse of criminology has been able to go on at this level. One has the impression that it is of such utility, is needed so urgently and rendered so vital for the working of the system, that it does not even need to seek a theoretical justification for itself, or even simply a coherent framework. It is entirely utilitarian.[35]

But 'utilitarian' seems to me too vague a term to comprehend this knowledge/power link, particularly in the light of the manifestly non-utilitarian nature of the deviancy control system. The term also does less than justice to the purely internal trajectory of academic knowledge. I am referring less to the liberal ideals of 'academic freedom' or 'uninterested pursuit of the truth' than to the incremental expansion of theoretical knowledge according to its own feedback loops. As a fellow academic, Foucault should not have been so astonished at the survival of criminology. The utility is internal (the journals, the jobs, the tenure decisions, the research applications and grants, the PhDs and the conferences) as well as geared to the system 'out there'. And the knowledge is much more disinterested than Foucault allows: as 'knowledge society' theorists suggest, intellectuals connected with state agencies are genuinely motivated by what Shils nicely called 'cognitive passion'.[36]

I will consider here two interdependent forms of criminological knowledge: on the one hand, evaluation and research and, on the other, testing and classification.

### What Works?

In criminology, cognitive passion used to be directed towards causation. To be sure, the quest was utilitarian (the correctional attitude was to find out the causes of crime in order to do something about it). But appreciation was also possible: it once seemed intellectually interesting to know why people committed crime. Now the Holy Grail of causation has been displaced by the Holy Grail of evaluation. Disillusioned with basic research and the quest for root causes, prepared to settle for limited intellectual horizons and constrained by the demands of funding agencies, criminologists started a decade ago asking the question, What works? As we saw when considering 'new behaviourism', the trend was to leave behind conventional causal questions and move in an even more explicitly technicist and correctional direction.

Programme evaluation and policy recommendation ('applied criminology') became the business of the day. This, undoubtedly, was where the research money lay, and criminologists have always followed what Raymond Mack once called the 'Reverse Midas Principle': whatever turns to gold, you touch. It is possible that evaluation research has already peaked — fewer innovative treatment programmes are being funded and so there is less to evaluate — and much academic criminology has stayed with more apparently 'academic' concerns. But in the less prestigious side of the discipline — criminal justice studies, private consultants, government agencies — criminology remains dominated by applied concerns.

The great advantage of the evaluation enterprise, is that it is not at all constrained by the lay public's naive utilitarian notion of what constitutes success and failure. In the same way as practitioners have ways to legitimate their failure to make things work very well, so evaluators develop strategies to deal with their failure to know what exactly does work. Like the search for the Golden Goose (to invoke another fable) the point is simply to keep hanging on to whoever last touched the source of power. The worse the crime problem becomes, the more professional growth can be justified. As David Bazelon, the Chief Judge of the US Court of Appeal reassured the Annual General Meeting of the American Society of Criminology in 1977: 'its subject matter alone makes American criminology a special profession. You have been charged with the understanding and management of our national nightmare. As our dreams have become more and more terrifying of late, so has your profession grown.'

What has been the special professional evaluation of correctional treatment? This was Martinson's original, famous 1974 conclusion (his 'bald summary' of 231 evaluation studies of rehabilitation in the correctional system): 'with few and isolated exceptions the rehabilitative efforts that have been reported so far have had no appreciable effect on recidivism.'[37] Programme after programme — intensive supervision, educational training, vocational training, group counselling, individual counselling — all produced inconclusive or ambiguous results. But, if the working language of helping and controlling has ways to cope with such ambiguities, so has the language of evaluation. The Golden Goose of 'effectiveness' has to keep its pursuers continually moving and hopeful. For Martinson and his colleagues, of course, never said 'nothing works'. They said either that most things work just as well as each other, or that the isolated instances of success produce no clear pattern to indicate the efficacy of any particular method. Moreover, 'it is just possible that some of our treatment programmes *are* working to some extent, but our research is so bad that it is incapable of telling.'[38]

Variations on this type of conclusion have appeared regularly over the last decade, and are now being reported for diversion and community control as well as rehabilitation in prison. Echoing Greenberg's earlier (1976) evaluation, Klein's 1979 review of 200 research reports concluded that all we can say is that some positive results are reported, some negative and some equivocal, and that the quality of evaluative research is weak.[39] Here is a typical evaluation finding. Placing status offenders in detention or a newer community based programme 'made no difference in terms of the numbers of subsequent offences and types of contact with the police or court. The youths in all groups seemed to improve about equally after intervention.'[40]

Not exactly 'nothing works' but rather 'we're not sure what causes the modest successes which have always been apparent.' There are two further findings which evaluation research often throws up. The first is that the best predictors of what works often lie in the offender rather than the mode of treatment. That is, a few simple variables such as offence record, employment history and educational level are the statistically most significant predictors of success. The second finding (which the more acute and honest of evaluators like Leslie Wilkins have been pointing out for many years) is that 'least is better'. The most complicated, expensive and intensive programmes are not any better, and sometimes worse, than the simplest. In cost-benefit terms, a fine is probably the best form of 'correctional treatment'. 'For the sick, the least is best', said Hippocrates, or in Illich's version: 'for a wide range of conditions, those who are treated least probably make the best progress.'[41]

To find clear statements of this kind actually recorded in the evaluation literature is, however, virtually impossible. The baroque language of the people-processing professions is matched by the equally obfuscating nature of research talk. No human being outside the research establishment can possibly grasp what goes on in producing an evaluation report or, even less, in producing models and guidelines for doing or writing evaluations. Organizations in the USA such as the Office of Development, Testing and Dissemination of the National Institute of Law Enforcement and Criminal Justice not only regularly produce such guidelines but publish glossaries on how to understand them. Evaluation talk is not nonsense but meta-nonsense, a more-or-less random arrangement in chapters, boxes, arrows and flowcharts of phrases such as: data collection points; needs assessment scales; goal progress charts; the hierarchical pyramid of goals, subgoals, basic objectives and action objective; programme completion criteria; programmatic activity evaluation forms; follow up assessment; outcome comparisons . . .

Now a certain amount of technical jargon is, of course, necessary and unavoidable. And the methodological problems of evaluation research are extremely complex — at some point even beyond the non-professional's grasp. But buried in the multi-variate-programme-outcome-analysis records, something like the following findings might be found. This — in descending order of certainty — is how you might explain the literature to an intelligent 10-year-old:

(1) most things don't work very well;
(2) some things work moderately;
(3) we're not sure what works better than anything else;
(4) 'type of offender' tells more about what might work than 'type of method';
(5) within the range of this uncertainty zone, doing less is probably better than doing more (outside this zone, the death penalty obviously 'works').

None of these rules should be particularly surprising. Earlier enthusiasts are now saying that it was crazy all along to believe that individual treatment could be effective. Radicals wearily note that surely no-one could expect the capitalist state to come up with any measure that could affect individual criminality. And evaluation pros, like Martinson, originally pointed out that the public anyway are not interested in whether an E group shows a lower recidivism rate than a C group; what it wants to know is whether the intervention reduced the overall crime rate.

Here is Ryan's savage conclusion from all this:

We could mindlessly double and redouble these billions poured down the 'criminal justice' rathole. We could spend another five or ten billion to build more prisons. We could increase our annual budget for police and prison guards from 10 billion to 20 billion. Or 40 billion. The results would scarcely be noticeable . . . the relationship between police and prisons on the one hand and crime and criminals on the other hand is so slight as to be almost non-existent.[42]

This angry rhetoric is a little exaggerated. But even if we reduce it to something like my child's guide, it should be apparent that the evaluation business is yet another endogenous form of system expansion. It can grow, without being very much affected by what happens 'out there'. The 'nothing works' fall out has certainly influenced criminal justice policy — mainly, as I describe in chapter 7, by diminishing the humane edge which the treatment model provided at its best. But this sort of influence emerged from external ideological and political changes rather than any drawing of logical conclusions from evidence.

The empirical demonstration of ineffectiveness has very little to do with the shape and size of the system. If we look not at the business of treating the offender (by any standards a difficult task) but psychotherapy with voluntary patients, there is no hint that professional growth could be curtailed by research showing the highly equivocal nature of therapeutic effectiveness. Let us look, for example, at Strupp and Hadley's famous comparison between 'specific' and 'non-specific' factors in psychotherapy.[43]

Students with various psychiatric symptoms (anxiety, depression), comparable to adults applying to a typical psychiatric outpatient clinic, were divided into three carefully matched groups. Group 1 were treated by highly experienced psychotherapists, selected for their clinical reputation and with some 23 years' average professional experience. Group 2 were treated by various college professors in subjects like English, history or mathematics. They had no clinical training and were selected on the basis of their reputation for warmth, trustworthiness and interest in students. Group 3 received no therapy at all, but were tested at intervals.

The results were clear enough. The young men treated by college professors (Group 2) showed on average as much improvement as the patients treated by experienced professional therapists. The improvements appeared during the treatment period and were maintained a year after follow-up. The no-treatment group also improved, but not as much. What works, it appeared, was not knowledge and skill but the 'healing effects of a benign human relationship'. Or, in the researchers' own reluctant words, 'it does seem fair to conclude that given a carefully specified and protected context, mature and competent individuals even in the absence of professional training, can engage appropriate patients in an interpersonal relationship whose outcome is therapeutic.'[44]

The point, again, is not that 'nothing works'. What most meta-evaluations of evaluation research show is that *most* patients who go through *any* form of psychotherapy gain something from it. As Luborsky and his colleagues suggest, the dodo-bird verdict is justified: 'everyone has won and all must have prizes.'[45] Their 1975 review of all existing reasonably controlled comparisons of psychotherapies with each other (and with other treatments) produced the classic 'tie score effect'. Most comparative studies show quite insignificant differences in the proportion of patients who improve by the end and a high proportion of patients who go through any of these therapies gain from them.[46]

In the criminal justice system, the only difference is that it is a *low* proportion who gain from what is done to them or who are stopped from committing further offences. The following example is shocking even if it is not representative of all criminal justice systems in the world today. British prison statistics for 1982 reveal that 66 per cent of all young males discharged in 1979 were reconvicted for an indictable (serious) offence within two years; for 14- to 16-year-olds sent to detention centres, the figure was 72 per cent; for 15- to 16-year-olds sent to Borstal training, 83 per cent; for 16- to 20-year-olds imprisoned, 69 per cent. The dodo-bird verdict will have to be slightly different for delinquency than for emotional disturbance. Not 'everyone has won and all must have prizes' but 'no-one has won and no-one can have prizes'.

This, needless to say, is not how the professionals see things. Over the whole decade since the public registered the Martinson effect massive intellectual resources have been devoted to neutralizing its more damaging implications. Endless research reports, polemics, and even an enquiry of the National Academy of Sciences, have suggested, variously, that:

• Martinson's original meta-evaluation was simply wrong,
• the 'nothing works' conclusion is far too sweeping, too pessimistic and out of date;
• effective forms of treatment are possible under the right conditions;
• recidivism should not be the only criterion for success.

Even Martinson himself is seen to have partially recanted by admitting that under different conditions the same programme might have different effects.

In any event, the current consensus among the evaluation professionals is said to be qualified, guarded and cautious.[47] Compared to the optimism of the sixties and the nihilism of the mid-to-late seventies, the prospects for effective treatment now seem a bit brighter. To be sure, most research is still mediocre and most rehabilitation efforts 'have probably been unsuccessful thus far relative to their overall target groups', but many programmes work with specified offenders under specified conditions. This is hardly a joyous message. Palmer (a leading *optimist*) provides the following summary of 'today's officially sanctioned position': 'no single correctional program (and therefore no broadly categorized method) has been unequivocally proven to reduce the recidivism of its target groups; that is, using very strict standards of evidence, none has been shown to work beyond almost all doubt. At any rate, none can be guaranteed to work.'[48]

To me, this sounds a great deal like 'no-one has won and no-one can have prizes.' But no matter. These statistical games, the nuances and glosses with which one can read this or that research report, the new tone of cautious optimism — all this is of no political significance. The real heart of the 'what works?' debate and real basis for system expansion, lies in the ideology of *classification* — the ideology which has always legitimated professional interest. The true ideal is proper matching. Results would be better if only we could find the right match between type of offender, type of treatment method, type of treatment setting and type of professional ('change agent'). As Palmer put it in his initial attack on Martinson, 'various methods of intervention are more likely to be associated with positive behavioural outcome (less recidivism) in relation to some offenders compared with others.'[49]

In the current jargon, the choice is between the BTA position (Basic Treatment Amenability), which asserts that certain offenders will respond to most methods and most offenders will respond to few if any methods, and the more optimistic DI position (Differential Intervention), which hopes to generalize about which method works with which offenders under which conditions.[50] But BTA or DI, the question is the same: not 'what works?', but 'what works, with what offender, where, by whom, how and why?' And to a question like this, there can only be one response: more intervention, more selection, more classification, more evaluation research. The further you get from the Golden Goose of success, the more frenetic and complicated does the pursuit become, the more impossible it is to let go.

It is here that power, knowledge and 'guild advantage' meet.

The practitioners' interest in continuing to do more or less what they have always done is complemented by the researchers' cognitive passion to find the right system of classification and matching. And in their complimentary quest, both types of professionals depend on exactly the same instrument – the test. Somewhere, they feel, there must be the right technique for discrimination, selection, diagnosis, screening, classification and matching. Without this, there is no intervention and no evaluation research. This is the only aspect of the control system where there are no ideological differences, where all interests coincide.

## Testing, Testing

Ever since the case history came into being, the people-processing professions have received a collective licence for gathering information. Foucault describes the significance of this historical moment as the point where the lives of ordinary people become individualized as well as the lives of kings, princes and generals. The examination allowed the process of judging people to be 'normalized'. Time (lateness), activity (inattention); speech (idle chatter) body (incorrect dress), are judged and made the objects of small-scale penal systems reproduced throughout society. The child, the patient, the madman and the prisoner enter into files, biographies and case records. The representation of real lives in writing is no longer confined to heroes. Quite the reverse: as power becomes more anonymous, those on whom it is exercised become more individualized. The moment when the human sciences are possible is when technology individualizes children more than adults, the sick rather than the healthy, the mad rather than the sane, the delinquent rather than the law abiding.[51] This was to be not cognitive passion for its own sake, but useful information as well. In every corner of care, control and health systems – social work reports, police files, psychiatric case histories, psychological diagnostic tests, institutional records – massive amounts of information about the individual deviant were collected and processed. If only we knew the right information, at the right time and could match it to the right method, then we would know what to do. Something would start to work.

Little of the critical work on professions and bureaucracies has come to terms with the significance of all this information. Influenced by visions of *Nineteen Eighty-Four*, most critics of the business of information gathering have concentrated on the harder, more political edge of the system. There is a massive literature on the political and civil libertarian issues of privacy, security, confidentiality and the right to know. Anxiety is directed at the technological possibilities of computerized data banks; the building-up of discrediting dossiers; the dangers of centralized access to all record systems (from schools, hospitals, clinics, welfare agencies, banks, credit-card companies); the use of surveillance systems for preventive policing and political control; the potential misuses of criminal justice systems such as SEARCH (System for Electronic Analysis and Retrieval of Criminal History).

This is the familiar territory of dystopian literature: the threat of creating an 'information prison' which is really another form of social control. Much of this anxiety might be justified (though the totalitarian potential of information gathering is perhaps weakened by the natural inefficiency of bureaucracy in dealing with all this information). At the soft end of the system, however, cognitive passion is largely unquestioned. The very same liberals who worry themselves about the political implications of knowledge gathering and storage, lose little sleep about the testing and research operations of the helping professions. For knowledge here appears not to be linked to the direct exercise of political power, but is part of the expert, professional and largely benevolent enterprise of classification. The softer and more benevolent the system appears, particularly when the medical model is invoked, the more rational and unquestionable appears the business of classification. Who could possibly object to the logic of collecting information, in order to reach the right 'diagnosis' and hence prescribe the right 'treatment'?

There is, indeed, little to be apprehensive about. Most of the information generated and stored in the system is less harmful than useless. It circulates in a self-contained system of knowledge and power where its primary function — as it has been for more than a century — is to allow the system to expand and diversify even further. The whole business of information gathering, diagnosis, classification, screening and matching is a classic example of professional interests at work.

Let me give an altogether banal contemporary example of the potential for growth in this information business. To make diversion work, a scientific form of bifurcation had to be found, that is a system which could sort out potential divertees from those destined for the hard end. One of the methods devised for the job was the 'pre-sentence investigation unit'. These appendanges not only increased and complicated the information from traditional social work or probation reports, but set up formal *teams* of investigators. As one enthusiastic team member reminds us: 'we all know the old adage that two heads are better than one and this concept is one of the axioms of the State of Washington's Pre Sentence Investigation Unit.'[52] Not just two heads, however, but many, many jobs: some probation and parole officers to investigate and dictate reports, and others there as 'experts in community resources'; a psychiatrist or psychologist, of course; the 'unit supervisor' making the final diagnosis and evaluation; and specialists in 'sexual deviance, alcoholism, negligent homicide, cultural and social anthropology'.

Orwell's terrible image of totalitarianism was the boot eternally trampling a human face. My vision of social control is much more mundane and assuring. It is the eternal case conference, diagnostic and allocations board or pre-sentence investigation unit. Serious-looking PhDs are sitting around a table. Each is studying the same computerized records, psychological profiles, case histories, neat files punched out on the word processor. The atmosphere is calm. Everyone present knows that no amount of criticism of individual treatment methods, no empirical research, no dodo-bird verdicts can slow the work down. The reverse is true. The more negative the results, the more manic and baroque the enterprise of selection becomes: more psychological tests, more investigation units, more pre-sentence reports, more post-sentence allocation centres, more contract forms, more case summaries, more referral notations, more prediction devices.

At some point, this is truly disinterested cognitive passion. For who can believe, after all these years, that rational, utilitarian goals really keep this system moving? At the hard end there *is* rationality. To refine the judgement of who should be sent to prison makes good ideological and economic sense. Principles such as selective incapacitation depend heavily on an efficient system of clinical or (better still) statistical prediction. It makes good sense to invest resources on perfecting such systems. But once this crude sorting out has been made — who is the hard core of the hard core — then all the other finer classifications have little rational point, for the simple reason that they cannot be matched to treatment modalities which 'work'.

At the periphery of the system, cognitive passion is perhaps neither interested nor disinterested. We are dealing more with ritual magic, incantations, dances, shamanism and divination. SIMBAD (Simulation As a Basis for Social Agents Decision) was a fine name for the computer program used by some probation departments in California to obtain probability estimates for success of disposition and treatment decisions. You feed in information about the offender and then magically receive a probability estimate of the success of each disposition.

These mythic journeys are increasingly organized by computers, statisticians and mathematical modellers. And, given the trend to behaviourism, it is likely that the information collected at the hard end will deal with crude behavioural details rather than the refined diagnostic categories of positivism (some two hundred categories were coded for SIMBAD). But, at the soft end, psychological information dominates. What are being cast during the ritual incantations are not bones but tests. At each stage of the process — diagnosing the client, allocating him to the right treatment modality, measuring progress during and after treatment — the grids, subtypes and subscales have got to be cast and then divined.[53]

And with what passion and ingenuity this is done! Imagine the budgets, personnel, resources, time and professional skill needed for the construction, pre-testing, application and evaluation of all those tests and then the reports, journal papers, doctoral theses, and cross-cultural validations. Each test evokes its own magical world: the Gough—Peterson Socialization Scale; the Minnesota Multi Phasic Personality Inventory; the Wunderlic Personnel Test; the Burse—Durkee Hostility Inventory; the Marlowe—Crown Social Desirability Scale; the Jesness Inventory; the Piers—Harris Self Esteem Measure; the Acceptable Behaviour Scale; the Criminal Behaviour Severity Index; the Assertion Inventory; the California Psychological Inventory; the Sarbin Scale for Measuring Conduct Impairment; the Mylonas Measurement of Attitudes Towards Law and Law Enforcement; the Crissman Moral Judgement Scale; the Nowicki—Strickland Locus of Control Scale . . .

Perhaps, after all, Foucault's 'astonishment' about the existence of criminology is justified. It is difficult to take seriously an intellectual 'discipline' whose members are doing something like this (a composite model of current soft-end evaluation research)

- they test experimental and control groups on a battery of instruments (like those listed above);
- they solemnly record and compute the results;
- they record what happens in a programme by using 'process assessment devices' such as 'life domain surveys', or 'intervention schedules';

- they discover that there are no before-and-after differences on any of tests between the E and C groups; and
- they end up calling for more research, finer instruments and a better matching of clients with treatment modalities and agents.

All this is what Illich has called (in a different context) 'shadow work'. It is more ritualistic and self-serving however than the 'phantom research' in medicine in which drug companies sponsor hundreds of research papers each year (spending on the author of each paper an average of $6,000 in honoraria and expenses) to show that trademarked products are superior to their generic equivalents.[54] The conclusion of most papers is that there are no medically significant differences. But this can be a useful finding, and the information on which it is based can be fully valid and reliable. The psychological information used in evaluation research, however — the raw material fed into consumers like SIMBAD — is usually of more dubious value. Here are two random examples of the sort of information on which classification, matching, treatment and evaluation are based.

First, in an 'educational centre' in Providence, to which diverted youths were committed, the staff (teachers, social workers, counsellors and administrators) maintained a 'Behaviour Observation Check System'.[55] Youths were allocated to four behaviour types identified as: (i) satisfactory (socially adjusted); (ii) needs some work (identifies with peer culture); (iii) needs a great deal of work (conforms to peer culture); (iv) unsatisfactory (anti-social, either aggressive or passive). Behaviour was monitored in areas like general appearance, foresight, resourcefulness, punctuality, dependability, participation, cooperation and response to criticism. For example, under 'Response to Criticism', there were the four possible classifications.

(1) Accepts constructive criticism in the manner in which it is given. Attempts to see its validity and strives to change in accordance with criticism when it is shown to be valid.
(2) Generally accepts constructive criticism. Sometimes argumentative but makes effort to change when convinced it is to his advantage to do so.
(3) Listens to constructive criticism attentively, generally accepts criticism but on his own terms. May appear to be responsive to go his own way.
(4) Not able to accept constructive criticism. Aggressive: may refuse to listen, become hostile or defensive. Passive: may

listen but demonstrates limited ability to understand or to respond in any positive way.

As the second example, here are some extracts from the 'Client's Residential Program Form' recommended as a *model* to follow when recording progress in half-way houses. These social evaluations are to be completed at the third staff meeting following a client's entrance into the programme and then again one week prior to his departure:

> *Level of awareness:* (1) very confused and imperceptive, (2) somewhat oblivious to social situation, (3) average level of alertness, (4) good degree of awareness, (5) very alert and perceptive . . .
>
> *Emotional responsiveness:* (1) dull, very little variation in feeling, (2) blunted, some variation in feeling, (3) emotions vary appropriately with situation, (4) somewhat exaggerated, (5) somewhat strong and fast: hot-headed . . .
>
> *Candor:* (1) positive efforts to deceive, (2) attempts to shade truth, (3) average level of honesty, (4) willing to reveal truth, (5) forthright and open.[56]

It might be objected that these are poor examples. More sophisticated psychology can surely generate better-quality information. This is no doubt true. But even if the information is totally comprehensive and accurate, the question is, what difference does it make to decisions or outcomes? That same guide to half-way house evaluation which takes such note of awareness, emotional responsiveness and candour also informs us that

> previous research suggests that significant relationships exist between programme completion (or success) as well as successful re-integration, and such variables as education, intelligence, marriage, sex age, employment skills, history of drugs or alcohol problems, community ties, length of time at the halfway house, history of psychiatric treatment, age at beginning of criminal career, number of prior incarcerations and type and length of criminal record.[57]

Given that 'programme completion (or success)' and 'successful reintegration' must naturally also be defined and measured according to an equally long list of variables, another way of saying all this is 'we haven't got the slightest idea why some people do better than others'.

The fact that collecting this information, particularly the finer psychological variety about emotions, awareness and moral character, is 'shadow work', has long ago been proved by another branch of academic psychology. Cognitive research on decision making suggests that the more complex the range of information presented to an individual, the more likely will judgements be made according to the most simple and obvious variables. This has been found time and time again. In criminal-justice decision making, in probation-officer recommendations or sentencing or parole-release decisions, the mass of information collected, the hundreds of variables from tests and life histories are of little or no importance. What counts are the crude variables of offence serious-ness, past record and social status. Silverman's summary of the research evidence was that all but 7–10 per cent of sentences imposed can be explained by court norms about *offence* and *prior record.*[58]

This is at the level of the individual decision maker. At the system level, we also know what happens when information be-comes too complex. The tension between individual need and standardized judgement simply becomes too much to manage. The system becomes arbitrary and irrational. Not only do none of those diagnoses and tests predict individualized treatment decisions, but even the 'rational' behaviourist criterion of of-fence seriousness can break down. A typical outcome is what Krisberg calls 'justice by geography': massive discrepancies in admission rates to institution, length of confinement, conditions and overcrowding not attributable to different rates or types of crime.[59]

Even if an absolutely foolproof way of classifying individuals could be worked out, the grid of all grids, on to which every offender could be placed, the exercise would be totally meaning-less unless each sub-class could be matched to the appropriate treatment or punitive 'modality'. An equally perfect way of classi-fying institutions, agencies and methods must, therefore, be devised. This was the problem which obsessed nineteenth-century prison managers (with their fine internal classifications of dis-ciplinary techniques) and their contemporary successors with their classification of different types of prisons (maximum, medium and minimum security; closed, semi-closed and open). Now the move to community demands a classification system to cover the whole correctional continuum. Particularly important, as we saw in chapter 2, is the degree of 'community basedness' of each agency.

So the agency as well as the individual has to be 'tested'. Teams of researchers descend on institutions examining not level of awareness, emotional responsiveness or candour, but size of building, colour of dining-room walls, number of permitted visitors, access to telephone and distance to the nearest grocery store. On this basis, the agency is placed on an 'institutionalization—normalization continuum'.[60] We learn, for example, from this research that 'forestry camps and ranches' fall below zero on 'extent and quality of community linkage', while 'children living with older sisters' score high on such variables. Another way is to rate institutions according to MEAP (Multiphasic Environmental Assessment Procedure), PASS (Program Analysis of Service Systems) or MARSY (Multicomponent Assessment for Residential Services for Youth).[61]

There can be no end to this business. The variety of human beings and what can be done to them defies perfect matching, especially when we have so little idea of 'what works'. But perhaps, as the progressive model of control policy assumes, one day things will get better.

'Shadow work', 'ritualism', 'magic', 'self-serving professional aggrandizement' . . . these are, after all, harsh judgements to make of the innocuous and well-intentioned business of testing and classifying. Let me turn again to psychology for a final and more charitable interpretation. 'The more complicated the better' is perhaps not just a rule to ensure indefinite occupational growth, but a deeply rooted psychological tendency. It is worth quoting at length from Watslawik's summary of one of Alex Bavelas's small group experiments.

In one experiment, two subjects, A and B, are seated facing a projection screen. There is a partition between them so that they cannot see each other, and they are requested not to communicate. They are then shown medical slides of healthy and sick cells and told that they must learn to recognize which is which by trial and error. In front of each of them are two buttons marked 'Healthy' and 'Sick', respectively, and two signal lights marked 'Right' and 'Wrong'. Every time a slide is projected they have to press one of the buttons, whereupon one of the two signal lights flashes on.

A gets true feedback; that is, the lights tell him whether his guess was indeed right or wrong. His situation is one of simple discrimination, and in the course of the experiment, most A subjects learn to distinguish healthy from sick cells with a fair degree of correctness (i.e., about 80 percent of the time).

B's situation is very different. His feedback is based not on his own guesses, but on A's. Therefore it does not matter what he decides about a particular slide; he is told 'right' if A guessed right, 'wrong' if A guessed wrong. B does not know this; he has been led to believe there is an order, that he has to discover this order, and that he can do so by making guesses and finding out if he was right or wrong. But as he asks the 'sphinx' he gets very confusing answers because he does not know that the sphinx is not talking to *him*. In other words, there is no way in which he can discover that the answers he gets are non-contingent – that is, have nothing to do with his questions – and that therefore he is not learning anything about his guesses. So he is searching for an order where there is none that *he* could discover.

A and B are eventually asked to discuss what they have come to consider the rules for distinguishing between healthy and sick cells. A's explanations are simple and concrete: B's are of necessity very subtle and complex – after all, he had to form his hypothesis on the basis of very tenuous and contradictory hunches.

The amazing thing is that A does not simply shrug off B's explanations as unnecessarily complicated or even absurd, but is impressed by their sophisticated 'brilliance'. A tends to feel inferior and vulnerable because of the pedestrian simplicity of his assumption, and the more complicated B's 'delusions', the more likely they are to convince A . . .

Before they take a second, identical test (but with new slides), A and B are asked to guess who will now do better than in his first test. All Bs and most As say that B will. In actual fact, B shows hardly any improvement, but comparatively speaking; seems to be doing better because A, who now shares at least some of B's abstruse ideas, performs significantly more poorly than the first time.

What Bavelas' ingenious experiment teaches us has far-reaching consequences: it shows that once a tentative explanation has taken hold of our minds, information to the contrary may produce not corrections but *elaborations* of the explanation. This means that the explanation becomes 'self-sealing'; it is a conjecture that cannot be refuted.[62]

The type of criminological knowledge useful for control systems is useful just because it is 'self-sealing' in this way. Policy makers veer between the fate of the hapless B with his non-contingent decisions and the even more pathetic A who becomes victim to eternal elaboration.

## TOWARDS THE CLASSIFIED SOCIETY

Let me return to those original early nineteenth-century transformations. But now, instead of seeing state centralization, segregation, mind control or professionalism as the crucial changes, imagine the enterprise of classification to be the centre of power.

The great projects of discipline, normalization, control, segregation and surveillance described by the historians of this transition were all projects of classification. Foucault's version of this history conveys this element most clearly. His theory is curiously close to functionalism, labelling theory and to Illich's notion of iatrogenic growth: the system is non-rational and non-utilitarian in that it creates and classifies deviance rather than seeks to eliminate it. Foucault, indeed, greatly exaggerates this irony: the prison system has *nothing* to do with turning offenders into honest citizens; it simply manufactures new criminals, drives offenders deeper into criminality and recruits them to the criminal class. The regrouping of delinquents into a 'clearly demarcated card-indexed milieu' is seen by Foucault as a typical episode in the mechanics of power: the prison fails, so now there takes place 'a strategic utilization of what had been experienced as a drawback'.[63]

There is no need, however, to accept all the implications of this rather crude type of left-functionalism to see how the emerging control system neither prevented nor eliminated crime but translated it into different terms. The unorderly and inefficient world of eighteenth-century crime control gave way to a regulated, ordered universe. The bifurcatory form became theorized and formalized: the criminal to be separated from the poor, the poor to be divided up into deserving and undeserving, the criminal then to be divided into bad and mad. The asylum, the closed institution, performed the initial sorting out. This was the roughest filter. Then, within the asylum, all sorts of elaborate and intricate systems of classification began to evolve. Students of nineteenth-century prisons describe institutions in which up to 29 separate categories of inmate were worked out.[64] The logical end of the process was solitary confinement – each individual in his own category. In the idealized panopticon, each one of these cells could be observed totally by a few unseen people. The exposure to cognitive passion was absolute – the smallest gestures, the merest words could be observed, described, classified and compared.

Eventually these elaborate systems inside broke down because of their sheer complexity. But the passion for classification remained, to be redefined and made scientific by the twentieth-century enterprise of scientific testing. The elaborate systems inside the prison are duplicated by the equally elaborate systems outside – the new 'continuum of community corrections' with all its fine gradations and notations.

The obsession with classification is truly baroque, something like the life work of a mid-European lepidopterist. And the whole enterprise is largely spurious, not just because of the difficulty of matching people to methods, but because changes in control policy keep demanding new schemes of classification. Each part of the system starts with its own selection criteria to accommodate the 'right' client around whom the regime or service was designed and for whom a particular professional specialism exists. But if there are not enough 'right' clients – not enough, that is who fit the selection criteria for the diversion agency, community correctional centre, half-way house or prison – then the norm changes. Other clients are admitted, the regime is altered accordingly and a new technology of selection has to be devised.

Like methods of punishment or treatment themselves, these classification systems may or may not 'work'. The category might be too broad or too narrow, the wrong candidate might be selected. Sometimes these mistakes can prove fatal, particularly at the output end where an offender might be classified as 'safe' to be released, but turns out to be dangerous. But these forms of failure are perfectly suited for the crime-control system. Unlike the failure of a correctional measure itself, the 'failure' of a classification system rarely evokes troublesome ideological questions and never threatens professional interests. It simply calls for more and better classification – an agenda which can be followed with total agreement from everyone. Liberals and conservatives, reformers and managers, psychologists and guards, all are committed to seeking further refinements to whichever bifurcation they are concerned with – soft or hard, treatable or untreatable, safe or dangerous. The non-contingent nature of these refinements matters not at all.

Nor do fads and fashions in penal philosophy matter very much. At first sight, the just-deserts movement and the attack on rehabilitation seem to threaten the whole edifice of individual classification. But the various judicial modes within classicism and the disciplinary or treatment modes within positivism are more complementary than they appear. At one point, Foucault gives a pleasing explanation of the 'furious desire' of judges to assess, diagnose, receive reports and listen to experts (even the 'chatter of criminology'): it was as if they were ashamed to pass sentence.[65] But as he shows, the need to classify runs deeper than this; I will try to simplify his tortuous and confusing 'history'.[66]

(1) The form of punishment in the great codification reforms of the eighteenth century simply refers the offence to a corpus of law which contains a single binary classification: the legal

opposition betwen permitted and forbidden, with prescribed categories of reaction.

(2) Though it has to appear general and universal, a precisely adapted code, in fact, is aimed at individualization. Punishment has to be finely calibrated 'with neither excesses nor loopholes, with neither a useless expenditure of power nor with timidity'. There was little psychological knowledge in the eighteenth century (tests, examinations, etc.) to supply this 'code-individualization link', so this Linnaeus-type taxonomy has to be found elsewhere. Criteria such as the repetition of the crime could be used to make the tactics of power more efficient.

(3) When the new disciplinary society emerges, so does a psychology of classification. The mind, not the body, the actor, not the act become the judicial object. The offender is examined, assessed and normalized — his 'soul' is brought before the court. This is not only to explain his action or to establish extenuating circumstances, nor to humanize the face of justice, but to reorganize yet again the economy of punishment. The new methods of punishment and treatment (aimed at changing the offender) have to be legalized. The individualized classifications, that is, have to be reproduced in the system as legal forms.

(4) The 'knowable man' now becomes the object of the human sciences. Inside and outside the court (but always sanctioned by the law) they begin testing, measuring, allocating each person to the correct space on which he can be differentiated.

At every stage, classification is deeply lodged in the framework of punishment. It is no less important for current deterrence theory (punish just enough to prevent repetition) or current just-deserts theory (punish just enough to redress the social balance). And even if they are not very good at matching, even if they are not too sure what works, and even if the court has a somewhat less than 'furious desire' to listen to them, the professional classifiers are still at work. In every judicial system we know, the number of social enquiry reports or recommendations submitted to the court grows incrementally. The soft/hard bifurcation makes the professional classifier even more important.

As we move away from sentencing into the punitive apparatus itself, the urge to classify remains. In prisons, the magic wand of classification has long been held out as the key to a successful system. If only those who mess up the regime could be weeded out (sent to special prisons, units or isolation centres), the system could go ahead with its business. All that has changed over the last century is the basis of the binary classification. It used to be 'moral character', sometimes it was 'treatability' or 'security risk', now it tends to be 'dangerousness'.

For example, at the end of the seventies, the Federal Bureau of Prisons set up a Task Force to investigate how to establish inmate 'custody level' in terms of dangerousness. They grouped the inmates according to 47 potentially significant factors from an initial list of 92 possibly relevant items, gathered from 329 staff. Institutions are grouped into a Security Designation Form according to 7 features, ending up with 6 security levels. Pertinent information is then teletyped to a central Designation Desk. Stepwise Multiple Regression is used to test validity. Each inmate has a Unit/Classification Team working with a Custody Classification Form.[67]

At the softer, community end, the classification business, as we have seen, lacks the rationality of models such as 'dangerousness', 'security risk' or 'incapacitation' (which can all be empirically validated). There are just endless pirouettes between psychological characteristics (self-esteem, conduct impairment, hostility to authority); composite categories (risk, amenability, proneness); treatment modalities (reality theory, camping, behaviour contracting); and places (7.8 on the normalization scale?). Even cruder legal categories become shifting and uncertain. One official study commissioned to solve the problem of *who* were the 'status offenders' to be deinstitutionalized, found that 46 classifications were being used, and that, for the most part, these had no effect on the selection of target groups.[68] This last project is an example of the convergence of academic with managerial and professional interests. There are workers who devise classification systems, others who operate them and meta-workers who classify these operations. Some professionals specialize entirely in the area. In one American enterprise, some 10 federal agencies, 31 task forces and 93 experts got together to study the impact of classification systems for children.[69]

To study the *impact* of classification systems though, is quite a different matter from joining the quest for the Golden Goose of systems that 'work'. For despite their apparently self-sealing logic, classification systems do indeed have an impact on the external world. Professional expansion is directed towards creating new categories of deviance and social problems, that is defining more people as belonging to special populations and then slotting them into one or other category. This is what labelling theory – correctly – means by the socially constructed nature of deviance. Professionals play a crucial role in making claims about the boundaries of the category and then ruling on who belongs to it.[70]

The logic of professionalism requires either that these boundaries be expanded to bring in new populations or that they be changed to relocate old populations. Types of deviance such as homosexuality, hyperactivity or drug abuse, the very nature of mental illness itself, categories such as dangerous, treatable or high-risk, have all been subject to this type of boundary adjustment. This is what happens in what sociologists variously call the 'politics of deviance', 'stigma contests', 'reality negotiations' and the 'power to criminalize'. But the real significance of classification lies in the form, not the content, the enterprise itself and not its end-results. The power to classify is the purest of all deposits of professionalism.

This is what Orwell meant when he said that the object of power is power. And this is what Foucault meant when reminding us that power is not just a force which excludes and says 'No', but a form of creation: 'we should not be content to say that power has a need for such and such a discovery, such and such a form of knowledge, but we should add that the exercise of power itself creates and causes to emerge new objects of knowledge and accumulates new bodies of information.'[71]

# 6
# Visions of Order

Any topic of interest in the social sciences has a peculiarly amorphous quality. It looks distinct, tangible, separate — empirically or conceptually — but the closer you examine it, the more it merges into its surrounding space. So it is with crime control. A matter of restricted scope, the subject of the parochial discipline of criminology, starts dissolving into much wider issues: political ideologies, the crisis in welfare liberalism, the nature of professional power, conceptions of human nature. This chapter embraces such dissolution: the deconstruction of crime control as a separate subject. We move into spaces which are not just amorphous, but imagined and imaginary.

## THE DYSTOPIAN ASSUMPTION

The beginning and the end of the nineteenth century marked two of the more utopian moments in crime-control history. At the beginning were those Great Transformations with which this book started. The founders of the penitentiary system in America and Europe were confident that they could devise a solution to the crime problem, a solution that would result in a better society. Rothman describes well this spirit of optimism, the explicit utopian thinking which informed the design of the asylums. And at the end of the century came the positivist 'revolution' in criminology. Whether it was genuinely innovatory or merely an elaborate justification of existing policy, the new 'science' of criminology took its message from the more general faith in scientific progress. Science and technology (and not just a belief in doing good) could solve social problems and create a new social order.

While these agendas are set by political and economic contingencies, the very idea that a social problem is solvable needs an appropriate belief system. Some beliefs are favourable and others unfavourable to planned intervention. [1] Those nineteenth-century moments of crime control contained favourable beliefs about two constants in the human predicament: human nature and the social order. The crime problem had always presented many awkward cognitive impediments to intervention: original sin, Calvinist ideas of predisposition, social Darwinism and the fatalism even within early biological versions of criminological positivism ('crime as destiny'). But once these beliefs could be neutralized, by-passed or forgotten, the way was open. If only the right combination of benevolence and technology could be found, even the worst of people could be changed and a better social order created.

We have already encountered some of the many twentieth-century assaults on these beliefs: pessimism about changing human nature, scepticism about organized benevolence, disenchantment with progress, distrust of technology, a willingness to settle for limited horizons. This was and is the new 'realism' of crime control. I want now to retrace these beliefs and counter-beliefs, and locate them in the wider context of utopian and dystopian visions. This is not in order to indulge in cheap futurology but rather to show how social-control ideology is deeply embedded in these more general predictions, fantasies, visions and expectations.

By the time that criminological positivism was establishing itself, the social sciences as a whole had taken it for granted that an analysis of the past and the present could be directed towards visualizing the future. As Kumar notes in his excellent guide to the sociology of industrial society: 'when sociology arrived in Europe early in the nineteenth century, it marked a strand of thinking about man and society that was increasingly directed towards the future.'[2] This strand became dominant as sociologists came to dwell on the Great Transformation which was to become their subject matter — the new social order of industrialism.

Not all this thinking, of course, was optimistic. We know Weber's forebodings about rationalization and bureaucracy, Marx's apocalyptic vision of what had to happen before the new social order could emerge. But an influential stream of these thinkers, represented by Comte, St Simon and the other 'prophets of progress', presented a much less complicated vision of the coming into being of the new social order. Social change was progressive; science and technology would usher in a new era; disease, misery and crime were capable of being vanquished.

With the obvious (though complicated) exception of Marx, few of these nineteenth-century social thinkers expressed themselves in the classic utopian form. Unlike in Plato's *Republic* or the original utopia of Thomas More, they were not constructing ideal societies. Theirs were not visions of what should be, but what is likely to be. And here, while never being quite as complacent as the literary and technological utopianists of their era, they were deeply influenced by the more general cultural optimism about science and technology.[3]

After the First World War, however, even this cautious optimism was to disappear. A bleaker, even apocalyptic world view became dominant. Ominous, irrational forces were at work which made human nature and social order far less amenable to change than had been thought. This was the 'sense of ending'. Moral and material progress were not the same; scientific advances would not necessarily bring happiness. All this is now seen as characteristic of the twentieth-century world view: cynicism, disillusionment, pessimism. This is the 'cheap wasteland philosophy' about which Saul Bellow's heroes muse so often.

In the social sciences, all those grand visions of progress and evolution were buried. Preoccupations became grandly abstract or minutely empirical. Within the limited fields that became known variously as social disorganization, social pathology, social problems and criminology, a degree of optimism remained. But it was only the degree needed to give credibility to the business of intervention. The evils of the big city, the disintegration of primary social control, the loss of community, the impersonality of technology — all such problems must get worse. Intervention could work, indeed it was desperately needed, but this was a rescue operation. The point was to save, treat or prevent the casualties of the machine. The social-problems industry remained the most optimistic part of the social sciences, but it was the optimism of the crusader, the muckraker, the lifesaver, and not the prophet of a new social order.

In the 1950s there was some sort of recovery. Industrialism seemed more resilient, and the new theorists of the 'managerial revolution', 'convergence' and the 'end of ideology' began to imply that the structural problems of industrialism were working themselves out.[4] A new note of complacency appeared which was not destined to last very long. By the 1960s the dark side of industrialism was rediscovered. It was not just the 'return' of ideology in the demands of Blacks and other ethnic minorities, gays and other groups labelled deviant, and the women's movement for a different place in the system, but a radical disenchantment with in-

dustrial progress itself. For many such groups, for the counter-
culture and the new left, and then for the ecology movement,
dystopia was already on the way. Most of all, the danger came
from the strong state; the quest for 'community' was an anti-
statist form of utopian thinking. The machine itself had to be
destroyed before it destroyed us. This, as I showed in chapter 4,
was the basis of the destructuring rhetoric. The old apparatus,
with its bureaucracies, institutions, professionals (words which
now acquired wholly negative meanings), had to be dismantled
or by-passed.

In the face of this apparent disintegration of the consensus,
theorists started constructing a new vision and a new ideology.
'Post-industrial society' was now on its way. This was claimed to
be a transformation which would eventually produce societies as
different from the classic industrial society of Marx, Weber and
Durkheim as theirs was in turn from early agrarian, pre-capitalist
formations. But as Kumar points out, neither the radical harbingers
of Future Shock, the Third Wave, the Greening of America nor
their more sober academic successors have shown just where this
qualitative leap is taking place.

For, despite the pretensions of post-industrial theorists, the
future which the real social world of 1984 indicates looks more
like an extension of the processes begun in the early nineteenth
century. Nothing very new needs to be added to that package of
concepts — formalization, rationalization, centralization, bureau-
cratization, professionalization — through which we understood
the coming of industrial society. Not a new social order, but more
of the same.

This, of course, was the burden of my account of the fate of
those radical destructuring movements. For what is true of the
social sciences and society in general, is no less true for criminology
and crime (and its control). The general literatures on futurology
and post-industrial society however, are remarkably silent about
crime and its control, while students of crime rarely articulate
more than a vague sense that things are getting worse.

Only one criminologist, Sykes, has formulated this sense more
exactly.[5] Conventional crime, he plausibly argues, is likely to continue increasing. Virtually every single causal indicator — economy,
ecology, family, education, values, immigration, population,
community — points to increasing rates of crime and delinquency.[6]
His scenario is familiar enough: middle-class flight to the suburbs;
decaying inner-city slums; unskilled and isolated minority groups;
chronic unemployment; zero economic growth; disintegration of

social ties; alienation and despair; abandonment of welfare ideologies; and so, more homicide, assault, robbery, larceny, rape. At
the same time, all sorts of other changes — in technology, property
relationships, corporate organization, political legitimacy — are
likely to increase the amount of 'unconventional crime': white-
collar crime, political crime, official lawlessness and political
corruption.

So much for crime. As for its control, beyond the assumption
that current policy has arrived at a turning point and that some
sort of crisis is ahead, Sykes presents a choice between pessimistic
and modestly optimistic alternatives:

> It is possible to envision a society marked by increasing violence and
> attacks on private property, by intolerance of any deviation from an
> obsessive morality, and by far reaching police surveillance coupled with
> a loss of civil liberties in a totalitarian social order. It is also possible
> (though admittedly more difficult in this disenchanted era) to envision
> a society with widespread acceptance of and conformity to the criminal
> law, a modest view of the proper reach of the State, and methods of
> law enforcement that are just, humane and effective.[7]

A linear projection from current control trends suggests changes
much more incremental and ambiguous. The assumptions which
Wilkins noted more than a decade ago still apply.[8] First, most
criminal-justice planning will continue to seek solutions by means
of more of the same. Second, the public will continue with the
mistaken and confused belief that because we do not like crime,
what we do about it will decrease it. The results of these assumptions will be a total breakdown of the criminal-justice system
(somewhere before the year 2000 Wilkins predicts), together with
increasing pressure for more and more control. The resultant forms
of control will be less noteworthy for their effects on crime than
their intrusive side-effects on ordinary citizens: a retreat into
fortress living; streets abandoned to outlaws; inconvenience and
erosion of civil liberty as a result of continual security checks and
surveillance systems. We have already seen this prediction from
several theoretical directions: for traditional law-and-order policies
based on doing something to individual offenders, 'the game is
almost up'. The next technology is the use of cybernetic planning
at the level of systems and environments in order to make the initial
*act* more difficult. The by-products might be unpleasant, but the
old punitive technology will soon be extinct.

Apart from these more imaginative excesses — crises, system
breakdown, desolation, totalitarianism — most crime-control predictions are only modestly pessimistic. An optimistic, utopian

element in crime-control thinking has always to be maintained:
the countervision of order, regulation and security which will
replace the imminent threat of breakdown and chaos. This vision
appeared in the early penitentiary movement, in the idealistic
excesses of scientific positivism, in the Continental social-defence
school and today, in the bland technicist criminology peddled
by international agencies to the Third World.[9] The visions of
chaos dominate; all that can be hoped for is a holding operation.
Genuine utopianism only remains on the extreme right with its
visions of environmental manipulation, psychotechnology or
genetic planning and the extreme left, with its prospect of a
'crime-free' society with the dissolution of capitalism. The dominant
tone is the realist right: 'I argue for a sober view of man and his
institutions that would permit reasonable things to be accomp-
lished, foolish things abandoned and utopian things forgotten.'[10]

What, though, can be learnt from the much richer world of
literary, philosophical and political utopias? This literature has
been well chronicled,[11] and so too has the expression of the
utopian form in science fiction and its eventual displacement by
anti-utopian and dystopian visions.[12] The transitional figure is
usually seen as H. G. Wells, the changes in his own long career
bridging the nineteenth-century utopias of Samuel Butler, William
Morris, Edward Bellamy and Jules Verne with the darker visions
of the twentieth century. After Wells, no more traditional utopias
were created; they were to come, if anywhere, from architects and
planners.

The key literary works of twentieth-century dystopianism
have passed into popular consciousness. In each case — unlike in
sociologies of the future — social control is a central theme. And
in each case there is a similar desolate vision of oppression, rigidity,
stifling conformity. In Zamyatin's *We* (published in 1924) people
are imprisoned in glass-walled cities and controlled as rigorously
as the weather. In Huxley's *Brave New World* (1932), genetic
control produces grades of humans designed to function according
to predetermined levels of intelligence; science makes life unde-
mandingly pleasant through mind-altering drugs; the very few
rebels are banished to a distant island. And then — most resonant
of all, of course — came Orwell's *Nineteen Eighty-Four*, a society
built around total control, with the proles segregated and the
middle class subject to surveillance and thought control. But the
element in *Nineteen Eighty-Four* which is so crucial to our theme
is that power is an end in itself. This sharply distinguishes it from
*We, Brave New World* and virtually the whole utopian tradition

where, whatever we might think of the results, the state is benevolent and justifies its policies in the name of the general social good.

By the early fifties, in any event, variants on the dystopian theme had become standard in 'genre' science fiction as well as more respectable literary forms. In a typical example, Vonnegut's *Player Piano* (published in 1952), society is dominated by superintelligent machines, materially prosperous, but regimented and spiritually empty. The vision became familiar: total social control with the hackneyed plot of the lone individual who somehow escapes conditioning, sees through all the lies and tries to escape. There is no hope of a collective political solution. In science fiction all that changes is the nature of the society's central obsession: nuclear disaster, overcrowding, pollution, crime. The enemies are no longer the old BEM's (Bug Eyed Monsters) from outer space — the symbols, some commentators argue, of communists in the Cold War — but are now within the society.

These 'visions of hell' in science fiction deserve genuine attention from students of social control.[13] They are not predictions of the future in the formal sense. True predictions are more linear: for example, as unemployment increases, so will crime increase. Science-fiction predictions are more imaginary. They involve speculation, guesswork, intuitive leaps. They predict futures rather than one future and allow you to imagine the extremes which might result if a particular value choice is followed through. Linear variables — like population or productivity, the type wisely used in criminology — are merely the flats and props, the background on which the visions are projected.

Science fiction is not a world which allows for easy systematization. A sense of these visions is best conveyed through a few random examples.

(1) Current illegalities (all forms of drug use, all sexual relationships) are decriminalized, but new problems and shortages (food, population growth, space, pollution) create new illegal markets and new crimes (hoarding, living in rooms too large); an exaggeration of current values also creates new crimes: 'conscious male chauvinism' becomes a punishable offence; old crimes like witchcraft reappear (in 2183),

(2) Current systems and ideologies of criminal justice break down completely, producing solutions such as: judging machines — analog computers which replace all human discretion; furies — robots who pursue and kill detected offenders; automatic on-the-spot justice by which offenders

are tried, sentenced and punished within a few minutes after the offence; bounty hunters: vigilantes who are paid cash rewards for killing anyone carrying out an armed robbery.

(3) New forms of punishment are devised or old ones revived: public executions are staged (in one story, there are mass 'Public Hatings' where the concentrated psychic energy of 70,000 minds burns the flesh off the offender's bones); offenders are implanted with telemachines (in one story, mobile prisons in the form of a three-walled halo which encases the offender and relentlessly accompanies him; if he stops moving the fourth wall joins itself and he is permanently sealed to death in a cube of impenetrable plastic); exile and banishment are also revived (as in Robert Silverberg's famous *Hawksbill Station*, where political deviants are banished back into time, condemned to eternal exile in a penal colony a billion years up the time line, somewhere in the early Paleozoic age).

The question is not whether these things could 'really' happen. As with Orwell's *Nineteen Eighty-Four*, or any species of utopian or anti-utopian thinking, these visions help clarify our values and preferences. Every form of social control, actual or idealized, embodies a moral vision of what should be. As my early chapters made clear, the system's sense of the future is not at all restricted to technical possibilities such as thought control, electronic surveillance or psychotechnology. I am talking about ideological rather than mechanical visions.

Take, for example, the idea that the perfect form of social control should avoid the cost, the physical segregation and the counter-productivity of the closed institution, but still entail moral judgement (stigma) and some real loss to the offender (justice). This is just the solution worked out in Silverberg's haunting story, *To See the Invisible Man*.[14] The prescribed punishment (for coldness) is to be pronounced invisible for a year or other fixed period. A luminous brand is placed on the forehead, no one is allowed to touch the offender, to speak to him, nor, after the first glance, to even look at him. The penalty for contact is to be sentenced to invisibility yourself. A perfect form of community control.

Exaggeration, fantasy, distortion, paranoia, panic mongering. . . No doubt. We must, however, understand these fictions, not to make predictions, but to confront the plaintive refrain which has run through the real stories of social control: 'that's not what we had in mind at all.' Perhaps not; perhaps good intentions do go fatefully wrong. But what is clear, is that many ideas which might seem repulsive to the liberal mind, were those embodied in classic *utopias*, not dystopias or anti-utopias.

In More's utopia, people are under constant observation by neighbours and magistrates. Society is governed by a set of rigid social controls; some deviations are punished by slavery; private political discussion is punished by death. In Bellamy's new society there is an inspectorate alert to any deviations. And so it goes on through virtually all the classic utopian literature: security, well-being, peace and, in socialist versions, equality. But, at the same time, there is suppression of individuality, stifling conformity, rigidity, smugness and complacency. This, of course, was the very combination satirized in the anti-utopias of Zamyatin, Huxley and Vonnegut.

This was not a vision which disturbed Bentham when he published his utopian panopticon plans in 1791 nor was it to worry Skinner's *Walden Two* of 1948. Here was perfect social control: an observed, synchronized society. Liberalism, as we well know, could absorb Bentham and it can even find Skinner appealing — the prospect of a world where people will naturally behave well, without punishment.[15] But we must now ground these visions, not in reality but in another and more specific set of visions — the city of the future. Here, dreams merge most visibly into nightmares, utopias into dystopias. Here too, we will glimpse the possibilities which my next and final chapter presents as real policy choices.

### THE CITY AS METAPHOR

Some time in the nineteenth century, the city began to be seen as a special, unique form of social life.[16] Before that, it appeared dominantly as a metaphor or paradigm, a model of society itself. Both these images survive. Alongside our concepts for understanding the uniqueness of the city (the business of all those special disciplines such as urban sociology, urban planning and urban geography), we are haunted by the old idea that the city stands for something. Today, invariably, it stands for disorder, chaos and breakdown. It is assumed that, unless we make radical changes (create a new *kind* of place? start again?), the city of the present — the iconography of violence, crime, insecurity, pollution, traffic congestion, overcrowding — is the society of the future. On the city streets lie the sharpest mirrors of dystopian imagery.

Cities, then, have never been just places, 'almost as soon as they were invented, they spawned a phantom version of themselves; an imaginative doppelganger that lived an independent life in the imagination of the human species at large. In other words, they stood for something.'[17] In the ancient world and then again with the re-emergence of city life in the later middle ages, the city tended to be conceived as a metaphor of order. The patterning of the city, its spatial arrangements, hierarchies, functional specifics, served as a mirror image of what the wider social reality could and should be like. The metaphor of the orderly city was so powerful that it could even serve as a mnemonic.[18] In Plato and Aristotle, then in the Heavenly City of St Augustine, the ordered city was a system for holding chaos at bay. The primordial city of these first utopias was a glimpse of eternal order, heaven on earth. The City of God became a symbolic representation of the universe itself. Here was the scheme of divine order: the temple and the palace at the centre.

As Mumford notes in his astute reading of the utopian literature, this picture was not entirely imaginary. It was an 'after image', an idealized form of the actual ancient city where divine order was embodied in every ritual and practice.[19] The ancient city was not simply the 'utopia' of later versions, but the most impressive and enduring of all utopias, actually embodying and even surpassing the ideal prescriptions of later fantasies.

But alongside the metaphor of order, the city was also used to construct metaphors and maps of hell. There were now secular infernos of crime and punishment, cities where vice and virtue would be stratified. In the City of the Wicked, all evil men were expected to form their own social order, and divine infernos were constructed to look like cities. With the Industrial Revolution, these metaphors gave way to reality and a darker, more complicated image emerged of the city as a problem, a form of evil in itself. This was the point at which social thinkers began constructing their now-familiar picture of urban life: impersonality, segmentalization, market rationality, degradation and anomie. From then onwards, the critique of the metropolis and the quest for community became central to sociological thought.

This was also the point at which the famous literary and political utopias of the nineteenth century were created by Bellamy, Fourier, Owen, Morris, Wells. As Mumford notes, there are close similarities between these visions and the more authoritarian utopias of the ancient and medieval cities. In both cases, we find 'isolation, stratification, fixation, regimentation, standardization, militarization'. And both visions merge into twentieth-century dystopias: 'one suddenly realizes that the distance between the positive ideal and the negative one was never so great as the advocates or admirers of utopia had professed.'[20] Again, the visions were not entirely imaginary; they drew on 'phantom versions' of previous realities.

But whatever the complex relationship between imagination, reality and after-image, the city could never again be used as a symbol of order. From every conceivable direction — anarchist, Marxist, liberal, humanist, conservative — intellectuals mounted their anti-urban attack. The metaphor of order could not be sustained nor (easily) could the tradition of thought that saw the city as the seat of civilization, the repository of grace and progress. Everything that was inhumane and degrading about the emergent industrial order (or capitalism) was to be found in the city. If there was order, it was an artificial, regimented, dehumanizing order. This was contrasted with the natural, organic order of the rural community and even its charming disorder: the irregular winding village lane, the casual conversations and family intimacies which took precedence over the market and the cash nexus. This was the alienation produced by the wrong sort of order. But the dominant vision was the anomie which resulted from too little order: the chaos and degradation of Hogarth, Dore, Dickens, Hugo, those unforgettable images of the areas of misery inhabited by the lumpen, the misfits, the Children of the Jago.

At the more theoretical level, of course, the vision was more complicated. Classical sociological thought contained a deep ambivalence about the city. Marx and Durkheim saw the possibilities for a new form of humanization, a different basis for social solidarity. Then, most notably, came Simmel's vision of the special kind of freedom that results in response to city conditions. The person could free his spirit (who I am) from his acts (what I usually do). This new freedom could be attained precisely because of the anonymity criticized in the anti-urban bias of intellectuals. Within the interstices of the metropolis, the 'I' could transcend mere routine.

But this is to anticipate a much later vision of the city. And, as we have so often seen, social-control thinking is never particularly sensitive to ambivalence. Such nuances would never have been picked up in the two major strands of nineteenth-century crime-control ideology: first, the notion that planning, regulation and classification could keep chaos at bay; second, the idealization of community, the vision of perfect social control in the paradise lost. Sometimes one theme dominated, sometimes the other. Eventually they became combined, symbiotically dependent on each other, in the powerful notion that the anomie and disorder caused by the replacement of natural and effective social control (community) by unnatural and ineffective social control (city, mass society) could be solved by the state. The state would have to compensate for the loss of community.

Before the great industrial cities had created their metaphors, planners and visionaries had, of course, already come together in the project with which this book opened: the closed institution as the answer to the impending problem of social control. Here would be constructed a simulated version, a working model, of what the good society should look like. This indeed was the City of the Wicked, but its order, discipline and hierarchy, its rows, tiers, lines, ceremonies of bell ringing and counting, could point us towards the good city. The perceived problem might have been (in the various versions I examined in chapter 1) an inchoate sense of disorder, a need to reinforce emerging class hierarchies and inculcate habits of work, a reproduction of a general disciplinary mode, but the result was the same.

Whether the planners of the penitentiary were influenced by earlier utopian visions, none of these historians tell us. Foucault, with a characteristic leap of imagination, conjures up the influence of two quite different after-images.[21] The first was the control over *leprosy*. The rituals of exile, banishment and exclusion, the marking and stigmatizing of the leper left behind the models for the Great Incarcerations. This was the political vision of the purified community. The second was control over the *plague*. The projects of surveillance, planning and record keeping that sorted out the contamination, confusion, and fear by distributing everyone into fixed spaces and rigid compartments, left behind the models of examination, classification and discipline. This was the political vision of the disciplined society.

These two projects 'came together' (mysteriously) in the nineteenth century. The prison is a space of exclusion, but it also is a space within which people are observed, partitioned, subject to timetables and disciplines. To all historians of the prison and asylum – whether or not they accept Foucault's fanciful archaeology – here was a form of 'moral architecture' – buildings designed not as ostentatious signs of wealth and power, not as fortresses for defence, but for the 'fabrication of virtue'.[22] If this was not clear enough in the prisons that were actually built, it was obvious in Bentham's fantasy of the panopticon. This was power and order in its pure utopian form – the 'simple idea' of using architecture to solve problems of morality, health, education and productivity.

Foucault's next imaginative leap, as we have seen, was to visualize 'panopticism' as a generalized principle, extended and dispersed throughout the social network. He fantasized the 'punitive city', as the utopia of the earlier judicial reformers: 'at the crossroads, in the gardens, at the side of roads being repaired or bridges built, in workshops open to all, in the depths of mines that may be visited, will be hundreds of tiny theatres of punishment.'[23] But this fantasy was never realized. Instead (again, mysteriously) came the disciplinary society, the carceral network in which power somehow 'circulated' through small-scale regional panopticons.

Again, there is no need to accept every baroque twist of Foucault's theory, to understand how the nineteenth-century city became the site for these larger visions of social order to be worked out, or to note how Bentham's vision in particular — hierarchy, surveillance, classification — carried an 'imaginary intensity which has persisted for 200 years'.[24] Other observers of the city, such as Marx and Engels, saw the problem of control in much more conventionally political terms. Following their line of thought, Hobsbawm, for example, has examined how the structure of cities might have affected the course of urban riots and insurrections, and what effect the fear of such movements might have had on urban structure.[25] The obvious questions to be asked were: How easily can the poor be mobilized, and suppressed? How vulnerable are centres of authority? Where are barracks and police stations located? What are optimal patterns of transportation? The most famous example of planning for control was, of course, the rebuilding of Paris and Vienna after the 1848 revolutions to take into account the needs for counter-insurgency: the wide, straight boulevards, for instance, along which artillery could fire and troops advance.

But, as Hobsbawn notes, this type of planning was never a dominant policy and in many cities did not occur at all. The powerful had no interest in politicizing the problem of social order, and the Victorian city became the site for a quite different set of plans and visions. The slums emerged not just as a solution (penal colonies to which the poor, the inadequate and the wicked could be sent) but as a problem: places where wickedness was being created. Historians have described how the slums of Victorian England became 'the mental landscape within which the middle class could recognise and articulate their own anxieties about urban existence'.[26] The solutions drew on the images of public health: cesspools of human misery, sewers of vice, cleaning up, germs and infections, isolation and segregation.[27]

For Foucault, the city was not a place for other metaphors, but was to provide a powerful spatial metaphor itself. Here could be observed the new dispersed discourse of power actually spreading itself out, passing through finer and finer channels. He continually uses the spatial metaphors of 'geopolitics' to describe the dispersal of discipline: city, archipelago, maps, streets, topology, vectors, landscapes.[28]

But however we view the emerging control systems — as responses to the dangerous classes, as attempts to recreate community, as exercises in the micro-physics of power or merely as part of the rationalization of the state — they could never leave behind any utopian after-images. Quite the contrary. As Mumford eloquently shows, here, already, is the real dystopia.[29] The dark shadow of the good city is the 'collective human machine': the dehumanized routine and suppression of autonomy, first imposed by the despotic monarch and the army, is now the 'invisible machine' of the modern technocratic state. Well before Foucault (and more clearly and simply), Mumford described how the utopian ideal of total control from above and absolute obedience below had never passed out of existence, but was reassembled in a different form after kingship by divine right was defeated. He also stressed that the new machine must be seen not in terms of its visible parts but the minute, intangible assembly of science, knowledge and administration. The new invisible machine is no longer an agent for creating heaven on earth, the holy city, but itself becomes the utopia which is worshipped and enlarged indefinitely.

It was just this horror of the invisible machine which was to produce the radical destructuring movements, the romantic impulses, the anti-industrial visions of the 1960s. So invisible was the machine, that its most benign parts (therapy, social work, humanitarianism) hid its most repressive operations. Here was Illich's foreboding of industrial nemesis: divine retribution for tampering with nature. The machine had to be exposed and taken apart. But alongside this vision of alienation (too much control), there lies, as in the nineteenth century, the more powerful vision of anomie (too little control). The fear is that the machine is breaking down by itself, and that 'outside', in the chaos of urban life, in the desolate city streets abandoned to the predators, lies the ultimate horror — chaos, disorder, entropy.

But this is to run ahead of the story. We must move from metaphors of the nineteenth-century city to the visions and plans of twentieth-century crime control.

PLANNING FOR ORDER

An archaeology of twentieth-century control ideologies would reveal the same combination of elements found in the previous century: after-images of the past, metaphors of the present and visions of the future.

The Progressive Era inherited the resonant images of cleansing and salvation. The city, like the sewers, had to be cleansed of undesirable elements. At the same time, the weak, the young, the defective and the vulnerable had to be saved, both from the city itself and from the hard edge of the control system. The Chicago School allowed for a more ambivalent vision. As Matza explains, they assumed pathology (and this eventually guided their preferred policies) but simultaneously provided evidence for diversity.[30] They drew from Simmel and their own journalistic feel for the city some sense of the urban potential for freedom and tolerance. Park (like Simmel) visualized a freedom not of identity, but of behaviour, not transcendental searching for selfhood but space to be an innovator, a deviant.

It was just this vision which was to give Goffman his only optimistic edge: the extraordinary human ability to create an identity in the cracks, the interstices of the system. And it was this vision that inspired the libertarians, labelling theorists and noninterventionists of the sixties to construct their visions of cultures of civility: areas of the city where deviance could become diversity, where people could do their thing without interference by the machine.[31]

To their radical critics, these cultures of civility were merely 'ghettoes of freedom', yet further evidence of repressive tolerance. In any event, it was the 'pathology' and not the 'diversity' of the Chicago School which was to influence social-control policy. Their dominant vision was the traditional one: deviance as the product of disorganization, a breakdown of social control, a fragmentation of the social bond. Within their complex moral geography of the city — those unforgettable concentric circles — the solution for the areas of disorganization was to restore community control.

This was solid liberal social reformism, not utopianism. To the same extent that the Chicagoans were not interested in macrosocial theory, they also did not attempt to construct visions of the good society. This has remained true of all modern strands of crime-control planning. Despite the obviously moral nature of the problem of crime, only a handful of criminologists have even tried to connect their plans, policies and preferences to some over-arching moral vision.[32] There was little utopian thinking, as we saw, in the general intellectual culture, so most criminologists settled for the realistic amelioration of a bleak future. Even good intentions go wrong, so let's settle for caution, realism, scepticism and, at the extreme, even nihilism.

Only in some sectors of urban planning and architecture, did some remnants of classic utopianism stay alive. Here, in the blue-prints of Frank Lloyd Wright and Le Corbusier, was a more ambitious vision of the future: the good city in the ideal society.[33] These writings are extraordinarily resonant to the student of social control. On the one hand, is the theme of the city as unnatural and immoral, the plans to remould it to resemble a village; on the other (especially in Le Corbusier) the idealized vision of machinery and mass production, the tower blocks in parks, the roads leading through parks to the Radiant City.

Le Corbusier is especially interesting. To his hostile critics, constructions like *Unite d'Habitation* exemplify perfectly the tendency for the anti-industrial motive (the return to community, the harmony of daily life and home, the cosmic harmony of man with nature) to create, paradoxically, the most artificial of en-vironments.[34] This is very similar to the critique of ersatz com-munity control, and Le Corbusier's admirers tell a classic tale of good intentions gone wrong. Gardiner notes that none of his cities were actually built (they got no further than drawing models); his imitators copied his outlines but not his underlying principles; his original vision never intended an epidemic of concrete towers surrounded by black asphalt and car parks.[35] Le Corbusier wanted order, but he also wanted space, easy communication, air, sunlight, grass and trees.

On the city streets, however, these visions of the good life must have looked as remote as the visions of the well-ordered asylum looked to its average inmates. From the end of the 1950s onwards, and with relentless momentum ever since, the cities became the arena for the 'crisis'. Architects and planners, urban renewers and developers, politicians and big business, capitalism itself were all to blame for the decline in the city. As metaphor and social fact, the city became identified with crime, racialism, poverty, unemploy-ment, discrimination, violence and insecurity. The city was a mnemonic not for order, but for the separate parts of a collective cultural nightmare:

- middle-class (meaning, in the USA, largely white) exodus to the suburbs;
- outward migration of shops, offices, factories;
- a live central business district but, just beyond, a dead space: houses abandoned, store fronts boarded up;
- whole blocks decayed, taken over by freaks, junkies, drop outs, winos, derelicts of all sorts;
- the inner city as a whole occupied by minority groups, the poor, the disadvantaged, the stigmatized;
- a few remaining middle-class fortresses, their occupants dodging the muggers and predators on the streets;
- blackboard jungle schools, scenes of violence, disorder and drug abuse;
- a physical landscape devastated by vandalism, graffiti and neglect.

I am not concerned with the factual basis of this scenario. The point is that over the last few decades it became so familiar, even so banal a part of popular consciousness, that it was difficult to even think of the future in any other terms.[36] My interest here is in the kind of counter-planning this vision evoked. In Britain where, of course, the full urban-crisis scenario took longer to establish, the period leading up to the radical conservatism of the Thatcher governments saw no drastic changes in social policy. The hard end remained hard while the soft end (welfare, care, social work) increased in more or less incremental fashion. The conservatism of the late seventies sharpened this bifurcatory line and inverted its priorities: law-and-order politics became dominant and welfare resources began to be drained.

In the USA, at the beginning of the sixties, liberal social planning entered a moment of optimism not again repeated in the subsequent twenty years. The hope that the Great Society could be built stimulated that famous series of reform programmes: War on Poverty, Urban Renewal, Mobilization for Youth. In addition to their conventional liberal reform ideology, these programmes contained many of the same radical elements as their destructuring counterparts: visions of decentralization, citizen participation, self-help. And they also contained conservative, social-control elements: placating, tokenism, informing, co-option, keeping trouble-makers off the streets. Today's judgements about the balance between these various elements and about ultimate matters of 'success' and 'failure' resolve themselves into familiar lines: reforms never tried properly, good intentions gone wrong, success, but in terms of regulation.

However we resolve this debate, it is clear that the actual (or putative) failure of these programmes to deal with crime on the streets or to confront the urban-crisis scenario, allowed older visions of order to become dominant. The subsequent liberal retreat from doing good meant little opposition to this dominance. Even at the time that liberal and radical alternatives were being suggested or implemented at the periphery (the soft end), the centre remained informed by the older vision. Official policy documents, for example, routinely invoked the urban-crisis scenario: the middle class locked in fortified high-rise cells or guarded compounds; slums as areas of terror completely out of police control; armed guards patrolling all public facilities. They used this as a warning of what might happen without 'effective public action'.[37]

What 'effective public action' meant, was a depoliticized version of those momentary nineteenth-century visions: reconstructing the city to meet the needs of social control. The spatial metaphors were simple and appealing: clean up the streets, the Safe Streets Acts, defensible space, residential security. This was just the move which futurists of crime control now regard as the way ahead: from older law-and-order responses directed at the individual offender, to dealing with systems, spaces, opportunities and environments. The idea was to manipulate the external environment to prevent the initial infraction. Concurrent liberal thinking could only offer programmes which were negative and abolitionist: decarceration, diversion, decreasing the intensity of intervention. Here was 'effective public action', something positive: continue with the older hard-edge policies directed at the individual offender (deterrence, incapacitation, just deserts) and, in the meantime, develop a technology of primary prevention. The attraction of preventive social control, moreover, was that at last there was the prospect of helping the potential victim.

The message became even more convincing when the safe-streets and target-hardening elements could be supplemented by invoking the rhetoric of community. For, after all, fortress living, closed-circuit television surveillance, armed guards patrolling schools, libraries and play grounds were simultaneously 'solutions' but also the very *problems* in the urban nightmares which were being constructed. The ideology of community offered something more palatable: citizen involvement in law enforcement, community policing, neighbourhood crime-prevention teams, block watches and whistle blowers.

The CPED movement (Crime Prevention Through Environmental Design) became the perfect combination of these trends. A dispassionate history of this movement remains to be written, but from its succeeding enthusiasts,[38] we can pick up its main appeal: urban environments can be designed or redesigned to reduce the opportunities for crime (or the fear of crime), but without resorting to the building of fortresses and the resulting deterioration of urban life. This is not just law enforcement and punishment and not just armed guards and big-brother surveillance, but the 'restoration' of informal social control and a way of helping ordinary citizens 'regain' control and take responsibility for their immediate environment.

Gardner sets out the three main conceptual models behind the CPED movements, all of them influenced by the dreadful realization that while the medieval fortress town has been a place of safe retreat against the external enemy, the enemy was now within the gates.[39]

(1) The notion of the *urban village*: originating in the Chicago School's model of urban disorganization and breakdown, and then revised in Jane Jacobs' eloquent picture of *The Death and Life of Great American Cities* (published in 1961), the stress is on recreating the social spaces for mutual recognition, surveillance ('the eyes on the street'), good neighbourliness, intimacy and communal responsibility. It assumes that a certain cultural homogeneity exists, or that this can be recreated.

(2) The ambivalent model of the *urban fortress*: reliance on technology, physical security and technical isolation from a hostile environment.

(3) The notion of *defensible space*, associated with the extremely influential work of Oscar Newman.[40]

It is here in the third model, that the social and the physical are combined: the ideal of the urban village comes together with the conscious planning of the physical environment in order to reduce crime and vandalism. Buildings, public-housing projects or estates and whole neighbourhoods are designed to allow for intensive monitoring and control by residents ('natural surveillance'); purely public areas are reduced or, at least, clear perceptual barriers created between communal, semi-public and private spaces; recognizable zones and hierarchies of interest are created by design and planning. The stress is on territoriality; proprietal interest and felt responsibility. More recently, Newman has extended his notion of defensible space to the wider ideal of a 'community of interests': the use of quota systems, allocations and housing subsidies to group people by common interest and life-style.

Current CPED thinking highlights one or other of these elements, combines them or tries to transcend them. But there is a common vision: territorial control, defensible space, close surveillance and, above all, the need to incorporate crime-control considerations into urban planning and design. Current evaluations of actual CPED programmes suggest only the most modest of gains in reducing crime rates.[41] But let us leave aside the question of effectiveness and concentrate on the vision.

There was undoubtedly a radical, humanistic edge to the movement. Note Newman's stress on matters of ownership, control and power; the support of local community against big-business interests, the question of the sheer unpleasantness of an environment conducive to crime. But there is a sense in which this vision of order is quite opposite to the premises of humanistic, utopian town planning. It is true that Jane Jacobs (and her predecessors) emphasized community cohesion, a sense of territory, mutual responsibility and a network of informal controls. In her often quoted words: 'the first thing to understand is that public peace . . . of cities is not kept primarily by the police . . . It is kept primarily by an intricate, almost unconscious network of voluntary controls and standards among the people themselves . . . and enforced by the people.'[42] But just because of this emphasis, humanists opposed the division of the city into specialized districts along functional lines. They argued, romantically perhaps, for diversity and tolerance, not conformity, for street activity and bustle, not just 'watching eyes'.

In practice, however, town planning — even of such humanistic utopian projects as the Garden City and the New Town — became a vision of order, a reaction to the dominant urban metaphors of disease, cancer, decaying blight, slum, apocalypse and death. As Jencks suggests, all this crisis-talk, the cancer metaphor, the 'eschatological and hysterical terms' in which urban problems were discussed, often exacerbated the deteriorating situation they were meant to cure. There was a 'metaphorical revenge', and the counter images of cleanliness and cosiness led planners to design 'salubrious and sterile' solutions, which were then condemned just as harshly.[43]

These contrasting visions — purity and order as opposed to a certain disorder and chaos — are captured in Sennet's critique of city life.[44] I will do no more than paraphrase this. The search for community, he argues, is indeed a response to real psychic needs —

for relatedness, intimacy, warmth, sharing, and fraternity, the possibility of creating somewhere in the city a life different from the impersonal machine. But this need stems from the specifically adolescent search for a purified identity: an attempt to steel oneself in advance against the unknown, the pain of uncertainty. Everything can be solved by 'planning': building a self-image (and a city to match it) which filters out all threats of the unknown, and wards off any sense of dissonance.

The myth is created of the purified community. But, for Sennet, these are 'pseudo' communities, with 'counterfeit' feelings. Their only sense of relatedness comes from feeling the same, from trying to exclude the others who are different (in terms of class, race or moral status). Their intolerance of ambiguity gives an exaggerated sense of threat and disorder. All this is quite different from the 'real' urban communities of decades ago, with their variety, complexity and chaos, their tolerance of disorder. Sennet describes the aim of city planning now as the simplification of social life, a hunger for total pre-planning to prevent anything unexpected: 'the essence of the purification mechanism is a fear of losing control.'[45] This is revealed by the flight to the suburbs, away from the richness of city life to the sanitized community with its intense private family and its rigid separation of social life (home, school, shopping centre).

Sennet's own preference is for a 'new anarchism', a new kind of urban confusion and tolerance for diversity and disorder. He constructs a genuine utopian vision, precisely opposite to that of the planners, crime controllers and environmental designers. Cities should be made *more* disorderly; there should be contact without sameness; we should actually look for and create places with a high level of tension and unease; people should be made to confront each other through various forms of non-violent contact; centralized social-control bodies, pre-planning and zoning should all be removed. A chapter on 'ordinary lives in disorder' presents a blueprint of what it might be to grow up in this sort of disordered urban milieu. This would be true growing up: abandoning the adolescent need for order and embracing the chaotic structure of human experience which can only be found in the dense, uncontrollable environment of the city.

Here, and in his later related writings,[46] Sennet, of course, is working out a broader critique of American society. The thesis is that social trouble comes not from the *decline* of the family, of privacy, of the small tribal unit. The problem is the *increased* intimacy and intensity of these forms, the consequent pressure on them and the corresponding decline of a meaningful public life. For him, the good life lay somewhere in the bustling streets and cafes of Europe in another century, in the anonymity of a true public space, in a world before the cults of intimacy, sincerity, authenticity and 'destructive *Gemeinschaft*'.

This is not utopian anti-modernism, not a glance back to the same mythic past which inspired the rhetoric of community control, but it is nonetheless a glance back to the past. Once again, reality conjures up different images, and the future conjures up different after-images.

Now it is time to go back again to the real world of crime control, this time to find the overall maps on to which these visions and plans are projected.

Let us go along with the standard assumption that crime, delinquency and allied social problems will continue to increase or at least stay much the same. Let us assume that no foreseeable innovations and permutations in existing control systems will radically 'solve' these problems. And let us also assume that the city, as image and reality, will be the territory where these futures will be most visible. Given these assumptions, it does not seem likely that much of the destructuring impulse will survive. That is to say, notions such as tolerating disorder, dismantling the machine and disestablishing the establishment will look even more quixotic than they do today. The response to real or perceived breakdown is to call for more regulation, order and control. Only anarchists, we are told, can be in favour of chaos. So, do more (which means more of the same) rather than less.

But how will these forms of social control be deployed in social space? At the end of chapter 2 I described two opposed forms of deployment: the older patterns of exclusion, stigma and segregation, and the 'new' counter-ideologies of integration and absorption. This difference is captured (a little more vividly) in Levi-Strauss's binary opposition between *vomiting out* and *swallowing up* as modes of deviancy control:

> If we studied societies from the outside, it would be tempting to distinguish two contrasting types: those which practise cannibalism — that is, which regard the absorption of certain individuals possessing dangerous powers as the only means of neutralising those powers and even of

turning them to advantage — and those which, like our own society, adopt what might be called the practice of *anthropemy* (from the Greek *emein*, to vomit); faced with the same problem the latter type of society has chosen the opposite solution, which consists of ejecting dangerous individuals from the social body and keeping them temporarily or permanently in isolation, away from all contact with their fellows, in establishments especially intended for this purpose.[47]

Let me convert this physiological metaphor into a spatial one. The vomiting-out mode stands for the possibility of separation, segregation, isolation, banishment, confinement. I will call this simply *exclusion*: temporarily or permanently, deviants are driven beyond social boundaries or separated out into their own designated spaces. The swallowing-up mode stands for the possibility of incorporation, integration or assimilation. This is *inclusion*: deviants are retained, as long as possible within conventional social boundaries and institutions, there to be absorbed. Modes of coping with unruliness in the classroom may serve as a crude illustration of these alternatives. Exclusion leads to measures such as expulsion; separate classes, schools, or units for designated troublemakers; special diagnostic labels such as 'hyperactivity' with treatments such as drugs. Inclusion leads to measures such as unobstructive techniques of assuring internal obedience; preventive conditioning by systems of reward and punishment aimed at all; deliberate extension of the boundaries of tolerance.

These are not, of course, total and exclusive alternatives and, anthropologists notwithstanding, whole cultures cannot easily be divided into inclusionary and exclusionary types. Most societies employ both modes of control, constantly oscillating between one and the other. Moreover, as I have consistently shown, reforms motivated by the inclusionary impulse often end up being exclusionary. This might happen when the decision about *whom* to include calls for an act of formal classification, which then immediately results in another form of separation. It is also by no means obvious that exclusion must be the more intensive and less tolerant mode. We might separate a group only to ignore it completely, while inclusion might entail massive efforts to achieve normative or psychic change. These are some of the social policy dilemmas which I raise in the next chapter. Here I want to project these abstractions onto a recognizable map of the future city.

The map is not the territory any more than the menu is the meal. But we need these maps for visualizing, knowing and planning. The elaborate classifications which early prison managers constructed within their institutions were 'atlases of vice', cities of the wicked in which every type of depravity was carefully separated out. At the end of the nineteenth century, phrenologists constructed maps of the head, plotting actual areas of good and evil.[48] Their social-reform counterparts were preoccupied with streets and sewers, plotting out like Mayhew, the domains and contours of poverty, despair and pathology. The Chicago School produced those famous moral maps of the city: concentric zones on to which grids of crime, delinquency, suicide and other forms of social disorganization were projected. Ecological analysis continued in criminology, and today's urban geographers, town planners and statisticians are all too busy with their maps of target areas, defensible spaces, high-crime zones, robbery-trip routes and spatial patterns of offenders. And in everyday perception and journalistic cliché, we give moral meanings to the territories of slum, downtown, safe streets, public park, suburb. This is how the word 'ghetto' is used. (It shows how language changes — nowhere in the modern world have there been ghettos of the type in which European Jews were forced to live.)

All these linguistic and metaphorical exercises share the common positivist obsession to differentiate and classify. This master impulse is obviously more compatible with the exclusionary mode, but let us see how these alternative spatial metaphors might work themselves out in the city.

### Inclusion

Foucault's 'punitive city' contained one part of the inclusive vision: social control was not concentrated and centralized, but dispersed throughout the social body. But in another way, this was not inclusion at all. The punishments were to take place in visible, open 'theatres' and therefore (presumably) would have been obtrusive and stigmatizing. In the control system actually created there was also 'dispersal' — but this was in the shadow of the great exclusionary institution of the prison and, moreover, each form of dispersal was simultaneously a way of classifying people, placing them into separate spaces.

A much more genuine, radical and 'purer' vision of inclusion lay behind the destructuring movements of the sixties. Every one of the messages was directed against exclusion and (if only by implication) in favour of inclusion: formal structures should be made less formal; central systems should be decentralized or dispersed; the professional power to exclude should be weakened; segregation in closed institutions should give way to integration in the open community; the visible and the stigmatizing should be rendered invisible and normal; the master institutions should not exclude their deviants but absorb them; the boundaries of control should blur or disappear into their surrounding space.

Forget, for the moment, the empirical results of the reforms inspired by the inclusionary message. This chapter deals with visions, not reality. We have to try to imagine, rather, how exactly the new inclusionary social order would deal with its deviants. Families, schools, work-places, neighbourhood blocks: would these all become 'tiny theatres' of social control, unobtrusively processing their 'own' deviants? Would formal agencies still remain, taking on a more limited role with more serious offenders, but in an 'inclusive' way?

Let us imagine the latter possibility in the city. Streets, blocks and neighbourhoods are not bounded institutions like families, schools or factories: a solution is needed to the problem of control without exclusion. We already know what such solutions look like: discreet surveillance, data banks, crime prevention through environmental design, community policing, secret agents, informers and decoys, defensible space. These systems constitute 'social control' primarily in the sense of observation, opportunity reduction, primary prevention and detection. Unless the system is totally successful, matters of adjudication, punishment and deployment still remain. And it was of course *total* success which the behaviourist utopias promised. The current system of preventive control reassembles much of the panopticon vision: visibility (you know about the TV screens and data banks); unverifiability (you do not know when you are being watched or checked); anonymity (it does not matter who is operating the system – it could be a computer); and the absence of force (you should want to be good).

But despite these facile similarities, it is quite obvious that nothing like this vision of total 'inclusive' surveillance has been assembled or even envisaged, nor is it likely to be. What is striking, though, is that the radical, 'humanist' edge of the inclusionary movement offered no alternative to these forms of control through surveillance. Again, what would inclusionary, integrative, or absorbing families, schools, neighbourhood or factories actually look like? It was, in fact, assumed from all sides that the preventive system would not and could not be a total success. The problem of what to do with the individual offender still remained.

Here, the solutions of the community-control movement were little more than permutations of the traditional model of probation:

counselling, service, treatment, reporting, observation — but trying to be more unobtrusive and invisible (as with the boy by the lake) and to blur the boundaries of control. Tracking, befriending, shadowing and even house arrest are just more imaginative variants of the same model.

The genuine futurists of crime control went only a little further. A widely quoted plan for 'restraint in the community', for example, would put on one side 'suspendees' (those threatened with a sentence, but otherwise ignored) and on the other, 'isolates' (the serious offenders who are humanely segregated).[49] This leaves 'restrainees': each is assigned to his own private field officer who has the sole function of reporting to the police when the restrainee is observed committing an offence. The restrainer has no direct contact with his target, indeed the restrainee does not even know his identity. This random element is close to the panopticon principle: the restrainee will always be in a state of uncertainty, not knowing what risks he runs. He is allowed to live freely, but if convicted of a new offence, then the next level of punishment will be unequivocally imposed.

Invisible community restraint could also be achieved — more cheaply and effectively, its proponents maintain — by the more sophisticated method of 'technological incapacitation'. The use of radio telemetry devices (externally worn or implanted and linked to a location-monitoring system which would limit the offender to designated areas) has been explicitly justified on inclusionary grounds. The offender's normal productive activity would not be inhibited (he goes to school, works, supports his family, pays taxes). There is no visible or identifiable stigma. The punishment is not permanent or disabling and there is no segregation, isolation or special institutions. Here is a newspaper account of a somewhat primitive version of the technology:

### Bleeper Could Cut Jail Numbers

An association has been set up in Britain to study the possibility of giving some criminals an alternative to jail by fitting them with an electronic device that emits a regular signal and enables their movements to be tracked by computer.

The Offender's Tag Association, launched by Mr Tom Stacey, a publisher and prison visitor, has the backing of Mr Carl den Brinker, the technical director of a leading electronics company, and the Rev Peter Timms, a former governor of Maidstone Prison.

A similar idea, which may be launched this week as a pilot scheme in Albuquerque, New Mexico, has caused controversy among lawyers and penal reformers in the United States.

Supporters say it would ease prison over-crowding, but opponents have declared that it will bring 1984 to Albuquerque a year early.

Mr Stacey said last week that there were important differences between his idea and the American version, which plans to make lesser offenders serve their time under a form of 'house arrest'.

He favours a scheme which would alert the authorities whenever an offender leaves a specified area. The signal would then be received in another zone.

Offenders would wear a 'bracelet' containing a tiny transmitter, giving out an inaudible electronically coded signal to provide an instant 'fix' on his whereabouts.

Mr Stacey believes that such a system would enable less serious offenders to continue living in the community, while meeting society's legitimate demands for protection.

He said that the system would have to be run by the police. Other members of the association, however, said it could be under the control of the probation service.

The idea has become technically feasible since the Government gave the go-ahead for the construction of a national network of cellular radio. A feasibility study carried out at Kent University showed that although technically possible, such a scheme would be prohibitively expensive.

A single channel allocated nationally on the cellular radio waveband would enable a theoretical maximum of 500 offenders to be monitored in each 'cell,' which covers a one-mile radius.

Four mini-computers would suffice for the whole of London, and in the early stages each offender's transmitter would cost between £700 and £1,000.

According to Mr Stacey, the idea could 'revolutionise the treatment of a large swathe of offenders in urban areas.' He added 'The advantages for the prison system are that it would reduce decisively the pressure on prison space and also on attitudes throughout the penal system.

In the United States Judge Jack Love has made himself a guinea pig for a similar idea by wearing an 'electronic leash' for the past three weeks.

A steel fetter that contains a miniaturised radio transmitter is riveted around his right ankle. Every 90 seconds it beeps a tell-tale report on the judge's whereabouts to a police computer in Albuquerque.

The judge is wearing the 5 oz gadget wherever he goes — in court, in his car, in the shower, in bed. It fits over his sock and his high western boot. 'Most time I just don't know it's there,' he said last week.

Starting this week, if the New Mexico Supreme Court approves, Judge Low will begin a 90-day pilot programme with up to 25 offenders on probation. Their movements would be monitored by the so-called 'snoop bracelet.'

The bracelet is riveted on by four steel bolts. But couldn't a wearer remove it with ease? 'Sure, said Judge Love. 'But the whole psychology of it is that he won't want to. This is the liberty card keeping him out of jail. The people who wear it, drunk drivers and so on, are going to be the people most frightened of going to jail.[50]

Leaving entirely aside questions about technical feasibility or moral desirability, note that such solutions are directed at an *extremely* limited part of the inclusionary vision: 'keeping people out of jail'. Even here, although the offender is neither banished nor as visibly stigmatized as a leper, he is surely every bit as classified as the actual or potential plague victim. In fact, systems such as Intensive Intermediate Treatment could come from Defoe's image of the 'plague city'[51]: regular reports to the supervising social worker, attendance for debriefing/decontamination sessions at the centre (for cognitive retraining, behaviour modification, improving self-concept), presence at an attendance centre to avoid sites of infection and contagion like the Saturday afternoon football game, night restriction or curfews, tracking for the rest of the time.

But however strange the after-images of some of its individual results, the point is that the inclusionary vision has never really been assembled as a whole. And, given its component parts (*Gemeinschaft* iconography, environmental design, restraint in the community), this is hardly a simple project. Even the most imaginative of science-fiction writers have not contemplated anything like it.[52]

To assemble the version of inclusion which emerged from the community-control movement, I will take the strategies and agencies described in chapter 2, and project them only slightly into the future. (Outsiders to this world might need reminding that these are all real programmes.) This would be the composite picture:

*Mr and Mrs Citizen, their son Joe and daughter Linda, leave their suburban home after breakfast, saying goodbye to Ron, a 15-year-old pre-delinquent who is living with them under the LAK (Look After a Kid) scheme. Ron will later take a bus downtown to the Community Correctional Centre, where he is to be given two hours of Vocational Guidance and later tested on the Interpersonal Maturity Level scale. Mr C. drops Joe off at the School Problems Evaluation Centre from where Joe will walk to school. In his class are five children who are bussed from a local Community Home, four from a Pre-Release Facility and three who, like Ron, live with families in the neighbourhood. Linda gets off next — at the GUIDE Centre (Girls Unit for Intensive Daytime Education) where she works as a Behavioural Contract Mediator. They drive past a Threequarter-way House, a Rape-Crisis Centre and then a Drug-Addict Cottage, where Mrs C. waves to a group of boys working in the garden. She knows them from some volunteer work she does in RODEO (Reduction of Delinquency Through Expansion of Opportunities). She gets off at a building which houses the Special Parole Unit, where she is in charge of a 5-year evaluation research project on the use of the HIM (Hill Interaction Matrix) in matching group treatment to client. Mr C. finally arrives at work, but will spend his lunch hour driving around the car again as this is his duty week on patrol with TIPS (Turn In a Pusher). On the way he picks up some camping equipment for the ACTION weekend hike (Accepting Challenge Through Interaction with Others and Nature) on which he is going with Ron, Linda and five other PINS (Persons In Need of Supervision) . . .*

Clearly, a lot of inclusionary *work* is going on here, and perhaps the anthropologist would see this as 'swallowing up'.

### Exclusion

Compared with the inclusionary mode — which appeared so prominently in recent progressive social-control talk — the exclusionary mode yields by far the more integrated set of plans and visions. It is undoubtedly easier to understand, it has a firmer historical and institutional base and it is psychologically more resonant and satisfying.

The final 'exclusion' of the death penalty aside, this mode of control was represented in pre-modern societies by such sanctions as banishment and physical stigmatization. Banishment offered total removal of the deviant while those sanctions which marked the offender permanently — branding on the forehead, cutting off thieves' hands or liars' tongues — were self-confirming forms of separation. These people could never be absorbed and could survive only by marginal activities. Whole sections of early cities contained these deviants, bound together by their stigma.

There is no need to chronicle here again the transition to the modes of exclusionary control so characteristic of the industrial age: the route through transportation and penal servitude, the retention of capital punishment and then the prison and the whole apparatus of modern corrections. The impulse to classify, separate, segregate and exclude constitutes the very heart of the system. But even if we step outside the formal apparatus — into the wider space of the city — the exclusionary ideal has retained its traditional resonance.

The resulting map, however, would yield neither the punitive city, nor the disciplinary society's invisible micro-systems of power, nor its contemporary equivalent, the 'integrated community-control continuum' in which the Citizen family were so busy. Instead, there would be the purified city — a landscape rigidly and visibly divided not in terms of its physical characteristics (rivers, bridges, streets) or social uses (shops, homes, schools, offices) but its moral attributes. There would be an exact geographical form to match degree of attributed stigma with intensity of social control.

When the Chicago School drew their maps, they implied a 'natural' patterning of social disorganization and consequent deviance, a shake up or drift inherent in the growth of the city which would produce that form. Later students of urban life, politics, and planning saw this process in more political terms: not natural ecological growth, but planned political outcomes. Starting not with problems of social control, but questions about race relations, social class, power or the fiscal crises, this literature contained powerful exclusionary images. There is the notion, for example, of the city as 'internal colony' exploited by centres of power elsewhere and descended on by suburbanites for work, entertainment and essential services. Let me list a few other of the images more relevant to the control question.

Sternlieb gives us 'the city as sandbox'.[53] The inner-city fears not exploitation (as in the colonial model) but indifference and abandonment. The city loses its jobs, its other economic functions, its role as a staging point for new immigrants, and becomes like a sandbox in which adults park their troublesome children. There the children can play, more or less undisturbed in their own territory. Government programmes — social, educational, welfare and health agencies — take the form of toys thrown to children. These have the symbolic functions of placebos — ways of placating the inhabitants (the poor, the racial minorities) who are left to play as the jobs, professions and services drift away to the suburbs.

Long gives us 'the city as reservation'.[54] The old inner cities, sites now of unemployment and underemployment, poor public services, chaotic and ineffective schools, justify their existence by finding a new role 'as an Indian reservation for the poor, the deviant, the unwanted and for those who make a business or career of managing them for the rest of society'. The choice for urban politicians is between accepting this model of the Indian reservation of inmates and keepers, economically dependent on transfer payments from the outside society in return for custodial services, or moving towards 'colonial emancipation', self-help and the development of a viable local economy. Organized central interests, as well as those of the local bureaucrats, keepers, professionals and the natives themselves, will be inclined to perpetuate the reservation model.

Then Hill, after reconsidering these visions created at the beginning of the seventies, gives us the 'pariah city'.[55] The political economies of the ageing central cities, he argues, already contain elements of the sandbox and the reservation: they are places for the economically disenfranchised labour force; many traditional jobs are absorbed by low-paid workers in and from the Third World; government funds (food stamps, housing, security and health payments) subsidize professional keepers or local slum landlords and merchants; containment and care becoming lucrative private businesses; a growing municipal bureaucracy is sustained by the plight of the poor; despair and apathy are rife. Hill questions some of this imagery. For him, the pariah city is not exactly an isolated reservation in the desert but the core of a complex system of economic institutions, mass media, transportation and politics. Even if the city stagnates, this nerve centre remains. The dominant tendency, he argues, is the state capitalist city, with its corporate management, technology and efficient capital accumulation.

But whatever the theoretical questionings,[56] the dominant image remains: the move to the suburbs; the old urban centres deserted and left to the socially marginal; a high degree of separation and exclusion within the city. All this sounds familiar to critics of decarceration. This is precisely their scenario for 'community care and treatment': decayed zones of the inner city inhabited by the old, confused and ill dumped from their institutions and' left to rot in broken-down welfare hotels or exploited in private nursing homes; psychotics wandering the streets 'locked in or locked out' of dilapidated boarding houses, barely able to cash their welfare checks, the prey of street criminals and a source of nuisance and alarm to local residents too poor to leave; an increasing ecological separation into 'deviant ghettos', 'sewers of human misery', garbage dumps for 'social junk' lost in the interstices of the city.[57]

All this might be termed exclusion through 'zones of neglect'. Our map would also have to show certain 'free zones' in which various forms of deviance or illegality (notably, the classic 'crimes without victims' — gambling, prostitution, drugs, pornography) would be tolerated or conveniently overlooked. This might be exclusion in the name of a vague liberal tolerance or, as Sykes suggests, the deliberate creation of 'combat zones' which can be kept under surveillance, thus allowing some degree of control over what cannot be entirely suppressed.[58] The standard model is the legal segregation of strip bars, X-movies, massage parlours and so on.

It is difficult to conceive of hermetic separation and exclusion, if only for the simple reason that the physical and the social do not coincide (even to the extent that they might have done in those maps of the Victorian city). And cultural or political differences will produce patterns unlike that of the central sandbox, reservation or pariah inner city. In Britain, for example, it has long been noted that the apparently 'clean' housing estate beyond the green belt and away from the inner-city slum may be the dumping ground for problem families and a source of crime. Or urban renewal may leave uneven pockets of poverty dotted throughout the city. Particular estates or high-rise blocks may become segregated versions of what their utopian planners might originally have visualized as forms of inclusion.

In addition, changes might occur through patterns of class struggle and accommodation.[59] Unlike in the medieval city, with its clear hierarchies, the poor might not accept what is being done for them (though a typical reaction — vandalizing and devastating their surroundings — might only increase their segregation). And the planners, lacking the homogeneous vision of their autocratic Victorian class, might be open to ideas other than continual segregation. Still, even in Britain, where the reservation scenario has not been established, radical visionaries see separation:

a distinct compartmentalization of the city, area by area. There is a hostile city centre, defended like a medieval keep by an urban motorway either looking like a moat, or fearsome battlements — the inhabitants gone. The horrific vision of a city forsaken by any life, with traffic circulating unendingly round its ring road . . . Surrounding this there are a series of enclosed camps, hemmed in by the arteries which once gave them life. People only enter and leave by controlled exit points to go to work . . . Then a further series of scattered encampments cluster the outer ring road, in the same state of isolation: workers commute to the city centre from outer suburbs, others travel out to the ring road factories. They never meet.[60]

If such radical criticism (and popular consciousness) tend towards exclusionary images of the city, this is even more apparent in science fiction. The overwhelming sense from these visions is a total separation and enclosure.[61] The forces of chaos, darkness and entropy — represented by crime, pollution, traffic congestion, or overpopulation — move inexorably closer and they have to be contained by barriers and enclosures. In one vision, the city regains its medieval role as fortress: the white middle classes occupy enclaves and sanctuaries in the inner city, undesirables and racial minorities are banished to reservations beyond the border. In the opposite vision — more dominant and corresponding more closely to what urban sociologists claim is already happening — the reservations are in the inner city and the white, the middle classes or the powerful have fled to sanitized suburbs beyond the city boundaries.

Writers' like Barry Malzberg and Robert Silverberg have, obsessively, produced permutations on these themes. Malzberg describes a Manhattan totally populated by a violent, malevolent and degraded class, the 'lumpen': one-tenth are there by choice, the rest as a penalty, or a result of idiocy, incompetence or a relationship with someone in these categories. Everyone else is 'outside'.[62] In Silverberg's 'Black is Beautiful', Blacks occupy a domed inner city and whites are commuters or come as tourists on helicopter buses to see how Blacks are managing their affairs.[63] It is like a city with an invisible wall. Silverberg and many others have also worked out a vision of lateral rather than horizontal separation. In *The World Inside*, people live in Urban Monads ('Urbmons'), thousand-floor buildings stratified into cities of different levels of status and intellectual ability.[64]

There is no shortage, then, of general visions of exclusion which correspond to dominant patterns of crime control. This correspondence might already be happening in movements such as CPED and defensible space. As Newman himself warned 10 years ago, the 'neat and workable' solution of letting urban core areas deteriorate, then putting a fence of police around them is 'done, though not talked about'. It might 'just happen' and become institutionalized. 'Remember that if all of us here are looking for solutions to crime problems, then this is one of the neatest, simplest, most effective — even though it is morally unacceptable — ways. There is a real danger that we will fall into the trap of accepting it when things become desperate.'[65]

CONCLUSION: DOMAINS OF CONTROL

I have given but a sample of the images and visions yielded by those two contrasting modes of control. First, there is *inclusion*, with its metaphors of penetration, integration and absorption, its apparatus of bleepers, screens and trackers, its utopia of the invisibly controlling city. Then there is *exclusion*, with its metaphors of banishment, isolation and separation, its apparatus of walls, reservations and barriers, its utopia of the visibly purified city.

As I will show in the next chapter, these images point to very real policy choices. But when put into practice, the contrasts cannot always be sustained. The two visions merge, with exclusion tending to dominate. Thus, the creation of forms of control informed by the inclusionary vision — those 'wider and different nets' — leads to new modes of separation. At the heart of the inclusive system administered by Mr and Mrs Citizen were tests, diagnostic devices, screening systems, labels and categories. Inclusionary principles such as tolerance and non-intervention can also find their expression in the rigid ecological separation of deviants. And the decentralization impulse — an attack on the exclusionary powers of professionals, bureaucracies and the central state itself — might result in repressively localistic, parochial and xenophobic institutions.[66] Starved of resources — because the shut-off valve on what flows into the neighbourhood or school is somewhere else — these institutions deteriorate and become themselves controlled through exclusion.

To understand these apparent paradoxes or unintended consequences, we must return to the same deposits of power discussed earlier. In particular, those questions about community and state become important — and both inclusion and exclusion reveal similar contradictions. Let me give some examples.

(1) The trouble with inclusion is that it is only utopian when it is explicitly anti-statist. Inclusion, self-help and community are all inconsistent — as the anarchist tradition correctly shows — with state regulation and ownership. Thus, when the principle of inclusion is taken over by the state, the result looks appalling — the perfectly functioning totalitarian society. If the inclusive community apart from the state looks like pure utopia, the inclusive state is pure dystopia.

(2) This is complicated by the question of ownership — the 'commodification of space' as Marx saw it. The public exclu-

sionary mode (deportation, imprisonment) is very different from the private exclusionary mode. To the extent that state intervention is being replaced by market mechanisms, new forms of private exclusion develop ('privatization'). With erosion of support for public institutions (school, welfare, police) and a decline of public services (whether garbage collection or health), the private sector not only offers replacement services (like private security) but 'commodifies' its own space. The pure market allows for increasing ecological separation based on life-styles, age, special needs, degrees of deviance: buildings, blocks neighbourhoods, even whole 'villages' (like Century City) which resemble medieval gated towns.

(3) To borrow Marxist terminology again, there is the 'fetishization of space'. Ever since the nineteenth-century ideal of moral architecture, reformers have exaggerated the extent to which social problems can be solved merely by reordering physical space. This is true whether the visions are inclusionary or exclusionary: the culture of diversity or the pariah city. This is to by-pass the central debate in urban sociology: the city as ecological, a system in itself, versus the city as political, merely a site for practices worked out elsewhere. These are the terms in which movements like neighbourhood justice or CPED need to be analysed.

(4) Then a final example of a paradox inherent in the inclusionary vision — a structural paradox which is not just a question of faulty implementation. When matters such as boundary blurring, integration and community control take place, the result is that more people get involved in the 'control problem'. In order to weaken, by-pass or replace the formal apparatus, more rather than less attention has to be given to the deviance question. In order to include rather than exclude, a set of judgements have to be made which 'normalizes' intervention in a greater range of human life. The result is not just more controllers (whether professionals or ordinary citizens) but also an extension of these methods to wider and wider populations. The price paid by ordinary people is to become either active participants or passive receivers in the business of social control.

It is difficult to know just how far this process of indefinite 'inclusion' might go. The type of theoretical problems I listed and (more important) all sorts of 'external' contingencies — political, economic, demographic — make any predictions extremely hazardous. But, as a conclusion to this chapter, let me try.

If we superimpose the newer 'inclusionary' controls onto the more traditional forms of exclusion (notably incarceration) and their counterparts in the city (reservations, sandboxes, or whatever), we arrive at the likeliest future of social control. It is a future of decisive and deepening bifurcation: on the soft side there is indefinite inclusion, on the hard side, rigid exclusion.

By 'soft', I mean mental health, the new growth therapies, middle-class 'thought crime', the tutelage of family life, the minor delinquent infractions. Here, inclusive control will be extended in two ways:

(1) there is the enterprise of inner space: new therapies, professions, specialities, movements and cults will continue to expand, taking in the unreached, the healthy neurotic, the potentially deviant and the ordinary citizen. More domains of inner life will be penetrated in the same way as stages of the biological lifespan have been medicalized (life from birth to death as a series of risk periods, each calling for professional observation, check-ups, tutelage, supervision and intervention) or psychologized (by being turned into a series of growth periods, life crises, identity transitions or 'passages').[67] The aim is to discourage anything from being casual — leisure, family, child rearing, sexuality. The cults of efficiency and happiness will offer themselves everywhere: posture, reflexes, orgasm, diet, breathing, dreams, relationships, psychic plumbing, child rearing. The end-point of this 'triumph of the therapeutic' is a 'colonization of the subjective' and a gradual coalescence of the therapeutic with mass culture itself.[68]

(2) Then there is the enterprise of social space. There will be an extension of those types of inclusionary work in which the Citizen family were involved: dispersed, invisible, integrative, and relatively non-stigmatizing. Schools, families, neighbourhoods, youth organizations and work-places will increasingly be exploited as sites for this type of control. More importantly, this sort of enterprise will become diagnostic, predictive and preventive. Urban environments and situations will become sites for behaviour control.

These later forms of intervention (CPED, target hardening, innovations in surveillance techniques, proactive policing) will of course, be more directed at hard rather than soft forms of deviance. But, at the hard end, exclusionary methods will continue to dominate. For one thing, it is virtually impossible even to visualize a society in which the invasion of subjective space and the preventive surveillance of social space can be so total and successful as to prevent all deviance. At their purest, these forms of inclusion work because they are voluntary or simply because they are not recognized to be social control. But they require a back-up sanction: if you do not take the initiative yourself or if we do not spot you in advance, this is what might happen to you.[69]

There are other far more important functions to exclusionary. control, however, than this purely instrumental back up. The bifurcatory principle itself — which, in the absence of evidence to the contrary I take to be a cultural universal — demands sorting out, separation and segregation. It is obvious that the inclusionary mode neither fulfils these symbolic functions nor answers the instrumental demand for a solution to hard-end crime.

At the symbolic level, social control must fulfil the functions of creating scapegoats, clarifying moral boundaries and reinforcing social solidarity. The primeval form of scapegoating directs aggression towards individuals not responsible for the group's frustration (which may be caused by external threat or internal discord). In the ancient Hebraic ritual, the high priest puts his hand on the goat, confesses injustices and sins, then the animal is driven out into the wilderness. This is to leave people feeling purified and solidified. These functions remain when societies move towards putting blame not on the community or its arbitrary 'representative' but on certain individuals who are then *properly* caused to suffer.

It is quite clear that neither the psychological functions of scapegoating (cleansing, reminding the righteous of their purity),[70] nor the classic social functions described by Durkheim (boundary maintenance, rule clarification, social solidarity) can be served by inclusionary control. Indeed, by not developing an alternative conception of stigma, by trying to abolish or downgrade all elements of ceremonial status degradation,[71] and by persisting in labelling-theory's touching faith that deviants are not, after all, very different from non-deviants, inclusionary controls are ill-equipped to foster social integration. The rituals of blaming are difficult to sustain: they lose their moral edge. Exclusionary control is symbolically much richer: stigma and status degradation are sharper, deviants are clearly seen as different from non-deviants and, above all, there is the promise that they will be vaporized, thrown down the chute or filed away, and not just keep coming back to be 'reintegrated'.

The purely instrumental, rather than symbolic, advantages of exclusion are even more obvious. Inclusion simply does not offer any solution to 'crime on the streets'. It is increasingly likely that bifurcatory separation will take more and more rigid forms and that those selected for the hard end — career criminals, dangerous offenders, recidivists, psychopaths, incorrigibles or whatever — will be subject to more and more punitive forms of exclusion. The rigid application of just deserts, long sentences in tougher prisons, selective incapacitation and a greater use of the death penalty, can be expected. We have noted the predictions: most projected economic, political and technological changes will lead to an increase in serious crimes to which society is vulnerable and a political ideology which will insist on a rigid bifurcatory and punitive agenda in order to command legitimacy.

In symbolic and instrumental terms, then, we can expect a future trade-off. As payment for voluntarily submitting to psychic help, for cooperating in all sorts of inclusionary projects and for tolerating a certain amount of inconvenience, the ordinary citizen will want to be reassured that the state means business. If I buy all the self-help books, become the foster parent of a troublesome child, spend my evenings patrolling my block, tolerate the crazy old ladies mumbling on the buses and let myself be frisked at airports, then I want to be sure that the exclusionary lines are properly and firmly drawn.

Leaving aside crime control in the formal sense, exclusion also fits better the realities, images, desired states and projected futures of the city. The utopian vision has always been homogeneity, conformity, stratification and separation. The point of exclusion is to create purified domains inhabited by just the right groups: not too old and not too young, not too blemished or disabled, not troublesome or noisy, not too poor, not with the wrong-coloured skin. This was the vision which Sennet criticized: unable to face up to diversity, the city tries to purge any form of unpleasantness. The 'innocent' scapegoat, the justly punished offender, the members of high-risk groups are all candidates for exclusion.

So, we arrive at a vision not too far from Orwell's. Middle-class thought crime is subject to inclusionary controls; when these fail and the party members present a political threat, then 'down the chute'. Working-class deviant behaviour is segregated away and contained; if the proles become threatening, they can be 'subjected like animals by a few simple rules'.

There is another resonant set of control images from twentieth-century fiction. This is Burroughs' vision of the soft machine, with its refined techniques of inclusionary control, blurring imperceptibly into the terrifying finality of the hard machine. There are pushers, agents, informers and charlatan doctors; there are the reconditioning centres, and the methods of autonomic obedience processing; there is Dr Shafer, the Lobotomy Kid, trying to produce the Complete All American De-Anxietized Man. All these agencies are *senders* (a key word for Burroughs). They are sending messages and this, in cybernetic terms, is the meaning of social control: 'nothing but the sending of messages which effectively change the behaviour of the recipients'.[72]

This type of language is important. It removes from 'control' its everyday connotations – dominate, manipulate, use as an instrument, impose one's will, govern another's movements – and allows the word to be used as if it were 'value free'. As Skinner explains: 'what is needed is more "intentional" control, not less, and this is an important engineering problem.'[73]

There is never the fear of too much control, but of too much chaos. If we feel we are losing control, we must try to take control. The senders start feedback loops which can never end; like drug addicts, they satisfy needs only to stimulate them further. Thus, 'control can never work . . . it can never be a means to anything but more control . . . like junk.'[74]

# 7

# What Is To Be Done?

I came to sociology by way of social work. My first training and career, that is, was devoted to the business of helping people. In various ways — with homeless old vagrants, with families coming to a child-guidance clinic, disturbed adolescents at a youth club, patients in a psychiatric hospital — I thought that I was doing good. And I very probably was. Eventually though, in the course of those usual biographical contingencies we later dignify with words such as 'conviction', I changed course. It seemed to me more interesting, more politically worthwhile, even more useful to start looking at the *real* causes, the *big* questions. So I became a sociologist.

No one better formulated this move than C. Wright Mills — the conversion of 'private troubles' into 'public issues'. I was powerfully impressed by this theoretical agenda, this type of attack on purely individualistic approaches to social problems. I remember also hearing at about this time a parable which Saul Alinsky, the radical American community organizer used to tell. It went something like this. A man is walking by the riverside when he notices a body floating down stream. A fisherman leaps into the river, pulls the body ashore, gives mouth to mouth resuscitation, saving the man's life. A few minutes later the same thing happens, then again and again. Eventually yet another body floats by. This time the fisherman completely ignores the drowning man and starts running upstream along the bank. The observer asks the fisherman what on earth is he doing? Why is he not trying to rescue this drowning body? 'This time,' replies the fisherman, 'I'm going upstream to find out who the hell is pushing these poor folks into the water.'

An impressive message to social workers: as long as you do nothing about original causes, you will continually just be pulling out bodies, mopping up the casualties. Here lay the promise of sociology: to get at structure, power, history and politics – the real stuff of social problems. But Alinsky had a twist to his story: while the fisherman was so busy running along the bank to find the ultimate source of the problem, who was going to help those poor wretches who continued to float down the river? As I moved further into sociology, this question continued to trouble me, and it still does. So I wrote worried and confused papers about why radical theories of crime and deviance seemed 'right', yet had undesirable, ambiguous or no implications at all for the individual business of helping (social work) or punishing (criminal justice).[1]

The problem seemed to be that the more successfully and radically social science changed your view of the world, the more indifferent it became to the fate of those individual bodies. It was not that social science did not help *understand* their fate. Quite the contrary. Theory and research became more and more sophisticated and in the areas of social life which interested me (crime, deviance, law, punishment) there were many sociological descriptions and explanations which were interesting and perfectly comprehensible. They made a difference to the way the world looked. But, as William James said, 'a difference that makes no difference is no difference'. I would deliver the same sort of message implicit in this book (without the ponderous analysis or the academic footnotes) to a group of social workers, and depart knowing that although everything I had said was right, it made no difference to my audience. Or else that it had made only the sort of difference which my colleagues assured me should make me proud: that these poor misguided social workers should now feel demoralized and frustrated about their work, and start looking for the 'real' issues (become sociologists?).

To the extent that I ever picked up these feelings (luckily my audiences were usually too sensible to be much influenced in this way) I became even more depressed and guilty. What a way to make a living: going round telling well-meaning people that what they were doing was no good! This was a shared cognitive experience for a large part of a generation of sociologists working in the social-problems area. We could draw on the vast literature around such issues as 'pure' versus 'applied' or 'committed' versus 'detached' social science, and criminologists arranged themselves along various axes of these standard debates. Some interpret their academic role in pure, theoretical, and intellectual terms; others openly align themselves with conservative forces; and yet others proclaim a committed, critical and radical role. Some stay outside the system, and talk about 'knowledge' (scientific or liberatory), others are attracted by 'power' and, as evaluators, advisers, consultants and policy makers, they are very much part of the system. Some want to solve the crime problem; some want to do justice; some still want to do good; some want to do nothing.

Aesthetically, I am closer to the traditional and privileged academic position. Despite the occasional psychic discomfort this entails, I am convinced that the role of the sociologist of crime and punishment is no different from that, say, of the sociologist of religion. We should not be priests, theologians or believers, and social scientists who have taken up equivalent positions in regard to crime are misguided. This is not to say that we can ever produce knowledge uncontaminated by power, nor that we should not be concerned with the analysis of power. But it is simply not our professional job to advise, consult, recommend or make decisions. Flattering and tempting as these tasks might sound, they belong to others.

This is not how most of my criminological colleagues see things. I have already noted the signs of technicism: the relative loss of interest in matters of causation, the endless quest for 'what works?', the invention of new ways to calibrate pain. This might be where the applied, professional role which I described in chapter 5 is leading. But technicist criminology is not the object of this chapter. My object, rather, is the very type of critical social-policy analysis which this book itself represents — its content, tone and characteristic biases. Not just the well-meaning activist but also the intellectual observer (that person watching Alinsky's fisherman) has to be interested in the bodies floating down the river. Part of *intellectual* work is to clarify the implications of your analysis. That is, to try to understand the type of differences which do make a difference. While my sociology draws me upstream, and to the public issues, my pragmatism directs me to the drowning bodies, to the private troubles. But leaving aside such pragmatic considerations, it is a simple matter of intellectual integrity and honesty to clarify the policy implications of social-problem analysis. This is especially so if this analysis contains intentional or unintentional distortions.

My aim in this chapter is to provide neither a handbook of practical recommendations on the one hand nor a set of lofty political platitudes on the other. The point is to clarify choices and values. And also to search our own stories for the same type of hidden agendas, deep structures and domain assumptions we so readily detect in the stories which others tell.

## THE INTELLECTUAL AS ADVERSARY

We have heard enough about the criminologist as technician, hired hand, and servant of the state, as informer and supplier of alibis, as producer of knowledge which legitimates power. But what of his supposed opposite — the radical intellectual who contemplates social-control matters with total criticism, detachment, alienation and even disgust?

Everything in my book so far has, more or less implicitly, supported this adversarial stance. As journalism, these pages come not from the 'gee whizz' tradition (impressed by everything), but from the 'aw nuts' tradition (impressed by nothing). As sociology, this has been a demystification job: things are not what they seem. Only those at the margins, those untouched by the mess and the power, have the necessary detachment to understand what is happening. Above all, only they can understand that things are not only not what they seem, but that they are much *worse* than they seem. In radical eschatology, no good at all can be found. All reforms, however liberal and well intentioned (indeed particularly when liberal and well intentioned) must lead to more repression and coercion. Contradictions increase and the system disintegrates, ultimately sowing the seeds of its own destruction. In a recent liberal world view (too moderate to be called 'eschatology'), the very basis of liberal reformism is open to similar doubt, benevolence itself is a highly suspect motive and its consequences invariably disastrous.

I have drawn on several versions of this type of adversarial pessimism (as opposed to the standard conservative pessimism which holds simultaneously to the views that things cannot be changed and that they were better before). Labelling theorists continue with their sceptical, ironical, even cynical and slightly world-weary view about the workings of social institutions. Marxists reject the possibility that much good can emerge from corporate capitalism (good is elsewhere, in systems of socialist legality, popular justice or the socialist society of the future). Maverick critics like Illich make their fatalistic, nihilistic predictions about all human services and helping professions (divine retribution will come for our unbounded desire for material goods, for our presumption to conquer nature and our absurd faith in technical solutions to human problems). Each of these streams of adversarial thought has worked out its own versions of the same two fateful paradoxes. First, that the cure might be worse than the disease[2] and, second, that most radical and oppositional attacks on the system will end up being absorbed, co-opted and even strengthening it.

Thus, we are told, things are worse than they seem, they are getting even worse and even the best of plans lead to the worst of consequences. I will use the terms 'analytical despair' and 'adversarial nihilism' to describe the complementary cognitive positions which lead to such conclusions. These are positions only too easy to sustain, not just because they fit the pessimistic and dystopian climate I mentioned in the last chapter, but because they come naturally to large sectors of the intelligentsia of Western social democracies. As Gouldner nicely suggests, the conservative and radical critique of intellectuals complement each other. The conservatives (like Shils) award them autonomy and condemn them for always being against prevailing culture and authority; the radicals (like Chomsky) see them as subservient to power and condemn them for not opposing the establishment. As Gouldner says, 'what it comes down to, then, is that the opponents of the system *cannot* change it, while the system's friends do not *want* to. Thus no rational change is possible.'[3]

But this is not the place to even begin to review the massive literature on this social group, on its history and the reasons for its disaffection. I want to make the more limited point that the adversarial role should itself be subject to analysis and demystification. The assumption that facts must always be unpleasant distorts the world as much as its opposite.

One major form of distortion is to compound the already distorting tendency in all sociology — whether Panglossian or deeply despairing — to overgeneralize. By concentrating on systems, structures, patterns and trends, by talking glibly of societies, systems and epochs, sociological analysis is often quite insensitive to variations, differences and exceptions. Not all the projects, programmes and strategies I described were relentlessly the same nor fitted equally into the general patterns I suggested. There were (and are) notable instances of destructuring reforms and community alternatives which have succeeded. Even in the case of dramatic overall failures to meet declared initial goals, some incidental successes were registered. Analytic despair dwells on the 70 per cent of clients in community agencies who would not anyway have been clients for incarceration; honesty demands that the other 30 per cent be given some attention. Adversarial nihilism questions the whole point of liberal reforms which end up being co-opted by the system; pragmatism looks for the gains which are made despite this co-option. The world may not be what it seems (if it were, Marx reminds us, there would be no need for science) but sometimes things might be better rather than worse than they seem.

Perhaps the most interesting example of the distortions produced by analytical despair and adversarial nihilism lies in the notion of unintended consequences. It is reflexly assumed that where a gap between official goals and actual consequences is to be found, this must be for the worst. The reform vision might have contained genuinely good (if muddled) elements but (for whatever reason) these good elements fade away and only the bad are left (threats to civil liberties, extension of state power, disguised coercion or whatever).

But in logical terms alone, the notion of unintended (or unanticipated) consequences must allow for positive as well as negative consequences. Why should these also not be 'ironies of social intervention'? Henshel has set out the main logical possibilities here: reforms turn out to be better than expected, (i) because unrecognized bad features of the previous condition are removed; or (ii) the reform turns out to have unrecognized beneficial features. Reforms turn out worse than expected because (i) unnoticed or unappreciated good features of the old arrangement are now lost; or (ii) because the reform itself turns out to have deleterious features.[4] It is the first two possibilities which we so often neglect.

In each case, needless to say, terms such as 'better' or 'worse', 'beneficial' or 'deleterious' imply a series of complex value judgements which may be quite specific to particular societies, historical periods and to whom is being affected by the reforms. But such judgements are absolutely unavoidable. The very vocabulary of social-problem intervention implies an initial state judged to be undesirable and an end state (the solution) which is supposed to make things better. The notion of intervention also demands an explicit comparison with what might have happened if nothing at all was done.

These are all, surely, banal enough points, though many sociologists reject the idea that the criterion of solubility should be at all important in defining social problems.[5] But this is a disingenuous position for those who also claim to be 'relevant' and, moreover, it leads to analytic distortions among those who claim 'purity'. Analytical integrity alone demands that social problems should not *in advance* be defined in such a way that no solution is possible, that all putative solutions must be worse than the initial state, and that all unintended consequences must be negative.

The combination of analytical despair and adversarial nihilism can lead radical critics of social-control policy into some strange directions. Consider the assumption of complexity (which I suggested in chapter 5 as an in-built cognitive bias in the professional world view). If, indeed, mere social reforms can never touch the real causes of social problems (which are fundamental, deeply rooted and complex), then reforms are doomed to failure in advance. This might be a correct analysis, but how are its implications to be distinguished from the conservative position that root causes (human nature and the social order) are beyond change? Here is a random example of what I mean. An altogether plausible analysis of the complex reasons why decarceration went wrong, concludes that such reforms 'simply reflect the wider economy of power relations under welfare state capitalism. Except for continued, perpetual tinkering at the organizational level among interested professionals in the crime control business, we cannot expect much change in this state. *After all, it is part of the order of things.*'6

This is analytically correct. But if nothing works because nothing can work, then perhaps nothing should be done at all? And perhaps ameliorative reforms should even be resisted on the grounds that they lull people into tranquillity and impede the realization of revolutionary social changes?

Or, consider the persistent tendency — my own included — to condemn a crime-control policy or programme simply by labelling it 'coercive' or 'punitive' and, hence, we are invited to conclude, a failure, unjust or inhumane. This is a peculiar stance, indeed, for intellectuals who subscribe to socialist or some other set of collective values. Only in the crudest forms of libertarianism and in the most romantic strains of labelling theory does it make sense to defend the exclusive rights of the individual against *any* form of imposition by the collective. In no other political philosophy or social theory can this be the way to resolve the relationship between the individual and society. It continually grieves me to see questions of punishment and individual moral responsibility posed in this way, particularly when it is implied that these are mere bourgeois issues which will quite obviously be resolved in the new social order.

This brings me to another type of adversarial distortion — the use of selective cognition and morality when comparing capitalist with other societies. I have written elsewhere about the example of popular or community justice.7 Starting with the assumption 'Beware the Greeks bringing gifts', all experiments in popular justice in capitalist societies are viewed with the greatest suspicion and subjected to the most rigorous analytical scrutiny – as forms of hidden coercion, net-widening, co-option or mystification. But certain forms of popular justice elsewhere, particularly in Third World revolutionary regimes, are often accepted with total credulity and their claims taken entirely at their face value.

This lack of synchronization between analytical rigour about your own society and romanticism about elsewhere is a familiar human and political failing, but the 'Beware the Greeks' mentality has some rather special and strange consequences when contemplating certain social-control reforms. For the bearers of the gifts were not always 'them' (the reformers, managers, professionals and politicians who used the destructuring rhetoric). They were often 'us' – the same radicals whose intellectual work fed this rhetoric.

We can respond in three ways to this poignant problem of failure (more or less mimicking those different theoretical models I described).

(1) We were right – we still agree with our original values, preferences and ideologies, but 'they' didn't understand us. The problem is implementation: the world is a complicated place and either bureaucratic imperatives or professional self-interest will mess things up.
(2) We blew it – yet again. Benevolent intentions are suspect and the whole business of doing good has to be re-evaluated.
(3) We told you so. This sort of 'tinkering' is bound to fail, things are always getting worse and nothing much good can come from this type of society; it is in 'the order of things'.

This chapter is largely a (self)-reflection about the third response. Its particular defect is that it does not confront the nature of the original values themselves. It is as if we were slightly embarrassed even to refer to them. They are dismissed as the product of false consciousness, inadequate theory (the 'sentimentalism' of labelling theory, the 'inversion' of left idealism) or the over-enthusiastic political commitment of youth.

That third response has another defect: perverse ethnocentrism which blocks out the realities of social control in other, especially socialist and communist, societies. Again and again – it would be tendentious to give examples – a general sociological point is made about 'capitalism' or 'liberalism' without any attempt to see whether this is not, after all, a more general social attribute or just *how* it differs in other societies or ideologies. Take the metaphor of the 'carceral archipelago' borrowed from Foucault and used by him to designate the way in which punishments are dispersed, yet cover the whole of a society. For some years now, this metaphor has been used to conceptualize Western control systems, and I believe that it is a good metaphor. But we have forgotten its origin in the real Gulag Archipelago. Foucault himself (in a way which does not endear him to orthodox Marxists) does not forget. He calls on radicals to confront the actual Gulag not by searching Marx and Lenin for errors, condemnations, deviations, misunderstandings and betrayals of theory and practice. For him, it is

> Rather a matter of asking what in those texts could have made the Gulag possible, what might even now continue to justify it and what makes its intolerable truth still accepted today. The Gulag problem must be posed not in terms of error (reduction of the problem to one of theory) but in terms of reality ... (this means) giving up the politics of inverted commas, not attempting to evade the problem by putting inverted commas whether damning or ironic around Soviet socialism.[8]

But leave aside the question of political criticism and the specific implications of the real Gulag. Even the most superficial sense of histories and societies outside North America and Western Europe should be enough to temper the enthusiasm with which specific judicial and punitive modes are so easily associated with crises in capitalism, changes in productive relations, cycles of unemployment, fiscal problems of the state, or whatever. This is not wrong politics but bad theory.

I have alluded to some of the reasons for this type of theoretical problem: analytical despair, over-generalization, adversarial nihilism, the culture of pessimism, political ethnocentrism. But perhaps there is an even deeper defence mechanism at work. Alongside the specifically conservative need for order and symmetry (which expresses itself in the quest for the purified city), intellectuals at various moments have been known to search for metaphysical absolutes and certainties. Isaiah Berlin has eloquently considered the Russian case.[9] He argues that at moments of historical crisis, people trade their doubts and agonies for deterministic views, for psychological cravings after 'essences' and certainties.

This is an illusory quest. A tough-minded world view (Berlin's 'pluralism') demands that we tolerate contradictions and inconsistencies. There can be no totally valid general solutions, only temporary expedients based on our clearly stated values and our sense of the uniqueness of each historical juncture. The question of crime generates absolute values — justice, social good, individual liberty, compassion — which are quite incompatible with each other and cannot be objectively ranked. Neither scientific nor political certainties can substitute for making difficult moral choices. Let me use the values of goodness and justice to illustrate the dangers of absolutism.

DOING GOOD AND DOING JUSTICE

There have recently been some startling changes of tactics, alliances and battlefields, but the basic conflicts in the politics of crime control are still expressed in traditional terms: soft versus hard, liberal versus conservative, treatment versus punishment or, more recently (and in many ways, more accurately), 'doing good' versus 'doing justice'. I do not intend to review here the massive current literature on this subject. The policy question I want to suggest is more limited: Just what sort of space for doing good and doing justice might actually be offered by emerging social-control systems? But before posing this question, some sense of the wider debate is needed.

In crime-control politics over the last few decades, the battle over doing good has been fought in two main areas: first, the somewhat restricted matter of the place of rehabilitation programmes in settings such as prisons and, second, the much wider issue of the legitimacy of rehabilitation as a primary aim of punishment. What has variously been termed the 'retreat from rehabilitation', the 'decline of the rehabilitative ideal' or the 'downfall of the therapeutic empire' over this period, has already been extensively described.[10] In chapter 4 I reviewed some of the reasons for this move, which of course overlapped with the destructuring impulse itself. These included distrust of the unchecked discretionary powers awarded to state officials, considerations of civil liberties, criticism of treatment as a mask for hypocrisy and coercion, and the perception that treatment was, anyway, not working.

Conservatives — so the story goes on — in the face of rising crime rates, general threats to order and traditional authority and then the apparent evidence that liberal solutions were played out, reaffirmed their traditional goals of deterrence, incapacitation and retribution by imposing harsh punishments. The liberal left 'capitulated', thinking that if the state could not be trusted to do good and if doing good anyway had ambiguous results, then we should, at least, let the system be fair, just, open and safe from abuse. So came the birth of the 'justice model' or the 'back to justice movement'.

But the next chapter of this story is already upon us. In the same way as the destructuring strategy was soon subject to 'first doubts and second thoughts', so the whole onslaught on rehabilitation and its supposed replacement by the justice model has turned out a terrible mistake. We blew it, yet again. The latest rallying call for 'real liberals' (as opposed to those now deemed treacherous and misguided 'justice model liberals') must be to re-affirm rehabilitation. In his passionate preface to a recent such call, Cressey mourns yet another episode in the tragic history of good intentions going wrong: 'the tragic irony involved as humanitarians, bent on reducing pain and suffering in the world, have recently convinced Americans to inflict more pain and suffering on criminals, even if doing so allows criminals to inflict more pain and suffering on the rest of us.'[11]

Cullen and Gilbert's 'real liberal' cry against the 'poverty of the justice model' and the 'corruption of benevolence' is indeed a resonant one. These are their main points:

(1) Whatever the flaws in the original rehabilitation model (ineffectiveness, civil-liberty abuses or whatever), it contained a hidden agenda of humane and decent values. Whether in the initial promise of the asylum movement, the visions of the progressive era, later psychiatric theories or positivist criminology itself, rehabilitation allowed the system to be humanized (it brought 'light into the darkness'). Even if treatment, strictly speaking, did not work, it imported into the prison all sorts of good things (education, counselling, relaxation of discipline) which served to ameliorate the pains of imprisonment.
(2) The justice model, on the other hand, is simply a movement to give renewed moral legitimacy to pure punishment. Perhaps the value of doing good was open to abuse and could only be imperfectly realized, but punishment can *never* bring good, even when it is carried out justly.
(3) By not questioning the basis of punishment, but simply computing how much of it is deserved, liberals have abandoned the whole debate to a political forum which is bound to be conservative.
(4) By basing policy only on the criminal act itself, the assumption is made that the state has not only no right, but no obliga-

tion to do anything about the offender's condition or background.

(5) In practice, the justice model has indeed turned out to be a masterpiece of unintended consequences. It has been totally co-opted into right-wing law-and-order politics and its visible 'success' in changing sentencing systems (making them fixed, mandatory, flat, presumptive, etc.) has only led to sentences which are longer, harsher and more unjust. In the process, prisons have become even more overcrowded and brutal than before.

(6) The overall attack on discretionary decision making has also turned out to be misplaced: this was precisely the way in which citizens could be protected from the hard edge of the state. When discretion goes, so does fairness, compassion and individuation, and in its place comes an abstract machine-like dispensation of fixed amounts of punishment.

In short, this is 'less a panacea than a Pandora's box': 'a criminal justice system rooted in retributive principles will be neither more just, more humane, nor more efficient than a system that at least ideologically, had offender reform as its goal.'[12] Cullen and Gilbert's new agenda for real liberals (and radicals) is to reaffirm rehabilitation. This time round, it is supposed to be a rehabilitation properly tempered by the need to curb the coercive powers of the state. We are told that, instead of giving way to despair, liberals should realize that rehabilitation is the only ideology which can be used to resist conservative policy and the only one which commits the state to care for the offender's needs and welfare. It is not enough for justice-model liberals to talk about the 'right' to decent conditions and treatment, nor to proclaim humanity as an end itself. This would only open criminal-justice politics to a struggle which the powerless are bound to lose. If the state was neglectful when it was supposed to provide services (rehabilitation was never *tried* properly) it will be even less diligent when it has no mandate to do so.

This is a persuasive programme. If I were interested in defending traditional liberalism I would not have any hesitation in joining this campaign. But then again I would have had no hesitation in joining the attacks on rehabilitation in the late sixties and proclaiming the value of justice (this is just what I did!). And I also might have supported the Fabian version of rehabilitation in Britain at the end of the fifties, spoken up for the Progressives in the twenties, supported the child-saving movement at the end of last century, even joined the ranks of the original asylum and penitentiary founders. And so, admirable as the notion of re-affirming rehabilitation might be, the banal question arises about why this particular new twist to the liberal ideal should not also meet a sorry end.

Cullen and Gilbert approvingly quote Thorsten Sellin's comment on the history of penal reform: 'beautiful theories have a way of turning into ugly practices.'[13] But why should this only be an epitaph for the justice model? This is what liberals said about doing good — and could say about anything that they once approved. Indeed, any policy, including the most anti-liberal, can be plausibly defended in this way. According to the *New York Times*, the latest 'quiet revolution' in the notion of what prisons are for is the recognition that *neither* rehabilitation nor deterrence works. A 'new theory of justice' has arrived: selective incapacitation of the worst career criminals. And a criminologist can be found to save the theory in advance from the judgement of history: according to Professsor Norval Morris, 'the danger of selective incapacitation is that it will be taken by the barbarians and misused'.[14]

I do not pretend to have an answer to this sort of silliness — this persistent assumption that theories are beautiful until the barbarians make them ugly. Perhaps, after all, there is no way of resolving the manifest contradictions between the lessons we learn from history and our moral obligations to state values, express preferences and make decisions — despite history. I very much agree with Rothman's statement of the 'exquisite diffi-culty' of applying the historian's analytic perspective (the ease with which you can do a hatchet job on deinstitutionalization) to the role of activist (placing your bets somewhere when talking about current alternatives to incarceration).[15]

But the activist's dilemmas aside, it is the theoretical crudity of the idealist separation of theory and practice which is so con-tinually striking in the history of crime control. Much self-con-sciously intellectual work is needed if we are to wake up from the dream of beautiful theories untouched by the pragmatics of power. One direction (combining two intellectual traditions which would certainly disown each other) would be to draw on classic American pragmatism and Foucault's theory of knowledge. Another less abstract route would be to examine the more general features of liberalism, instead of embarking on yet another round of burying then resurrecting liberal crime theory. How genuine is the paradox that neo-liberals and neo-conservatives currently find themselves

on the same side? And is that recurrent sense of bewilderment –
reviewing the past and then discovering that you have arrived too
late or that someone has messed up your ideas – peculiar to the
history of crime control or endemic in liberal ideology?[16] After
all the openings provided by labelling and then radical theory,
mainstream criminology appears once again to be insulating
itself from these wider debates.

There is also danger in that cognitive need for certainty, often
just as apparent in liberalism as in Marxism (where it is more usually
noticed). How absurd have been the cycles of fashion in crime-
control ideology: rehabilitation to justice then back to rehabilitation; psychiatrists then lawyers then back to psychiatrists; needs
then rights then needs again; determinism, free will then back to
determinism; institution then community, then again institution.
These oscillations are justified by an analytic despair which
pronounces absolute failure each time and therefore the need to
rush in a different direction. Thus the 'reaffirming rehabilitation'
movement (about to take off in the next few years) is total and
certain in its condemnation of the reactionary nature of the justice
model. But good empirical research can show that:

- the direct causal link between determinate sentencing and larger
  prison populations is *not* inevitable;[17]
- average sentence length does not always increase;
- reforms can succeed in making release dates non-contingent on
  participation in treatment programmes;
- these reforms continue to be supported by the prisoners' movement;[18] and that
- sentencing changes, anyway, probably correlate more closely
  with wider political and economic changes than with theoretical 'models'.

But leaving aside empirical questions, these leaps of fashion are
classic examples of what Jacoby terms 'social amnesia'. Each time
we move – to community, justice, treatment, or whatever – we
repress the reasons which inspired the last move. Let us look
again at the question of reaffirming rehabilitation. Not content
to revive rehabilitation as a value in itself or else as an ideology to
use in the struggle against conservatism, Cullen and Gilbert have
to make the very same essentialist claims against 'punishment' and
about the 'real' purposes of the criminal justice system which
started the last round of reforms moving. Thus, 'the goal of the
criminal justice system should be to improve rather than damage

an offender and that for society's own welfare, criminal punishment should reflect not our basest instincts (vengeance) but our most noble values,'[19] or (about punishment) 'at its most it provides a fleeting moment of satisfaction as one's thirst for vengeance is quenched.'[20]

But why is this type of absolutist rhetoric necessary? In the face of centuries of debate and any number of good arguments tồ the contrary, I see no reason for anyone to accept that 'the' goal of criminal justice should be to improve the offender. As it stands, the claim is ridiculous. And since when is punishment merely a matter of base, emotional vengeance? This sort of rhetoric would be enough to make me an unrepentant 'justice-model liberal'.

This leads me from the case for doing good to the claims for doing justice. Here I take a somewhat unusual supporting text — not two sociologists reaffirming rehabilitation, but a psychiatrist reaffirming justice. In his compelling account, *The Killing of Bonnie Garland*, Gaylin provides a model liberal argument for doing justice — as a positive social value (beyond 'base vengeance') and as a counter to liberal versions of doing good.[21] The details of the case do not concern me here: how Richard Herrin hammered his girl-friend to death; how the working of a defence claiming 'extreme emotional disturbance' excused him from maximum responsibility and led to the reduction of the charge to manslaughter; and how organized religion (the local Catholic church), psychoanalytical ideology and the adversarial trial system, all conspired to reach a verdict which placed individual welfare beyond social needs.

This is the essence of Gaylin's case: that organized good-will, empathy, compassion and the doctrine of psychic determinism usurped the feelings due to the victim as representative of the community. Not rehabilitation, but justice has to be 'reaffirmed', as an honourable moral value in itself and not merely something which the law mechanically requires. Gaylin insists that this moralistic idea is not the same as the notion of equity which lay behind the 'back to justice model' (of which he was one of the original advocates!). Justice is not just measurable fairness, impartiality and equity (this should have been called the 'equity model' rather than the 'justice model'), but a broader, more social and less tangible sense of 'rightness'. While the insanity defence (and similar notions from the rehabilitative model) have operated historically to bring a compassionate limit to the concept of human responsibility and a greater sense of relativism (and hence a more humane

concept of justice), no organized system of justice can be constructed from the point of view of individual need and welfare.

As Gaylin is aware, he is defending two very traditional moralistic principles: personal responsibility and the moral purpose of
law. These are principles of justice which come from a different
tradition to those of individuation, doing good, and rehabilitation. The newer tradition comes from a more enlightened,
scientific, humanistic and optimistic world view. In Richard Herrin's
case, certain expressions of this world view — individual rights,
compassion, psychic determinism — allowed an unbridled individualism to triumph which can only threaten the social good. If
people lose their sense that 'things are working' and that they are
living in a 'fair and just' society, this can generate 'anger and
outrage' which, in turn, leads to abandoning all humanitarian concerns for criminals and beyond that for disadvantaged groups in
general.[22]

I have quoted Gaylin's case because it so attractively counter-
poses the claims of doing justice against doing good, while staying
well within the liberal consensus. It loses its moral force the
moment we step outside this consensus. If the state is patently
not 'fair and just' if things are obviously not 'working', then there
is no sense of 'rightness' to be confirmed by the law. The three
major elements of the Marxist case against the liberal version of
the justice model all make sense. First, that the model gathered
momentum because it was sustained by a climate of political and
economic conservatism, retrenchment and despair — it was an
ideology that could allow coercion to be disguised as fairness.
Second (as the 'new rehabilitationists' suggest), the consequences
have largely been in the direction of harsher and more unjust
punishment. And third (and more important to me, because I
am concerned with the idea itself and not its origins or consequences), the formal notion of justice is contradicted by the presence of substantive injustice, inequality and exploitation, all of
which must seriously question those principles of individual
responsibility and moral legitimacy.

But in pragmatic terms, a nihilistic abandonment of the possibilities of doing justice in the here-and-now are no more justified
than the Gadarene rush away from doing good. As Greenberg
correctly argues, the justice model made perfect political sense
(and still continues to do so) as a way of dealing with immediate
grievances and injustices.[23] Analytical insight about the model's
origins, 'essence' or even consequences, should not lead to that

species of political quiescence in which 'once the observation has been made that the justice model is bourgeois and arises from the material relations of capitalism, nothing more is to be said or done.'[24] Each historically specific demand, whether for civil liberties in the sixties or justice in the seventies, must be judged in its own terms. Similarly, for each current demand 'it is little solace to someone who is not even being treated equally to be told that the demand for equality is bourgeois and therefore inadvisable.'[25]

Unlike the attractive but somewhat socially disembodied liberal idea of justice, Greenberg suggests a socialist programme which would: (i) endorse a principle of punishment and responsibility (within clear limits based on the nature of the violation and allowing for mitigating circumstances); (ii) be committed to abolishing the criminogenic features of the system which conservatives are committed to preserving; and (iii) be encouraged to think about questions of protection from state repression in socialist societies.

If the second part of this programme distinguishes it from conservatism and neo-liberalism, the third part is equally important as a counter to leftist romanticism about legal control in countries which call themselves socialist. This century's history of popular justice, revolutionary justice and socialist legality has by no means been uniform, but its dominant traces have been shamefully transparent. To go on mouthing these slogans as if nothing had happened is not only dishonest but it also — as Greenberg notes — removes the possibility of offering a concrete compelling vision that things need not be as they are. My preference is to be pragmatic about short-term possibilities but to be genuinely utopian about constructing long-term alternatives.

By way of this selective and somewhat breathless survey of the traditional terrain of criminal-justice politics, I can now state my position in shorthand. That is to say, offer a guiding criterion for evaluating 'community control' and other such forms of control which this book has covered. I term this criterion *moral pragmatism.*

The 'moral' element affirms doing good and doing justice as values in themselves. By 'doing good' I mean not just individual concern about private troubles but a commitment to the socialist reform of the public issues which cause these troubles. By 'doing justice' I mean not equity or retribution but the sense of the rightness and fairness of punishment for the collective good. By 'values in themselves' I mean that both utilitarian and strategic considerations should, where possible, be secondary to attaining these values for their own sake and whatever their other results. Or — in negative terms — utilitarian aims such as reducing crime should not be achieved at the cost of sacrificing cherished values. And while strategic goals are certainly justifiable, for example using the struggle for justice as a way of exposing injustice and using benevolence as a way of exposing inhumanity, these goals should not override immediate human needs.

The 'pragmatic' element stands against all forms of premature theoretical and political closure, all quests for cognitive certainty which rule out certain solutions as being conceptually impure or politically inadmissible. If the guiding values of social intervention are made clear (justice, good or whatever else might be offered) then the only question is: what difference does this particular policy make? Each proffered solution must thus be weighed up in terms of its consistency or inconsistency with preferred values, the alternative solutions realistically available at the moment of choice, and the likelihood of the programme being able to realize (intentionally or otherwise) the desired goals with the minimum cost.

A programme which comes near to this vision is Nils Christie's.[26] In order to escape the long historical oscillation between either changing the offender or inflicting a just measure of pain (those beautiful theories which always get into the hands of barbarians), Christie tries to abandon utilitarianism in favour of a clear moral position. Punishment must be understood, without euphemism, to mean the delivery of pain; the moral position is to reduce or severely restrict the use of man-inflicted pain in order to achieve social control.

With this definition and programme, Christie then re-reviews the history of classical and positivist criminology. Because his criteria are clear ('morally pragmatic' as I would see them), each stage or current option can be evaluated without either mindless progressivism (everything gets better) or analytic despair (everything gets worse). He sees gains in neo-classicism, for example – in its exposure of injustices in a system which pretended to treat people, its honest confrontation with the problem of pain, the protection it promised against unjust pain delivery, and the way it allowed values to be made more explicit. He also sees a loss, however, in neo-classicism's elevation of the criminal *act* to sole importance. This opened up the hidden agenda of simply inflicting more pain, created (like the theory of general deterrence) the illusion that there can be an abstract, simple and 'scientific' solution to crime and, above all, denied the legitimacy of the values (kindness, compassion) and the knowledge (limits to human autonomy) which dictated the hidden agenda of positivism.

In trying to imagine the knowledge and power which would be 'conditions for a low level of pain infliction', Christie arrives, significantly, at much the sort of vision which lay behind the destructuring movements of the sixties. He believes that social control should be genuinely decentralized (that is, it should replace and not just supplement the control repertoire and do so with local agents vulnerable and exposed to the community); systems of expertise and professional knowledge should be broken up; the euphemistic language of 'treatment' should be abandoned; the state should take on a minimal role. Right against the spirit of utilitarian thinking which sees treatment in terms of measurable cure, general deterrence in terms of measurable crime prevention, and justice in terms of calculated market exchange, Christie is defending an absolute theory of punishment, that is, an expressive rather than an instrumental theory. Punishment, in Christie's simile, should be like mourning – expressive and visible.

I offer something like Christie's expressive idea of punishment and his moral absolutism about pain reduction, together with my own criterion of moral pragmatism, not as panaceas, but as counters to utilitarian criminology. Nearly two centuries of scientific crime control have left a record of sustained failure for two perfectly obvious sociological reasons: first, the control system is not designed to work because it fulfils other more important social functions,[27] or because 'effectiveness' conflicts with other more important values; second, the major causes of crime are too deep-rooted for the control system to touch. Instead of being an invitation to do much the same or nothing at all, however, the historical record should invite us to consider other goals.

### INSIDE THE SYSTEM – AGAIN

We can now return to the machine and to the stories of my early chapters. This time, though, certain cognitive styles (analytical despair, the need for certainty, adversarial nihilism and the like) will be put aside. And the somewhat different lens of moral pragmatism will be used to search for possibilities and openings which were previously less apparent.

The matter of motives (paradoxically, because they are always more opaque) might be easier to resolve than the matter of consequences. Somewhere between the total credulity which greets good intentions and beautiful theories, and the total incredulity which dismisses them as fairy tales, each claim to do good or to do justice must be confronted on its own merit. This does not mean 'at its face value'. There is still the need to look for hidden agendas, undeclared interests, unlikely coalitions and uncontrollable forces. Social life being what it is, there is no reason to suppose that decarceration, delegalization, community justice, etc. will be informed by simple and transparent motives. Without some measure of analytical awareness, we are doomed to accept ritualistically — like the most naive of participants in interpersonal life — such motivational accounts as 'I only meant well', 'I didn't mean to do it' and 'I didn't know any better'. But with analytical awareness only, and no set of value preference nor any sense of historically specific judgement, we are doomed to eternal condemnation of self and others.

Evaluating the end-state itself is a much more difficult business because of the lack of fully agreed-upon criteria for success. Let me evade the question of the general social good or the collective sense of justice and try to imagine the real or potential difference which recent control practices might make to the individual (the body in the river, 'I, myself' in Kafka's corridor). The question is whether good or just things could happen in spite of (and even sometimes because of) net widening, intensification, dispersal or blurring.

Easiest to deal with, are the clear cases of acknowledged success in meeting initial goals. At scattered points in the system are agencies and programmes which were set up as radical alternatives and have satisfied their founders and clients. Take the example of rape-crisis centres. Influenced by ideas from the women's movement and the new left, informed by principles such as self-help, localism, community control, indigenous concern and anti-professionalism, these organizations have to a large extent retained their initial creative, radical and alternative edge. Despite their chronic organizational problems, their internal conflicts (between volunteer and professional or dependency and independency), their status as an arena for ideological conflict,[28] and even their co-option (for example, in the USA, into District Attorney offices), they conform closely enough to the original vision. In providing supportive services to the victims they are doing good, and in changing law enforcement priorities about the offender, they are doing justice.

Of course the conditions for this sort of success are quite distinctive: the strong counter-ideology of feminism, the right combination of pressure-group politics with self-interest, the relative absence of bureaucratic counter-interests. But this is hardly a reason to ignore such cases. Combining them with allied successes — shelters for battered women, counselling networks for gays, other self-help and support groups such as some ex-offender organizations, 'hot-line' communication systems for reporting problems, some neighbourhood youth projects — they should be opportunities to make valid generalizations and arrive at informed policy choices.

Similarly, even to its harshest critics, the informal justice movement has generated some interesting experiments: restitution programmes, mediation projects, advisory sentencing panels made of local residents (including sometimes the victim) and others. All my analytical generalizations still apply, but in the immediate sense these projects might clarify rather than obscure moral values, they might expose more ordinary people to the nature of the formal machine, and remind them that the state has no monopoly on justice.

Beyond these more visible exceptions, there is a less tangible sense in which the sheer proliferation of new agencies might be preferable to the stark alternatives of the old system. This would clearly be true for the justice model in its original more radical form. This required more mild sanctions for offences of intermediate seriousnesness. An appreciable number of offenders sent to these new options as a genuine alternative to release or imprisonment by no means look like 'cream puff cases' to their victims.

The question of doing good is more difficult to resolve, though clearly there are some programmes of community treatment and diversion, which are genuine alternatives to incarceration and are also more humane. To this extent, they might succeed in avoiding the harsh, stigmatizing and brutalizing effects of 'hard-end' institutions. This may happen not because of the quality of the 'services' but (as their original proponents sometimes claimed), simply because the new networks are more flexible. Or, to use a less euphemistic term, they are more *vague*. It is precisely the disguised, masked and blurred attributes of these agencies that allow good things to happen which before might have been more scrutinized and, therefore, more controlled. To the extent that it is not an imposed addition, the soft machine might be preferable to the hard machine just because it is softer. Radical eschatology often comes close to the position that open coercion is always better than hidden coercion. And it is certainly true that some offenders (I would suspect *all* offenders) would prefer not to be called 'clients' and would indeed like to 'know exactly where they stand'. I have an absolute value preference against euphemism, but I also have to concede that there are pragmatic possibilities in the creation of vague social institutions.

Vagueness, disguise and boundary blurring are not positive values in themselves. They can easily lead to the most undesirable consequences: violations of civil liberties, unchecked discretion, professional imperialism. But it is also possible that institutions with less visible margins would allow better things to happen around the edges. Some of those terrible sounding 'agents of social control', instead of being disguised storm-troopers of the state, might be able to deploy more resources along those margins, create more opportunities, and provide more services to groups who need them most.

In a curious and largely unintended way, community agencies might discover these needs and be able to respond to them. For at least a hundred years, positivist crime-control systems have used methods — identification, differentiation and surveillance — which cannot really 'fail'. Those who find themselves in the carceral network — in the interstices of all those centres, agencies, clinics and services — come from much the same social groups who have always been caught up (with some new shallow-enders thrown in). The depredations of white-collar, organized and government crime aside (a large aside!), the standard classificatory devices of positivism are more or less reliable: losers, misfits, troublemakers, outcasts and other members of the social underclass can be identified. This is just what the system has always done. More research on 'background variables' is hardly needed to show the main contours of deprivation, desperation, unhappiness, blocked opportunity and the like which can be sensed from an hour's visit to a prison.

My point is simply this: some good might be done, if only by chance, to those who are now being recycled into the soft machine. Not necessarily in the sense of stopping them committing another crime, and certainly not in the sense of even touching the real sources of inequality, exploitation, and deprivation. How absurd to think that 'community control' could do any of this. The good that might be done, would be to touch the 'incidental' problems which the positivist filter cannot but pick up: alcoholism, chronic ill-health, illiteracy and learning disability, psychological disturbance, ignorance or powerlessness about claiming welfare rights, legal problems, homelessness, etc.

The sheer statistical chance that community projects might be able to function in this way are increased, as I have suggested, by their very looseness and vagueness, by the fact that most of them do not actually have the slightest idea what they are doing. By being — however ambiguously — 'in' the community rather than behind closed walls, it is sometimes easier to assemble a package deal of useful services. All this was particularly true when community projects were first set up. In the heyday of the community-control movement when, in the USA, organizations like LEAA had large budgets to throw around, many of these projects were conscious attempts at window dressing. They indeed were actually called 'exemplary projects', and were designed to prove to sceptics that community could 'work'. They were well financed, invariably overstaffed and offered a wide range of services. Much of this funding has now dried up and these organizations are showing their harder side, have gone private or have disappeared completely.

Thus, instead of talking *only* about net widening or disguised coercion, the case can still be made for channelling welfare resources into genuine soft-end projects, certainly if this is an alternative to an escalating prison-building programme.

At their best, and especially when they were over-staffed with non-custodial professionals, these exemplary projects offered wide-ranging and useful services. Educational programmes, for example, provided facilities for individual tuition, small classes and personally tailored curricula. Or high-technology medical services were offered. Other projects unambiguously solved (and still do) such clear short-term needs as homelessness, for example the NACRO chain of hostels in England. Or else roles of advocate (acting on behalf of the client) and intermediary (putting the client in touch with other agencies) were developed — things which are usually more workable in community than custodial settings. Often what is done is banal enough: getting kids on to baseball or football teams, helping them open a savings account, sending them off to the Boy Scouts or the YMCA, giving out phone numbers of counselling services, sexual advisory clinics, or abortion agencies. . .

A simple anthology of these activities reveals this: the clients (reluctant as they are to be 'clients') are being offered (though sometimes it is an offer they can't refuse) the very range of services, facilities and contacts which the middle class takes for granted. All these matters are part of the environment in which the middle-class youth grows up — you can purchase them on the market, your parents 'know someone' who provides them, you are totally surrounded by advocates and intermediaries. In this sense, middle-class kids who get into trouble have always had their own system of diversion: access to counsellors, therapists, lawyers, or friends of the family who could help them stay out of the system, protect them from its hard edge or 'minimize penetration' (as they say in the diversion business).

At their best (and the majority fall dismally short of this), these are the sort of resources which diversion or community agencies could provide. Naturally, their clients have to pay a price which their middle-class counterparts do not: instead of being kept out of the system, they are kept in. In exchange for paying the market price you have to submit to labelling, compulsion and surveillance and you have to put up with diagnostic tests, classification schemes, evaluation research and tedious hours spent answering questions from psychologists. Still, a morally pragmatic approach to social intervention compels us to consider the cost-benefit ratio of all this — in human and political terms.

When we move from services, resources and contacts to the less tangible and more dubious benefits of therapy and rehabilitation, such considerations are even more difficult. There can be some general consensus about the value of literacy, for example, and hence the pragmatic gain of achieving this in a diversion agency. Therapeutic imperialism, on the other hand, is open to all sorts of intrinsic moral and political objections as well as lacking established criteria of individual success. At one level, it could again be argued that the extension of the therapeutic enterprise is merely an egalitarian provision to the working class of a resource which the middle class could always get. And it is surely true that if providing empathy, achieving relief from chronic anxiety and depression, and allowing for insight and self-awareness are good in themselves, then they should be available to all. Why should the working class delinquent also not be given such opportunities? There is a bizarre stream in radical political thought which seems to suggest that self-awareness is a bourgeois value and that the poor and the oppressed have no psychic lives at all.

The real objections to therapy in these community settings is the coercive price which might have to be paid and, hence, the diminished chances of any good being done at all. In addition, of course, what is usually provided these days is not insight or self-awareness but the dehumanizing psychology of behaviourism. The strategies established by the growth-and-awareness movements of the sixties — silly, superficial, intellectually thin and politically reactionary as they often may be — are loosely derived from a psychodynamic model which offers richer human possibilities than behaviourism. And there is little that is positively harmful in participating in a transactional analysis group. The egalitarian claim is more difficult to evaluate. When these services appear under the rubrics of community control or treatment, they are no more the 'same' as their middle-class derivatives than the medical or educational services in the Third World are the same as those exported from the West. The new clients receive an ersatz version of the original, administered by low-status and less-motivated professionals, and are more exposed to the annoyance of evaluation and experimentation.

Besides the services which are officially provided, community agencies might allow for all sorts of other hidden and unintended benefits. The genuine quest for community — perverted as it usually is by the official status of the agency — might unwittingly be realized within its interstices. When people come to these places, they seek and find (from each other and the staff) talk, friendship and intimacy. Or they simply want time out — adults from their spouses, their children and their work (or the dole queue), kids from their school and parents. In these circumstances, 'community control' or 'community treatment' provides little control or treatment, but some components of community.

Even if the agency or the agents do not deliver this (and might not even be aware of it), the vagueness of the new system makes it malleable enough to be exploited in this way. For generations, prisoners have managed to subvert the regime, to adapt it ingeniously to their own purposes and to acquire their own forms of 'resocialization'. The looseness of certain community agencies makes them even more suitable for these purposes. In the USA, for some years now, many forms of neighbourhood intervention have become major unofficial opportunity structures for local residents and have been absorbed into the local hidden economy and polity.[29] Offenders have built up a stake in the soft part of the system: being supported while searching for a job, finding new hustles, making a legitimate career as an ex-con or ex-addict in the new self-help agencies. 'Decentralization' was seen in political terms not as rebuilding small *Gemeinschaft* villages, but as an attempt to recreate (often not very successfully) the same local political machine based on patronage and services which brought power and mobility to earlier immigrant groups. The soft end of the system became a 'new career' (as one project was actually called).

And it is unlikely that the gobbledegook of the new Controltalk fools anyone. On the contrary, it provides a hip, sophisticated vocabulary well suited to manipulation by (rather than of) the client. The 'soft machine' is not a particularly efficient form of conditioning. As long as human beings can reflect on what is happening to them, they soon enough pick up the key survival skill: to know when you are being conned.

In some cases, the clients might not even have to work very hard to develop techniques of survival, subversion or exploitation. The project's staff might be committed to an anti-establishment strategy which makes them only too willing to collude with their clients in finding loopholes in the system. They are also living in the 'interstices', and their personal life-style and political commitment may lead them to sympathy and even solidarity with their underdog clients. As I suggested in chapter 5, professional power (and the professional 'ethic' of autonomy) can easily be used in these circumstances to benefit the individual. The new 'controllers' have been drawn from a cohort of graduates who were exposed to labelling theory and counter-cultural values and who know that hard control was not working. They have 'occupational self-interest', to be sure, in these new jobs built around the soft social-work vocabulary, but they are also sincere and have a need not to think of themselves as punitive (which is why they were so bewildered and resentful about the attack on treatment in the name of justice).

Workers of equally marginal status have also been recruited into the new neighbourhood-justice projects, and here the possibility presents itself of them arriving at just decisions which might have been less likely in the formal judicial system. Even the most hostile critics of current experiments in 'popular' or 'auxiliary' justice, concede that these new activists are less likely to be mystified by state justice agencies and might become 'angrily aware' about corruption, racism and inefficiency.[30]

To summarize: alongside an analytical view of current social-control systems, can be placed a more pragmatic sense about possibilities for realizing preferred values. There is some point in drawing attention to exceptions, unintended benefits and strategic loopholes. Individual gains may be registered, despite an overall system which must be judged with the deepest misgivings. As Brecht said: 'even bribed judges sometimes give correct verdicts.'

### MEANS AND ENDS

The original reformers and the current managers of the emerging system claim to be responding to real needs in the community or to be uncovering new needs. In a sense, they are correct. The social reaction to crime does not only reinforce social solidarity (as left and right functionalists suggest) but has the opposite 'latent function' — to expose the cracks and wounds in the social body. As the prospects get bleaker for a genuinely caring welfare state, the awful tragedy is that someone has to commit an offence (or be considered 'at risk') before the state will provide the services it should have provided anyway. But should crime-control systems be used in this way?

I argued earlier for doing good and doing justice as positive social values to 'counter' purely utilitarian crime-control theory. As it stands, this argument has two enormous flaws. The first is that it does nothing to resolve the inevitable clash of values between goodness and justice. Here I can only restate the difficulty of finding a fixed and absolute ordering of priorities. Each policy decision becomes an arena for clarifying these values and knowing where they compete.

The second flaw is that utilitarianism can never be really avoided: crime-control systems are utilitarian by definition. Social policy is the choice of means to achieve ends (even if these ends are themselves largely expressive or symbolic). The declared purpose of the crime-control system (and its mimesis in academic criminology) is to reduce or prevent crime. The blatant historical failure of either the system or the discipline to deliver the utilitarian goods — in the form of a crime-control policy that 'works' — cannot itself be an argument against utilitarian thinking. We can state in analytical terms that the 'real' purpose of the system is something else (endless classification, increased discipline, norm clarification or whatever), or even show that in-built failure is the required condition for the system and discipline to thrive. But it would be an irrelevant type of crime-control politics that deliberately rejected common-sense utilitarian criteria, as if to assert that such matters as death, injury, loss or insecurity as a result of criminal victimization are of no importance at all.

In a whole range of crimes and delinquencies too obvious to enumerate, we have to accept the most utilitarian of all common-sense justifications for punishment, namely, deterrence. And in those same examples, doing good for the individual offender must have very low priority, both in instrumental and expressive terms. One of the most banal of criminological truisms — again, the type stated on the first pages of textbooks and then forgotten (as I have throughout this book) — is that there are different types of crime and that no policy or causal generalizations can cover them all. The claim, for example, that *the* goal of the criminal justice system should be to improve 'the offender' is not worth considering for such offences as corporate crime or the vast bulk of traffic offences.

Such general debates, though, are beyond the scope of this book. I merely want to consider how the utilitarian question of effectiveness might apply to our various community and destructuring reforms. My anti-utilitarian preference dictates here that moral values which are cherished as ends in themselves, should not be relabelled as 'means' for the instrumental enterprise of crime control. Doing so would only be to devalue these values, and to lead to their abandonment if the official purposes of the system are then not achieved.

Take community crime-prevention projects as an example. Let us assume that a particular project (and this is close enough to the standard research finding about *all* such projects[31]) fails to reduce crime in the target neighbourhood, but succeeds in achieving what are variously conceived as 'means', 'incidental effects', 'intervening variables' or 'intermediate links'. That is to say, there is objectively the same amount of crime in the neighbourhood (or even more) but fear of crime is reduced (or held constant while increases are registered everywhere else); there is less apathy, helplessness and isolation; a deteriorating area has been revitalized; people are happier and more involved in their neighbourhood. And let us say that these effects have indisputably been produced by setting up services, facilities and agencies which are valued in themselves: playgrounds for kids; democratic tenants associations; shelters for battered women and rape victims; counselling, legal aid and restitution for other victims; escort services for the elderly . . .

My point is that, under these circumstances, the failure of the project to reduce crime is irrelevant. Under other circumstances, of course (the far more frequent result), not only is there standard utilitarian failure, but all those means, variables, links and effects are either without any value or are actually harmful. An example of a 'valueless means' would be to introduce a new form of psychological classification. This would neither reduce crime nor do any good for anybody (except the psychologists administering the test). An example of a harmful effect as a result of a community crime project, would be an increase in paranoia, hostility to strangers, and garrison living, despite no objective drop in the crime rate. In both such examples, the programmes should be scrapped without further thought (sadly, an unlikely outcome).

But where desired values are achieved — and this too, requires objective evidence and not just a vague feeling of self-satisfaction — then we are perpetrating great cruelty if we abandon a good policy on the grounds that it does not reduce crime. This is simply to assign too much importance to crime. We build adventure playgrounds because we believe in this, and not because it might reduce vandalism. Similarly (to talk about less measurable matters), if we are against inequality, racism and exploitation, our convictions should not be weakened in the slightest by the demonstration of low correlation coefficients with official crime rates.

The choice here is between two quite different political options. One would be the strategic use of social-control resources as an opportunity for welfare improvement — deliberately seeking out, for example, the type of gains from the soft machine that I have just described. The alternative would be to divert scarce resources right away from the system and devote them to policies (family, educational, community, health, fiscal, etc.) which are not justified in control terms at all. To pursue my simple example: the first strategy would be to use the excuse of 'vandalism prevention' in order to build adventure playgrounds for kids living in high-rise apartments; the second would be to forget about vandalism and simply build the playgrounds as part of a neighbourhood project.

The advantage of the first strategy is (sadly) that it is politically more appealing and hence more likely to attract the scarce resources which have not been consumed by hard-end law-and-order budgets. Its corresponding disadvantage is that it is more vulnerable to pseudo-scientific attacks of the 'nothing works' type and will be readily abandoned if it cannot be politically justified in crude utilitarian terms. The advantage of the second strategy is its integrity, its direct appeal to values and its ability to be defended in its own terms — of which none of which elements, of course, has the slightest appeal to right-wing politicians controlling monetarist economies.

Still — romantically — I am in favour of the second strategy. It offers, instead of planning for order and control, the opportunity to plan for human happiness and fulfilment. Colin Ward's beautiful book, *The Child in the City* contains 220 pages of ideas about what growing up in the city could and should be like, and nowhere is any policy justified as a form of delinquency prevention.[32] He talks about making cities more accessible, negotiable and useful for children; about allowing streets, neighbourhoods and public transport to be exciting and stimulating; about increasing opportunities for self-respect and confidence; about the possibilities of involvement and exploration in ways which are not predatory and harmful to others; about increasing control over physical and social space.

These might look like the same 'subjects' which are talked about in the literature on community control, and it would be nice to think that a realization of this sort of vision would reduce much predatory delinquency. But these imaginative possibilities appear not at all in the public discourse of social policy, and are distorted into 'means' in the grimly utilitarian projects of criminology. I have read thousands of books, articles and research reports about community control. I can remember very few instances of 'community' and 'growing up' being presented except as means to achieve order and control or to allow for a more decent separation of soft from hard offenders.

But the abiding ideology of community control draws on genuine psychic and social needs. It is easy enough to trace the mythical elements in this ideology, see how it is exploited and note how its reproductions are so appallingly different from the original. All this, however, hardly diminishes the reality of the quest. I believe that if people are offered the opportunity of experiencing community (or, shall we say, growing up in the type of city which Ward imagines) then they would like the idea, *even if* it did not guarantee efficient crime control. But this is hardly the stuff of which social-control policy in the 1980s is made. Professionalism, anti-utopianism, realistic utilitarianism, cost-benefit analysis, planning for the purified city: these better fit the dominant mood.

From all the tales about community control, one image remains vividly in my mind. As part of neighbourhood crime-control programmes in New York and other cities, projects with names such as 'Block Mothers' or 'Helping Hands to Children' were developed. Local residents were taught how to help children in trouble, how to approach them and calm them down if they were frightened or had been threatened. After this training, each resident would receive a decal − a large red clasped hand sign − to display conspicuously in the window. Neighbourhood children would be told that these were safe places to go for refuge − if running away from home, threatened by violence or just to talk to somebody.

No fine moral sensibility is needed to grasp what is bad about growing up in a neighbourhood where you fear the stranger in the street, and can only trust a neighbour whose benevolence is professionally certified and displayed.

### EXCLUSION AND INCLUSION – AGAIN

I have not written about the whole problem of crime and punishment. My allusions to conservative, liberal and radical positions or my account of doing justice and doing good were addressed only to the limited matter of the institutional patterns in which certain offender populations are deployed. Criminal justice politics (and allied ways of looking at the same issues – in literature, jurisprudence, sociology of law, political philosophy) involve complex issues and whole substantive areas which I have hardly even touched upon.

For all its complexity, though, and its centuries of unresolved and unresolvable debates, crime control occupies a curiously restricted place in the whole terrain of social policy. This is because it makes crime too important. All competing policies, whether based on rehabilitation, social reform, just-deserts, deterrence or incapacitation, remain within the closed circle of the offence or the offender. I want to end this book by suggesting a way of clarifying policy choices which does not start with the supposed nature of crime or the supposed purposes of punishment. This is not because crime is 'unimportant': its material and human consequences, together with the vast apparatus of people, resources and ideas which make up the control system, testify otherwise. It is rather, as therapists sometimes have to tell their patients or Zen masters their disciples, that we have to take a problem less seriously in order to solve it: 'if I am to help someone else to see that a false problem is false, I must pretend that I am taking his problem seriously. What I am actually taking seriously is his suffering, but he must be led to believe that it is what he considers as his problem.'[33]

My suggestion is to return to those contrasting visions of social control that I described in the last chapter – to see them, however, not as visions but as concrete and pragmatic policy alternatives for every single form of deviance. The history of social control can be told in many ways, and one way would be to rewrite it as a choice between exclusion and inclusion. No iron law of political, economic or historical inevitability has determined which of these alternatives have been chosen at any particular time, nor is there any technique for making or predicting future choices. The issues are too complex for such certainties. What we have seen are cycles, periodic reactions and counter-reactions, changes of emphasis, sustained moves in directions which are then abandoned.

To remember what these choices include and imply, let me use the old trick of listing some synonyms and equivalents from a Thesaurus. *Exclusion* means banishment and expulsion, segregation and isolation, designation, signification and classification, stigmatization. The nearest single word is 'separation', which conveys not just the sense of physical or social exclusion but also the setting up of a separate, that is 'exclusive', category. *Inclusion* means integration, assimilation, accommodation, normalization, toleration, absorption, engulfment, incorporation. The last word — incorporation — is probably the nearest single synonym.

Thus, to rewrite that history condensed into chapter 1, those original features of early nineteenth-century control systems (state centralization, classification, and institutional segregation) were all great projects of exclusion. The 1960s, on the other hand, were a time when the inclusionary impulse seemed to dominate. This was the positive as well as abolitionist message of the destructuring movements: integration in the community rather than segregation in the closed institution; decentralizing, weakening or diverting from various systems of exclusion, classification and control; even accommodation or non-intervention. 'Exclude less, include more' could have been the slogan of all these movements.

The intentions might have been complex and even suspect, the visions naive and even misguided, the results paradoxical and even malignant. The inclusionary impulse nonetheless sensed what was wrong with the old (and now stronger) exclusionary system. If this vision of alternatives seemed attractive then, it is no less attractive now. Instead of forgetting, denying or repressing our original values, we must either explicitly repudiate them or, as I believe is still possible, cautiously reaffirm them:

- it still makes some sense to look for more humane, just and effective alternatives to such exclusionary institutions as prisons
- mutual aid, fraternity and good-neighbourliness still sound better than dependence on bureaucracies and professions;
- cities should be places which everyone can share and where disorder can be tolerated, rather than being divided up into sanitized zones;
- the vision of 'community' responds to genuine psychic and social needs;
- some way must be found to halt the seemingly inexorable process by which society keeps classifying, controlling, excluding more and more groups according to age, sex, race, behaviour, moral status, ability or psychic state.

But it must be 'cautious' reaffirmation because we know the flaws in the 'beautiful theory' of inclusion.

(1) It fails to confront the moral issues of guilt, wrong-doing, punishment and responsibility and the empirical issues of harm, danger and fear which are raised by the problem of crime. By favouring a naive individualism, it does not give enough space to legitimate collective interests.

(2) In terms of 'doing good', the non-interventionist, abolitionist message of inclusion can easily provide a benevolent licence for neglect. A conservative *laissez faire* state can now use inclusionary slogans to abdicate responsibility for caring for its weaker citizens. And in terms of 'doing justice', conservative law-and-order policies will fill the instrumental and symbolic gaps left by non-interventionist policies about crime.

(3) Inclusionary policies can inadvertently lead to the establishment of new agencies and professionals whose very existence and traditional modes of operation lead to new forms of exclusion. The project of normalizing people is carried out in such a way as to classify and 'problematize' them even further. The dispersal of social control which follows the attempt to break up centralized concentrations of exclusionary power, might draw new (that is, previously 'included') populations into the orbit of social control.

(4) Inclusion does not confront the uncomfortable facts of human diversity. People are different not just in the labels attached to them. And the attachment of labels might anyway be the only way to create a social policy genuinely responsive to human needs.

It is this last flaw which is hardest for the inclusionary vision to confront. For many of us (and this is why labelling theory was so attractive) the positivist doctrine of 'differentiation' — the notion that deviants were different from non-deviants in any way other than the labels — had to be denied. Metaphysically this denial remains valid. Practically speaking also, as Scull nicely remarks, the quiet reabsorption into the community of many recently decanted inmates is scarcely surprising as 'many of those subject to processing by the official agencies of social control have been virtually indistinguishable from their neighbours who have been left alone.'[34]

But not always. Where differences do exist, it by no means follows that non-exclusionary forms of welfare and control are better. This is why critics of community control in such areas as mental illness are correct in exposing the negative consequences of shifting the burden to the less-visible, less-equipped inclusionary institutions of society. These were precisely the institutions which ejected the deviant in the first place and where, in the 'positivist' sense, the real differences and conflicts appeared which gave rise to the labelling.

If the positivist version of differentiation sometimes leads to malignant forms of exclusion, then the old socialist version — 'from each according to his abilities to each according to his needs' — need not. To identify needs, we require some form of classification and to satisfy needs, some form of exclusion. Compare the examples of the recent 'discoveries' of 'hyperkinesis' and family violence. In the first case, the medicalization of classroom deviance sanctioned a series of malignant forms of exclusion: unchecked professional power, isolation in special units, massive drug control (with damaging side-effects), abuses of civil liberties, the individualization of a social problem. But the 'discovery' of the problem of family violence over this same period — first battered children, then battered women — is an example of the benign consequences of exclusion. That is to say, it was only the professional, public and political creation of a separate category that allowed any social intervention.

These are examples, of course, of very different types of deviant or problematic behaviour, and this is just my point. It is very difficult to make rules about which types of behaviour or people require inclusionary and which exclusionary policies. We could identify many groups among the handicapped, the weak and the sick, those who have no power and are unlikely ever to have power, for whom it is obviously not in their interests to be normalized, incorporated or tolerated. They *need* — in the rhetoric of benevolence — to be exclusively labelled and they might even *want* to be physically separated.

But there are groups with much more potential power — like sexual and racial minorities that could manoeuvre themselves into a political 'stigma contest' — who have a quite different interest in separate recognition.[35] These groups might ultimately be seeking full inclusion into the social body, but at their most successful they were not saying 'we are just like everyone else'. They proudly proclaim their differences and their particular interests, even their 'deviance', rather than calling for the dissolution of all social categories.

I doubt, however, whether generalizations of this sort can be sustained for very long. For one thing, there are different forms of exclusion. The potentially strong, like the gay movement, might want separate recognition but will strongly oppose the exclusionary labelling power given to mental-health professionals. It might, however, be in the best interests of the weak to have their own exclusive professional labellers and caretakers. Then within each category there might be legitimate conflicts between inclusion and exclusion. In mental-retardation policy, for example, a major controversy is whether to improve exclusive institutions or else to move towards what is actually called 'normalization' (leaving the child in his or her family, ordinary school, neighbourhood). It is also easy enough to envisage whole exclusive communities whose internal organization is inclusive. Two examples (both discussed by Christie) would be the famous Christiana island in Denmark (a community like a medieval town, where the counter-culture is in control and which 'includes' all sorts of freaks, druggies, crazies and runaways) or various self-contained villages for mentally defectives who look after themselves and exclude professionals.

The choice in every instance is pragmatic and depends on our values. The 'flaw' in the inclusionary vision, for example, which leads to more deviants being created and more control work being required, is not a flaw if there are pragmatic gains from this process. And the prospect of inclusion — families looking after their mentally ill members, schools tolerating disruptive pupils, citizens spending their spare time sitting on dispute panels, neighbourhoods where diversity, disorder and tension are encouraged — is open to quite opposite evaluations. To some, the prospect is appalling, to others, this is a vision of the Good Society.

Nor are these value choices fixed for ever. It might be possible at any one time to construct an ad hoc 'spectrum of noxiousness',[36] through which local communities rate the social desirability of the deviants they are supposed to be 'reintegrating'. Such measures will usually show a low tolerance for the project of inclusion. But, as the Frankfurt School always reminds us, we cannot assume that attitudes like exclusion or intolerance are fixed human needs which can be objectified, fetishized and used as an excuse for resisting innovation. These attitudes are products of particular social relationships which can be changed. Moreover, we have very little understanding about matters such as tolerance. How much will people accept? How disorderly can a city be?

Undoubtedly, 'inclusion versus exclusion' implies policy alternatives which are much too absolute and simple. Values might be better clarified if we try to imagine degrees of inclusiveness for each category of socially problematic populations created by industrial society. For this is the central problem of welfare and control: how large concentrations of power — in the state, polity, and economy — generate superfluous people, embarrassing, residual or marginal populations, and simultaneously generate demands for their control and management.

This is to talk of 'social junk' — to use Spitzer's vivid distinction — rather than 'social dynamite'. The junk populations are 'only', helpless, sick, incompetent, and awkward; the inclusion/exclusion choice can more readily be made with reference to private troubles, to doing good. The choice, for example, between institution or hostel or family for the mentally retarded child, need refer only to the individual and his immediate milieu. The dynamite populations, however, and those to whom moral culpability can be assigned, raise quite different considerations. Crime-control policy — when, how much and what ways to exclude — must primarily be made with reference to the collective interest. For this reason, as much as I have blurred these terms, crime control is different from other forms of 'social control'. The choice between exclusion and inclusion is, above all else, a political decision determined by the nature of the state.

Nevertheless, different as the actual governing criterion is, the dimensions of choice at each stage of the system are the same. At the macro-level, Do we construct exclusive or inclusive systems? At the micro-level, Do we exclude or include this particular individual? Thus, at the initial stage of notifying, detecting and screening, the choice is between a centralized, rationalized and bureaucratic police force or neighbourhood police directly controlled by or consisting of local residents. At the stage of judging and sentencing, the choice is between a formal, rationalized and centralized judicial system or various forms of informal, community, popular or neighbourhood justice. And at the stage of the punitive control apparatus itself, the choice is between highly exclusive controls (such as banishment, imprisonment and the death penalty) or various less-exclusive modes: traditional ones such as fines, suspended sentences or probation, and the newer ones which have been the subject of this book.

Over and above such operational choices, however, there is the most important exclusionary consideration of all: why and how the action in question is classified as a crime in the first place. Crime, as Christie reminds us, is not 'a thing' to be controlled, it is a concept applicable to those situations where it is possible and in the interests of one or several parties to apply it. We can create crime by creating the systems which ask for this word. This is to repeat something no more and no less than Durkheim's idea of crime as a social fact. It is an idea which labelling theory expresses in terms of a 'society' that creates rules, and Marxist theory in terms of a 'state' that has the power to criminalize.

So, at last, we come back to sociology. To me, this means coming back to the political philosophy most consistent with sociology, namely anarchism. In the last instance (as they say) it is the nature of the state which shapes the nature of crime control. A quite different theoretical agenda could also be constructed that does not give the state such a privileged position, that sees the real force of social control as lying right outside the formal punitive system — in consumer culture, welfarism, family, education, systems of private regulation and civic law. Indeed, the difference between state and market control might well be the crucial theoretical issue for the future.

But theoretical agendas, public issues, systems of power, deep structures, social facts and ultimate causes have not been the subjects of this chapter. I have moved from this realm to such matters as private troubles, drowning bodies, unpredictable exceptions and moral choices. In political terms, the differences between these realms are sometimes expressed as: revolution rather than reform, radicalism against liberalism, long-term goals and short-term possibilities. For some of us, this schizoid split between two worlds of awareness, is reproduced in our personalities. Therefore, this chapter.

# Appendix: On Constructing a Glossary of Controltalk

In the appendix to *Nineteen Eighty-Four*, Orwell explains the principles of 'Newspeak', 'Doublethink' and 'Ingsoc'. 'The purpose of Newspeak was not only to provide a medium of expression for the world view and mental habits proper to the devotees of Ingsoc, but to make all other modes of thought impossible'.[1] By inventing new words, eliminating undesirable words and stripping remaining ones of unorthodox and secondary connotations, Newspeak functions 'not so much to express meanings as to destroy them.'[2]

Here, as everywhere else, Orwell is the moralist and political analyst, not the futurologist or science-fiction writer. He was always concerned with the anaesthetic function of political language: how words might insulate their users and listeners from experiencing fully the meaning of what they are saying and doing. He thought that political speech and writing had already become 'a defence of the indefensible', that political language had come to consist largely of 'euphemism, question begging and sheer cloudy vagueness.'[3] His original examples have become only too banal: 'pacification', 'transfer of population', 'elimination of undesirable elements'. In each instance, 'such phraseology is needed if one wants to name things without calling up mental pictures of them.'[4]

The ways in which this type of political language functions as a form of social control are obvious. Such structured bad faith ensures conformity to the right 'world view and mental habits' and it also allows indefensible forms of control to look more defensible. This was part of the achievement of mass literacy: the separation of words and objects. So we have the structured hypocrisy which Naipaul's hero (see p. 114) found so characteristic of Western civilization: saying one thing, but meaning or doing something else.

Social-control ideologies depend heavily on key words which have powerful symbolic meanings cut off from actual concrete reality: 'law and order', 'decent people', 'treatment', 'community', 'socialist legality', 'popular justice'. In each case, a conscious mental effort has to be made to conjure up exact things, people, places and processes. This is why Burroughs wrote: 'an essential feature of the Western control machine is to make language as *non-pictorial* as possible, to separate words as far as possible from objects or observable processes.'[5]

All this is more transparent if we are talking about political or 'hard-end' forms of control: 'interrogation' is used for example, when the more pictorial 'torture' is meant (though who, even Orwell, could have imagined the 'State Research Bureau' — Idi Amin's organized murder squad?) At the softer, benevolent parts of the system, however, the conscious mental effort to translate words into objects is much harder.

In chapter 5 I quoted extensively Edelman's indispensable guide to this subject: how therapeutic language functions to disguise the political elements (status, authority and power) intrinsic to the helping professions.[6] He shows how various professional terms, syntactic forms and scientific metaphors justify a hierarchy of power. These 'mythic cognitive structures' or 'rhetorical evocations' are used to classify clients and justify regulating their lives: 'when the power of professionals over people is at stake, the language employed implies that the professional has ways to ascertain who are dangerous, sick or inadequate; that he or she knows how to render them harmless, rehabilitate them or both; and that the procedures for diagnosis and treatment are too specialized for the lay public to understand or judge them.'[7]

The use of therapeutic language is not simple deception: 'many clients want help, virtually all professionls think they are providing it, and sometimes they do.'[8] We must not search for deliberate deception, but we must abandon the naive idea that words like 'pre-delinquent', 'resocialization' or 'in need of care and protection' actually stand for particular persons, objects, behaviour or procedures. These words are symbols, elaborate cognitive structures that are full of ambivalence and ambiguity, and that combine facts with beliefs, perceptions, emotions, habits and predictions.

Edelman goes on to examine the political uses of language in psychiatry, social work, psychiatric nursing, public-school education and law enforcement. Most of his examples, though, are drawn from the special vocabulary of therapy used in more-or-less coercive settings. Here, the control functions of language are particularly potent. To routinely use the term 'therapy' as suffix or qualifier, to label a common activity as though it were a medical one 'is to establish superior and subordinate roles, to make it clear who gives orders and who takes them and to justify in advance the inhibitions placed on the subordinate class'.[9] So subtle is this linguistic evocation of the entire political system, that both sides — the powerful and powerless, the definers and the defined, the helpers and the helped — can play out their roles without thinking in political terms, or feeling any resentment. Ambivalence, value conflict or moral doubt about coercion or constraint, can be resolved by defining all practices as help or treatment.

The power of professional language is such that for the outsider to redefine these practices in everyday, common-sense or pictorial terms would be seen as shocking. (Edelman's somewhat extreme example is the sobbing patient in a psychiatric ward being required as part of her 'therapy' to scrub a shower-room floor repeatedly with a toothbrush, while two 'psychiatric technicians' stand over her shouting directions, calling her stupid and pouring dirty water on the floor.) A crude 'phenomenological' description of such practices or a mere change of words ('punishment' instead of 'negative reinforcement') would be regarded as a distortion, and quite rightly so from the professional point of view. My observer's view of the language of, for example, behaviour therapy as a sub-class of Newspeak ('not so much to express meanings as to destroy them') would be dismissed as disengenousness, naivety or pathetic ignorance about the theory and its practice. Or else, to use Bernstein's standard distinction, I would be using a restricted linguistic code when really an elaborated code is called for.

Building on this restricted/elaborated distinction, Gouldner reminds us that professionals are members of a special speech community.[10] The distinctive cultural capital of the New Class is a speech code based on justification, reflexivity and truth claims, rather than appeal to traditional authority. They are 'guild masters of an invisible pedagogy . . . Speech becomes impersonal. Speakers hide behind their speech. Speech seems to be disembodied, decontextualized and self grounded.'[11]

By authorizing for themselves this technical language as the standard of all serious speech, professionals forbid any appeal to common sense ('Hang on, isn't she suffering?') or traditional morality ('Is what you're doing right?'). And, every bit as important, not only what professionals do is anaesthetized in this way, but also what 'deviants' do. This is the argument against the 'triumph of the therapeutic'.

But this is to raise cryptically all sorts of considerations well beyond the point of this appendix. My purpose is simply to call for serious attention to be paid to the nature and functions of Controltalk: the language of punishing, treating and helping This would have to include psychiatry and psychology, law enforcement, corrections and criminology, medicine and social work, research, testing and evaluation.

In these introductory remarks I have done little more than paraphrase a few social scientific accounts — Edelman on political language, Gouldner on the new class — that are useful in analysing Controltalk. There are obviously many other areas which might be helpful: sociolinguistics, ethnomethodological work on legal psychiatric language, discourse analysis. Little of this work, however, says much more than Orwell originally did, and none of it says it as clearly.

Controltalk resembles Newspeak, though there are some important differences. Newspeak tried to shrink the language by eliminating words which were too complex and ambiguous. Controltalk, however, increases rather than decreases the vocabulary, or substitutes elaborated-code for restricted-code words. And there are few examples in Controltalk of deliberate doublethink ('joycamp' for forced labour camp, Ministry of Peace for Ministry of War). Therapeutic language more often blurs rather than inverts reality.

But these are random comments. In place of the serious study which is needed, what follows is a classification of four main types of Controltalk, with some comments and a few examples drawn from the areas covered by this book.

Why is a study of Controltalk 'needed'? Not because ridicule, criticism or 'demystification' will change the professional world view. It is far too deeply rooted for that to happen. Rather, because such a project of self-awareness might help to clarify the moral tactical and political choices in working out a policy towards crime and delinquency. Other things being equal (they seldom are), I would always prefer a form of justice in which values, conflicts and injustices become open and visible, and a form of welfare which is unashamed to talk about such matters as kindness and compassion. Controltalk prevents this.

### EUPHEMISM

The most natural and also most complex, form of Controltalk is euphemism. From positivist criminology onwards, progressive crime-control ideology has developed a special vocabulary to soften or disguise the essential (and defining) feature of punishment systems — the planned infliction of pain. 'Substitution of mild or vague expression for harsh or blunt one', is the standard dictionary definition of euphemism.

Christie has provided the most subtle moral analysis of euphemism in crime control theory and practice.[12] 'Client', 'inmate', 'treatment', 'correctional centre', and the like are indeed euphemisms — substitutes for the harsh and blunt realities of prison life. But there are often 'kind thoughts behind kind words'; prisoners might feel better if not constantly reminded of their status: 'maybe kind words create a kind world'.[13] It is better sometimes to use euphemism. The hidden agenda of positivism — understanding, kindness, compassion — might be preferable to the hidden agenda of neo-classicism — hurt people more.

But we pay a price for euphemism. Punishment is *intended* to be painful. Prisoners, Christie reminds us, are not supposed to be happy; nor are they even in the most sterile, modern, comfortable Scandinavian prison. The opposite of punishment is not treatment, but reward. Through language and ceremony, through boundary blurring, through the 'invisible pedagogy of professionalism', crime control is rendered clean and hygienic, purged of all suffering and misery. Christie suggests that the term 'pain delivery' should be used instead (community pain agencies?). If inflicting pain is dissonant with our ideals, and if we want to reduce such infliction, then we must bring this value conflict out into the open, not give it an 'innocent somnabulistic insulation'.

Euphemism, though, is the most subtle of all types of Controltalk to detect because of the changing contexts in which words are used. 'Asylum', 'house of refuge' and 'sanctuary' did historically carry a voluntary meaning which is now usually absent. Words like 'agency' and 'service', although too bland

and anodyne to be strictly accurate (crime-control 'services' are not services at all), have become too commonplace to find substitutes. In some cultures, words like 'segregation', 'isolation', 'solitude' or 'confinement' carry more negative connotations than they do in others.

It is extremely difficult, therefore, to make a list of words which are unambiguously euphemistic. What follows are a few examples (in alphabetical order) of *usually* euphemistic terms.

**Adjustment centre:** punishment block, isolation block, segregation block, security housing unit.

**Anecdotal records:** dossiers, files.

**Behavioural units:** also support classes, sanctuaries, withdrawal groups, educational guidance centres, rescue units, opportunity groups, havens, adjustment units, pastoral care unit or special unit. These are all names used in Britain for places to send pupils who will not behave in the classroom (they are known in the trade as 'sinbins').

**Care:** often does mean 'care', but also means locking up as 'in care' or 'taking into care'. In Britain a 'care order' refers to the legal permission given to social workers to remove a child from home and place him in an institution.

**Client:** the most universal of all euphemisms. The word clearly implies self-referral, and this applies to not a single offender, prisoner or delinquent.

**Community:** see chapters 2 and 4.

**Contract:** the term is taken from behaviour therapy to refer to the 'agreement' between an offender and whatever authority is in control of him/her. A contract, however, is a voluntary agreement between two parties.

**Correctional counsellors:** guards, wardens.

**Correctional facilities:** prisons.

**Cottage:** the term originates from the ideology of the institution as a surrogate community. It is used to describe wings or cell blocks of an institution.

**Diversion:** see chapter 2.

**Drop-out:** used increasingly to describe those expelled from a community programme; people cannot 'drop out' of settings which they are legally compelled to attend.

**Finding:** as in 'making a finding of delinquency'; means convicted or sentenced.

**Home visit:** it could mean home visit, but it could also mean search or interrogation.

**Hard-core:** a long list of words has been developed (including many I have used myself in this book such as 'deep end') to describe either serious offenders, those who are not deterred or treated or who foul up on their programme. These include: incorrigible, unreachable, untreatable, bottom of the barrel. These sometimes overlap (quite innacurately) with certain criminological terms such as persistent offender, recidivist, career criminal and dangerous offender and (less frequently these days) psychiatric classifications such as psychopath or sociopath.

**Hearing:** also 'panel' — trial.

**Placement:** can mean placement in a hostel or foster home, but more often means incarceration as in 'intensive placement' or 'short-term intensive placement'.

**Pre-delinquent:** there is a long list of synonyms, usually borrowed from the medical or psychiatric model, to refer to children/youth who have not committed any offence. These include: potential delinquent, at risk, pre-delinquent, hidden delinquent, delinquent-prone or even latent delinquent. These terms all mean non-delinquent.

**Quiet room:** solitary confinement.

**Referred:** can mean 'referred' in the neutral sense of being sent from one agency to another, but it often simply means being charged with a criminal offence. Note also 'petition filed on his behalf'.

**Training school:** there is a long list of similar terms — 'approved schools', 'community homes', 'residential treatment centre' — all used at one time to describe prisons for juveniles.

### MEDICALISM AND PSYCHOLOGISM

A special and influential form of Controltalk, one which serves the same general functions as euphemism, derives from the medical model of deviance.[14] In its strong form, it appears in psychiatry, clinical psychology and various forms of therapy, in its weaker form in counselling and social work, and its most discredited (but still influential form) in the deeper ends of the crime-control system.

I have already noted Edelman's account of the special potency of therapeutic language: justifying hierarchy and restraint, neutralizing resistance, insulating its users from moral ambivalence and value conflict. In addition, it renders the most banal of everyday activities into complex, professional 'treatment modalities.' It would be tendentious to list and then explain what each of the following really means: environmental therapy, bibliotherapy, milieu therapy, music therapy, dance therapy, art therapy, occupational therapy, recreational therapy, work therapy, and so on.

A separate glossary would have to be constructed for the language of behaviourism. Again, the main examples are too familiar to list, though their very familiarity has rendered them more opaque. In particular, there are terms such as **Negative reinforcement; Aversion therapy; Aversive conditioning** which cover the deliberate infliction of pain on another human being, whether through electric shock, beating, nausea-producing drugs, sensory deprivation, or restricted diet ('Behaviour Mod: Meat Loaf').

In addition to the specific language of behaviour modification, there is the more important way in which medical and psychiatric models have redefined the essence of deviance, rule-breaking and immorality. Most notably, even when the medical analogy has been discarded, its conceptual logic is still influential: prediction, diagnosis, symptoms, prognosis, treatment. Then there has been the use of psychiatric terminology to create new categories of deviance, the best documented recent example being 'hyperkinesis' or 'hyperactivity'.[15]

In the control system itself, the psychodynamic model has left behind such technical phrases as **Acting out** and is indirectly responsible for the practice of stringing together simple words into complicated diagnoses, such as **Adolescent running away reaction.**

Here is an extract from an article entitled 'Behavioural Techniques For Sociopathic Clients': 'in certain refractory cases deliberate painful applications are an absolutely necessary part of treatment . . . The concept of punishment is largely a semantic philosophical problem which may be avoided in practice by substituting new phrases such as "aversive conditioning" or "negative consequences".'[16]

ACRONYMS

Newspeak contained a great number of abbreviations. This was not just to save time, but was a technique to convey a particular ideology and meaning. Orwell's examples came from the telescoped words and phrases used in totalitarian regimes, 'Comintern' giving a more simple administrative connotation than the ideologically loaded 'Communist International': 'it was perceived that in thus abbreviating a name, one narrowed and subtly altered its meaning by cutting out most of the associations that would otherwise cling to it.'[17]

In Controltalk, particularly the usage perfected in the USA over the last 20 years, the acronym is the most popular method of cutting out wrong associations. This is an ideal way of rendering language non-pictorial. It is more powerful than simple abbreviation because it requires two stages of decoding: first, you have to work out what the letters stand for, then you have to decipher the words themselves (which are often euphemisms, psychobabble or plain gibberish) before you arrive at that elusive mental image.

At the beginning of chapter 2 (p. 41), I gave an illustrative list of such acronyms (GUIDE, RODEO, START, READY, TARGET, STAY, CREST and so on) and I will not decode them all here. But here are some particularly elusive examples.

**ARD:** Accelerated Rehabilitation Disposition. Each component word here is totally opaque, though 'accelerated' perhaps does convey something about this diversion programme for first offenders charged with non-violent crimes.

**PREP:** Preparation Through Responsive Educational Programs.

**PICA:** Programming Interpersonal Curricula For Adolescents. Both PREP and PICA are token economy programmes used in schools. 'Underachievers' and 'behavioural problems' earn or lose points, depending on how well they improve their social and academic skills.

**VISA:** Volunteers to Influence Student Achievements. Teachers of 1st and 2nd grade children (6- or 7-year-olds) are asked to identify 'potential delinquents' for assignment to Big Brother counsellors (one of the criteria for rating potential delinquency was 'father away from home').

**WHISP:** Willowbrook-Harbour Intensive Supervision Project. We can see a *place*, but what can 'Intensive Supervision' mean?

**START:** Short Term Adolescent Residential Training. .

**STAY:** Short Term Aid to Youth. This STAY is a START programme, but the 'clients' go home at night.

**CPI:** Critical Period Intervention. An extremely non-pictorial name indeed, for a programme to identify (by diagnostic tests) youths 'susceptible to drug abuse'.

Would that all acronyms were as unambiguous as **TIP** (Turn In a Pusher) . . .

TECHNOBABBLE

The helping, healing and punishing professions deal with the everyday world and there is, therefore, less room for them to invent the genuinely technical vocabulary of a nuclear physicist, electronic engineer, biochemist or even architect. Nevertheless, they have developed a small and specialized vocabulary which is wholly esoteric, that is, virtually incomprehensible to the outsider.

This technobabble can sometimes be understood in Gouldner's terms: the infrastructure of modern technical language which challenges the old élites and authorities. The language must imply that 'the established hierarchy is only a semblance and that the deeper, more important distinction is between those who speak and understand truly and those who do not.'[18] More simply though, this language originates in the same way as the argot and slang of various sub-cultures. It shows that you are 'wise', that you have inside knowledge, and it enables you to communicate secretly even in front of your clients. More simply, certain technical abbreviations save wasting time on the whole description. This jargon becomes fetishized with use, and sometimes its original meaning is forgotten.

In every case, though, outsiders can have little sense — certainly little pictorial sense — of the procedures, places and objects which the vocabulary conveys.

I will list three somewhat different forms of technobabble.

(1) Neologisms or abbreviations — usually of legal or medical procedures. **Sectioned** refers to the use of a particular section of the Mental Health Act (in Britain) for the compulsory commitment of a patient. (As in 'we had to section her'). Similarly, patients or clients may be **Number fived** (or whatever the appropriate legal sub-clause).

(2) Jargon to make quite simple matters sound very complicated. For example, **Naturally related community resources** means family members used in various programmes of tracking, counselling or behaviour modification. Similarly, there is **Youth nominated peer**, which means friend.

(3) Then there are examples of the convoluted use of language in technical reports written by people who cannot write English. Their opposite is the type of plain English which Orwell tried to encourage. Evaluation reports are the most fertile source of these horrors:

- 'At this point, the programmatic activity evaluation recording ` was initiated': someone started to look at what we were doing.
- 'Service delivery modality': what we were doing.
- 'The outcome variables appear only poorly related to the initially determined programme objectives': we don't know what happened.
- 'The operational criteria of success were not attained at a significant level': the project didn't do too well.

# Notes and References

I use several references published by the National Institute of Law Enforcement and Criminal Justice, Law Enforcement Assistance Administration, US Department of Justice, US Government Printing Office, Washington DC. To save space, these are all cited as 'Washington DC: NILECJ'.

## INTRODUCTION

1. For some different versions of this debate, see Stanley Cohen and Andrew Scull (eds), *Social Control and the State: Comparative and Historical Essays*, (Oxford: Martin Robertson, 1983).
2. See Joan Higgins, 'Social Control Theories of Social Policy', *Journal of Social Policy*, 9, 1 (January 1980).
3. Neal Shover, *A Sociology of American Corrections*, (Homewood, Ill.: Jersey Press, 1979), p. 36.
4. The best theoretical guide remains David Matza, *Becoming Deviant*, (Englewood Cliffs, NJ: Prentice Hall, 1968): the story in Britain was told in Stanley Cohen, 'Criminology and the Sociology of Deviance in Britain: A Recent History and Current Report', in P. Rock and M. McIntosh (eds), *Deviance and Social Control*, (London: Tavistock, 1974), pp. 1–40.
5. See the introduction to Cohen and Scull, *Social Control and the State* and Morris Janowitz, 'Sociological Theory and Social Control', *American Journal of Sociology*, 81, 1 (1975), pp. 82–108.
6. Gary T. Marx, 'Ironies of Social Control', *Social Problems*, 28, 3 (February 1981), pp. 221–66.
7. A useful guide to these changes is Geoffrey Pearson, *The Deviant Imagination: Psychiatry, Social Work and Social Change*, (London: Macmillan, 1975). On radical social work particularly, see Jeffrey Galper, *Social Work Practice: A Radical Perspective*, (Englewood Cliffs, NJ: Prentice Hall, 1980).
8. I concentrate in this book on *Discipline and Punish* which is the third of Foucault's trilogy (following *Madness and Society* and *The Birth of the*

*Clinic*) tracing the ideology of control institutions (lunatic asylums; teaching hospitals; prisons) and the human sciences symbiotically linked with them (psychiatry; clinical medicine; criminology and penology).

9. Andrew T. Scull, *Decarceration: Community Treatment and the Deviant — A Radical View*, (Englewood Cliffs, NJ: Prentice Hall, 1977).

10. Jacques Donzelot, *The Policing of Families*, (New York: Pantheon, 1979); Robert Castel et al., *The Psychiatric Society*, (New York: Columbia University Press, 1981).

11. Nicholas Kittrie, *The Right to be Different*, (Baltimore: Johns Hopkins Press, 1971); Thomas Szasz, *The Manufacture of Madness*, (New York: Dell, 1970); Martin L. Gross, *The Psychological Society*, (New York: Simon and Schuster, 1978); Peter Schrag, *Mind Control*, (London: Marion Boyers, 1980).

12. For example, see Philip Rieff, Russell Jacoby, Richard Sennet and, most recently and notably, Christopher Lasch, *The Culture of Narcissism*, (New York: W. W. Norton, 1978), *Haven in a Heartless World: The Family Besieged*, (New York: Basic Books, 1977), and 'Life in the Therapeutic State', *New York Review of Books*, XXVII, 10 (June 12, 1980) pp. 24–32.

13. Note, for example, the total absence of crime and deviance in Bell's standard work: Daniel Bell, *The Coming of Post Industrial Society: A Venture in Social Forecasting*, (New York: Basic Books, 1973). The only sustained attempt in criminology to predict the future of crime (but not of its control) is Gresham Sykes, *The Future of Crime*, (Washington DC: National Institute of Mental Health, 1980).

14. As Kumar notes in his excellent guide to the prophesies of classical social theory and contemporary post-industrialism: 'Even the most routine science fiction writer has more imagination and understanding than was revealed in the technocratic, jargon-ridden, commission reports, think tank projections and social forecasts through which I dutifully plodded.' Krishan Kumar, *Prophecy and Progress: The Sociology of Industrial and Post-Industrial Society*, (Harmondsworth: Penguin, 1978), p. 7.

15. Michel Foucault, 'Prison Talk', in C. Gordon (ed.), *Michel Foucault Power/ Knowledge: Selected Interviews and Other Writings, 1972–1977*, (Brighton: Harvester Press, 1980), p. 52.

### 1  THE MASTER PATTERNS

1. The key revisionist histories are (in order of publication): David J. Rothman, *The Discovery of the Asylum: Social Order and Disorder in the New Republic*, (Boston: Little Brown, 1971); Michel Foucault, *Discipline and Punish: The Birth of the Prison*, (London: Allen Lane, 1977); Michael Ignatieff, *A Just Measure of Pain: The Penitentiary in the Industrial Revolution*, (London: Macmillan, 1978); and Dario Melossi and Massimo Pavarini, *The Prison and the Factory: Origins of the Penitentiary System*, (London: Macmillan, 1981). The first three elements in my

condensation of this history are well set out in Andrew Scull, *Decarceration: Community Treatment and the Deviant*, (New Jersey: Prentice Hall, 1977) chapter 2, and Steven Spitzer and Andrew Scull, 'Social Control in Historical Perspective: From Private to Public Responses to Crime', in D. F. Greenberg (ed.), *Corrections and Punishment*, (Beverly Hills; Sage, 1977), pp. 265—86.

2. For an excellent analysis of such agreements and disagreements, see M. Ignatieff, 'State, Civil Society and Total Institution: A Critique of Recent Social Histories of Punishment', in M. Tonry and N. Morris (eds), *Crime and Justice: an Annual Review of Research*, (Chicago: University of Chicago Press, 1981, vol. 3. This paper is reprinted in Stanley Cohen and Andrew Scull (eds), *Social Control and the Modern State: Comparative and Historical Essays*, (Oxford: Martin Robertson, 1983), a book which also contains a number of other evaluations of this literature.

3. Rothman has claimed, however, that although his subsequent work was indeed informed by such current issues, he wrote *The Discovery of the Asylum* exclusively as a historian, with little awareness of contemporary political happenings in the USA or of prison and mental hospital conditions: Dorothy Chunn and Russell Smandych, 'An Interview with David Rothman', *Canadian Criminology Forum*, 4 (Spring 1982), pp. 152—62. This claim is partly contradicted by the explicit political moral with which Rothman ends the books and the fact that he had already read Goffman's *Asylums*; see Andrew Scull, 'Competing Accounts of the Rise of the Asylum: A Response to Rothman', *Canadian Criminology Forum*, 5 (1982), pp. 62—5.

4. Note, for example: 'Our initial interest in the history of prisons was aroused during the late 1960's at a time when this institution in Italy (and elsewhere) was thrown into a deep crisis.' Melossi and Pavarini, *The Prison and the Factory*, p. 1.

5. Ignatieff, 'State, Society and Total Institutions . . . ', p. 155.

6. A good (that is, not simple-minded) version of this story is Blake McKelvey, *American Prisons: A History of Good Intentions*, (Montclair NJ: Patterson Smith, 1977).

7. David J. Rothman, *Conscience and Convenience: The Asylum and its Alternatives in Progressive America*, (Boston: Little Brown, 1980). Rothman has usefully summarized this history in *Incarceration and Its Alternatives in 20th Century America*, (Washington, DC: NILECJ, 1980).

8. David J. Rothman, 'Introduction' and 'The State as Parent', in W. Gaylin et al., *Doing Good: The Limits of Benevolence*, (New York: Pantheon 1978).

9. Rothman, *Conscience and Convenience*, p. 11.

10. A fascinating post-Rothman account of the same history has been provided by Cullen and Gilbert. Dismayed by what they see as the betrayal of 'real' liberalism by those disenchanted liberals who so easily abandoned the rehabilitative ideal in favour of a return to justice, they have rewritten a progressivist history in such a way as to defend it from this subsequent

betrayal! See Frances T. Cullen and Karen E. Gilbert, *Reaffirming Rehabilitation*, (Cincinatti: Anderson Publishing Co., 1983), Especially chapter 3, 'The Rise of Rehabilitation'.

11. George Rusche and Otto Kirchheimer, *Punishment and the Social Structure*, (New York: Russell and Russell, 1938). Relatively neglected in the years after its original publication, this work was taken up more seriously only in the 1970s.

12. This process is summarized in Steven Spitzer, 'The Rationalization of Crime Control in Capitalist Society', *Contemporary Crises*, 3, (April 1979), pp. 187—206. See also Spitzer and Scull, 'Social Control in Historical Perspective.'

13. In addition to Melossi and Pavarini's *The Prison and the Factory*, see D. Melossi, 'Institutions of Social Control and the Capitalist Organization of Work', in B. Fine at al. (eds), *Capitalism and the Rule of Law*, (London: Hutchinson, 1979), pp. 90—9.

14. Melossi and Pavarini, *The Prison and Factory*, p. 145.

15. Melossi, 'Institutions of Social Control', p. 98.

16. Michael Ignatieff, 'State, Society and Total Institutions' and 'Class Interests and the Penitentiary: A Response to Rothman', *Canadian Criminology Forum*, 5 (1982), p. 66.

17. In addition to *Discipline and Punish*, see various chapters, (especially 'Prison Talk') in Colin Gordon (ed.), *Michel Foucault: Power/Knowledge: Selected Interviews and other Writings, 1972—1977*, (Brighton: Harvester Press, 1980). An exemplary summary of Foucault's position is Alan Sheridan, *Michel Foucault: The Will To Truth*, (London: Tavistock, 1980).

18. Foucault, *Discipline and Punish*, p. 220.

19. *Ibid.*, p. 268.

20. *Ibid.*, p. 271.

21. *Ibid.*, p. 272.

22. For the reasons I gave in the introduction, I cannot deal here with such debates as Foucault's proximity to functionalism. Another (much less noticed) resemblance is to labelling theory: first, in his account of the generation of deviant categories and, second, in his notion of the ironical way in which control systems produce the deviants which they 'need'.

23. Foucault, *Discipline and Punish*, p. 221.

24. This is a selection of criticisms to be found in David Brion Davis, 'The Crime of Reform', *New York Review of Books*, 26 June, 1980, pp. 14—17; Christopher Lasch, 'Review of *Conscience and Convenience*', *The Nation*, 14 June, 1980, pp. 29—30; and Andrew Scull, 'Progressive Dreams, Progressive Nightmares: Social Control in 20th Century America', *Stanford Law Review*, 33 (1981), pp. 301—16. *Conscience and Convenience* has justifiably attracted harsher criticism than Rothman's earlier book. In *The Discovery of the Asylum*, the account of the reform enterprise is much less internalist and much more grounded in the political position and aims of the reformers.

25. The growing revisionist history of social control (for a bibliographical

guide, see the various papers in Cohen and Scull, *Social Control and the State*) deals, of course, with many institutions other than the prison. On juvenile justice, for example, note Anthony Platt's *The Child Savers: The Invention of Delinquency*, (Chicago: University of Chicago Press, 1969), a revisionist history which, in the second edition of the book (1977) becomes more 'disciplinary'. For a particularly interesting attempt (using the same case) to add the variable 'revealed preference' to the contrast between 'stated intentions' and 'revealed outcomes', see Steven G. Schlossman, *Love and the American Delinquent: The Theory and Practise of Progressive Juvenile Justice, 1825–1920*, (Chicago: University of Chicago Press, 1977) and Steven L. Schlossman and Stephanie Wallach, 'The Crime of Precocious Sexuality: Female Juvenile Delinquency in the Progressive Era', *Harvard Educational Review*, 48, 1 (1978), pp. 65–94.

26. Isaiah Berlin, 'Alexander Herzen', in *Russian Thinkers*, (London: Hogarth Press, 1978), p. 193.

27. As 'a former though unrepentent member' of the revisionist school however, Ignatieff ('State, Society and Total Institutions') has provided an interesting self-critique of these claims, concentrating particularly on what he sees as the exaggerated role assigned to the state as the punitive regulator of deviant behaviour.

28. The contemporary significance of this point will be discussed in chapter 5. For a relevant historical analysis of the capture of deviancy control by experts, see Scull's work on nineteenth-century psychiatry: Andrew Scull, *Museums of Madness: The Social Organization of Insanity in Nineteenth Century England*, (London: Allen Lane, 1979).

29. Foucault, *Discipline and Punish*, p. 27.

30. Documented, each in its own way, by all the revisionist histories. See also Scull, *Decarceration*, chapter 7.

31. Andrew Scull, 'Community Corrections: Panacea, Progress or Pretense?', in R. Abel (ed.), *The Politics of Informal Justice*, (New York: Academic Press, 1982), vol. one, p. 101. By the beginning of the 1970s, David Rothman could write an article entitled 'Of Prisons, Asylums and Other Decaying Institutions' in *Public Interest*, 26 (Winter 1972), pp. 3–17. For a useful guide to the search for alternatives to prisons, see James R. Brantley, *Alternatives to Institutionalization: A Definitive Bibliography* (Washington DC: NILECJ, May 1979) – 2198 entries are listed.

32. Scull, *Decarceration* p. 42.

33. The ideologies (and consequences) of informalism and delegalization, are well charted by Richard Abel in his 'Introduction' and 'The Contradictions of Informal Justice' in Abel, *The Politics of Informal Justice* and 'Delegalization: A Critical Review of its Ideology, Manifestations and Social Consequences', in E. Blankenburg et al. (eds), *Alternative Rechtsformen und Alternativem zum Recht – Jahrbuch fur Rechtssociologie und Rechtstheorie*, (Opladen: Westdeutscher Verlag, 1979), pp. 27–42. An example of an enthusiastic and totally uncritical version of the same tale, is Benedict Alper and Lawrence Nichols, *Beyond the Courtroom:*

*Programs in Community Justice and Conflict Resolution*, (Lexington, Mass: D. C. Heath and Co., 1982).

34. Abel, *The Politics of Informal Justice* and 'Delegalization'.
35. The influence of sentimental anarchism on the deinstitutionalization movement is beautifully analysed by Bernard Beck, 'The Limits of Deinstitutionalization' in M. Lewis (ed.), *Research in Social Problems and Public Policy*, (Greenwich: JAI Press, 1979), vol. one, pp. 1—14.
36. The most quoted of the early sceptics were: on community corrections, David Greenberg, 'Problems in Community Corrections', *Issues in Criminology*, 10, 1 (Spring 1975); on mental illness particularly, Scull, *Decarceration* (for an up-to-date review of the myth of deinstitutionalization, see the Afterword of the second edition of *Decarceration*, (Cambridge: Polity Press, 1984) and various papers by Scull in the *American Behavioral Scientist*, July—August, 1981); on diversion, Thomas Blomberg, 'Diversion and Accelerated Social Control', *Journal of Criminal Law and Criminology*, 68, 2 (June, 1977), pp. 274—82.
37. James Austin and Barry Krisberg, 'Wider, Stronger and Different Nets: The Dialectics of Criminal Justice Reform', *Journal of Research in Crime and Delinquency*, 18, 1 (January 1981), pp. 165—96. The informal justice movement — given its more ambitious pretensions — has been the object of even deeper scepticism than the community corrections field. Destructuring, we were told, is bogus (nothing much has become informal, decentralized or non-coercive), state control has been extended; conflict neutralized; state resources distributed in favour of the advantaged; the interests of the professions advanced. See Abel, *The Politics of Informal Justice* and 'Conservative Conflict and the Reproduction of Capitalism: The Role of Informal Justice', *International Journal of Sociology of Law*, 9 (1981), pp. 215—67.
38. For an example of such poignant self-reflection, see Edwin M. Lemert, 'Diversion in Juvenile Justice: What Hath Been Wrought?', *Journal of Research in Crime and Delinquency*, 18, (January 1981), pp. 34—45.
39. James Austin and Barry Krisberg, 'The Unmet Promise of Alternatives to Incarceration', *Crime and Delinquency*, 28, 3 (July 1982), pp. 374—409.
40. Abel's volumes evaluating the informalism movement eloquently carry this message. See my review 'The Deeper Structures of the Law or "Beware the Rulers Bearing Justice" ', *Contemporary Crises*, 8 (January 1984), pp. 83—93.

2  INSIDE THE SYSTEM

1. One early textbook, Vernon Fox, *Community Based Corrections*, (Englewood Cliffs, NJ: Prentice Hall, 1977), listed 142 types of 'service'. And a three-year follow-up study of 570 juveniles moving through the Massachusetts Departmental Youth Service showed that, collectively, they experienced 132 different programmes: R. B. Coates et al., *Diversity in a*

*Youth Correctional System: Handling Delinquents in Massachusetts*, (Cambridge Mass: Ballinger, 1978).

2. Our bewildered cultural dummy might also be helped by the *Criminal Justice Thesaurus* published regularly by the National Institute of Justice.

3. Note, for example, Rothman's comments about the early twentieth-century impact of the psychiatric ideology on the criminal justice system: 'rationales and practices that initially promised to be less onerous nevertheless served to encourage the extension of state authority. The impact of the ideology was to expand intervention, not to restrict it.' David T. Rothman, 'Behaviour Modification in Total Institutions: A Historical Overview', *Hastings Centre Report*, 5 (February 1975), p. 19.

4. Here, as throughout this chapter, I draw on the following excellent evaluations of deinstitutionalization and community control: James Austin and Barry Krisberg, 'Wider, Stronger and Different Nets: The Dialectics of Criminal Justice Reform', *Journal of Research in Crime and Delinquency*, 18, 1, (January 1981), pp. 165–96, and 'The Unmet Promise of Alternatives to Incarceration', *Crime and Delinquency*, 28, 3 (July 1982), pp. 374–409; John Hylton, 'The Growth of Punishment: Imprisonment and Community Corrections in Canada', *Crime and Social Justice*, 15 (1981), pp. 18–28, *Reintegrating the Offender: Assessing the Impact of Community Corrections*, (Washington DC: University Press of America, 1981), 'Community Corrections and Social Control: The Case of Saskatchewan, Canada', *Contemporary Crises*, 5, 2 (April 1981), pp. 193–215, and 'Rhetoric and Reality: A Critical Appraisal of Community Correctional Programs', *Crime and Delinquency*, 28, 3 (July 1982), pp. 341–73, Paul Lerman, "Trends and Issues in the De-Institutionalization of Youths in Trouble', *Crime and Delinquency*, 26, 3 (July 1980), pp. 281–98; Andrew Rutherford and Osman Bengur, *Community Based Alternatives to Juvenile Incarceration*, (Washington DC: NILECJ, October 1976) Malcolm W. Klein, 'Deinstitutionalization and Diversion of Juvenile Offenders: A Litany of Impediments', in N. Morris and M. Tonry (eds), *Crime and Justice: An Annual Review of Research*, (Chicago: University of Chicago Press, 1979), vol. 1, pp. 145–201.

5. Unless otherwise stated all these statistics are drawn from the following sources. For England: Annual Reports of the Work of the Prison Department; 'Digests' and 'Briefings' published by NACRO (National Association for the Care and Resettlement of Offenders), 1979–83. For the USA: T. Flanagan and M. McCleod (eds), *Sourcebook of Criminal Justice Statistics 1982*, (Washington DC: Bureau of Justice Statistics, 1983), *Report to the Nation on Crime and Justice: The Data*, (Washington DC: Bureau of Justice Statistics, 1982), I. . . . et al., *American Prisons and Jails, Population Trends and Projections*, (Washington DC: National Institute of Justice, 1980), vol. II, and Barry Krisberg and Ira Schwarz, *Rethinking Juvenile Justice*, (Unpublished MS. National Council of Research on Crime and Delinquency, 1982). For Canada, Janet B. L. Chan and Richard V. Ericson, *Decarceration and the Economy of Penal*

*Reform*, (Centre of Criminology, University of Toronto, 1981). All these sources contain detailed information on recent patterns of imprisonment.

6. See David Downes, The Origins and Consequences of Dutch Penal Policy Since 1945', *British Journal of Criminology*, 22 (October 1982), 325–57.

7. Robert Vintner et al. (eds), *Time Out: A National Study of Juvenile Correctional Programs*, (Ann Arbor, Mich: National Assessment of Juvenile Corrections, University of Michigan, 1976).

8. For a series of detailed case studies of the effects of the DSO programme, see Joel F. Handler and Julie Zatz (eds), *Neither Angels Nor Thieves: Studies in the Deinstitutionalization of Status Offenders*, (Washington DC: National Academy Press, 1982).

9. The classic study of the California projects is Paul Lerman's *Community Treatment and Social Control: A Critical Analysis of Juvenile Correctional Policy*, (Chicago: University of Chicago Press, 1975). See also Sheldon Messinger, 'Confinement in the Community: A Selective Assessment of Paul Lerman's "Community Treatment and Social Control"', *Journal of Research in Crime and Delinquency*, 13, 1 (1976), pp. 82–92; and E. M. Lemert and F. Dill, *Offenders in the Community: The Probation Subsidy in California*, (Lexington: D. C. Heath & Co., 1978).

10. David H. Thorpe et al., *Out of Care: The Community Support of Juvenile Offenders*, (London: George Allen and Unwin, 1980). For further analysis, see Andrew Rutherford, *A Statute Backfires: The Escalation of Youth Incarceration in England During the 1970's*, (London: Justice for Children, 1980).

11. Barbara Hudson, 'Against The Ethos: Incarceration in the Era of Decarceration', (Unpublished Paper, International Symposium on the Impact of Criminal Justice Reform, San Francisco, 1983).

12. This shallow-end/deep-end argument was nicely used by Rutherford and Bengur in *Community Based Alternatives*.

13. Klein, 'Deinstutionalization and Diversion', pp. 162–6.

14. The deinstitutionalization and diversion strategies usually overlap. But, in addition to the general literature on community control cited in note 4, I have relied on the following evaluations of diversion: Thomas Blomberg, 'Diversion and Accelerated Social Control', *Journal of Criminal Law and Criminology*, 68, 2 (June 1977), pp. 274–82, 'Diversion from Juvenile Court: A Review of the Evidence', in F. Faust and P. Brantingham (eds), *Juvenile Justice Philosophy*, (Minneapolis: West Publishing Co., 1978) and 'Widening the Net: An Anomaly in the Evaluation of Diversion Programmes', in Malcom Klein and Katherine Teilmann (eds), *Handbook of Criminal Justice Evaluation*, (Beverly Hills: Sage, 1980); Marvin Bohnstedt, 'Answers to Three Questions about Juvenile Diversion'. *Journal of Research in Crime and Delinquency*, 15, 1 (January 1978), pp. 109–23; Bruce Bullington et al., 'A Critique of Diversionary Juvenile Justice', *Crime and Delinquency*, 24, 1 (January 1978), pp. 59–71; Donald Cressey and Robert McDermott, *Diversion From the*

*Juvenile Justice System*, (Washington DC: NILECJ, 1974; Franklyn W. Dunford, 'Police Diversion — An Illusion?', *Criminology*, 15, 3 (November 1977), pp. 335—52; Malcolm Klein et al., 'The Explosion of Police Diversion Programs: Evaluating the Structural Dimensions of a Social Fad', in M. Klein (ed.), *The Juvenile Justice System* (Beverly Hills: Sage, 1976); Andrew Rutherford and Robert McDermott, *Juvenile Diversion*, (Washington DC: NILECJ, 1976). On Britain, see Alison Morris, 'Diversion of Juvenile Offenders from the Criminal Justice System', in N. Tutt (ed.), *Alternative Strategies for Coping With Crime*, (Oxford: Basil Blackwell, 1978), and Robert Adams and Jim Thomas et al. (eds). *A Measure of Diversion? Case Studies in Intermediate Treatment*, (Leicester: National Youth Bureau, 1981).

15. Cressey and McDermott, *Diversion from the Juvenile Justice System*, pp. 3—4.

16. Klein, 'De-institutionalization and Diversion', p. 153.

17. Note here the literature on various forms of restitution and victim compensation schemes. For example, J. Hudson and B. Galaway (eds), *Victims, Offenders and Alternative Sanctions*, (Lexington Mass: Lexington Books, 1980). The British experience with such schemes shows a more genuine development of alternatives, the American a tendency to use them as supplements to other penalties.

18. D. C. McBride and S. G. Dalton, 'Criminal Justice — Diversion for whom?', in A. Cohn (ed.), *Criminal Justice Planning and Development*, (Beverly Hills: Sage, 1977), pp. 103—16.

19. Lemert, 'Diversion in Juvenile Justice', p. 17.

20. In addition to the general literature, note particularly the fascinating system research on the Illinois Status Offender Services, see Irving A. Spergel et al., 'De-institutionalization of Status Offenders: Individual Outcome and System Effects', *Journal of Research in Crime and Delinquency*, 28 (January 1981), pp. 4—33 and 'Response of Organization and Community to a Deinstitutionalization Strategy', *Crime and Delinquency*, 28, 3 (July 1982), pp. 426—49. The research demonstrates clearly that females are now subject to more intense processing because of the new options. Spergel and his colleagues also suggest that the ISOS had the least effect in the most affluent communities and that in the poorer fragmented communities where it was most active, it actually *inhibited* the development of natural means of informal control in the community.

21. Quoted in Thorpe et al., *Out of Care*, p. 82.

22. For speculation on how the community strategy might feed back to the internal organization of the prison, see Stanley Cohen, 'Prisons and the Future of Control Systems: From Concentration to Dispersal', in M. Fitzgerald (ed.), *Welfare in Action*, (London: Routledge, 1977).

23 See Stanley Cohen and Laurie Taylor, *Prison Secrets*, (London: National Council of Civil Liberties, 1978).

24. National Institute of Mental Health, *Community Based Correctional*

*Programs: Models and Practices*, (Washington DC: US Government Printing Office, 1971), p. 1.

25. See Coates et al., *Diversity in a Youth Correctional System*; and Jean Ann Linney, 'Alternative Facilities for Youth in Trouble: Descriptive Analysis of a Strategically Selected Sample' and Appendix C: 'Multicomponent Assessment for Residential Services for Youth', both in Handler and Zatz, *Neither Angels Nor Thieves*, pp. 127–75 and 740–79. Linney's research shows that average PASS ratings did indeed improve following 'deinstitutionalization', that is the institutions began to look more normal and comfortable. . But it was also apparent that a secure, isolated facility could offer a 'normalizing' internal experience, while a group home, with its 'seeming openness and small size' could be restrictive and regimented internally.

26. H. B. Bradley, 'Community Based Treatment for Young Adult Offenders', *Crime and Delinquency*, 15, 3 (1969), p. 369.

27. For a survey, see R. P. Seiter et al., *Halfway Houses*, (Washington DC: NILECJ, 1977).

28. Described in Charles Silverman, *Criminal Violence, Criminal Justice*, (New York: Random House, 1978), pp. 417–23.

29. Fox, *Community Based Corrections*, pp. 62–3.

30. See Colin Thomas, 'Supervision in the Community', *Howard Journal of Criminology and Crime Prevention*, 18, 1 (1978), pp. 23–31.

31. N. Hinton, 'Intermediate Treatment', in L. Blom Cooper (ed.), *Progress in Penal Reform*, (Oxford: Oxford University Press, 1974), p. 239. For other sources on the ideology of IT see Thorpe et al., *Out of Care*, Ray Jones and Andrew Kerslake, *Intermediate Treatment and Social Work*, (London: Heinemann, 1979) and, in particular, the regular 'Aspects' and 'Briefings' on IT published between 1978 and 1983 by the Youth Social Work Unit, National Youth Bureau (Leicester).

32. J. A. Pratt, 'Intermediate Treatment and the Normalization Crisis', *Howard Journals*, 22, 1 (1983), pp. 19–37.

33. National Advisory Commission on Criminal Justice Standards, quoted in G. R. Perlstein and T. R. Phelps (eds), *Alternatives to Prison: Community Based Corrections*, (California: Goodyear Publishing Co. 1975), p. 74.

34. For a sensitive account of the plight of the mentally ill tracked in this way – the 'forfeited' patients whom nobody wants – see Gary Whitmer, 'From Hospitals to Jails: The Fate of California's Deinstitutionalized Mentally Ill', *American Journal of Orthopsychiatry*, 50, 1 (January 1980), pp. 65–75.

35. Paul Lerman, 'Child Welfare, the Private Sector and Community Based Corrections', *Crime and Delinquency*, 30, 1 (January 1984), pp. 5–38.

36. Steven Spitzer and Andrew Scull, 'Social Control in Historical Perspective: From Private to Public Responses to Crime', in D. F. Greenberg (ed.), *Corrections and Punishment*, (Beverly Hills: Sage, 1977), pp. 265–86 and 'Privatisation and Capitalist Development: The Case of the

Private Police', *Social Problems*, 25, 1 (October 1977), pp. 18–29.

37. Andrew Scull, 'A New Trade in Lunacy: The Re-modification of the Mental Patient', *American Behavioral Scientist*, 24, 6 (July/August 1981), pp. 741–54.

38. Note here the series of Rand Corporation studies on the impact of fiscal cutbacks in the criminal justice system: W. E. Walker et al., *The Impact of Proposition 13 on Local Criminal Justice Agencies: Emerging Patterns*, (Santa Monica: Rand Corporation, 1980), and J. M. Chaiken et al., *Fiscal Limitation in California: Initial Effects on the Criminal Justice System*, (Santa Monica: Rand Corporation, no date). As well as the degree of 'privatization', this research suggests that 'a leaner and smaller public sector may also turn out to be meaner and harsher'.

39. See Carol Warren, 'New Forms of Social Control: The Myth of Deinstitutionalization', *American Behavioral Scientist*, 24, 6 (July–August 1981), pp. 724–40.

40 Lerman, 'Child Welfare, the Private Sector'.

41. Joanne A. Arnaud and Timothy Mack, 'The Deinstitutionalization of Status Offenders in Massachusetts: The Role of the Private Sector', in Handler and Zatz, *Neither Angels Nor Thieves*, pp. 335–71.

42. See Chester J. Kulis, 'Profit in the Presentence Report', *Federal Probation*, 47, 4 (December 1983), pp. 11–16. His melodramatic vision is of private operators 'rising phoenix-like' from a criminal justice system 'charred' by budget cuts and staff layoffs.

43. For references to these and similar bright ideas, see Charles A. Lindquist, 'The Private Sector in Corrections: Contracting Probation Services from Community Organizations', *Federal Probation*, 44, 1 (March 1980), pp. 58–63.

44. This process is well described in Rutherford and McDermott, *Juvenile Diversion*. 'Non legal' becomes 'para-legal', 'para-legal' becomes 'legal'.

45. See A. A. Cain et al., *Para legals – a Selected Bibliography*, (Washington DC: NILECJ, 1979).

46. Spitzer and Scull, 'Privatization and Capitalist Development'. And see Clifford D. Shearing and Philip C. Stenning, 'Modern Private Security: its Growth and Implications', in M. Tonry and N. Morris (eds), *Crime and Justice: An Annual Review of Research*, (Chicago: University of Chicago Press, 1981), vol. 3, pp. 193–245 and 'Private Security: Implications for Social Control', *Social Problems*, 30, 5 (June 1985), pp. 493–506.

47. Shearing and Stenning, 'Private Security', p. 496.

48. See Gary T. Marx, 'Thoughts on a Neglected Category of Social Movement Participant: The Agent Provocateur and the Informant', *American Journal of Sociology*, 80, 2 (September 1974), pp. 402–42.

49. Notably Gary Marx, whose various writings on the subject I rely upon here: 'The New Police Undercover Work', *Urban Life and Culture*, 8, 4 (1980), pp. 400–46, 'Who Really Gets Stung? Some Issues Raised by the New Police Undercover Work', *Crime and Delinquency*, 28, (April 1982), pp. 165–93 and *The Expansion and Changing Form of American Secret*

*Police Practices*, unpublished MS. (Massachusetts Institute of Technology, 1982).

50. For approved examples of these new forms of policing, see L. Bickman, et al., *Citizen Crime Reporting Projects*, (Washington, DC: NILECJ, 1977) and R. K. Yin et al., *Citizen Patrol Projects*, (Washington DC: NILECJ, 1977).

51. On the problems of these developments (and an attempt to distinguish them from 'genuine' forms of popular justice) see James F. Brady, 'Towards a Popular Justice in the United States: The Dialectics of Community Action', *Contemporary Crises*, 5, 2 (April 1981), pp. 155–92.

52. Greenberg, 'Problems in Community Corrections', p. 8.

53. Dunford, 'Police Diversion', p. 350.

54. Messinger, 'Confinement in the Community', p. 84–5.

55. See Rutherford and Bengur, 'Community Based Alternatives', p. 4. The (admittedly extreme) example they cite of something called 'community treatment', consisted of 25 full-time staff, 15 clients and was located on the fourth floor of a 1000-bed public hospital.

56. For examples of this sort of regime, see Seiter et al., *Halfway Houses*.

57. D. Boorkman et al., *An Exemplary Project: Community Based Corrections in Des Moines*, (Washington DC: NILECJ, 1976). For a more general impression of community correctional centres, see R. M. Carter et al., *Community Correctional Centers: Program Models*, (Washington DC: National Institute of Justice, 1980).

58. R. Ku and C. Blew, *A University's Approach to Delinquency Prevention: The Adolescent Diversion Project*, (Washington DC: NILECJ, 1977). Note that both my examples – Fort Des Moines and the ADP – were among the 20 'exemplary projects' selected by the LEEA for their effectiveness and adaptability.

59. This programme was hailed by John Conrad as 'News of the Future' in *Federal Probation*, 47, 4 (December 1983), pp. 54–5.

60. For general information, see *Intensive Intermediate Treatment*, (Leicester: Youth Social Unit, National Youth Bureau, July 1983). On the Coventry PACE project, see Alistair Crine, 'A Lifeline For Young Offenders', *Community Care*, 10 February 1983.

61. Michael E. Smith, 'Will the Real Alternatives Please Stand Up', (Unpublished Paper, Colloquium on Prison Overcrowding Crisis, New York University Review of Law and Social Change, March 1983).

62. Lest it be thought that I am prejudiced against behaviourism (which I most certainly am) here is an example of another type of 'treatment modality in the community'. Three 'sociopathic' girls were taken from a corrective school and 'voluntarily committed' to a psychiatric hospital unit where they were administered minimal daily doses of insulin to instil hunger and anxiety. Each girl was then assigned to a 'selective maternal companion' with whom she 'interacted spontaneously' 5 hours daily for 6 months. 'Close dependent relationships developed, changes in identification took place and there was some suggestion that super ego changes

are possible.' This is cited, without a hint of criticism or comment, by Marguerite Warren, *Correctional Treatment in Community Settings: A Report of Current Research*, (Washington DC: National Institute of Mental Health, 1974).

63. *Project Crest: Counselling for Juveniles on Probation*, (Washington: US Department of Justice, 1980).

64. Foucault, *Discipline and Punish*, p. 211.

65. Lamar T. Empey, *Alternatives to Incarceration*, (Washington DC: US Government Printing Office, 1967).

66. I could, a little melodramatically, describe the system's effect on its surrounding space as 'prisonization', 'institutionalization' or — to invent an even more clumsy term — 'controlization'. These processes are similar to Lindheim's notion of the 'hospitalization of space' (as used by Illich to describe the medical colonization of everyday areas of social life).

67. D. Skoler, 'Future Trends in Juvenile and Adult Community Based Corrections', in Perlstein and Phelps, *Alternatives to Prison*, p. 11.

68. Christopher Lasch, *Haven in a Heartless World: The Family Besieged*, (New York: Basic Books, 1977).

69. The following references give some sense of the literature. In the USA: J. M. McPartland and F. L. McDill (eds), *Violence in Schools: Perspectives, Programs and Positions*, (Lexington Mass: D. C. Heath and Co., 1977); Robert J. Rubel, *Unruly School: Disorders Disruptions and Crimes*, (Lexington Mass: D. C. Heath and Co., 1977), and 'HEW's [Health Education and Welfare] Safe School Study — what it says and what it means for teachers and administrators', (Maryland, Institute for Reduction of Crime, 1978); Robert Rubel et al., *Crime and Disruption in Schools: A Selected Bibiliography*, (Washington DC: NILECJ, 1969); S. D. Vestermark and P. D. Blauvelt, *Controlling Crime in the School — A Complete Security Handbook for Administrators*, (West Nyack NY: Parker Publishing Co., 1978); National Institute of Education, *Violent Schools — Safe Schools: The Safe Schools Study*, Report to Congress, (Washington DC: US Govt. Printing Office, 1978). In England: J. W. Docking, *Control and Discipline in Schools: Perspectives and Approaches*, (London: Harper & Row Ltd., 1980) and Del Tatum, *Disruptive Pupils in School and Units*, (Chichester: John Wiley, 1982).

70. See Peter Schrag and Diane Divoky, *The Myth of the Hyperactive Child*, (New York: Pantheon, 1975).

71. Department of Education and Science, *Behavioural Units* and *Truancy and Behavioural Problems in Urban Schools*, (London: DES, 1978).

72. Here are a few sample questions from an Institute publicity leaflet aimed at selling its security package to schools: 'Although you feel that the percentage of unruly children hasn't changed much over the years, you also feel that your control over them is slipping away;' 'Your usual administrative remedies such as suspension and detention, don't seem to work anymore, either with individuals or the overall group of unruly pupils;' 'Because courts are limiting how you can discipline students, you are

now alienating your teaching staff as you are forced to return borderline students to their classrooms'.

73. See John Winterdyk and Ronald Roesch, 'A Wilderness Experiential Program as an Alternative for Probationers: An Evaluation', *Canadian Journal of Criminology*, 24, (January 1982), pp. 39–51.

74. See J. T. S. Duncan, *Citizen Crime Prevention Tactics: A Literature Review and Selected Bibliography*, (Washington DC: National Criminal Justice Reference Service, 1980).

75. Anthony Sorrentino, *How to Organize the Neighbourhood for Delinquency Prevention*, (New York: Human Sciences Press, 1979).

76. See Anthony F. Bottoms, 'Some Neglected Features of Modern Penal Systems', in D. Garland and P. Young (eds), *The Power to Punish*, (London: Heinemann, 1983).

77. Foucault, *Discipline and Punish*, p. 113.

78. The term 'bifurcation' was used by Bottoms to refer to the split in modern British penal policy towards adult offenders: new tough measures for the really serious or dangerous offender, a more lenient line towards the 'ordinary' offender. See Anthony Bottoms, 'Reflections on the Renaissance of Dangerousness', *Howard Journal of Penology and Crime Prevention*, 16, 2 (1977), especially pp. 88–91.


3  DEPOSITS OF POWER


1. As Bottoms notes, in order to account for such matters as changes in imprisonment rates, it is not particularly important which of these explanations is correct: Anthony Bottoms, 'Neglected Features of Contemporary Penal Systems', in D. Garland and P. Young (eds), *The Power to Punish*, (London: Heinemann, 1983), pp. 166–202.

2. See, for example, David Biles, 'Crime and Imprisonment', *British Journal of Criminology*, 23, 2 (April 1983), pp. 166–72.

3. Kenneth Carlson et al., *American Prisons and Jails*, (Washington DC: National Institute of Justice, 1980), vol. 2, *Population Trends and Projections*, p. 50.

4. Malcolm Klein, 'Deinstitutionalization and Diversion of Juvenile Offenders A Litany of Impediments', in N. Morris and M. Tonry (eds), *Crime and Justice: An Annual Review of Research*, (Chicago: University of Chicago Press, 1979), vol. 1, pp. 145–201.

5. Edwin M. Lemert, 'Diversion in Juvenile Justice: What Hath Been Wrought?', *Journal of Research in Crime and Delinquency*, 18, 1 (January 1981), pp. 34–46.

6. *Ibid.*, p. 45.

7. D. H. Thorpe et al., *Out of Care: The Community Support of Juvenile Offenders*, (London: George Allen & Unwin, 1980), p. 3.

8. Joel Handler and Julie Zatz, 'The Implementation System: Characteristics and Change', in Handler and Zatz (eds), *Neither Angels Nor Thieves: Studies in the Deinstitutionalization of Status Offenders*, (Washington DC: National Academy Press, 1982).

9. Klein, 'Deinstitutionalization and Diversion'.

10. James Austin and Barry Krisberg, 'Wider, Stronger and Different Nets: The Dialectics of Criminal Justice Reform', *Journal of Research in Crime and Delinquency*, 18, 1 (January 1981), pp. 165–96.

11. *Ibid.*, p. 166.

12. Andrew Rutherford and Robert McDermott, *Juvenile Diversion*, (Washington DC: NILECJ, 1976), p. 13.

13. Lemert, 'Diversion in Juvenile Justice', p. 40.

14. Irving Spergel, et al., 'De-institutionalization of Status Offenders: Individual Outcome and System Effects', *Journal of Research in Crime and Delinquency*, 18, (January 1981), pp. 4–33. For a more optimistic evaluation of the DSO programme, see Handler and Zatz (eds), *Neither Angels Nor Thieves*.

15. M. Rein and F. Rabinowitz, 'Implementation: A Theoretical Perspective' in W. Burnham and M. Weinberg (eds), *American Politics and Public Policy*, (Cambridge Mass: MIT Press, 1978).

16. David Greenberg and Drew Humphreys, 'The Cooptation of Fixed Sentencing Reform', *Crime and Delinquency*, 26, 2 (April 1980), pp. 206–25.

17. Peter Schrag, *Mind Control*, (New York: Pantheon, 1978), p. 11.

18. David Greenberg, 'Problems in Community Corrections', *Issues in Criminology*, 10, 1 (Spring 1975), p. 23.

19. Thorpe et al., *Out of Care*, p. 22.

20. *Ibid.*

21. *Ibid.*, p. 128.

22. Klein, 'Deinstitutionalization and Diversion', p. 190.

23. Richard Abel (ed.), *The Politics of Informal Justice*, (2 vols, New York: Academic Press, 1982), vol. 1 *The American Experience*, vol. 2 *Comparative Studies*.

24. Steven Spitzer, 'The Rationalization of Crime Control in Capitalist Society', *Contemporary Crises*, 3 (April 1979), p. 201.

25. Andrew Scull, *Decarceration: Community Treatment and the Deviant – A Radical View*, (New Jersey: Prentice Hall, 1977). For Scull's later reflections on and modifications of his original thesis, see the 'Afterword' to the second edition of *Decarceration* (Cambridge: Polity Press, 1984), and 'Community Corrections: Panacea Progress or Pretence?' – different versions in Abel, *The Politics of Informal Justice*, pp. 99–118 and Garland and Young, *The Power to Punish*, pp. 146–65.

26. The combination of the increased use of community alternatives together with (i) uninterrupted increases in crime-control budgets and employment rates; (ii) an upward trend in welfare spending in proportion to the total budget; and (iii) growing government deficits, is well documented in the Canadian case. See, Janet Chan and Richard Ericson,

*Decarceration and the Economy of Penal Reform*, (Toronto: Centre of Criminology, University of Toronto, 1981).

27. Paul Lerman, 'Trends and Issues in the Deinstitutionalization of Youth in Trouble', *Crime and Delinquency*, 27, 3 (July 1980), pp. 281–98 and 'Child Welfare, the Private Sector and Community Based Corrections', *Crime and Delinquency*, 30, 1 (January 1984), pp. 5–38.

28. This is the account provided by Steven Spitzer, 'Towards a Marxian Theory of Deviance', *Social Problems*, 22, 5 (June 1975) pp. 638–51. An important, and often quoted source, about the increased production of the 'human detritus' of capitalist urbanism and the consequent expansion of all sorts of control institutions to clear the market place of everyone but the 'economically active' is Harry Braverman, *Labour and Monopoly Capitalism: The Degradation of Work in the Twentieth Century*, (New York: Monthly Review Press, 1974). See especially pp. 279–80.

29. I am paraphrasing here Dario Melossi's two papers: 'Institutions of Social Control and the Capitalist Organization of Work', in B. Fine et al. (eds), *Capitalism and the Rule of Law*, (London: Hutchinson, 1979) and 'Strategies of Social Control in Capitalism: A Comment on Recent Work', *Contemporary Crises*, 4, 4 (October 1980), pp. 381–402.

30. Melossi, 'Strategies of Social Control', p. 396.

31. Stuart Hall et al., *Policing the Crisis: Mugging the State and Law and Order*, (London: Macmillan, 1978); Stuart Hall, 'Moving Right', *Socialist Review*, 11, 1 (1981), pp. 113–37; Ian Taylor, 'The Law and Order Issue in the British General Election and the Canadian Federal Election of 1979: Crime, Populism and the State', *Canadian Journal of Sociology*, 15, 3 (Summer 1980), pp. 285–311 and *Law and Order: Arguments For Socialism*, (London: Macmillan, 1981).

32. Marilyn Dixon, 'World Capitalist Crisis and the Rise of the New Right', *Contemporary Marxism*, 4 (1981), pp. 1–10; Raymond Michalowski, 'The Politics of the Right', *Crime and Social Justice*, 15 (Summer 1981), pp. 29–35; Tony Platt and Paul Takagi, 'Intellectuals for Law and Order: A Critique of the New "Realists"', *Crime and Social Justice*, 8 (Winter 1977), pp. 1–6 and 'Law and Order in the 1980s'; Editorial in *Crime and Social Justice*, 15 (Summer 1980), pp. 1–6 (see also the rest of this issue devoted to the 'rise of the right'); Tony Platt, 'Managing the Crisis: Austerity and the Penal System', *Contemporary Marxism*, 4 (1981), pp. 29–39.

33. See R. S. Ratner and J. L. McMullan, 'Social Control and the Rise of the "Exceptional State" in Britain, the United States and Canada', *Crime and Social Justice*, 19 (Summer 1983), pp. 31–43.

34. Bertram Gross, *Friendly Fascism: The New Force of Power in America*, (New York: M. Evans and Co., 1960).

35. Taylor, *Law and Order*, p. 78.

36. Abel, 'The Contradictions of Informal Justice', p. 305.

37. For a crude version of this 'endless repression' theory, including the curious thesis that the criminal justice system grows because there is little room

elsewhere for capitalism to develop, see the writings of Richard Quinney, for example *Class, State and Crime* (London: Longman, 1977).

38. For a review of the evidence on the massive state finding of soft, community based delinquency programmes, see Frank Hellum, 'Juvenile Justice: The Second Revolution', *Crime and Delinquency*, vol. 25, No. 3, (July 1979), pp. 299–317.

39. Chann and Ericson, *Decarceration and the Economy of Penal Reform*, p. 21.

40. Spitzer, 'Towards a Marxian Theory of Deviance', p. 648.

41. Platt and Takagi, 'Intellectuals for Law and Order', p. 10.

42. Lerman, 'Child Welfare, the Private Sector and Community Based Corrections'.

43. Greenberg and Humphreys, 'The Co-optation of Fixed Sentencing Reform'.

44. V. S. Naipaul, *A Bend in the River*, (Harmondsworth: Penguin, 1980), pp. 22–3.

## 4   STORIES OF CHANGE

1. On the sociology of nostalgia, see Fred Davis, *Yearning For Yesterday: a sociology of nostalgia*, (London: Collier Macmillan; 1979).

2. Robert A. Nisbet, *The Quest for Community*, (New York: Oxford University Press, 1962) and *The Sociological Tradition*, (New York: Basic Books, 1966). Nisbet quotes Marx as the only dissenting voice among the founding fathers who warned against the romanticism of the community ideal. Writing in 1853 about the village community in India, Marx (while deploring the 'sickening loss' of the traditional community as a consequence of English colonialism) noted also 'we must not forget that these idyllic village communities, inoffensive though they must appear, had always been the solid foundation of Oriental depotism, that they restrained the human mind within the smallest possible compass, making it the unwitting tool of superstition, enslaving it beneath traditional rules, depriving it of all grandeur and historical energies.' Despite his warning, though, few contemporary heirs to the Marxist traditions have really questioned the idealization of community.

3. This theme is usefully reviewed by Raymond Plant, *Community and Ideology: an essay in applied social philosophy*, (London: Routledge & Kegan Paul, 1974).

4. *Ibid.*, pp. 47–8.

5. C. Wright Mills, 'The Professional Ideology of Social Pathologists', *American Journal of Sociology*, 46, 2 (September 1943), pp. 165–80.

6. Bernard Beck, 'The Limits of Deinstitutionalization', in M. Lewis (ed.), *Research in Social Problems and Public Policy*, 1 (Greenwich: JAI Press, 1979), pp. 1–14.

7. On recent strategies for creating free enclaves of self, see Stanley Cohen and Laurie Taylor, *Escape Attempts: the Theory and Practice of Resistance to Everyday Life*, (London: Allen Lane. 1977).

8. Beck, 'The Limits of Deinstitutionalization', p. 5.

9. For an excellent account of the misreadings of anthropology in the informal justice movement, see Sally Engel Merry, 'The Social Organization of Mediation in Nonindustrial Societies: Implications for Informal Community Justice in America', in R. Abel (ed.), *The Politics of Informal Justice*, (New York: Academic Press, 1982), vol. 2, *Comparative Studies*, pp. 17–45. On the more general problems of transferring social-control ideologies back and forth between industrial and non-industrial societies, see Stanley Cohen, 'Western Crime Control Models in the Third World: Benign or Malignant?' in R. Simon and S. Spitzer (eds), *Research in Law, Deviance and Social Control*, (Greenwich: JAI Press, 1982). vol. 4.

10. Abel, *The Politics of Informal Justice*, introduction.

11. For a review of this history (that is, of the E. P. Thompson school) and an account of the changes in law enforcement, see David Philips, '"A Just Measure of Crime, Authority, Hunters and Blue Locusts", the Revisionist Social History of Crime and Law in Britain, 1780–1850', in S. Cohen and A. Scull (eds), *Social Control and the State State Comparative and Historical Essays*, (Oxford: Martin Robertson, 1983) and '"A New Engine of Power and Authority", The Institutionalization of Law Enforcement in England 1780–1830', in V. A. Gatrell et al. (eds), *Crime and Law: The Social History of Crime in Western Europe since 1500*, (London: Europa, 1980).

12. Beck, 'The Limits of Deinstitutionalization', pp. 8–9. See also Scull's various writings on decarceration for similar characterizations of social-control talk.

13. Beck, 'The Limits of Deinstitutionalization', p. 9.

14. Only the anarchist tradition is consistent here: building community is a means to reduce state intervention. The necessary and sufficient conditions for community are the absence of political specialization and of any concentration of force. See Michael Taylor, *Community, Anarchy and Liberty*, (London: Cambridge Press, 1982).

15. Philip Abrams, 'Social Change, Social Networks and Neighbourhood Care', *Social Work Service*, 22 (February 1980), pp. 12–23.

16. Beck, 'The Limits of Deinstitutionalization', pp. 7–8.

17. See Thomas Mathieson, 'The Future of Control Systems: The Case of Norway', *International Journal of the Sociology of Law*, 8 (1980), pp. 149–64. Mathiesen sees a master shift from individualistic modes of explanation that explain property crime in terms of a rational, individual response to the environment (material need) to more collective social modes that see property crime at a time of economic growth as due to weakened social control, which needs to be strengthened. The problem with this account, is that punitive cellular confinement (which for Mathieson exemplifies the first phase) was actually also justified by the notion of weak social control.

18. William Ryan, *Blaming the Victim*, revised edn, (New York: Random House, 1976), p. 8

19. Boaventura de Sousa Santos, 'Law and Community: The Changing Nature of State Power in Late Capitalism', in R. Abel (ed.), *The Politics of Informal Justice*, vol. 1, *The American Experience*, pp. 249–66.

20. William Gaylin et al., *Doing Good: The Limits of Benevolence* (New York: Pantheon, 1978). See particularly Rothman's 'Introduction' and 'The State as Parent'.

21. Steven Marcus, 'Their Brothers' Keepers: An Episode from English History', in Gaylin, *Doing Good*, p. 42. Note How Trilling's eloquent warning (in 1947) against Marxism is now used to warn about liberalism: 'some paradox in our nature leads us, once we have made our fellow men the objects of our enlightened interest, to go on to make them the objects of our pity, then of our wisdom, ultimately of our coercion', quoted by Rothman in *Doing Good*, p. 72.

22. Rothman, *Doing Good*, pp. 73–4.

23. William Gaylin and David Rothman, 'Introduction' to Andrew von Hirsh, *Doing Justice: The Choice of Punishments*, (New York: Hill and Wang, 1976), p. xi.

24. Ronaly Bayer, 'Crime, Punishment and the Decline of Liberal Optimism', *Crime and Delinquency*, 27, 2 (April 1981), pp. 169–90.

25. For this reason, critics like Sedgewick allege that such movements as anti-psychiatry and the decarceration of the mentally ill, were 'really' conservative. Neither civil liberties, nor the left adoption of critiques such as Laing's nor the movement to 'alternative' therapies can confront the central problem of the asylum: 'how to create the economic means of employment, the material apparatus of housing, the ethical structure of fellowship and solidarity for those who through various forms of mental disability cannot purchase these benefits as commodities in the market place' — Peter Sedgewick, *Psychopolitics* (London: Pluto Press, 1982), p. 219.

26. I rely, in this section, on Peter Steinfels, *The Neo-conservatives: The Men Who Are Changing American Politics*, (New York: Simon & Schuster, 1979) and Michael Waltzer, *Radical Principles*, (New York: Basic Books, 1980).

27. Tony Platt and Paul Takagi, 'Intellectuals for Law and Order: A Critique of the New Realists', *Crime and Social Justice*, vol. 7, (Fall–Winter, 1977), p. 11.

28. Taylor, *Law and Order: Arguments for Socialism*, (London: Macmillan, 1981).

29. Waltzer, *Radical Principles*.

30. For a persuasive account of this process in terms of the gradual *disappearance* of a public form of political and social life, see Richard Sennet, *The Fall of Public Man*, (London: Oxford University Press, 1978).

31. William Burroughs, *The Naked Lunch*, (London: Calder, 1964), p. 44.

32. Jacques Donzelot, *The Policing of Families*, (New York: Pantheon Books, 1979).

33. *Ibid.*, p. 98.
34. Christopher Lasch, *Haven In a Heartless World: the Family Besieged*, (New York: Basic Books, 1977). See also his review 'Life in the therapeutic state', *New York Review of Books*, xxvii, 10 (12 June 1980), pp. 24—32.
35. Clifford D. Shearing and Philip C. Stenning, 'Private Security: Implications for Social Control', *Social Problems*, 30, 5 (June 1983), pp. 493—506.
36. Francis T. Cullen and Karen T. Gilbert, *Reaffirming Rehabilitation*, (Cincinatti: Anderson Publishing Co. 1980), p. 19. See the whole of their chapter four, 'Attacking Rehabilitation', pp. 89—149.
37. Nils Christie, *Limits to Pain*, (Oxford: Martin Robertson, 1981), p. 52.
38. James Austin and Barry Krisberg, 'Wider Stronger and Different Nets: The Dialectics of Criminal Justice Reform', *Journal of Research in Crime and Delinquency*, 18, 1 (January 1981), p. 167.
39. Richard Abel, 'Conservative Conflict and the Reproduction of Capitalism: The Role of Informal Justice', *International Journal of Sociology of Law*, 9 (1981), pp. 215—67.
40. Marc Galanter, 'Justice in Many Rooms: Courts, Private Ordering and Indigenous Law', *Journal of Legal Pluralism*, 19 (1981), pp 1—47.
41. The standard critique of the therapeutic state became Nicholas Kittrie, *The Right to be Different : Deviance and Enforced Therapy* (Baltimore: Johns Hopkins Press, 1971). A popular description of the thought control scenario (neurological control of violence, drug control, medicalization of political dissent etc) is Peter Schrag, *Mind Control*, (New York: Pantheon, 1978).
42. George Orwell, *Nineteen Eighty-Four* (London: Secker and Warburg, 1949). Page references are to the Penguin edition (Harmondsworth, 1954), p. 203.
43. Bertram Gross, *Friendly Fascism: The New Face of Power in America*, (New York: M. Evans and Co., 1980); Jeff Gerth, 'The Americanization of *1984*', in Richard Quinney (ed.), *Criminal Justice in America: A Critical Understanding*, (Boston: Little Brown & Co., 1974), pp. 213—28.
44. Orwell, *Nineteen Eighty-Four*, pp. 60—1.
45. David J. Rothman, 'Behaviour Modification in Total Institutions: A Historical Overview', *Hastings Centre Report*, 5 (February 1975), pp. 17—24.
46. See, for example, this group of writings: Paul Gendrau and Robert Ross, 'Effective Correctional Treatment: Bibliotherapy for Cynics', *Crime and Delinquency*, 25, 4 (October 1979), pp. 463—89 and 'Offender Rehabilitation: The Appeal of Success', *Federal Probation*, 45, 4 (December 1981), pp. 45—7; Robert Ross and H. Bryan McKay, 'Behavioural Approaches to Treatment in Corrections: Requiem for a Panacea', *Canadian Journal of Criminology and Corrections*, 20, 3 (July 1978), pp. 279—95 and Robert Ross and Paul Gendreau, *Effective Correctional Treatment*, (Toronto: Butterworth, 1980).
47. Ross and McKay, 'Behavioral Approaches'.

48. For the flavour of behaviourist talk here, see such journals as *Behaviourism, Behaviour Modification; Criminal Justice and Behaviour; Journal of Applied Behavioural Analysis.* A recent sympathetic, but modest, review of the uses of behaviour therapy on young offenders in and out of the community is Philip Feldman (ed.) *Developments in the Study of Criminal Behaviour,* (London: John Wiley and Sons, 1982), vol. 1, *The Prevention and Control of Offending.*

49. Judith Wilks and Robert Martinson, 'Is the Treatment of Criminal Offenders Really Necessary?' *Federal Probation,* 40, 1 (March 1970), pp. 3–9.

50. The most quoted enthusiasts were Barton L. Ingraham and Gerald W. Smith, 'The Use of Electronics in the Observation and Control of Human Behaviour and Its Possible Use in Rehabilitation and Corrections', *Issues in Criminology,* 7, 2 (Fall 1972), pp. 35–53.

51. M. W. Lehtinen, 'Technological Incapacitation: A Neglected Alternative', *Quarterly Journal of Corrections,* 2 (Winter 1978), pp. 31–8.

52. For an effective demolition of the more theatrical claims and unrealistic fears about thought control — the vision of an 'electroligarchy' where people could be enslaved by controlling them from within their own brains — see Elliot S. Valenstein, *Brain Control: A Critical Examination of Brain Stimulation and Psychosurgery,* (New York: John Wiley and Sons, 1976). Valenstein is critical both of his neurological colleagues and their uninformed social-science critics for crude extrapolations from animal experiments and for propagating the quite unwarranted idea that *specific* functions or actions (like aggression) can be controlled by electrodes or other such techniques.

53. See for example, S. Yochelson and S. E. Samenow, *The Criminal Personality,* (New York: Jason Aronson, 1976), vol. 1.

54. A. E. Bottoms, 'Reflections on the renaissance of dangerousness', *Howard Journal of Penology and Crime Prevention,* 16, 2 (1977), pp. 70–96.

55. Edward K. Morris, 'Applied Behavior Analysis for Criminal Justice Practice: Some Current Dimensions', *Criminal Justice and Behavior,* 7, 2 (June 1980), p. 135.

56. See notably, the work of Leslie T. Wilkins, for example 'Crime and Criminal Justice at the Turn of the Century', *Annals,* 208 (July 1973), pp. 13–20.

57. C. R. Jeffrey, *Crime Control Through Environmental Design,* (Beverly Hills: Sage, 1977), p. 40.

58. R. V. Clarke and P. Mayhew (eds), *Designing Out Crime,* (London: HMSO, 1980).

59. On various early LEAA projects, see *Crime Prevention Through Environment Design,* (Washington DC: LEAA, 1976) and W. D. Wallace (ed.), *Crime Prevention Through Environmental Design — Annotated Bibliography* (Westinghouse Electrical Corporation, 1976). I return to this work in chapter 6.

60. A selecton of this sort of work may be found in C. Ray Jeffrey (ed.),

'Criminal Behaviour and the Physical Environment', *American Behavioural Scientist*, 20, 2 (November–December 1976).

61. For a good account of the changing world views which support social-problem intervention, see Richard Henshel, *Reacting to Social Problems*, (Ontario: Longman Canada, 1976).

62. Mordecai Rotenberg, *Damnation and Deviance: The Protestant Ethic and the Spirit of Failure*, (New York: Free Press, 1978).

63. David J. Rothman, 'Prisons: The Failure Model', *Nation*, (21 December 1974), p. 647.

64. James Q. Wilson, 'Crime and the Criminologists', *Commentary*, (July 1974), p. 49. Wilson's full argument is to be found in *Thinking About Crime*, (New York: Basic Books, 1975).

65. This has been made clear recently by one of its leading ideologues: James Q. Wilson, '"What Works?" Revisited: New Findings on Criminal Rehabilitation', *The Public Interest*, 61 (Fall 1980), pp. 3–17.

66. *Ibid*, p. 13.

67. Marvin E. Wolfgang, 'Change and Stability in Criminal Justice', in E. Sagarin (ed.), *Criminology: New Concerns*, (Beverly Hills: Sage, 1979). p. 69.

68. Donald R. Cressey, 'Criminological Theory, Social Science and the Repression of Crime', in Sagarin (ed.), *Criminology*, p. 45, and 'Criminology in the 1980s', *Criminal News*, the Newsletter of Criminology Section, American Sociological Association, (Spring 1982), p. 4.

69. Amitai Etzioni, 'Human beings are not very easy to change after all', *Saturday Review*, (3 June, 1972); reprinted in *Annual Editions: Readings In Social Problems*, (California: Dushkin, 1973).

70. Gagnon and Davison remark on the exquisite irony of using methods such as token-economy regimes in institutions like prisons and mental hospitals. The original asylum founders thought they were designing havens for disturbed citizens to recover from the brutal competitiveness of the economic order. Here the poor, the marginal, those at the end of a career of downward mobility could find a refuge of order and discipline, away from the pressures which had driven them crazy: The token economy also attempts to restore order, but by deliberately reproducing the very set of conditions earlier thought to be pathogenic: the market economy. See John Gagnon and Gerald Davison, 'Asylums, the Token Economy and the Metrics of Mental Life', *Behaviour Therapy*, 6 (1976), pp. 528–34. But there might be no irony here. Behaviourism shares with pure capitalist ideology the idea that people work only for gains in wealth and power – positive reinforcement. This is a degrading and brutal assumption, but is more acceptable than the Freudian possibility that work might be connected with internal psychic satisfaction.

71. See Harvey Wheeler (ed.), *Beyond the Punitive Society*, (London: Wildwood House, 1973). Wheeler also reminds us that classic liberalism was a theory of negative government – maximizing liberty by minimizing restraints. You leave things alone up to the point where you have to

punish. Skinner, by contrast, is in favour of a positive, interventionist state: the point of operant reinforcement (like much current crime-control ideology) is not to wait and then punish, but to do something first.

72. Michel Foucault, *Discipline and Punish*, (London: Allen Lane, 1977), p. 223.

73. Robert Castel et al., *The Psychiatric Society*, (New York: Columbia University Press, 1982). For accessible criticisms of the over-reach of contemporary (American) psychiatry, see Martin L. Gross, *The Psychological Society*, (New York: Simon and Schuster, 1978) and Schrag, *Mind Control*. For a good summary of the recent critical histories of psychiatry, see David Ingleby, 'Mental Health and the Social Order', in Cohen and Scull (eds), *Social Control and the State*, pp. 141–88.

74. Christopher Lasch, *The Culture of Narcissism*, (New York: W. W. Norton, 1978). Such critics have noted that 'third stream', post-Freudian psychologies are even more incongruent than classic Freudianism with the ideal of community. The ego-centred notion of self-actualization implies that once the individual has broken away from traditional communal restraints (family, status, citizenship) he owes nothing to society. Society is merely an outside force acting on the individual; social roles are alienated forms of behaviour. So 'community treatment' not only takes place in settings far removed from the traditional community, but is informed by a therapeutic ethic quite incompatible with such communal ideals as fraternity, mutual aid and cooperation. See Philip Rieff, *The Triumph of the Therapeutic*, (New York: Harper and Row, 1966), chapter 3, 'Community and Therapy'; and Russell Jacoby, *Social Amnesia*, (Brighton: Harvester Press, 1977).

75. Wolfgang, 'Change and Stability in Criminal Justice', p. 69. Note, however, that the new cognitive paradigm in psychology is not quite the same as the behaviourism favoured by the criminal justice system. Though 'cognitive psychology' is not at all Freudian, it overlays on behaviourism certain mentalistic concepts which are closer to William James's old definition of psychology as 'the science of mental life'. For a popular survey of these developments, see Jonathan Miller, *States of Mind*, (New York: Pantheon, 1983).

76. Scull, 'Community Corrections: Panacea, Progress or Pretense?' in Abel (ed.), *The Politics of Informal Justice*, p. 100.

77. Howard S. Becker, 'Whose Side Are We On?', *Social Problems*, 14, 3 (1967), pp. 239–47.

78. David Garland and Peter Young (eds), *The Power to Punish*, (London: Heinemann, 1983), 'Introduction'.

79. Murray Edelman, *The Symbolic Uses of Politics*, (Urbana: University of Illinois Press, 1964).

80. Peter Sedgewick, *Psychopolitics*, (London: Pluto Press, 1982), p. 137.

81. Amitai Etzioni, 'The Grand Shaman', *Psychology Today*, (November 1972), pp. 88–94.

82. Edmond R. Leach, *Political Systems of Highland Burma: A Study of Kachin Social Structure*, (London: Athlone Press, 1970), original edn, 1954.
83. *Ibid.*, pp. 265–6.
84. *Ibid.*, p. 281.
85. *Ibid.*, pp. 286–7.


5  THE PROFESSIONALS


1. For a useful summary of the post-industrial society literature, see Krishan Kumar, *Prophecy and Progress: The Sociology of Industrial and Post Industrial Societies*, (Harmondsworth: Penguin, 1978).
2. Pat Walker (ed.), *Between Labour and Capital*, (Boston: South End Press, 1979).
3. Alvin Gouldner, *The Future of the Intellectuals and the Rise of the New Class*, (London: Macmillan, 1979).
4. *Ibid.*, p. 8.
5. See Eliot Freidson, *Professional Dominance*, (New York: 1970), and Magali S. Larson, *The Rise of Professionalism: A Sociological Analysis*, (Berkely: University of California Press, 1977).
6. Gouldner, *The Future of the Intellectuals*, p. 21.
7. James Finlayson, *Urban Devastation: The Planning of Incarceration*, (Solidarity Pamphlet, no date).
8. Peter Sedgewick, *Psychopolitics*, (London: Pluto Press, 1982), p. 138.
9. Paul Willis, *Learning To Labour*, (Westmead: Saxon House, 1977), p. 176.
10. See Geoffrey Pearson, *The Deviant Imagination: Psychiatry, Social Work and Social Change*, (London: Macmillan, 1975).
11. On the early history of psychiatry, see Andrew Scull, *Museums of Madness: The Social Organization of Insanity in 19th Century England*, (London: Allen Lane, 1979) and, more generally, David Ingleby, 'Mental Health and Social Order', in S. Cohen and A. Scull (eds), *Social Control and the State: Comparative and Historical Essays*, (Oxford: Martin Robertson, 1983). On the medical profession in general, see Eliot Freidson, *Profession of Medicine*, (New York: Dodd Mead, 1970).
12. Lasch, however, notes an interesting paradox. On the one hand, the helping professions have 'besieged' the family and made ordinary people more dependent on them. On the other, the ultimate triumph of the therapeutic (the lodging of therapeutic modes of thought more deeply into the public mind) may have *weakened* the special monopoly and power of the psychiatric profession. See Christopher Lasch, *Haven in a Heartless World*, (New York: Basic Books, 1977).
13. See Robert Castel et al., *The Psychiatric Society* (New York: Columbia University Press, 1982), and Peter Schrag, *Mind Control*, (London: Marion Boyars, 1980).

14. But see the statistical sources cited in chapter 2 for data on: (a) the overall growth of criminal justice expenditure and manpower; (b) the particular growth in the correctional sector (in the USA in 1979, this was 45 per cent of state justice budgets, a 15 per cent rise from the previous year), which outpaces the increase in inmates; and (c) the expansion of the community and private sectors, especially under welfare or psychiatric authority.

15. In the USA, this expansion was most apparent when increased Federal crime-control budgets in the sixties began funnelling more money into LEEP (the Law Enforcement Education Programme under LEAA). From 1969–76, a total of $234.7 million in LEAA funds was awarded to more than 1000 colleges and universities. An estimated 290,000 staff went back to school under these programmes. By 1974/5 some 75 per cent of applicants for correctional officer jobs in the Federal Bureau of Prisons had bachelor degrees. See Neal Shover, *A Sociology of American Corrections*, (Homewood Ill.: Dorsey Press, 1979), chapter 6.

16. Carol Warren, 'New Forms of Social Control: The Myth of De-institutionalization', *American Behavioural Scientist*, 24, 6 (July–August 1981), pp. 724–40.

17. See Andrew Scull's 'Afterword' to the new edition of his *Decarceration: Community Treatment and the Deviant*, (Oxford: Martin Robertson, 1984).

18. Ivan Illich, *Limits to Medicine – Medical Nemesis: The Expropriation of Health*, (Harmondsworth: Penguin, 1977).

19. *Ibid.*, p. 49.

20. Harry Bakwin, 'Pseudodoxia Pediatrica', *New England Journal of Medicine*, 232 (1945), pp. 691–7, quoted in Illich, *Limits to Medicine*, p. 100.

21. The clearest statement of this claim in the deviancy literature remains the work of Kai T. Erikson, 'Notes on the Sociology of Deviance', *Social Problems*, 9 (1962), pp. 307–14 and *Wayward Puritans*, (New York: Wiley, 1966). In contemporary criminology, the work of Blumstein and his colleagues on the 'stability of punishment hypothesis' raises many of the same issues.

22. David Dery and Stanley Cohen, 'On Defining Juvenile Delinquency as a Policy Problem', in D. Dery, *Problem Definition in Policy Analysis*, (University of Kansas Press, 1984).

23. John R. Seeley, 'The Non-Petty Politics of Social Science Policy', unpublished paper, quoted in Schrag, *Mind Control*, p. 249.

24. Illich, *Limits to Medicine*, p. 123.

25. Jacques Donzelot, *The Policing of Families*, (New York: Pantheon Books, 1979), pp. 150–2.

26. Richard Abel, 'The Contradictions of Informal Justice' in R. Abel (ed.), *The Politics of Informal Justice*, (New York: Academic Press, 1982), see vol. 1, *The American Experience*, pp. 301–4. In the USA there is now a Society of Professionals in Dispute Resolution.

27. See Richard Henshel, *Reacting to Social Problems*, (Ontario: Longman, Canada, 1976), pp. 150–1.

28. Kumar, *Prophecy and Progress*, p. 266.

29. Murray Edelman, *Political Language: Words That Succeed and Policies that Fail*, (New York: Academic Press, 1977), pp. 16–20.

30. *Ibid.*, p. 59. This whole chapter of Edelman's book, 'The Political Language of the Helping Professions', is essential reading.

31. *Ibid.*, p. 60.

32. *Ibid.*, pp. 62–3.

33. *Ibid.*, p. 67.

34. For some exquisite examples of this sort of talk see various papers in Joan King (ed.), *Control Without Custody*, (Cambridge: Institute of Criminology, 1976). This volume contains a nice exception to my generalization that the treatment rhetoric is less used in Britain than America. According to J. S. Adams, sitting around in a Day Training Centre in Liverpool listening to music written by people in depressed areas (comparing brass band music from the depressed North East to the Beatles) is now apparently 'music therapy'. Psycho-babble is increasingly used in Intermediate Treatment; 'crisis intervention', 'short-term residential experience'.

35. Michel Foucault, 'Prison Talk', in C. Gordon (ed.), *Michel Foucault, Power/Knowledge: Selected Interviews and Other Writings 1972–1977*, (Brighton: Harvester Press, 1980), pp. 47–8.

36. Edward Shils, 'Privacy and Power', in *Center and Periphery: Essays in Macrosociology*, (Chicago: University of Chicago Press, 1975), pp. 317–44.

37. Robert Martinson, 'What Works? Questions and Answers about Prison Reform', *The Public Interest*, (Spring 1974), p. 25.

38. *Ibid.*, p. 52.

39. David Greenberg, 'The Correctional Effects of Corrections: A Survey of Evaluations', in D. Greenberg (ed.), *Corrections and Punishment*, (Beverly Hills: Sage, 1976); Malcolm Klein, 'Deinstitutionalization and Diversion of Juvenile Offenders: A Litany of Impediments', in N. Morris and M. Tonry (eds.), *Crime and Justice: An Annual Review of Research*, (Chicago: University of Chicago Press, 1979), vol. 1; see also John Hylton, 'Rhetoric and Reality: A Critical Appraisal of Community Correctional Programs', *Crime and Delinquency*, 28, 3 (July 1982), pp. 341–73.

40. Irving Spergel et al., 'Response of Organization and Community to a Deinstitutionalization Strategy', *Crime and Delinquency*, 28, 3 (1982), pp. 426–49.

41. Illich, *Limits to Medicine*, p. 88.

42. William Ryan, *Blaming the Victim*, (New York: Random House, 1976), p. 332.

43. H. Strupp and S. W. Hadley, 'Specific versus nonspecific Factors in Psychotherapy', *Archives of General Psychiatry*, 36 (September 1979), pp. 1125–36.

44. *Ibid.*, p. 1136. By 'engage appropriate patients in an interpersonal relationship whose outcome is therapeutic' is meant 'help'.
45. L. Luborsky et al., 'Comparative Studies of Psychotherapies: Is It True That "Everyone Has Won And All Must Have Prizes"?', *Archives of General Psychiatry*, 32 (August 1975), pp. 995–1008. The dodo-bird's verdict after judging the race in *Alice in Wonderland* was originally used in a 1936 paper by Saul Rosenzweig on the same subject: 'Some implicit common factors in diverse methods of psychotherapy'.
46. In statistical terms, if a high proportion of all patients improve, it is more difficult to achieve a significant difference between various forms of treatment.
47. Ted Palmer, 'The "Effectiveness" Issue Today: An Overview', *Federal Probation*, 46, 2 (June 1983), pp. 3–10.
48. *Ibid.*, p. 4.
49. Ted Palmer, 'Martinson Revisited', *Journal of Research in Crime and Delinquency*, 12 (1975), pp. 133–52.
50. Palmer, 'The 'Effectiveness' Issue', p. 5.
51. Michel Foucault, *Discipline and Punish*, (London: Allen Lane, 1977), pp. 184–94.
52. Chuck Wright, 'Team Approach to Presentence', *Federal Probation*, 43 (March 1979), p. 21.
53. For example, in terms of the 'problem profile approach' devised in assessment centres in Britain, see Masud Hoghughi et al., *Assessing Problem Children: Issues and Practice*, (London: Andre Deutsch, 1980).
54. Illich, *Limits to Medicine*, p. 84.
55. *Providence Educational Center: An Exemplary Project*, (Washington DC: LEAA, 1977), Appendix C-17.
56. Harry E. Allen et al., *Halfway Houses*, (Washington DC; LEAA, 1978), pp. 48–51.
57. *Ibid.*, p. 37.
58. Charles Silverman, *Criminal Violence, Criminal Justice*, (New York: Random House, 1978), pp. 291–3.
59. Barry Krisberg, 'Youth in Confinement: Justice By Geography', (San Francisco: NCCD Research Centre, no date).
60. R. B. Coates et al., *Diversity in a Youth Correctional System*, (Cambridge Mass: Bollinger, 1978). This is one of a whole series of publications by members of the Harvard Center for Criminal Justice devoted to the deinstitutionalization programme of the Massachusetts Department of Youth Services.
61. Jean Ann Linney, 'Multicomponent Assessment for Residential Services for Youth' (MARSY), in J. Handler and J. Zatz (eds.), *Neither Angels Nor Thieves: Studies in the Deinstitutionalization of Status Offenders*, (Washington DC: National Academy Press, 1982), pp. 740–79.
62. Paul Watzlawick, *How Real is Real? Confusion, Disinformation, Communication*, (New York: Random House, 1976), pp. 48–51.
63. Foucault, 'Prison Talk', p. 40.

64. Robin Evans, *The Fabrication of Virtue: English Prison Architecture 1750–1840*, (Cambridge: Cambridge University Press, 1982).

65. Foucault, *Discipline and Punish*, p. 304.

66. The following points are my composite summary of the argument scattered throughout *Discipline and Punish*; I have not given exact page references.

67. For a summary of this project, see R. B. Levinson and J. D. Williams, 'Inmate Classification: Security/Custody Considerations', *Federal Probation*, 43, 1 (March 1979), pp. 37–43.

68. Cited by Klein, 'De-institutionalization and Diversion', p. 161.

69. Nicholas Hobbs, *The Future of Children*, 2 vols, (San Francisco: Jossey Bass Publishers, 1975), vol. 1, *Categories, Labels and their Consequences*, vol. 2, *Issues in the Classification of Children*.

70. The 'claims making' theory of social problems is set out in Malcolm Spector and John Kitsuse, *Constructing Social Problems*, (Menlo Park, California: Cummings, 1977).

71. Foucault, 'Prison Talk', p. 51.

## 6 VISIONS OF ORDER

1. One of the few social-problems texts that examines the role of belief systems in justifying intervention is Richard Henshel, *Reacting to Social Problems*, (Ontario: Longman Canada, 1976).

2. Krishan Kumar, *Prophecy and Progress: The Sociology of Industrial and Post Industrial Society*, (Harmondsworth Penguin, 1978), p. 14.

3. On the themes of optimism and pessimism in sociology, see more generally, Lewis Killian, 'Optimism and Pessimism in Sociological Analysis', *American Sociologist*, V (1971), pp. 281–6.

4. For a guide to this literature and that of post-industrialism, see again Kumar, 'Prophecy and Progress'. The enjoyable standard criticism of the 'sunshine boys' of sociology, was Dusky Lee Smith, 'The Sunshine Boys: Toward a Sociology of Happiness, *The Activist*, 14 (Spring 1964), pp. 166–77.

5. Gresham Sykes, *The Future of Crime*, (National Institute of Mental Health, Washington DC: US Government Printing Office, 1980).

6. There is, however, one variable – changing age-structure – which could reduce the level of crime. For some years, American criminologists have predicted that with ageing of the baby-boom cohort, crime rates would decline. For the past three years, this has already been happening and is likely to continue for at least the next decade, the usual 'other things being equal'.

7. Sykes, *The Future of Crime*, p. 7.

8. Leslie T. Wilkins, 'Crime in the World of 1990', *Futures*, (September 1970), pp. 203–14 and 'Crime and Criminal Justice at the Turn of the Century', *Annals*, 208 (July 1973), pp. 13–20.

9. Stanley Cohen, 'Western Crime Control Models in the Third World: Benign or Malignant?', in S. Spitzer and R. Simon (eds), *Research in Law, Deviance and Social Control*, (Connecticut: JAI Press, 1982), vol. 4.

10. James Q. Wilson, *Thinking About Crime*, (New York: Random House, 1975), pp. 222–3.

11. Most notably in the Manuels' massive recent volume: Frank G. and Fritzie P. Manuel, *Utopian Thought in the Western World*, (Oxford: Basil Blackwell, 1979).

12. See, for example, Mark R. Hillegas, *The Future as Nightmare: H. G. Wells and the Anti Utopians*, (New York: Oxford University Press, 1967); Fred Polak, *The Image of the Future*, (Amsterdam; Elsevier, 1973), Chad Walsh, *From Utopias to Nightmare*, (New York: Harper and Row, 1962). For some interesting general comparisons between utopian and science fiction forms see Raymond Williams, 'Utopia and science fiction', in P. Parrinder (ed.), *Science Fiction: A Critical Guide*, (London: Longman, 1979). I use 'utopia' and 'dystopia' throughout this chapter in the rather loose and non-technical sense of visions of good places and bad places.

13. The uninitiated might try the following anthologies: Hans Santesson (ed.), *Crime Prevention in the Thirtieth Century*, (New York: Walker Publishing Co., 1969) and Joseph D. Olander and Martin Harry Greenberg (eds), *Criminal Justice Through Science Fiction*, (New York: New Viewpoints, 1977). Major science-fiction writers who have given explicit attention to deviance and social control include Theodore Sturgeon, Robert Silverberg, Alfred Bester, John Brunner and Ray Bradbury. Outside the genre, Antony Burgess's *A Clockwork Orange* is probably the best known. My subsequent examples all appear in these sources.

14. First published in 1962 and reprinted in *The Best of Robert Silverberg*, (London: Futura Publications, 1978). This collection also contains *Hawksbill Station*.

15. For these, and quite opposite, views on Skinner's utopia see Harvey Wheeler (ed.), *Beyond The Punitive Society*, (London: Wildwood House, 1973).

16. I have drawn, in this section, upon Richard Sennett's useful collection *Classical Essays on the Culture of Cities*, (New Jersey: Prentice Hall, 1969).

17. Jonathan Miller, 'Introduction to Metaphoropolis', *Architectural Design*, 38 (December 1968), p. 570. See also in same issue, D. P. Walker, 'Poneropolis', pp. 581–96.

18. Francis Yates, 'Architecture and the Art of Memory', *Architectural Design*, 38 (December 1968), pp. 573–8.

19. Lewis Munford, 'Utopia, the City and the Machine', in Frank F. Manuel (ed.), *Utopias and Utopian Thought*, (London: Souvenir Press, 1973), p. 151.

20. *Ibid.*, p. 9.

21. Michel Foucault, *Discipline and Punish: The Birth of the Prison*, (London: Allen Lane, 1977), pp. 195–200.

22. Robin Evans, *The Fabrication of Virtue: English Prison Architecture, 1750–1840*, (Cambridge: Cambridge University Press, 1982).

23. Foucault, *Discipline and Punish*, p. 113.

24. *Ibid.*, p. 205.

25. Eric Hobsbawn, 'Cities and Insurrections', *Architectural Design*, 38 (December 1968), pp. 579–88.

26. Gareth Stedman-Jones, *Outcast London*, (London: Oxford University Press, 1971), p. 151.

27. See Geoffrey Pearson, *The Deviant Imagination*, (London: Macmillan, 1975), pp. 149–76 for an analysis of this type of nineteenth-century social-control imagery.

28. Besides *Discipline and Punish* itself, see also the interview with Foucault, 'Questions on Geography', in C. Gordon (ed.), *Power/Knowledge: Selected Interviews and Other Writings By Michel Foucault, 1972–1979*, (Brighton: Harvester Press, 1980), pp. 63–77.

29. Mumford, 'Utopia, the City and the Machine', pp. 17–22.

30. David Matza, *Becoming Deviant*, (Englewood Cliffs NJ: Prentice Hall, 1969); see especially pp. 45–9 on 'The Chicago Dilemma'. Matza's exegesis of the Chicago School and functionalism is essential to understand the theoretical basis of deviance and Controltalk.

31. Howard S. Becker (ed.), *Culture and Civility in San Francisco*, (Chicago: Aldine, 1971).

32. The most important exceptions in criminology are Nils Christie's vision of a 'pain-reduced' society (which I discuss in chapter 7) and the Marxist vision of a 'crime-free' society. In general political thinking, the anarchist tradition has been the only one consistently interested in linking crime control to visions of the good society. On the pragmatics of this tradition, see Colin Ward, *Anarchy in Action*, (London: Allen and Unwin, 1973) for a much too idealistic account, see L. Tift and D. Sullivan, *The Struggle to be Human: Crime, Criminology and Anarchism*, (Orkney: Cienfuegos Press, 1980).

33. For an introductory collection of visions of the future city by planners and social scientists, see Andrew Blowers et al. (eds), *The Future of Cities*, (London: Hutchinson, 1974).

34. Jencks deals with these criticisms and paradoxes in terms of the 'multivalence' of Le Corbusier's work. See Charles Jencks, *Modern Movements in Architecture*, (Harmondsworth: Penguin, 1973), pp. 14–19, 24–26 and chapter 4.

35. Stephen Gardiner, *Le Corbusier*, (London: Fontana, 1974), especially pp. 111–20.

36. Two good collections of such science-fiction visions produced in the sixties and seventies, are Roger Elwood (ed.), *Future City*, (New York: Pocket Books, 1974), and Ralph Clem et al. (eds), *The City 2000 A.D.: Urban Life Through Science Fiction*, (Greenwich: Fawcett, 1976).

37. *To Establish Justice, to Ensure Domestic Tranquility. Final Report of the National Commission on the Causes and Prevention of Violence*

(Washington DC: US Government Printing Office, 1969), p. 46.

38. For example, Shlomo Angel, *Discouraging Crime Through City Planning*, (Berkeley: Institute of Urban and Regional Development, 1968); Richard A. Gardner, *Design for Safe Neighbourhoods: The Environmental Security Planning and Design Process*, (Washington DC: LEAA, September 1978); and Clarence R. Jeffrey, *Crime Prevention Through Environmental Design*, (California: Sage, 1977). The actual results of CPED projects are usefully reviewed in Charles A. Murray, 'The Physical Environment and the Community Control of Crime', in James Q. Wilson (ed.), *Crime and Public Policy*, (San Francisco: ICS Press, 1983), pp. 107–24.

39. Gardner, *Design for Safe Neighbourhoods*, pp. 11–17.

40. Oscar Newman, *Defensible Space: Crime Prevention through Urban Design*, (New York: Macmillan, 1972), *Architectural Design For Crime Prevention*, (Washington DC: US Government Printing Office, 1973), *Design Guidelines For Creating Defensible Space*, (Washington DC: LEAA, 1975) and *Community of Interest*, (New York: Anchor Press, 1980).

41. Murray, 'The Physical Environment and the Community Control of Crime'.

42. Jane Jacobs, *The Death and Life of Great American Cities*, (New York: Vintage Books, 1961).

43. Jencks, *Modern Movements in Architecture*, pp. 245 and 299–303.

44. Richard Sennet, *The Uses of Disorder: Personal Identity and City Life*, (New York: Alfred Knopf, 1970).

45. *Ibid.*, p. 98.

46. Richard Sennet, 'Destructive Gemeinschaft', in N. Birnbaum (ed.), *Beyond The Crisis*, (New York: Oxford University Press, 1977), pp. 171–97, and *The Fall of Public Man*, (London: Oxford University Press, 1978). Note also the complementary argument in Lasch's writing on the family.

47. Claude Levi-Strauss, *Tristes Tropiques*, (Harmondsworth: Penguin, 1977) p. 508.

48. Valenstein nicely describes contemporary visions of thought control as 'modern phrenology based on the belief that the brain is organized into neat functional compartments that conform to our social needs'. See Elliot Valenstein, *Brain Control: A Critical Evaluation of Brain Stimulation and Psychosurgery*, (New York: John Wiley, 1976), pp. 350–1.

49. Judith Wilks and Robert Martinson, 'Is the Treatment of Criminal Offenders Really Necessary?', *Federal Probation*, 40, 1 (March 1976), pp. 3–9.

50. Hugo Davenport and William Scobie, 'Bleeper Could Cut Jail Numbers', *The Observer*, 10 April 1983. On the original Albuquerque experiment, see 'Wearing A Jail Cell Around Your Ankle', *Newsweek*, 21 March 1983.

51. I am grateful to Barbara Hudson for drawing my attention to this comparison.

52. Note, though, Alfred Bester's solution in *The Demolished Man*: the control system overall is exclusionary, but experts trained in extra sensory perception ('espers') can detect (and therefore prevent) any hint of

deviant thoughts or intentions in another person's mind. See Alfred Bester, *The Demolished Man*, (Harmondsworth: Penguin, 1966).

53. George Sternlieb, 'The City as Sandbox', *The Public Interest*, 25 (Fall 1971), pp. 14–21.

54. Norton E. Long, 'The City as Reservation', *The Public Interest*, 25 (Fall 1971), pp. 22–38.

55. Richard Child Hill, 'Fiscal Collapse and Political Struggle in Decaying Central Cities in the United States', in W. K. Tabb and L. Sawers (eds), *Marxism and the Metropolis: New Perspectives in Urban Political Economy*, (New York: Oxford University Press, 1979), pp. 213–40.

56. For a recent summary, see Roger Friedland, *Power and Crisis in the City*, (London: Macmillan, 1982).

57. Andrew Scull,. *Decarceration: Community Treatment and the Deviant*, (Englewood Cliffs NJ: Prentice Hall, 1977), pp. 1–2.

58. Sykes, *The Future of Crime*, p. 18.

59. James Finlayson, *Urban Devastation: The Planning of Incarceration*, (Solidarity Pamphlet, no date).

60. *Ibid.*, p. 21.

61. For examples, see Elwood (ed.) *Future City*, and Clem (ed.), *The City, 2000 AD*.

62. Barry Malzberg, *The Destruction of the Temple*, (London: New English Library, 1975). Part of this story appears also as 'City Lights, City Nights' under Malzberg's pen name, K. M. O'Donnell, in Elwood (ed.), *Future City*.

63. Robert Silverberg, 'Black is Beautiful', in Clem (ed.), *The City, 2000 AD*.

64. Robert Silverberg, *The World Outside*, (London: Granada, 1978).

65. Oscar Newman, 'Defensible Space', in *Policy Development Seminar on Architecture, Design and Criminal Justice*, (Washington DC: LEAA, 1975), p. 52. Note Newman's alternative: 'dispersing the ghettoes' – moving 'the core of the crime problem' into other areas by mixing in a quota of 20–30 per cent of low-income families.

66. William Ryan, *Blaming the Victim*, (New York: Random House, 1976), pp. 336.

67. Ivan Illich, *Limits to Medicine*, (Harmondsworth: Penguin, 1977), pp. 85–96.

68. Joel Kovol, 'Therapy in Late Capitalism', *Telos*, 30 (Winter 1976–77), pp. 73–92.

69. In the Urbmon of 2381 when your threshold for 'thwarting acceptance' begins to dip, you turn yourself in to 'consolers' or 'blessmen', moral engineers who help you adjust to reality. You must do this *before* things get really uncontrollable, which leads to countersocial behaviour – which means 'down the chute': Silverberg, *The World Inside*.

70. See Russel Eisenman, 'Scapegoating as Social Control', *Journal of Psychology*, 61 (1965), pp. 203–9.

71. See Harold Garfinkel, 'Conditions of Successful Degradation Ceremonies', *American Journal of Sociology*, LXI (March 1956), pp. 420–24.

72. This type of cybernetic language is used by Tony Tanner to describe how Burroughs (and similar modern writers) deal with the fear of entropy and chaos. See Tony Tanner, *City of Words: American Fiction 1950–1970*, (London: Jonathan Cape, 1971), especially chapters 5 and 6.

73. B. F. Skinner, *Beyond Freedom and Dignity*, (London: Jonathan Cape, 1972), p. 177.

74. William Burroughs, *The Naked Lunch*, (London: Calder, 1959), p. 164.

### 7  WHAT IS TO BE DONE?

1. Stanley Cohen, 'It's Allright For You To Talk: Political and Sociological Manifestos for Social Work Action,' in R. Bailey and M. Brake (eds), *Radical Social Work*, (London: Edward Arnold, 1975), and 'Guilt, Justice and Tolerance: Some Old Concepts For a New Criminology', in D. Downes and P. Rock (eds), *Deviant Interpretations*, (Oxford: Martin Robertson, 1979).

2. For a liberal version of this view of social policy (with some telling examples), see Sam D. Spieber, *Fatal Remedies: The Ironies of Social Intervention*, (New York: Plenum Press, 1981).

3. Alvin W. Gouldner, *The Future of the Intellectuals and the Rise of the New Class*, (London: Macmillan, 1979), p. 41.

4. Richard L. Henshel, *Reaching to Social Problems*, (Ontario: Longman, Canada, 1976) chapter 3.

5. For a defence of the solubility criterion, see David Deri and Stanley Cohen, 'On Defining Juvenile Delinquency as a Policy Problem', in D. Deri, *Problem Definition in Policy Analysis*, (University Press of Kansas, 1984).

6. Janet B. Chan and Richard V. Ericson, *Decarceration and the Economy of Penal Reform*, (Toronto: Centre of Criminology, University of Toronto, 1981), p. 68, my emphasis.

7. Stanley Cohen, 'The Deeper Structures of the Law or "Beware the Rulers Bearing Justice"', *Contemporary Crises*, 8 (January 1984), pp. 83–93.

8. Michel Foucault, 'Powers and Strategies', in C. Gordon (ed.), *Michel Foucault: Power/Knowledge: Selected Interviews and Other Writings*, (Brighton: Harvester Press, 1980), pp. 135–6.

9. Isaiah Berlin, *Russian Thinkers*, (London: Hogarth Press, 1978) (note Aileen Kelley's excellent Introduction, 'A Complex Vision', pp. xiii–xxiv); and *Against the Current: Essays in the History of Ideas*, (London: Hogarth Press, 1979). See, particularly, Berlin's various essays (in these volumes) on Alexander Herzen whom (at the risk of sounding pretentious) I would recommend as the soundest of moral and political guides to evaluating social policy.

10. Note, for example, Francis Allen, *The Decline of the Rehabilitative Ideal*, (New Haven: Yale University Press, 1981).

11. Donald Cressey, Foreword to Francis T. Cullen and Karen E. Gilbert,

*Re-Affirming Rehabilitation*, (Cincinatti: Anderson Publishing Co. 1982), p. xi.

12. Cullen and Gilbert, *Re-Affirming Rehabilitation*, p. 152.

13. *Ibid.*, p. 151.

14. Tamar Lewin, 'Making Punishment Fit Future Crime', *New York Times*, 14 November 1982.

15. In Dorothy Chunn and Russell Smandych, 'An Interview with David Rothman', *Canadian Criminology Forum*, 4 (Spring 1982), pp. 152–62.

16. As Trilling reminded us: 'liberalism is always being surprised.' See Lionel Trilling, *The Liberal Imagination*, new edition (Oxford: Oxford University Press, 1951).

17. On the methodological problems of finding these sorts of overarching connections between reform movements and patterns of imprisonment, see the series of studies by Richard Berk, Sheldon Messinger and their colleagues on the California system, e.g. Richard Berk et al., 'Prisons as Self Regulating Systems', *Law and Society Review*, 17, 4 (1983), pp. 547–86.

18. Lynne Goodstein, 'Sentencing Reform and the Correctional System: A Case Study of the Implementation of Minnesota's Determinate Sentencing Law', *Law and Policy Quarterly*, 5, 4 (October 1983), pp. 478–501. Prisoners actually raised $15,000 to support a campaign to make sentencing guidelines apply retroactively to them.

19. Cullen and Gilbert, *Reaffirming Rehabilitation*, p. 20.

20. *Ibid.*, p. 283.

21. Willard Gaylin, *The Killing of Bonnie Garland: A Question of Justice*, (New York: Penguin Books, 1983). This is a model piece of work in another respect as well: a blending of concern for private troubles with a sensitivity to public issues.

22. *Ibid.*, p. 341.

23. David Greenberg, 'Reflections on the Justice Model Debate', *Contemporary Crises*, 7 (November 1983), pp. 313–27.

24. *Ibid.*, p. 318.

25. *Ibid.*, p. 321.

26. Nils Christie, *Limits to Pain*, (Oxford: Martin Robertson, 1981).

27. This, of course, is the familiar Durkheimian argument about the functional necessity of social control. It is mentioned in every criminology textbook, and then its implications are totally ignored. For a concise restatement of the non-obvious nature of the argument, see Randall Collins, *Sociological Insight: An Introduction to Non Obvious Sociology*, (New York: Oxford University Press, 1982), chapter 4, 'The Normalcy of Crime'.

28. Menachem and Delilah Amir, 'Rape Crisis Centers as an Arena for Ideological Conflict', (Unpublished Paper, 1982).

29. For a nice example, see Joan Moore, *Homeboys: Gangs, Drugs and Prison in the Barrios of Los Angeles*, (Philadelphia: Temple University Press, 1978).

30. James F. Brady, 'Towards a Popular Justice in the United States: The Dialectics of Community Action', *Contemporary Crises*, 5, 2 (April 1981), pp. 155–92. To Brady, though, auxiliary justice is 'merely' liberal, populist, and no challenge to the existing legal order as well as a 'depressing example of co-option, containment and manipulation by the capitalist state'. For a more favourable view of the potential of local community mediators and tribunals to create a 'needs-based' concept of justice, see Dennis Longmire, 'A Popular Justice System: A Radical Alternative to the Traditional Justice System', *Contemporary Crises*, 5, 1 (January 1981), pp. 15–30. This debate (see also the exchange between Brady and Longmire in *Contemporary Crises*, January 1981, pp. 31–42) illustrates nicely the difference between uncompromising Marxism and liberal reformism.
31. Charles A. Murray, 'The Physical Environment and the Community Control of Crime', in J. Q. Wilson (ed.), *Crime and Public Policy*, (San Francisco: ICS Press, 1983), pp. 107–22.
32. Colin Ward, *The Child in the City*, (Harmondsworth: Penguin Books, 1979).
33. Alan W. Watts, *Psychotherapy East and West*, (New York: Mentor Books, 1963), p. 50.
34. Andrew Scull, 'Community Corrections: Panacea, Progress or Pretence?', in D. Garland and P. Young (eds), *The Power to Punish*, (London: Heinemann, 1983), p. 154.
35. Edwin Schur, *The Politics of Deviance: Stigma Contests and the Uses of Power*, (New Jersey: Prentice Hall, 1980).
36. A phrase coined by a community-services manager to describe local resistance to decarceration, cited in Joanne Arnaud and Timothy Mack, 'The Deinstitutionalization of Status Offenders in Massachusetts', in J. Handler and J. Zatz (eds), *Neither Angels nor Thieves*, (Washington DC: National Academy Press, 1982), p. 351. Apparently mentally retarded children were the most unwelcome on this spectrum.

## APPENDIX

1. George Orwell, *Nineteen Eighty-Four*, (Harmondsworth: Penguin, 1954), p. 241.
2. *Ibid.*, p. 245.
3. George Orwell, 'Politics and the English Language', in *The Penguin Essays of George Orwell* (Harmondsworth: Penguin, 1984).
4. *Ibid.*, p. 362.
5. William Burroughs, 'Prisoners of the Earth Come Out', in *The Job: Interviews With William Burroughs By Daniel Odier*, (London: Jonathan Cape, 1970), p. 48. This whole interview (pp. 51–104) is a wonderful example of Burroughs' paranoid sense of images and words as instruments of control.

6. Murray Edelman, 'The Political Language of the Helping Professions', chapter 4 in his *Political Language: Words That Succeed and Policies that Fail*, (New York: Academic Press, 1977), pp. 57–75.

7. *Ibid.*, p. 60.

8. *Ibid.*, p. 61.

9. *Ibid.*, p. 60.

10. Alvin W. Gouldner, *The Future of Intellectuals and the Rise of the New Class*, (London: Macmillan, 1979).

11. *Ibid.*, p. 29.

12. Nils Christie, *Limits to Pain*, (Oxford: Martin Robertson, 1981).

13. *Ibid.*, p. 14.

14. It therefore must be understood not in linguistic terms alone, but in terms of the overall 'medicalization' of deviance. For a useful recent introduction to the subject, see Peter Conrad and Joseph W. Schneider, *Deviance and Medicalization: From Badness to Sickness*, (St Louis: C. V. Mosby Co., 1980).

15. Peter Schrag and Diane Divoky, *The Myth of the Hyperactive Child*, (New York: Pantheon, 1975), and Steven Box, 'Where Have All the Naughty Children Gone?' in National Deviancy Conference, *Permissiveness and Control*, (Basingstoke: Macmillan, 1979).

16. Richard D. Perlow, 'Behavioural Techniques For Sociopathic Clients', *Federal Probation*, 39 (March 1971), p. 4.

17. Orwell, *Nineteen Eighty-Four*, p. 247.

18. Gouldner, *The Future of Intellectuals*, p. 59.

# Index